ECONOMIC DEVELOPMENT

READINGS IN THEORY AND PRACTICE

C. VAN EATON

ECONOMIC DEVELOPMENT

READINGS IN THEORY AND PRACTICE

Edited by

THEODORE MORGAN
GEORGE W. BETZ

University of Wisconsin, and Economic
Research Centre, University of Singapore

WADSWORTH PUBLISHING COMPANY, INC.
BELMONT, CALIFORNIA

Preface

Only a few years ago, useful articles and other readings in economic development were scarce. But in the past dozen years, increasing work in the field has produced a rapidly mushrooming volume of material. Concurrently, public and professional interest in the economic problems and possibilities for economic advance in less-developed countries has intensified. Colleges and universities are offering more and more courses in economic development.

This anthology represents an effort to put together in one convenient volume a balanced group of articles and excerpts, adapted to the needs of students and specialists in the field. The aim is to present the most useful collection possible of materials on less-developed economies, which will, altogether, illuminate and give insight to the complete range of fact, theory, and policy.

The following types of readings have received special emphasis: distinguished contributions, with which all students in the field ought to be acquainted; significant contributions to controversies, which are numerous in this unsettled subject; outstanding papers published in foreign and less-known sources, and so not readily available in the United States; and useful summaries.

We have checked our judgment and improved our choices by drawing on the advice of George B. Baldwin, P. T. Bauer, Reynold E. Carlson, Rendigs Fels, Benjamin Higgins, Michael Hoffman, Bert Hoselitz, Simon Kuznets, Wilfred Malenbaum, Max Millikan, Harry T. Oshima, Kenneth Parsons, Hans Singer, and William O. Thweatt. We are indebted to each for his assistance.

Contents

4 International Trade and Economic Growth

5 Education and Growth

6 Unemployment

7 Development Policy

An Approach, 289

Aid, 315

Population, 318

Financial Matters, 353

Development Administration, 381

The Impulse to Modernize, 391

Plans and Planning, 400

Author Index

Part One: Central Problems of Economic Growth

Historical Experience of Economic Development

H. J. Habbakkuk

1

The factors favourable to development are so varied and have historically combined in so many different ways that I see no possibility of isolating a small number of crucial variables. All I propose to do is to consider the historical experience on four points where it seems to me to have particular relevance to the problem of development at the present day.

The first point relates to the initiating factor in development. Here if one has to single out one influence, priority must be given to the widening of markets. Under the pressure of demand, old attitudes were modified, social obstacles to growth were removed, new methods were invented and specific bottlenecks—shortages in entrepreneurial skill, in skilled labour and capital— were overcome.[1] There are it is true some cases where the capacity to respond to widening markets was temporarily checked by some particular shortage. But if one confines one's attention to those areas which were

Excerpted from "Historical Experience of Economic Development," chapter 6 in E.A.G. Robinson, ed., *Problems in Economic Development*, proceedings of a conference held by the International Economic Association; Macmillan, London, and St. Martin's Press, New York, 1965. Reprinted by permission of the author and publisher. The author is at Oxford University.

[1]See A.K. Cairncross, *Factors in Economic Development* (London, 1962), chapter 13.

1

successful in developing in the century before 1914, the main dynamic was provided by increases in market possibilities rather than by independent changes in the supply of factors of production. The shortage it proved most difficult to alleviate was that of entrepreneurs. In countries with a long history of previous growth a supply was readily forthcoming from a wide variety of sources, from landowners, merchants and small masters in industry of the prefactory type. In a country which lacked an adequate class of indigenous entrepreneurs, but where other factors were favourable, entrepreneurs were imported. The foreign entrepreneurs called forth local entrepreneurial ability; they stimulated competition and imitation and they provided opportunities for local inhabitants to acquire industrial techniques and administrative experience. In the successful nineteenth-century industrializations even this shortage proved to be very short-lived, once a stimulus had come from the side of demand.

The increase in market possibilities arose in a variety of ways. The orders from government-sponsored railways—directed to local industry by a tariff or by more direct means—provided a market for nascent heavy industry in a number of countries. In some cases steps were taken to secure for the local industries the domestic market in goods which had previously been imported; and once a wide range of industries had been established, there were possibilities of a cumulative process of balanced growth. But the possibilities were restricted in the early stages of economic growth, which are the stages of most interest in the present context. This is why in several of the most successful of the older industrializations exports played an important role and in a number of them foreign demand was the source of a substantial part of the initial impetus.

Potential export markets were so much greater than the domestic market that an area which had a marked advantage in a particular line of production could expand on the basis of exports in a way which would have been impossible had it been restricted to the domestic market. The expansion of the export sector drew resources away from sectors of low productivity and underemployment; it afforded some economies of scale; it stimulated investment in other sectors; and where it put pressure on domestic resources it stimulated invention and innovation.[2] The export sector was sometimes a manufacturing industry; thus cotton textile exports played a crucial role in the early industrialization of Britain and Japan. But the most striking instances of growth ignited by expansion of exports were the regions of recent settlement. In these areas the expansion of exports provided the stimulus for the development of their resources—not only the direct stimulus of an increase in income but the galvanizing effects of foreign contacts; it also enabled these areas to import the capital necessary for the purpose.

A large part of the economic growth of the nineteenth century can be explained in these terms: by a process of transmission from the more

[2]C.P. Kindleberger, 'Foreign Trade and Economic Growth', *Economic History Review*, second series, XIV, No. 2, December 1961, pp. 289-91.

advanced areas and their increased demand for imports. This growth did not necessarily take the form of industrialization. The comparative advantage of some areas was so decidedly in primary production that industry was inhibited, except for the processing of raw materials and the manufacture of the simpler consumer goods. But in most of them the increase in incomes sooner or later generated a local market sufficiently large to support a significant industrial base.

It is often argued that the circumstances which made international trade so effective an engine of growth in the nineteenth century were essentially temporary. Clearly, in principle, the rapid growth of one area is capable of inhibiting as well as stimulating growth in less-developed regions. Were the circumstances, which in the nineteenth century ensured that growth in one region exerted a powerful stimulus over a wide area, peculiar to a bygone phase of growth?

There is one sense in which nineteenth-century developments were unique, the importance of textile exports as a generator of growth. Both Britain and Japan exported textiles to areas which were sufficiently developed to afford such imports but not sufficiently developed to make their own textiles. This stage of development was from its very nature temporary and it is unlikely that textile exports will ever again be a springboard for industrialization.

The nineteenth-century experience was exceptional in a more fundamental sense. The regions of recent settlement—simply because they were areas of abundant land—had a very decisive relative advantage *vis-à-vis* the industrial areas in the production of foodstuffs. Since they were nearly all in the temperate latitudes, these regions produced many of the same foodstuffs as were produced in the industrial countries. As a result, primary production in the overseas regions expanded not only because industrial incomes were growing but because there was a contraction in the agriculture of the industrial areas taken as a whole.[3] The regions of recent settlement were also particularly attractive to European migrants and these migrants were a powerful factor in the diffusion of advanced technology. Moreover, the fact that these areas were peopled from Europe and shared European institutions facilitated a movement of capital. Most of them also were—again because of the abundance of land—areas where incomes were high from the start and where therefore there was a substantial market for manufactured goods, goods moreover of the same general type as those produced in the older industrial areas.

The poorer, more densely populated and long-settled areas of primary production also enjoyed a greatly increased demand for their products in this period: cocoa, palm oil and ground-nuts from West Africa, for example, coffee from Ceylon, tin and rubber from Malaya. The reaction of these areas did not of course fall into a uniform pattern—there was indeed a great diversity of response—but there are certain characteristics common to most of them. The increase in exports from such areas was often considerable; in the

[3]Cairncross, *op. cit.* p. 197.

last thirty years of the nineteenth century, for example, the value of Burma's exports increased by an average of 5 per cent per annum. But in general the increase was achieved by an increase in the total resources employed in production and did not lead to cumulative improvements in productivity. It is easy to underestimate the changes in these countries produced as a result of the increase in exports, but as a broad generalization it remains true that in their case international trade as an engine of growth did not generate enough power to stimulate a cumulative expansion.

Why did these economies fail to respond more vigorously to the stimulus of foreign demand? The answer does not seem to be primarily the absence of overhead capital, for at least some of these areas, e.g. India, were provided with railways and port facilities; and banking systems were also introduced. One reason that has been suggested was that these areas were not capable of replacing the primary production of the more advanced areas. While Australian and North American wheat expanded at the expense of European wheat production, tropical products had to depend for their market exclusively upon such increases of demand as flowed from the rise of income and change of taste in the advanced economies.[4] This was certainly an important difference. But as we have already said, the demand for the products of these undeveloped areas was in many cases increasing rapidly. I am inclined to think that a more important difference is in the technological characteristics of the production functions of the commodities which these areas produced for export. These technological characteristics influenced the extent to which an export sector induced subsequent developments because they determined the nature of the inflows of labour and capital and the distribution of income within a particular region.[5] And it has been plausibly argued that the export of a plantation type commodity was less likely to stimulate growth than a grain crop or the production of livestock, commodities better suited to production by family-size farms. One can think of several other explanations of greater or less force according to the particular area in question. But one explanation which seems to be fairly generally relevant is the persistence in these areas of traditional agrarian structures unfavourable to the transmission of the impulses derived from foreign trade.

The implication of the historical experience on this point is not that export sectors did not still have an important role to play in development but only that they are unlikely to promote vigorous growth without extensive changes in agrarian structure.

This leads to the second point at which historical experience bears with particular relevance on the present: the role of agriculture. All the successful nineteenth-century industrializations were accompanied in their early stages by an increase in agricultural output, and in the countries of Europe—which

[4] Cairncross, *op. cit.* p. 197.

[5] R.E. Baldwin, 'Patterns of Development in Newly Settled Regions', *The Manchester School*, XXIV, No. 2, May 1956.

are the most relevant for the purpose—this increase involved in many cases not only the introduction of new techniques but the transformation of the system of land tenure and ownership. This increase in agricultural output is not to be regarded as a pre-condition of growth, if only because it usually accompanied rather than preceded the acceleration of growth. It is rather a part of the growth which requires explanation, but an essential part in the sense that, with the possible exception of Holland in the seventeenth century, there are no cases of successful growth where unresponsiveness of domestic agriculture was made good by imports of agricultural products. Even Britain and Japan did not begin to rely heavily upon such imports until relatively late in their development.

This coincidence of successful development and agrarian improvement does not seem to be accidental. For agrarian improvement performed certain functions which could not have been performed by imports of food, even if these had been available on very favourable terms. Broadly speaking, it performed four functions. (a) It facilitated the supply of labour to industry; for even where there was surplus labour, in some sense, in agriculture, before the transformation of the agrarian structure, it was often not available to industry, or was available only on terms which gave small dispersed handicraft industry an advantage in relation to factory industry. (b) The increase in agricultural productivity facilitated investment. Where the government taxed agriculture in order to promote industry, the higher the level of productivity in agriculture the easier the burden was to bear. Where the finance for industrial investment was derived mainly from industrial profits, the increase in agricultural productivity prevented the appearance of the curb on accumulation most feared by Ricardo: the rise in the subsistence wage as a growing population pressed on limited supplies of land. (c) In some cases, the agrarian improvements made possible an expansion of exports which helped to pay for imports of machinery and raw materials. (d) Finally, the increase in agricultural productivity provided a domestic market for industrial goods, and thus a basis for the establishment of new industries.

The relative importance of these functions varied from country to country. Agricultural reform was important in releasing labour for the towns in Russia and Germany; in Russia and Japan agriculture was taxed to support industry; exports of raw silk in the case of Japan and grain in the case of Russia earned foreign exchange at a critical stage in their industrialization. But the function of agricultural improvement which seems to have been of the most general importance was the creation of a domestic market for local industries in the earliest and most difficult stages of their growth. The importance of this consideration is most clearly seen in the case of India in the later nineteenth and early twentieth centuries—a country which had many of the prerequisites for industrialization (a railway system, indigenous and foreign entrepreneurs, raw materials; and abundant labour) but where agricultural production between the 1880s and the 1930s seems to have remained virtually constant in face of a population increase of nearly one hundred million.

The responsiveness of agriculture in Europe was partly the result of the fact that techniques were available, particularly the introduction of artificial grasses and root-crops. These were primarily land-saving improvements; the open-field system, under which a large part of the cultivatable land was left fallow each year—a system which had developed during the centuries in which Europe was sparsely populated—afforded considerable opportunities for raising the productivity of land by the introduction of new crops. But these crops also raised the productivity of labour, because they reduced the seasonalness of agricultural work.

But there is the additional point that, in some areas, the agrarian structure was well suited for the introduction of the new techniques. In England, particularly, well before the Industrial Revolution, there were relatively large farms, worked for the market by tenant farmers who had considerable supplies of capital. The existence of this type of agrarian structure was one of the factors most favourable to England's economic development. It is true, of course, that this structure was itself the result of the earlier growth in the English economy, but it was of critical importance that, in the eighteenth century, when other conditions were favourable for an acceleration of growth, the process was not halted by an inelasticity in the agriculture sector. Where peasant proprietorship was the dominant form of agricultural enterprise, and even more where share-cropping prevailed, the agricultural sector acted as a damper on growth—not so powerful as to preclude growth where other conditions were favourable, but strong enough to impede growth even, for example, in France and Italy. There are a great many reasons why the economic history of southern Europe was so much less successful than that of the north in the nineteenth century, but one reason is that there was less scope for increasing agricultural productivity. It is not merely that the new root-crops and grasses were not suited to the climate of these regions. Because they were, in general, densely populated in relation to resources there was no reserve of capacity in their agriculture such as was represented by the fallows of open-field agriculture.

There is probably some contrast between the effectiveness of the techniques available for raising agricultural productivity in open-field Europe in the eighteenth and nineteenth centuries and those now available in most contemporary under-developed areas. The introduction of root-crops and grasses promised a large increase in productivity for the expenditure of quite a modest amount of capital. But the technical possibilities for agricultural productivity in contemporary under-developed areas are nevertheless very considerable, in some cases greater than those of nineteenth-century Europe. The really striking contrast is not in the technical possibilities but in the power of the social obstacles to their introduction. In England, the main social obstacles to the introduction of new techniques had been decisively weakened well before the Industrial Revolution: agriculture was in the hands of capitalist tenant-farmers. In countries like Germany and Russia, where serfdom, the fragmentation of holdings and communal rights of ownership or cultivation still survived, the reform of the agrarian social structure was undertaken by the state and pushed through rapidly and with relatively small regard for individual interests, which were sacrificed to the aim of increasing the efficiency of agriculture. Thus the existence of state authority, capable of transforming the agrarian structure and anxious to do so, was one condition of the elasticity of food supplies in the earlier phases of European industrialization.

But not only was the agriculture of most Western European countries unusually responsive to an increase of demand. There were also influences working on population which ensured that the forces making for an increase in *per capita* incomes were not entirely neutralized by an increase in numbers. This is the third point on which history is illuminating.

In most parts of pre-industrial Europe (and in those parts of the world which were settled from Europe) there were powerful and long-established mechanisms tending to keep the increase of population in line with resources. The central part of these mechanisms was the age at marriage and the frequency of marriage. From very early in European history, the social unit was the nuclear family—the husband and wife and their children—as opposed to the extended family or kinship group. In the nuclear family, the individual man was responsible for the support of his wife and their children. Thus marriage was, from early times, associated with the setting up of a separate household, and there was a strong tendency for a man to marry only when he could support a separate household, and support it at a conventional standard of living well above the physiological minimum. It is not my intention to trace the roots of the nuclear family back into European history, but I am sure that this institution (and the attitudes to marriage which it implied) was of immense importance in European economic development. It provided a rough-and-ready mechanism which limited the power of population growth to depress living standards; and in favourable circumstances it made it possible to retain permanently an increase in *per capita* incomes. For though such an increase had a tendency to stimulate population growth, it also raised men's notions about the standard of living which they expected before they embarked on marriage.

This is one respect in which European experience differed from those areas, e.g. India and China, where some form of kinship group or extended family prevailed—the family which covered several generations or several degrees of relationship. In these extended families, the obligation to support children was much more widely diffused than in the nuclear family, much less firmly fixed on the father; and the obligation to have children, in order to extend and continue the group was much more powerful. Marriage was not directly linked, as in Western Europe, to the establishment of a new household; the newly married couple took their place in the existing family household. As a result the age at marriage in such areas was lower and the incidence of marriage higher than in Europe. This seems to have been a difference of long standing and to provide the principal reason why the living standards of India and China were below those of Europe before the Industrial Revolution. Compared with pre-industrial Western Europe, population growth in countries such as India or China was, therefore, determined more by variations in mortality than by variations in fertility, and for this among other reasons it responded more rapidly to any improvement in economic conditions. There was therefore a much more serious population barrier to economic growth.

There is a second feature of European demographic history which is relevant to economic development. The marked and continuous fall in European death rates did not start until the later nineteenth century, and European death rates did not reach very low levels until the end of that century. By this time many parts of Europe had already experienced a long period of economic growth. Moreover, by the time death rates had reached low levels, birth rates were already falling. The fall in birth rates was, at least in part, the result of attitudes towards family size and marriage which were of long standing and which ensured that when an increased number of children survived their early years, fewer would be born.

By contrast, the under-developed regions of the contemporary world have experienced a much more rapid fall in death rates; this fall has been the result of foreign medical techniques introduced without major changes in economic standards or in social attitudes; the fall in death rates has taken place before any fall in birth rates, and without demographic mechanisms which in the advanced countries helped to adjust the rate of population increase by a reduction in birth rates.

Nineteenth-century Europe was favoured by a third exceptional circumstance. Where population growth did press heavily on resources, the existence in the temperate zones of great regions of unsettled and fertile land provided opportunities for migration, and emigration mitigated the fall in living standards in some areas and helped to make possible a rise in living standards in others.

Thus if we ask why, in nineteenth-century Europe, the forces making for an increase in *per capita* incomes were not frustrated by pressure of population, the explanation lies not only in the strength of these forces but in three circumstances relating to population: the European family structure; the timing of the fall in death rates; and unusually favourable opportunities for emigration. The crucial point seems to be that Western European birth rates, on the eve of industrialization, were already lower than those now prevailing in many under-developed regions, and that a sustained and marked fall in European death rates did not start until the economies of Western Europe had already acquired momentum. It was for this reason that the forces making for an increase in *per capita* incomes—forces which were initially of very modest strength—were able to persist. Attention is generally concentrated on the fact that European industrializations were accompanied by a rapid rise in population—a doubling, for example, in the U.K. between 1800 and 1860, and in Germany in the last seventy years or so of the nineteenth century. But it is perhaps more significant that, as a result of restraints on population growth, population was smaller, in relation to resources, in most parts of pre-industrial Europe than in contemporary undeveloped areas.

It is clear that a great many circumstances were responsible for the economic development of Europe, but, if I had to select the two most important circumstances, I should choose the two I have just dealt with: the responsiveness of the agricultural sector and the restraints on population growth. It was because of these that the widening of market possibilities was not brought to a halt but stimulated a cumulative process of expansion. This is the justification for supposing, as a very rough-and-ready generalization, that what had previously delayed European development was not so much inadequate productive capacity as inadequate demand. The characteristic situation in contemporary under-developed countries is obviously different. There the existence of inflationary pressures suggests not a deficiency of demand but bottlenecks on the supply side.

The historical record suggests a fourth reflection. Economic development in the last hundred and fifty years has been predominantly confined to Europe and the countries settled from Europe—with the important exception of Japan. Even within this region, development has been limited. The U.S.A., Germany, the U.K., France and Russia accounted for approximately 80 per cent of the world's manufacturing production in 1870; though the proportions between them changed greatly, they still accounted for about 75 per cent on the eve of the Second World War.[6] Or, to take another indication, Western Europe and the areas settled from it in North America and Australasia accounted for 57 per cent of the world's incomes in 1938 and for not far short of two-thirds in 1949.[7] Moreover most of the countries which were successful in developing enjoyed *per capita* incomes well above those of the contemporary under-developed areas, even before the classic industrial revolution. Many of them, too, had already exhibited a capacity for technical progress. Thus, for example, progress towards manufacture by interchangeable parts was made in Sweden, France and the U.S.A. *before* these countries felt the impact of the new English technology. France had a strong scientific tradition; and even in Russia, which was the most backward of the major European countries in the nineteenth century, there were centres of scientific research from the time of Lomonosov. Thus the diffusion of technology which has taken place since the later eighteenth century has only been markedly successful in regions which had some similarities even before the Industrial Revolution.

The only striking exception to the generalization is Japan, which, starting from a state of economic life less developed than that of any European country on the eve of industrialization, grew very rapidly from the 1880s onwards. The growth is the more remarkable since, at least until after the First World War, the producer-goods industries—which played a large part in other late industrializations—were not of much importance. Even in the case of Japan, however, there are certain similarities to the European experience.

[6]*Industrialisation and World Trade* (League of Nations, 1945).

[7]S. Kuznets, 'Quantitative Aspects of the Economic Growth of Nations: I. Levels and Variability of Rates of Growth', *Economic Development and Cultural Change*, V, No. 1, October 1956, p. 17.

In the first place agricultural productivity increased rapidly. Mr. Johnston has estimated that between the 1880s and the 1910s output per head in Japanese agriculture more than doubled.[8] It is true that this increase was achieved within an agrarian structure based on small units of cultivation, and by increasing intensity of cultivation often achieved under the threat of starvation. On the other hand, in this case too the increase in agricultural productivity was preceded by agrarian reforms. The content of the agrarian reforms of the Meiji regime was different from that of the European reforms associated with the abolition of serfdom; but by converting feudal payments in kind into fixed money payments the Meiji reforms gave Japanese cultivators the means as well as the incentive to increase output. Again, though rice cultivation was the predominant form of agriculture, there is this similarity with the European experience—that technical methods of increasing output were available which were relatively inexpensive in capital (in the Japanese case, improved seeds and fertilizers). This increase in agricultural productivity made a direct contribution to raising the level of income per head; it released population for employment in industrial pursuits; it contributed to the growth of the Japanese domestic market; and it made possible a rapid expansion in exports (especially raw silk) which enabled Japan to import machinery and raw materials.

The economic development of Japan took place in the face of a rapid increase in population. The population doubled between 1880 and 1935. This is, it is true, no greater an increase than in the U.K. in a comparable period of her industrialization, but Japan was very much more densely populated in 1880, in relation to natural resources, than the U.K. in 1800. The development of Japan does therefore show that even a country which is densely populated at the start can generate enough momentum to break through the 'population barrier'. The circumstances which made it possible in this particular case warrant much closer examination than is possible in a short paper. But it must be remembered that even after eighty years of rapid industrialization, real output per head in Japan is still far below that of most of the industrialized countries of Europe. Moreover, the disparity would certainly have been greater had not Japan not begun to exhibit some of the demographic traits of the more industrialized countries.

I have concentrated in this paper on the early stages of economic development rather than on the factors which determine variations in the rate of development of advanced economies. My impression is that, in these early stages the influences which may be broadly defined as social were of greater importance than the strictly economic factors. Some of the most important social influences have not been touched on at all, e.g. those which determined the degree of prestige attached to economic achievement in any given society, the sources from which entrepreneurs were drawn and the amount of optimism they showed.

[8]Bruce F. Johnston, 'Agricultural Productivity and Economic Development in Japan', *Journal of Political Economy*, LIX (1951).

The Present Underdeveloped Countries and Past Growth Patterns

Simon Kuznets

2   Much of the writing and thinking on problems of economic growth in underdeveloped countries is unconsciously steeped in the social and economic background of the developed Western nations, and there is a temptation to extrapolate from the past growth patterns of these nations to the growth problems and potentials of the underdeveloped areas. An emphasis on the differences, viewed as obstacles to such extrapolation, may contribute to a more realistic appraisal of the magnitude and recalcitrance of the problems.

Summary Results of Comparisons

1. The present levels of per capita product in the underdeveloped countries are much lower than were those in the developed countries in their preindustrialization phase.

Excerpted from a paper with this title presented at the University of Texas in April 1958. Reprinted from Easton Nelson, ed., *Economic Growth: Rationale, Problems, Cases,* University of Texas Press, Austin, 1960, by permission of the author and publisher. The author is professor of economics at Harvard University.

11

This statement can be supported by a variety of evidence and appears to be true, except in reference to Japan, where per capita income before industrialization was as low as in most of Asia today. The preindustrialization phase may be defined either as the decade when the share of the labor force in agriculture was at least six tenths of the total and was just ready to begin its downward movement, or as the decade just before those which Professor W. W. Rostow characterizes as the "take-off into self-sustained growth."[1] In either case, the evidence that we have on the presently developed countries—in Western and Central Europe, in North America, and in Oceania—shows that the per capita incomes in their preindustrial phases were already much higher than those now prevailing in the underdeveloped countries. They ranged well above $200 (in 1952–54 prices) compared with the present well below $100 for the populous underdeveloped countries of Asia and Africa. Even in Russia, per capita income around 1885 was probably more than $150 (in 1952–54 prices), on the assumption that the present level is about $500.[2]

2. The supply of agricultural land per capita is much lower in most underdeveloped countries today than in most presently developed countries even today, let alone their preindustrial phase. Comparison of the supply of agricultural land per agricultural worker would yield similar findings.

This statement conforms to our general knowledge of the higher density of population settlement and the greater pressure of population on land in such countries as China, India, Pakistan, and Indonesia than in the older Western European countries now or even more before their industrialization, not to mention the vast empty spaces of Canada, the United States, and other Western European offshoots overseas or for that matter of the USSR. Statistical evidence assembled by Colin Clark relates agricultural land (reduced to standard units) to male workers in agriculture, and yields ratios of 1.2 workers per land unit for the United States, slightly more than 3 in USSR, about 10 in Germany and France, and as many as 31 in India and Pakistan, 25 in China, and 73 in Egypt (post-World War II).[3] More directly relevant are the data provided by Professor Bert F. Hoselitz on the density of agricultural settlement in countries with more than half of the active labor force in agriculture, which show that in England and Wales in 1688 and in many European countries in the mid-nineteenth century the number of hectares per male worker (or household) ranged mostly between 5 and 10, whereas similar calculations for Asian countries and Egypt today show a range from well below 1 to at most 2.5 hectares.[4]

[1]See *The Economic Journal*, LXVI, 261 (March 1956), pp. 25-83, particularly the table of dates on p. 31.

[2]This statement is based on the long-term rates of growth shown for Russia in my paper, "Quantitative Aspects of the Economic Growth of Nations: I. Levels and Variability of Rates of Growth," *Economic Development and Cultural Change*, V, 1 (October 1956), Appendix Table 13, p. 81.

[3]See his *Conditions of Economic Progress*, 3d ed. (London, 1957), Table XXXIII, following p. 308.

[4]See his "Population Pressure, Industrialization and Social Mobility," *Population Studies*, XI, 2 (November 1957), Table I, p. 126.

3. The lower per capita (and per worker) income in the underdeveloped countries—relative to that in the preindustrialization phase of the presently developed countries—is probably due largely to the lower productivity of the agricultural sector.

We have no direct confirmation at hand, but several items of indirect evidence strongly support this statement. First and most telling, is the lower supply of agricultural land per worker noted above. Second, cross-section comparisons for recent years indicate that the shortage of per worker income in the agricultural sector relative to that in the nonagricultural sector is negatively associated with real national product per capita or per worker. This association suggests that the shortage of per worker income in the agricultural sector relative to that in the nonagricultural sector in the underdeveloped countries today is greater than it was in the preindustrial phase of presently developed countries. Third, the nonagricultural sector in even the underdeveloped countries includes some modern industries that were nonexistent in the mid-nineteenth century or earlier. It may well be that per worker income in the nonagricultural sector of the underdeveloped countries is today as high as per worker income in the nonagricultural sector in the preindustrialization phase of currently developed countries. On this possibly extreme assumption, per worker income in the agricultural sector in the underdeveloped countries must be one fourth or one third of per worker income in agriculture in the currently developed countries in their preindustrialization phase (much lower than the one third to one half for *total* income per worker).

4. Inequality in the size distribution of income in the underdeveloped countries today is as wide as, if not wider than, it was in the presently developed countries in their preindustrialization phase.

Here again we have only indirect evidence. First, limited statistical data suggest that today the inequality in income distribution in the underdeveloped countries is distinctly wider than in the developed countries.[5] Although this may be due in part to the reduction in income inequality in the process of growth of the developed countries, there is some indication that with industrialization, inequality first widened and then contracted, so that inequality in the phases *preceding* industrialization may not have been as wide as that during the early phases of industrial growth. Second, the very wide difference suggested under point 3 between per worker income in the agricultural and nonagricultural sectors in the underdeveloped countries, a difference wider than that in the preindustrialization phase of currently developed countries, also suggests wider inequality in the size distribution of total income.

Even if relative inequality in the size distribution of income in the underdeveloped countries today were no wider than it was in the pre-industrialization phase of the currently developed countries, or even if it

---

[5]See Theodore Morgan, "Distribution of Income in Ceylon, Puerto Rico, the United States and the United Kingdom," *Economic Journal*, XVIII (December 1953), pp. 821–834, and subsequent discussion by Harry Oshima and Theodore Morgan in *ibid.*, LXVI (March 1956), pp. 156–164.

were slightly narrower, the appreciably lower income per capita in the underdeveloped countries would aggravate the economic and social implications. For if average income per capita is so low, the majority of the population with incomes significantly below the countrywide average must exist at distressingly low standards of living, and the contrast must be striking between, on the one hand, these large masses of agricultural cultivators and of low-paid *lumpen* proletariat in the few cities and, on the other, the small groups that, either by control of property rights or by attachment to a few economically favorable sectors, manage to secure relatively high per capita incomes.

5. Social and political concomitants of the low-income structure of the underdeveloped countries today appear to constitute more formidable obstacles to economic growth than they did in the preindustrialization phase of presently developed countries.

The vast array of diverse evidence on the point can hardly be summarized here, nor do we claim that these social and political patterns are necessarily consequences of the low-income structure and attributable to it alone. But at the risk of "economocentricity," it can be argued that the low economic base was a factor in producing the social and political results and a few illustrations will elucidate the point.

First, the crude birth rates in underdeveloped countries, even in recent years, are at least 40 per 1,000, and in many cases well above.[6] Rates as high as these or even higher apparently characterized the United States in the early decades of the nineteenth century, possibly Canada, and other "empty" lands overseas. But in the older countries in Western, Central, and Northern Europe, the birth rates in the preindustrialization phase were already down to the middle 30's, and in some cases close to 30 per 1,000. In other words, part of the process of demographic transition had already taken place; birth rates were as high as those in underdeveloped countries today only when the ratio of population to resources was extremely favorable. Obviously, rapid population growth under the conditions prevailing in underdeveloped countries today is an obstacle to accumulation of capital and to economic growth, as it was in the older European countries in their preindustrialization phase.

Second, let us disregard for the moment literacy rates, which are distressingly low in the underdeveloped countries today, and probably well below those in the currently developed countries in their pre-industrialization phase. An even more important problem for many is linguistic and cultural disunity, a problem particularly acute for both the large population units like India and China and for the smaller ones in which groups with different antecedents have been brought together. Without claiming that economic factors predominate, one can argue that the persistingly low level of economic performance and, as part and

[6]See, for example, United Nations, *Report on the World Social Situation* (New York, 1957), particularly pp. 6–10.

parcel of it, of communication and transportation, has played an important role. No such major problem of linguistic and cultural unity or literacy appears to have plagued the currently developed countries during their preindustrial phase.

Third, a weak political structure is in large measure predetermined by low and unequal incomes, backwardness of transportation and communication, and linguistic and cultural disunity, if by a strong political structure one means a complex of associations culminating in an efficient sovereign government, checked and guided by underlying voluntary organizations. The cleavage between the masses of population struggling for a meager subsistence and the small groups at the top—precluding a widely graded bridge of "middle" classes—certainly militates against a strong political structure and easily leads to dictatorial or oligarchical regimes, which are often unstable and unresponsive to basic economic problems. In all these respects, the situation in the preindustrial phase of the currently developed countries, again with the possible exception of Japan, was far different in the effective interplay between the government and the interests of the population, and in the much greater influence of the various groups in the population upon the basic decisions made by the state in order to facilitate economic growth.

6. Most underdeveloped countries have attained political independence only recently, after decades of colonial status or political inferiority to the advanced countries that limited their independence. This was not true of the currently developed countries in their preindustrial phase; industrialization followed a long period of political independence.

This statement is a partial explanation of the weaknesses in the social and political structure of underdeveloped countries today and to that extent is a corroboration of point 5. But there is an important additional element in it. Insofar as their political independence has recently been won only after a prolonged struggle—and is thus an outcome of decades of opposition to the advanced countries, viewed as imperialists and aggressors—not only were economic problems neglected but the native leadership was trained in political conflict rather than in economic statesmanship. There was also a negative association between the forms of advanced economic operation, as practiced by the invaders and aggressors, and its products as reflected in a higher material standard of living: the higher standard was favored, but the forms of organization which made it possible were hated. A similar condition may have existed in the development of some of the presently developed countries: for example, a distinctive minority may have been associated with a revolutionary economic process that necessitated disruptive changes and adversely affected established interests. But such an association could not have been so widely and distinctly felt as are those in the underdeveloped countries, which have had a long history as colonies or inferior political units. Neither could the disruptive effects of the advanced elements in the economy have been as great, nor in some respects as painful, as those resulting from the introduction of Western methods and practices into a social and political framework whose historical roots were radically different from those of the West.

7. The populations in underdeveloped countries today are inheritors of civilizations quite distinctive from and independent of European civilization. Yet it is European civilization that through centuries of geographical, political, and intellectual expansion has provided the matrix of modern economic growth. All presently developed countries, with the exception of Japan, are either old members of the European civilization, its offshoots overseas, or its offshoots on land toward the East.

This statement is again part of the explanation of the weaknesses in the social and political structure of underdeveloped countries today. But it is useful to recall that the European community went through a series of revolutions from the fifteenth century (to set the initial date as late as possible) to the eighteenth, antedating the agricultural and industrial revolutions in eighteenth-century England which ushered in the industrial system, the vehicle of modern economic growth. The intellectual revolution with the introduction of science, the moral revolution with the secularization of Christo-Judaic religions, the geographical revolution with expansion to the East and the West, the political revolution with the formation of national states, all occurred within the context of European civilization, not in Asia, Africa, or the Americas; and they occurred long before the modern industrial system was born. Whether or not these antecedents were indispensable is unimportant here since we are not concerned with a general theory of the causes of modern economic growth. Our point is simply that participation in this long process of change before the emergence of the industrial system meant *gradual* adaptation, an opportunity to develop within the existing social and political framework the new institutions necessary to exploit the potentials provided by these intellectual, moral, geographical, and political revolutions. Thus when the presently developed countries within the European orbit reached their preindustrialization phase, they already possessed a variety of social, political, and economic institutions, and particularly a prevailing set of views and scale of values that permitted them to make the further adjustments which industrialization brought in its wake or that were essential concomitants.

The present situation in the underdeveloped countries is in sharp contrast. They are the inheritors of different civilizations, the possessors of social, economic, and political institutions with roots that go far back and represent a heritage of adjustment to a different series of historical events, lacking the same kind of geographical, intellectual, and political revolutions, yet possibly containing a wide variety of other marked changes. These changes, however, are *not* the matrix out of which modern economic growth emerges. Consequently, there is no continuity between the adjustments that may have occurred in these underdeveloped areas before their invasion by the aggressive and expanding European civilization and the adjustments that are needed to take advantage of the potentials of modern economic growth. Some of these other civilizations did indeed reach highly impressive levels: after all, China in the seventeenth or early eighteenth century was a political unit that, in size of population and efficiency of administration, dwarfed even the largest European unit of the day; and some of the accomplishments of the native Indian civilizations were far in advance of anything that the European civilization could produce at the time. But this very success, the specific adaptation of the social and cultural patterns to the potential (e.g., the development in China of the non-phonetic written language to overcome the problem of diversities of spoken languages, or in India of the caste system) becomes a serious obstacle in their response to an entirely different range of technological potentials, calling for a markedly different set of social and cultural behavior patterns.

Growth Rates in the Less and More
Developed Parts of the World

3

Table 1.   Estimated Average Annual Growth Rates of Developed and Less Developed Countries, Summary by Region (In 1965 prices)

Region	1965 Region Weight	Percent Change in Total GNP				Percent Change in GNP per Capita					Current Rate of Population Growth
		1950-1955	1955-1960	1960-1966	1957-8 Av. to 1965-6 Av.	1955-1960	1960-1966	Change from Preceding Year 1965	Change from Preceding Year 1966	1957-8 Av. to 1965-6 Av.	
Less Developed Countries											
Total[a]	100.0	5.0	4.4	4.8	4.7	2.1	2.3	1.2	2.4	2.3	2.5
Latin America	32.0	5.1	4.9	4.5	4.6	2.0	1.6	2.2	1.1	1.7	2.9
Near East	13.0		5.6	6.4	6.2	3.3	3.9	3.4	2.9	3.7	2.4
South Asia	22.6	3.6	4.2	3.8	4.2	2.1	1.4	-4.8	3.1	1.8	2.5
East Asia											
Including Indonesia	12.6		3.8	4.9	4.6	1.3	2.3	4.2	2.2	2.0	2.7
Excluding Indonesia	8.9		5.0	6.3	6.2	2.2	3.4	4.4	3.3	3.3	3.0
Africa	10.5			3.4	3.7		1.1	1.6	-0.3	1.4	2.4
Other[b]	9.3			8.0	6.0		6.4	5.7	7.4	4.4	1.6
Developed Countries											
Total Including U.S.	100.0	4.7	3.4	5.0	4.8	2.2	3.8	3.9	3.7	3.6	1.1
Total Excluding U.S.	48.6	5.2	4.9	5.1	5.3	3.9	4.0	2.9	3.1	4.2	1.1
United States	51.4	4.3	2.2	4.8	4.3	0.5	3.4	4.6	4.2	2.8	1.2
Europe	35.7	5.0	4.5	4.5	4.7	3.7	3.5	2.7	2.6	3.8	0.9
Other Developed Countries	12.9	6.2	6.1	7.0	6.9	4.6	5.6	3.6	4.7	5.5	1.4

aThese estimated growth rates for the less developed countries are based on trend data.
bLargely Spain and Puerto Rico.
Source: Adapted from Gross National Product: Growth Rates and Trend Data, Agency for International Development, Statistics and Reports Division, RC-W-138, March 31, 1967.

Table 2.   Latin America: Estimated Average Annual Growth Rates

Region and Country	Percent Change in Total GNP 1950-1955	1955-1960	1960-1966	1961-1966	1957-8 Av. to 1965-6 Av.	Percent Change in GNP per Capita 1955-1960	1960-1966	Change from Preceding Year 1965	1966	1961-1966	1957-8 Av. to 1965-6 Av.	Current Rate of Population Growth
Costa Rica	7.6	4.7	4.9	5.8	4.7	1.0	1.1	3.1	2.8	2.0	0.9	3.8
El Salvador	4.5	4.0	6.4	6.8	5.6	0.9	3.2	0.7	2.2	3.6	2.5	3.2
Guatemala	2.3	5.2	6.5	7.1	5.7	1.9	3.2	3.7	3.0	3.8	2.4	3.3
Honduras		5.3	3.8	4.5	3.9	2.2	0.7	3.6	3.0	1.4	0.8	3.1
Nicaragua	8.3	2.3	7.8	8.2	5.9	-0.6	4.6	5.0	2.7	5.0	2.8	3.0
Central American Economic Commission	4.6	4.5	6.0	6.6	5.3	1.3	2.7	3.1	3.0	3.3	2.0	3.3
Argentina	3.0	3.1	2.6	1.8	2.7		1.0	6.3	-2.5	0.2	1.1	1.6
Bolivia	5.7	5.9	5.0	5.6	4.2	1.3	2.7	3.1	3.0	3.3	1.9	2.4
Brazil	3.0	4.2	4.2	3.7	5.1	2.8	1.2	1.8	0.4	0.7	2.1	3.0
Chile	5.5	4.0	4.5	4.6	3.9	1.6	2.1	3.2	3.3	2.2	1.4	2.4
Colombia	6.7	5.5	4.5	4.6	4.7	1.1	1.6	0.3	2.8	1.6	1.8	3.6
Dominican Republic	5.3	4.6	1.7	3.2	2.1	1.9	-1.9	-14.2	-0.4	-0.4	-1.5	3.4
Ecuador	6.2	6.1	4.3	4.9	4.5	1.4	1.0	0.0	0.9	1.6	1.3	3.5
Mexico	4.0	5.8	6.1	6.7	5.9	2.8	2.7	1.8	3.3	3.2	2.5	3.2
Panama	2.9	2.4	8.0	7.4	7.2	2.9	4.8	4.5	3.7	4.1	4.1	2.6
Paraguay	6.0	4.3	4.6	4.4	3.7	0.2	1.8	3.8	1.4	1.7	1.2	3.1
Peru		4.3	6.5	6.2	6.3	1.6	3.4	0.8	3.0	3.1	3.3	3.4
Uruguay		0.0	0.4	-0.1	0.1	-1.4	-1.0	-0.2	-0.7	-1.5	-1.3	1.4
Venezuela	9.0	7.2	5.0	5.8	5.2	3.2	1.6	1.4	1.5	2.4	1.7	3.4
18 Latin American Republics — Total	5.1	4.9	4.5	4.4	4.6	2.0	1.6	2.2	1.1	1.5	1.7	2.9
Jamaica			4.8	5.0			2.8	2.0	2.3	2.8		2.6
Trinidad and Tobago		6.0	6.0	6.1			3.0	3.5	2.5	3.1		3.0

Source: Agency for International Development, *op cit.*

Table 3.   Near East and South Asia: Estimated
Annual Growth Rates

Region and Country	Percent Change in Total GNP				Percent Change in GNP per Capita					Current Rate of Population Growth
	1950-1955	1955-1960	1960-1966	1957-8 Av. to 1965-6 Av.	1955-1960	1960-1966	Change from Preceding Year		1957-8 Av. to 1965-6 Av.	
							1965	1966		
Cyprus			5.5			4.6	18.1	2.5		1.5
Greece	7.0	5.3	8.8	7.2	4.4	8.3	6.9	8.9	6.6	0.5
Iraq		6.3	6.2	6.1	3.6	3.1	5.5	1.7	2.8	3.2
Israel	13.1	9.0	8.4	9.2	5.1	4.5	3.4	-1.3	5.6	2.6
Jordan		12.1	8.3	8.5	9.3	5.4	0.8	-1.4	5.7	3.0
Turkey	6.3	5.2	4.9	4.5	2.3	2.4	2.7	5.7	1.9	2.5
Near East – Total		5.6	6.4	6.2	3.3	3.9	3.4	2.9	3.7	2.4
Ceylon			3.0			0.4	-0.5	0.7		2.9
India	3.9		3.5	4.0	2.3	1.1	-6.4	3.3	1.7	2.4
Pakistan	1.7		5.5	5.2	1.3	2.9	2.2	2.0	2.6	2.6
South Asia – Total	3.6		3.8	4.2	2.1	1.4	-4.8	3.1	1.8	2.5

Source: Agency for International Development, *op. cit.*

Table 4.   East Asia and Africa: Estimated
Average Annual Growth Rates

Region and Country	Percent Change in Total GNP				Percent Change in GNP per Capita					Current Rate of Population Growth
	1950-1955	1955-1960	1960-1966	1957-8 Av. to 1965-6 Av.	1955-1960	1960-1966	Change from Preceding Year 1965	Change from Preceding Year 1966	1957-8 Av. to 1965-6 Av.	
Burma	7.0	5.7	2.0	3.7	3.9	-0.1	2.1	-4.0	1.7	2.1
China (Taiwan)		4.6	9.7	9.1	1.8	6.8	9.4	4.5	6.1	2.8
Korea			7.5	6.3		4.7	5.3	7.3	3.5	2.8
Malaysia			6.1			3.1	4.9	2.3		3.0
Philippines	6.9	4.5	4.8	4.7	1.5	1.4	1.9	1.6	1.4	3.4
Thailand			7.2	7.5		4.1	3.3	4.8	4.5	3.1
East Asia LDC's – Total										
Including Indonesia		3.8	4.9	4.6	1.3	2.3	4.2	2.2	2.0	2.7
Excluding Indonesia		5.0	6.3	6.2	2.2	3.4	4.4	3.3	3.3	3.0
Japan		9.8	9.3	9.9	8.9	8.3	2.7	6.8	8.9	1.0
Ethiopia			3.5a			2.1	2.1	2.1		1.4
Ghana			1.8			-0.9	2.5	-5.9		2.7
Kenya			4.5			1.6	-0.5	3.4		3.0
Morocco		0.2	2.3	3.8	-2.6	-0.5	-1.4	-4.9	0.9	3.1
Nigeria			5.0	2.3		2.9	4.5	3.2	-0.5	2.1
Rhodesia		5.8	0.5	4.8	2.5	-2.7	2.7	-10.8	2.8	3.2
Sudan			3.6	2.4		0.8	-0.6	1.9	-0.8	2.9
Tanganyika			4.2	4.3		2.3	1.3	5.0	1.5	1.9
Tunisia			4.5			2.4	3.6	-0.5		2.5
Uganda			3.5	3.4			1.4	0.5	0.9	2.5
Zambia		9.9	6.5	7.6			21.8	0.1	4.7	2.9
Africa LDC's – Total			3.4	3.7		1.1	1.6	-0.3	1.4	2.4
South Africa		4.0	5.7	4.9	1.6	3.4	2.7	2.4	2.5	2.3

aAnnual growth 1961-1966.
Source: Agency for International Development, op. cit.

Table 5a.   Less Developed Countries: Ranking by
Growth Rates, 1960 to 1966

Per Capita Gross National Product

Country	Rate	Country	Rate
Greece	8.3	*Average (Weighted)*	2.3
Spain	7.7		
China (Taiwan)	6.8	Tanganyika	2.3
Jordan	5.4	Chile	2.1
		Ethiopia	2.1
		Paraguay	1.8
Panama	4.8		
Korea	4.7	Colombia	1.6
Cyprus	4.6	Kenya	1.6
Nicaragua	4.6	Venezuela	1.6
		Philippines	1.4
Israel	4.5	Brazil	1.2
Thailand	4.1	Costa Rica	1.1
Zambia	3.6	India	1.1
Peru	3.4	Argentina	1.0
El Salvador	3.2	Ecuador	1.0
Guatemala	3.2	Uganda	1.0
Malaysia	3.1	Sudan	0.8
Iraq	3.1	Honduras	0.7
		Ceylon	0.4
Nigeria	2.9	Burma	−0.1
Pakistan	2.9	Morocco	−0.5
Bolivia	2.7	Ghana	−0.9
Mexico	2.7		
		Uruguay	−1.0
Tunisia	2.4	Dominican Republic	−1.9
Turkey	2.4	Rhodesia	−2.7

Source: Agency for International Development, *op. cit.*

Table 5b.   Less Developed Countries: Ranking
by Growth Rates, 1960 to 1966

Total Gross National Product

Country	Rate	Country	Rate
China (Taiwan)	9.7	Average (Weighted)	4.8
Greece	8.8		
Spain	8.5	Philippines	4.8
Israel	8.4	Paraguay	4.6
		Chile	4.5
Jordan	8.3	Colombia	4.5
Panama	8.0		
Nicaragua	7.8	Kenya	4.5
Korea	7.5	Tunisia	4.5
		Ecuador	4.3
Thailand	7.2	Brazil	4.2
Guatemala	6.5		
Peru	6.5	Tanganyika	4.2
Zambia	6.5	Honduras	3.8
		Sudan	3.6
El Salvador	6.4	Ethiopia	3.5
Iraq	6.2		
Malaysia	6.1	India	3.5
Mexico	6.1	Uganda	3.5
		Ceylon	3.0
Cyprus	5.5	Argentina	2.6
Pakistan	5.5		
Bolivia	5.0	Morocco	2.3
Nigeria	5.0	Burma	2.0
		Ghana	1.8
		Dominican Republic	1.7
Venezuela	5.0		
Costa Rica	4.9	Rhodesia	0.5
Turkey	4.9	Uruguay	0.4

Source: Agency for International Development, *op. cit.*

Table 6.   Developed Countries: Ranking by
Growth Rates, 1960 to 1966

Total Gross National Product

Country	Rate	Country	Rate
Japan	9.3	Sweden	4.8
Portugal	6.7	United States	4.8
South Africa	5.7	Belgium	4.7
Canada	5.6		
Norway	5.3	New Zealand	4.7
Iceland	5.2	Denmark	4.6
France	5.1	Germany	4.6
Average excluding			
U.S. (Weighted)	5.1		
Italy	5.1	Australia	4.2
		Austria	4.1
Average including		Ireland	3.5
U.S. (Weighted)	5.0		
Netherlands	4.9	Luxembourg	3.2
Switzerland	4.9	United Kingdom	3.0

Per Capita Gross National Product

Country	Rate	Country	Rate
Japan	8.3	Iceland	3.5
Portugal	5.8	Netherlands	3.5
Norway	4.5	South Africa	3.4
Italy	4.3		
Sweden	4.1	United States	3.4
Average excluding		Germany	3.3
U.S. (Weighted)	4.0	Ireland	3.2
Belgium	4.0		
Canada	3.8	Switzerland	3.0
Denmark	3.8	New Zealand	2.7
Average including		Australia	2.2
U.S. (Weighted)	3.8		
France	3.8	United Kingdom	2.2
Austria	3.5	Luxembourg	2.1

Source: Agency for International Development, *op. cit.*

Table 7. Comparisons between Developed and
Less Developed Areas by Region

Item	Unit	Developed Areas[a]		Less Developed Non-Communist Areas				
		Total	United States	Total	Africa	Far East	Latin America	Near East and South Asia
Population								
Total (mid-1965)	Millions	628	195	1,560	250	280	230	760
Annual Growth	Percent	1.3	1.5	2.5	2.3	2.7	2.9	2.4
Persons per Square Mile	Number	50	54	60	20	20	30	180
Land								
Total Area	1,000 Sq. mi.	12,400	3,620	26,250	10,800	1,560	7,710	4,330
Agricultural Land	% of Area	39	47	24	26	17	24	30
Acres per Capita	Number	5	6	2.7	7.6	0.6	5.2	1.1
Gross National Product								
Total GNP (1964)	$ Billions	1,200	628	240	27	30	71	86
Annual Growth (1957-58 to 1964-65)[b]	Percent	4.7	4.0	4.7	3.4	4.4	4.4	4.9
GNP per Capita (1964)	Dollars	1,950	3,270	160	115	110	325	115
Food Production								
Production Index (1965)	1957-59 = 100	115	116	121	117	128	126	119
Per Capita Production Index (1965)	1957-59 = 100	106	104	102	100	107	103	101
Electric Power per Capita	KWH per Year	3,530	5,540	150	80	90	400	80
Foreign Trade (value basis)								
Total Exports, f.o.b. (1964)	$ Billions	115.4	26.6	35.8	6.6	6.0	9.9	9.1
Annual Growth, 1959-1964	Percent	9.2	8.5	6.3	8.9	3.3	5.1	6.8

Table 7. Comparisons between Developed and Less Developed Areas by Region (Continued)

Item	Unit	Developed Areas[a]		Less Developed Non-Communist Areas				
		Total	United States	Total	Africa	Far East	Latin America	Near East and South Asia
Foreign Trade (value basis) (continued)								
Total Imports, c.i.f. (1964)	$ Billions	120.0	20.3	38.5	6.4	7.4	8.6	10.1
Annual Growth, 1959-1964	Percent	9.3	3.6	6.1	4.3	2.5	3.6	7.7
Health								
Life Expectancy	Years	70	70	47	40	42	55	47
Calories per Day	Calories	2,920	3,090	2,250	2,355	2,160	2,560	2,130
People per Physician	Number	800	730	4,300	19,100	5,400	1,600	4,900
Education								
Literacy	Percent	96	98	37	18	57	67	25
Pupils as Percent of Population[c]	Percent	18	23	11	8	15	15	10

[a]Generally the industrial countries of Western Europe, United States, Canada, Australia, New Zealand, Japan, and South Africa.
[b]Based on data in constant 1962 prices.
[c]Primary and Secondary students only.

General Note on Main Sources Used:
Population, land, foreign trade, and education — Publications of United Nations and its specialized agencies; AID reports.
GNP — Official government reports and AID estimates.
Food — Economic Research Service, USDA.
Electric power — Publications of UN and US Federal Power Commission.
Health — UN, USDA, and official government publications.
Source: Compiled in *Selected Economic Data for the Less Developed Countries*, Agency for International Development, Statistics and Reports Division, June 1966, page 8.

International Comparisons of Income Levels: A Suggested New Measure

W. Beckerman
R. Bacon

4 ... The difficulties of obtaining reliable estimates by conventional methods are, as is well known, very great indeed. These difficulties are of two main kinds. First, in most developing countries it is very difficult to construct national accounts in national currencies because of the absence of adequate statistical services, and of the inherent difficulty of obtaining reliable statistical information from a population much of which may be illiterate in the usual sense of the word as well as innumerate.

Secondly, even where reasonably reliable national accounts estimates are available in national prices, these are usually quite inadequate as a basis for international comparisons of relative real incomes because of the inappropriateness of exchange rates as an indicator of the relative internal purchasing powers of the currencies. The reasons for this are, of course, fairly obvious, and in the studies by Gilbert and Kravis[1]

An excerpt from an article in the *Economic Journal,* Sept. 1966. Reprinted by permission of the authors and publisher. The authors are at Balliol College and Nuffield College respectively, Oxford University.

[1] Milton Gilbert and Irving Kravis, *An International Comparison of National Products and the Purchasing Power of Currencies* (Paris, O.E.E.C., 1954).

and Gilbert and Associates[2] explicit measures of the discrepancy between internal purchasing power parities and exchange rates have been provided. Furthermore, in many developing countries (*e.g.,* where multiple exchange rates are used, or where the "free" market rate differs from the official rate) it is not even possible to identify what the exchange rate is.

A related issue is the reliability, for any given country, of its estimates of the growth rate of income over time. Morgernstern's criticisms[3] of the interpretation of comparative growth data may be challenged in its application to developed countries. Hence, quite apart from the difficulties of assessing the level of income of underdeveloped countries relative to each other or to developed countries it is also very difficult to assess how rapidly they are making progress, and hence the effectiveness of their own policies or of aid policies in those countries.

Faced with such a situation, various attempts have been made to fill the gap.[4] These attempts are of two main kinds. The first, following the work of Bennett,[5] consists of the use of "non-monetary indicators," such as calories consumed, infant mortality rates, stock of physicians, stocks of telephone or transport equipment, cement consumption and so on. The procedure is basically to rank countries according to the index of each indicator (with, say, the U.S. level + 100), and then simply to average the indices of all the indicators. Various refinements may be adopted, as in the study by Cseh-Szombathy[6] or Niewiaroski,[7] but the end result is still impossible to interpret in terms of the fundamental welfare or productivity constructs of economic theory, which are based on the need to combine different indicators according to their relative marginal satisfactions or marginal costs. That is, the weighting pattern used in the various indices produced so far on the basis of non-monetary indicators has no theoretical justification, or even clear interpretation, whatsoever.[8]

The second line of approach has been that originated by Colin Clark[9] and later vastly refined and improved in the pioneering work of Milton Gilbert and Irving Kravis, in which the problems of international deflation of the monetary values (in national currencies) of national product and its

[2]Milton Gilbert and Associates, *Comparative National Products and Price Levels* (Paris: O.E.E.C., 1958).

[3]O. Morgernstern, *On the Accuracy of Economic Observations* (2nd edition) (Princeton and Oxford, 1963).

[4]A survey of work in this field is given in Wilfred Beckerman, *International Comparisons of Real Incomes,* O.E.C.D. Development Centre (Paris, 1966).

[5]M. K. Bennett, "International Disparities in Consumption Levels," *American Economic Review,* September 1951.

[6]L. Cseh-Szombathy, "Comparing Synthetic Indicators for International Comparisons of the Standard of Living Using Index Numbers Expressed in Natural Units of Measure," in *The Standard of Living: Some Problems of Analysis and of International Comparison,* Hungarian Academy of Science (Budapest, 1962).

[7]D. H. Niewiaroski, *The Level of Living of Nations: Meaning and Measurement* (roneoed) I.B.R.D., Washington, July 1964.

[8]For fuller discussion of this see W. Beckerman, *op. cit.*

[9]Colin Clark, *The Conditions of Economic Progress* (Macmillan, 1937).

components were approached in conceptually exactly the same way as the deflation over time of the national accounts data for a given country. This approach is clearly the only satisfactory approach from a theoretical point of view. However, the resources required for such an operation are considerable, even when it is limited to a few advanced countries where basic statistics are in reasonably good shape. It is possible that it can be extended, given time and considerable resources, to a few developing countries, either along the original Gilbert and Kravis lines or following the alternative, but comparable, method used by Paige and Bombach.[10] But it is quite beyond the realm of possibility to apply these methods to all the eighty or so developing countries in the world.

Outline of the Method Used

The object of this paper is to propose and describe an alternative method of measurement that appears to be theoretically valid, potentially very accurate and, at the same time, almost costless.[11] The results obtained by this method so far are also shown. There are various obvious improvements that might be made and, as further equations are tested and more control data eventually become available, the basic equations used will be modified and improved; but in the light of the correlation coefficients obtained it does appear that considerable use can be made of the main results already obtained.

The rationale of the method used has been briefly indicated elsewhere.[12] In this paper we shall spell this out in more detail and, in particular, consider some of the main technical statistical queries that might arise. The other main additional feature of this paper is that by virtue of further results obtained, estimates are now shown for eighty countries, and the estimates are probably more accurate than those shown hitherto.

The basis of the method used is as follows. We start from the position that it is only the national accountant's measure of income or consumption that is intelligible in terms of the fundamental concepts of economic theory (in which indifference surfaces and production possibility surfaces are defined in terms of economic goods and services), as it is only such a measure which weights together the various components (such as meat consumed, auto-mobiles purchased, etc.) in terms of their relative satisfactions or costs to the economy. It may well be—in fact, it certainly is—true that defined widely, "standards of welfare and degrees of happiness" include many other factors in life, some quantitative (such as non-market transactions for which no satisfactory imputation can be made) and some non-quantitative, such as

[10]Deborah Paige and Gottfried Bombach, *A Comparison of National Output and Productivity of the United States and the United Kingdom* (O.E.E.C., 1959).

[11]Most of the costs, namely those of programming the basic computations, have already been incurred. The marginal costs of further refinement and application of these computations are small.

[12]W. Beckerman, *op. cit.*

spiritual contentment, but this, though important, is beside the point here, and the "non-monetary approach" as pursued by Bennett and others is no more help in providing an all-embracing measure of welfare in this sense than in providing a valid measure of economic welfare or output in the sense that economists are interested in. In other words, we are not interested here in the conceptual issues of the units in which the production boundaries should be drawn, or the limits on these boundaries, but solely in how to measure what is inside the boundary as conventionally drawn and in terms of the usual theoretical definition of the unit. . . .

The procedure adopted has been as follows. First we have independent direct estimates of relative "real" consumption per head in the nine Gilbert and Associates countries for two years, 1950 and 1955, plus estimates for four additional countries . . . For those countries and years we have prepared values of several "non-monetary" indicators of the type used by Bennett and others. From preliminary analysis we have selected those indicators which, taken by themselves, appeared to show reasonable correlation with the twenty-two independent observations of "real" consumption per head. With the aid of a computer we have then found which combination of indicators, and which forms of the equations linking them to real consumption per head, give the best results, in terms of the multiple correlation coefficients (adjusted for the degrees of freedom) and the standard errors of the regression coefficients. We also varied the number of country observations used, partly because for some countries (notably China and the U.S.S.R.) it was not possible to obtain data on all the most useful non-monetary indicators, and partly to examine the effects on the results.

The results are discussed in detail later in the paper, and it must suffice at this stage to say that the size of the correlation coefficients obtained (some of 0.990 and above), given that they are also adjusted for degrees of freedom, is extremely reassuring. In fact, such correlations must be very rare in cross-section data in economics. It has been said that if one found, in economics, correlations as strong as those found between smoking and lung-cancer one would sit up and take them seriously. The above results seem to be in this category. . . .

[The best relationships turned out to be variants on the following double-log equation:]

$$\log X_1 = b_1 + b_2 X_2 + \cdots + b_n \log X_n$$

where X_1 = "real" private consumption per head (per annum) relative to the United States (on geometric average of the United States and national price weights);

X_2 = annual apparent crude steel consumption per head (kilograms);
X_3 = annual cement production per head (metric tons x 10);
X_4 = annual number of domestic letters sent per head;
X_5 = stock of radio receivers per head x 10;
X_6 = stock of telephones per head x 10;

X_7 = stock of road vehicles (commercial and domestic) per head x 100;

X_8 = annual meat consumption per head (kilograms). . . .

What may appear at first sight to be a remarkably good correlation result is not really remarkable at all, for all it means is that, of the hundreds of items one could envisage, we have identified five or six that satisfy these conditions sufficiently well that, when taken together, a very high $\bar{R}^2$ is obtained. Such a result is by no means surprising.

The final results are shown in the table below:

Table 1.   *Estimated Levels of "Real" Consumption*
per Head in 1960 (United Kingdom = 100)

Country	Index	Rank	Country	Index	Rank
United States	140	1	Hungary	21	41
Sweden	125	2	Cyprus	21	42
Canada	108	3	Greece	21	43
Australia	106	4	Brazil	20	44
United Kingdom	100	5	Colombia	20	45
Switzerland	96	6	Bulgaria	18	46
New Zealand	95	7	Fed. of Rhodesia	18	47
Denmark	87	8	Malaya	18	48
West Germany	86	9	Mauritius	16	49
Norway	83	10	Turkey	16	50
France	75	11	China (mainland)	15	51
Belgium	74	12	Iraq	15	52
Netherlands	73	13	Syria	14	53
Finland	67	14	Peru	13	54
Austria	66	15	Morocco	13	55
Italy	53	16	Tunisia	13	56
Iceland	48	17	Taiwan	12	57
Ireland	47	18	Iran	12	58
Japan	46	19	Jordan	11	59
Czechoslovakia	45	20	U.A.R.	10	60
Israel	45	21	Ceylon	9	61
South Africa	42	22	Ecuador	8	62
Argentina	39	23	Dominican Rep.	8	63
East Germany	38	24	Ghana	8	64
Malta	35	25	Saudi Arabia	7	65
U.S.S.R.	35	26	Paraguay	7	66
Spain	34	27	Albania	7	67
Lebanon	31	28	Bolivia	6	68
Venezuela	31	29	Thailand	6	69
Uruguay	30	30	Cambodia	6	70
Portugal	28	31	Korean Rep.	6	71
Chile	27	32	Congo	5	72
Hong Kong	27	33	India	5	73
Singapore	24	34	Nigeria	4	74
Poland	22	35	Indonesia	4	75
Algeria	22	36	Pakistan	4	76
Cuba	22	37	Haiti	2	77
Roumania	22	38	Sudan	2	78
Yugoslavia	22	39	Burma	2	79
Mexico	22	40	Ethiopia	1	80

Total Investment versus
Official Investment

John W. Kendrick

5 Development and improvement of economic accounts is a
never-ending task. Since the first national income estimates were prepared by
Sir William Petty in 1665, there have been gradual improvements in concepts,
definitions, data availability, estimating methodology, and structuring of the
accounting framework. . . . Economic accounts inevitably reflect the interests
and theoretical predilections of each generation. A generation ago, when
national income statistics were first being put into their modern accounting
mold by Stone and Meade in the United Kingdom with guidance from
Keynes, interest centered on economic fluctuations and the theory of income
determination. National product was defined largely with reference to market
activity, and the key investment component was taken to comprise chiefly
business investment.

Excerpted from the 47th Annual Report of the National Bureau of Economic
Research, June 1967. The title of the Report is *Contributions to Economic Knowledge
through Research*. Reprinted by permission of the National Bureau of Economic
Research and the author. The author is a member of the research staff of the National
Bureau, and professor of economics at George Washington University.

In part reflecting the usefulness of income theory and of economic accounts as background for countercyclical policy formulation, there has been a shift of interest in recent years more to problems of economic growth and development. In studying the growth of a given economy, or comparing levels, structure, and growth of different economies, it is apparent that major types of nonmarket production must be considered in addition to the restricted national product measures. There has been scattered work on various types of nonmarket productive activity not now included in the official estimates. I am trying to develop systematically imputed incomes for all the major categories of this type so as to obtain orders of magnitude and of temporal changes in relation to GNP.

Also since World War II, economists have been taking a broader view of investment as the central element in economic growth. Increasingly, we view investment as comprising not only business capital outlays but also household and government expenditures for structures, equipment, and inventories; intangible outlays for research and development, education and training, health, and mobility; even the costs of rearing children to working age. Considerable research is going on in each of these areas. Currently at the National Bureau, Thomas Juster is continuing his work on household capital formation, and Gary Becker and Victor Fuchs are pushing forward research on education and health investment.

But no one has been looking at *total* investment, which I would define as all outlays that enhance future output- and income-producing capacity. My work involves pulling together and developing estimates for all types of investment or "quasi-investment" by sector, and analyzing the new total saving and investment functions that emerge from the expanded definitions. The over-all view is important since each type of investment competes for the limited resources released by gross saving. To each should be applied the principles governing efficient use of investment funds.

This work on total investment and the expansion of imputations has inevitably involved me independently in some restructuring of the U.S. national income accounts—particularly the setting up of separate current and saving-investment accounts for each sector. . . .

I shall now briefly summarize some of the estimates of order of magnitude which have thus far emerged from my study, and indicate plans for additional work. Limitations of space prevent me from developing further the concepts, or detailing here the sources and methods of estimation.

Additional Imputations

As estimated by the Department of Commerce, GNP already includes a number of types of imputed incomes, shown in Table 1. These comprised 8.6 per cent of the total in 1929 and 7.3 per cent in 1965. The drop in the ratio chiefly reflects the relative decline of the farm economy and of its production for own use. But the several activities for which the Commerce Department

Table 1. Imputed Values in U.S. Gross National
Product, Official and Selected
Experimental Imputations

	1929		1965	
	Billions of Dollars	Percentage of Official GNP	Billions of Dollars	Percentage of Official GNP
Market GNP (excluding imputations)	94.2	91.4	631.6	92.7
Official imputations, total	8.9	8.6	49.6	7.3
Space rental value	5.9	5.7	39.4	5.8
Financial services	1.3	1.3	7.8	1.1
Farm consumption	1.1	1.1	0.2	0.03
Payments in kind	0.6	0.6	2.2	0.3
Official GNP	103.1	100.0	681.2	100.0
Imputations for consistency with total investment, total	22.6	21.9	210.4	30.9
Business investments charged to current expense	2.5	2.4	26.2	3.9
Student compensation	5.7	5.5	65.1	9.6
Rentals on capital goods Households and institutions	10.8	10.5	71.3	10.5
Governments	3.5	3.4	47.8	7.0
Other imputations, total	48.0	46.6	174.8	25.7
Housewives' services	44.5	43.2	144.4	21.2
Volunteer labor	0.9	0.9	14.2	2.1
Consumption charged to business expense	2.6	2.5	16.2	2.4

Source: Department of Commerce and National Bureau of Economic Research.

prepares imputations were selected more or less arbitrarily, for admittedly pragmatic reasons. What happens when imputations are expanded to cover all major nonmarket economic activities? The first and biggest conceptual problem one faces in endeavoring to answer this question is to define economic activity. As a rough first approximation, one may define it as activity undertaken primarily for the sake of obtaining the resulting income or product, in contrast to noneconomic activity, such as play, which is pursued primarily for its own sake.

The first group of additional imputations shown in the table is required to make the GNP consistent with the expanded investment concept, introduced earlier. The largest item is the estimated gross rental value of capital goods owned by the nonbusiness sectors. This involved estimating the net stock of durable goods owned by households, nonprofit institutions, and governments as a basis for imputing a net interest charge and estimating depreciation annually. Repair and maintenance cost is already included in the official estimates. Our procedure merely extends uniformly the principle already applied by the Commerce Department to owner-occupied houses.

Compensation for schoolwork was estimated by imputing to students 14 years of age and over the average earnings of persons in the same age-sex-color groupings with the same attained educational levels. Not only is imputed student compensation the largest part of educational investment but it has risen markedly relative to national product.

Business investments charged to current expense include the small tool and other tangible capital outlays included in GNP by the Commerce Department prior to the 1965 conceptual revision. But the major portion of the category represents intangible investments, primarily research and development and employee training. Estimates of the latter item are rough, but data on business-financed R & D are relatively good since 1953. Because of the intangibles, the category as a whole has risen markedly since 1929 as a portion of GNP. Taken as a whole, the imputations just discussed rose from about 22 per cent of GNP in 1929 to more than 30 per cent in 1965.

The several further types of imputed incomes shown in the table can be estimated only with large probable margins of error. Consumption charged to business expense includes "expense-account living," welfare services for employees, and entertainment financed by advertising. The data on volunteer labor services are fragmentary, but it is hoped that a recent Labor Department survey will provide a benchmark in this area.

By far the largest category of unpaid work is housewives' services. A surprisingly large amount of scattered data exists with respect to time spent on various types of housework, to which we have imputed the average compensation in the market place for similar work. But we have not yet included all types of housework in the estimates, nor the unpaid work performed by household members other than housewives. Expansion of the category may result in substantially reducing its relative decline, which now reflects chiefly the increasing labor force participation of women.

We have refrained from summing the additional imputations at this stage, since they are incomplete as well as preliminary. Also, there are possible offsets to the imputations, such as commutation costs and other work-connected expenses now included in "final" consumption expenditures.

It is apparent, however, that the tentative imputations presented here would enlarge GNP in 1965 to more than one trillion dollars, over 50 per cent above the official estimate of $681 billion. Significance should not be attached to the apparent decline in the relative importance of the additional imputations as a whole, in view of their still incomplete coverage.

Total Investment

There are three main points that stand out with respect to our total investment estimates for the economy as a whole, as compared with the official estimates, even though our estimates are still preliminary. They are much higher; they have grown in relation to GNP; and they have shown less cyclical amplitude of fluctuation. In comparing total investment with GNP we use the official GNP adjusted for consistency with the new investment estimates, as noted above. We shall look first at each of the major investment

Table 2.   Total Tangible and Intangible Investments
in Relation to Adjusted U.S. Gross
National Product

	1929		1965	
	Billions of Dollars	*Percentage of GNP*	*Billions of Dollars*	*Percentage of GNP*
Gross tangible domestic investment		23.5		24.8
Structures	11.5	9.1	75.2	8.4
Durable equipment	15.7	12.5	131.2	14.7
Change in inventories	2.4	1.9	15.0	1.7
Net foreign investment	0.8	0.6	4.2	0.5
Intangible investment		13.9		22.0
Education and training	11.0	8.8	120.6	13.5
Medical and health	3.7	3.0	38.9	4.4
Research and development	0.3	0.2	21.0	2.4
Mobility costs	2.4	1.9	15.7	1.8
Rearing costs (households)	9.8	7.8	54.2	6.0
Total gross investment				
Including rearing costs	57.6	45.8	475.8	53.4
Excluding rearing costs	47.8	38.0	421.6	47.4
GNP adjusted for consistency with total investment estimates	125.7	100.0	891.6	100.0
Addendum, official estimates				
Gross investment	17.0	16.5	110.7	16.3
GNP	103.1	100.0	681.2	100.0

Source: Department of Commerce and National Bureau of Economic Research.
Note: Detail may not add to totals due to rounding.

categories shown in Table 2, noting briefly the concepts and quality of the estimates.

Purchases of structures and durable equipment by households and governments are actually Commerce Department estimates, reclassified into separate capital accounts for each of the nonbusiness sectors. When purchases of residential units for owner occupancy are counted as part of household investment, tangible investments of the nonbusiness sectors somewhat exceed those made by business, and have grown a little faster since 1929. Aggregate tangible investment, however, has grown only slightly in relation to adjusted GNP.

The relative increase in total investment has been due chiefly to marked growth in the three major types of intangible investment. The largest relative increase has come in research and development, estimates for which are reasonably good.

The largest class of intangible investment, education and training, has increased more than 50 per cent faster than GNP since 1929, and now absorbs almost as much money as all durable equipment. Estimates of formal education costs are firmly based, but data on worker training leave much to be desired.

Medical and health outlays have also increased by almost 50 per cent more than GNP. The estimates for this category are reasonably good, but the difficulty lies in determining how much of medical and health outlay represents investment. Income-producing capacity has been greatly enhanced by increased longevity, reduced time lost from illness, and possibly by increased vitality. But some health expenditure may be called maintenance. Not knowing how to draw the dividing line, we have included all medical and health expenditure in the table.

Mobility costs are relatively small and, judging from rough estimates, have not risen in relation to GNP. Yet there can be no doubt that expenditures for geographical and occupational mobility have raised personal incomes and contributed to economic growth—thus meriting the label of investment.

More controversial is the suggestion for including the costs of rearing children to working age as investment.[1] But one may look at total investment with or without "tangible human investment," according to taste.

Exclusive of rearing cost, total gross investment has grown from less than 40 per cent to almost 50 per cent of adjusted GNP between 1929 and 1965. In other words, as real income per capita has risen, the tendency has been for individuals and organizations to increase the percentage of gross income allocated to forward-looking outlays. Including rearing costs, more than half of GNP in recent years has been devoted to gross investment. The 1965 total of around $475 billion is more than four times the Commerce Department estimate of $111 billion, which represents 15 per cent of official GNP (see Table 2).

It should be kept in mind that our estimates are *gross* of capital consumption. It is possible that our subsequent *net* investment estimates will represent a smaller proportion of NNP, and a smaller multiple of the Commerce net investment estimates, since much of the investment we have added to the official estimates comprises relatively shortlived capital.

In terms of sectors, as shown in Table 3, total gross investments by business, households and nonprofit institutions, and net foreign investment have not varied much in relation to GNP in years of high-level activity. All of the increase has come in the public sector. But attention needs to be paid also to the effect on each sector's investment of change in its gross disposable income. We then see that the relative increase in public investment was largely due to a doubling of public revenues in relation to GNP, although in the government sector gross investment also increased somewhat as a proportion of revenue. The gross disposable income of households and institutions, in contrast, declined from 79 to 68 per cent of GNP from 1929 to 1965, but this was offset by an increase in the investment proportion of disposable income from 35 to 43 per cent. In the case of business, gross retained income

[1] See John W. Kendrick, "Restructuring the National Income Accounts for Investment and Growth Analysis," *Statistisk Tidskrift*, Stockholm, 1966:5.

Table 3. Disposable Receipts and Expenditures, Current and Capital, by Sector of the U.S. Economy

	1929			1965		
	Billions of Dollars	Percentage of Adjusted GNP	Percentage of Sector Revenue	Billions of Dollars	Percentage of Adjusted GNP	Percentage of Sector Revenue
Gross disposable personal income[a]	98.9	78.7	100.0	602.7	67.6	100.0
Current consumption expenditures	62.2		62.9	332.3		55.1
Total investment	34.6	27.6	35.0	260.6	29.2	43.2
Net financial investment	2.1		2.1	9.8		1.6
Gross business retained income[a]	12.7	10.1	100.0	100.5	11.3	100.0
Total investment	15.7	12.5	123.7	107.8	12.1	107.3
Net financial investment	-3.0		-23.7	-7.3		-7.3
Gross government receipts[a]	13.0	10.4	100.0	187.2	21.0	100.0
Current purchases	5.6		42.7	80.7		43.1
Total investment	6.5	5.2	49.8	103.2	11.6	55.2
Net financial investment	1.0		7.5	3.2		1.7
Net foreign transfers	0.4	0.3		2.8	0.3	
Net exports	1.1	0.9		7.0	0.8	
Net foreign claims	-0.8	-0.6		-4.2	-0.5	
Total income	125.0	99.4		893.2	100.2	
Statistical discrepancy	0.7	0.6		-1.6	-0.2	
Total GNP, adjusted	125.7	100.0		891.6	100.0	

Note: Detail may not add to totals due to rounding; percentages are based on more detail than shown.
[a] Gross of capital consumption, but net of transfers to other sectors.
Source: Department of Commerce and National Bureau of Economic Research.

comprised a fairly stable proportion of GNP in good years, despite the increase in income taxes, and the proportion of total investment to gross retained income showed no pronounced trend, though there was a decline from 124 per cent to 107 per cent between 1929 and 1965.

In all post-World War II recession years, intangible investments continued to rise, more than offsetting drops in tangible investment, except in 1949. Between 1929 and 1933, intangible investment fell by one-third, compared with a decline of 80 per cent in tangible investment. In 1938, intangible investment was the same as in 1937, while tangible investment fell by more than 20 per cent.

Inequalities

Lauchlin Currie

6 Why, with all the benefits of science and invention, and with great aid and investment programs, are the developing countries, even in the relatively favored group we are here studying, finding it so difficult to achieve minimum standards ...? In Mexico, Colombia, Peru, Brazil, and other countries, millions and millions of country people are on a bare subsistence basis, practically outside the money economy, with a standard of living in basic essentials lower than that we have just been considering.

... The natural resources of the countries under discussion are certainly sufficient for a decent minimum standard of living. It is true that the large size of a population in itself necessitates expenditures (wells and privies, for example, are not acceptable in cities), but up to a certain point, largeness permits economies of scale. Moreover, as we have seen from our example, large stocks of accumulated or imported capital are not necessary for the attainment of a decent minimum standard. A great portion of the elements of such a standard can be created internally (housing, food, clothing, furniture and miscellaneous goods, beer, and tobacco, health, and education), though if

From chapter 3 of *Accelerating Development, The Necessity and the Means,* by L. Currie. Copyright © 1966 McGraw-Hill, Inc. Used by permission of McGraw-Hill Book Company. Lauchlin Currie is professor of economics at the University of Bogota.

advantage is to be taken of modern techniques, import requirements of specialized machinery must be larger. Even here, it may pay to use country resources less efficiently (say by protecting an industry) if the alternative is nonutilization of such resources.[1]

It is in three other factors that significant differences appear—the little work that is actually done, the complexity of the economy with concomitant lack of understanding of its functioning, and the gross and widening inequality.

Where half the population is engaged in growing food and fibers for the other half, despite the coexistence of mechanized, technical farming, one may be sure that the work of the bulk of the rural people is of such little economic value that we would be justified in calling them unemployed, at least in an economic sense. Where their condition differs from the Canadian subsistence farmers described above is in diet, housing, health, and education. To stay alive without work is not difficult in a tropical or semitropical country. On the other hand, the incidence of intestinal parasites and amoebas is very high, and these lower not only initiative but resistance to other diseases.

A combination of factors brings about wide and growing inequality. A very small minority has a monopoly of education and skills, and these people intermarry and exercise great influence. Poor public administration, inadequate tax enforcement, and chronic inflation conspire to make these wealthy property holders still wealthier. This group in turn has attempted to make its peace with the organized urban workers by providing relatively high fringe benefits in the labor laws and by granting frequent wage advances and extralegal benefits which are not difficult to pass along to the consumer. Thus there are two types of inequality: the traditional one between the propertied classes and the workers, and the newer one between the organized workers on the one hand and the self-employed and casual laborers—mostly rural people—on the other.

The importance of the distribution of income in developing countries is not always fully appreciated. It is difficult to cite statistics on this inequality. However, Carl S. Shoup et al.[2] estimated that in Venezuela the 43 percent of the population that is rural earned 10 percent of the income and that members of independent professions averaged 80,000 Bs (around US$24,000) and petroleum workers 20,000 Bs (US$6,000), as contrasted with an average of 900 Bs. (US$270) earned by agriculturalists (Shoup, pp. 24-26). The authors conclude: "Given the very low income and inheritance taxes in Venezuela, these inequalities in ownership can be perpetuated and perhaps even intensified, in a way that is hardly possible in countries with much more severe taxation" (p. 32). Milton Taylor et al.[3] arrived at a similar conclusion

[1] . . . This argument is strongly presented by Sidney Dell in *Trade Blocs and Common Markets*, Constable & Co., Ltd., London, 1963, pp. 162-163.

[2] *The Fiscal System of Venezuela*, The Johns Hopkins Press, Baltimore, 1959.

[3] *Fiscal Survey of Colombia*, published for the Joint Tax Program by the Johns Hopkins Press, Baltimore, 1965, p. 2. This excellent study arrived too late for me to use it as extensively as I otherwise would have liked to do.

in Colombia for the distribution of income within the labor force. For 1961 it was estimated that the lowest quartile of the labor force received 5 percent of the income while the upper quartile received 65 percent.

Gross inequality is usually deplored because it offends one's concepts of social justice. Occasionally it is defended as encouraging saving. It is doubtless true that much of the saving is done by the wealthy, especially in a country with an inadequately enforced progressive income tax system. But it is also true in the countries under discussion that great inequality in income leads to great inequality in consumption. Well-to-do Latin Americans do travel a lot, and their children are educated abroad for at least part of the time. Their houses are usually luxurious, and they all have one or two cars and the full complement of other consumer durable goods. They have an abundance of servants. The socially expensive pattern of suburban living and individual driving to work, and the consequent necessity of devoting more and more of the scanty national savings to urban roads, is already apparent. In short, the pattern of effective demand is strongly affected, or one might say distorted, by wide and growing inequality in income. A good part of the labor of the community is for a new lord of the manor. His effective demand leads to the diversion of investment to dacron plants, while millions may have scanty clothing of native cotton; to the import or local assembly of cars, while public buses are unbelievably overcrowded. Hundreds of thousands with very poor housing are engaged in constructing costly homes for a relative few. If any thought is given to this, it is defended as providing work. The "money veil" prevents its full significance from being grasped.

Inequality of income has other harmful effects. In the absence of quantitative restrictions on foreign exchange, it leads to excessive imports of luxury goods (in relation to available exchange resources), to heavy personal expenditures abroad, to the export of capital as a measure of caution or prudence, and to a large business in contraband.[4] On balance, it would appear that developing countries pay a heavy and generally unrecognized price for the savings of the wealthy.

The second form of inequality—that between the organized city worker and the self-employed countryman—likewise has its effect on the pattern of demand, though of course to much less degree. This type of inequality is harmful more in dampening down the rate of growth in demand for goods of mass consumption and in preventing the benefits of growing efficiency in manufacturing from being shared in any way by the self-employed rural portion of the population.

[4]An interesting argument made by William McGreevey in an as yet unpublished Ph.D. thesis, Massachusetts Institute of Technology, 1965, "The Development of Colombia," is that for a long period in Colombian history the growing of tobacco, a plantation crop, led to great inequality, luxury consumption abroad, and little accompanying industrial development, and that toward the end of the nineteenth century the introduction of coffee, a small man's crop, ushered in the transition to development. Whether or not this actually was the explanation, it is a logically defensible point of view despite the fact that a plantation crop could theoretically give rise to more savings than a small-peasant-holding crop. The point might be made of pre-Civil War cultivation in the United States in both the South and the North.

In developed countries, the contribution to continuing unemployment made by "wage inflation" resulting from strongly organized unions in industries that do not have much difficulty in passing along increases in costs has long been recognized, and the concept has recently been extended to other incomes. It has not been generally appreciated[5] that this phenomenon has its counterpart in developing countries. There it slows up industrialization and obstructs mobility of labor by causing demand, production, and employment opportunities to be less than they otherwise would be.[6]

This type of inequality has some curious results in encouraging over-mechanization in industry and undermechanization in agriculture. For example, at a certain point in the rise of white-collar workers' salaries, it will "pay" to install costly imported office machinery. If earnings had risen more in line with the overall growth in productivity, it would not have paid, and the exchange resources could have been spent on other things. The displacement of workers by machines often makes little sense from an overall national point of view if human resources are inadequately utilized. The machine may merely add to the disguised unemployment. Similarly, the low rural earnings delay the point when it pays to use more and better machinery. Thus this type of inequality also distorts the pattern of demand and the allocation of investment resources.

Another consequence of intense poverty combined with great inequality can be readily seen in the bitterness and resentment involved in wage negotiations and labor relations. Demands have little to do with the value of the work performed or prevailing incomes of the disguised unemployed. Negotiations are conducted by the union leaders in terms of "equity" or "justice" (the poor versus the rich), and the basis of comparison is the highest wages paid (in Venezuela and Colombia, by the foreign oil companies). Foreign companies are special targets because they are foreign, they are fearful of their public relations, and their foreign personnel live so obviously at a far higher standard of living than the workers.

Where it is possible to meet union demands by rises in prices, this is done. In other cases, it may prove possible to contract the work out to small operators who can disregard the Labor Code and resist any attempts at unionization. In the case of a foreign firm in Colombia needing a supply of cut logs, it was found that the cost of acquiring them by purchase from smaller operators was one-fifth the cost of direct cutting by the company.

[5]But see R.S. Eckaus, "The Factor Proportions Problem in Underdeveloped Areas," *American Economic Review*, 1955, pp. 539-565. Also Jan Tinbergen, *The Design of Development*, Johns Hopkins Press, Baltimore, 1958. The existence of a much higher level of wages in industry in developing countries was recognized by Gunnar Myrdal, but instead of examining the implications for the growth of effective demand, he cited this as a justification for even higher customs protection. *Economic Theory and Underdeveloped Regions*, University Paperbacks ed., Methuen & Co., Ltd., London, 1957, p. 95.

[6]It may be objected that by widening the spread between incomes, wage inflation encourages mobility. True, it does make mobility more desirable, but it does not create more jobs, and country people cannot offer their labor at a cheaper rate in organized industries.

The explanation lay almost entirely in wage rates and fringe benefits. In fields where the system of contracting can be employed, it is very difficult for companies guaranteeing steady employment at much higher levels of remuneration to compete. The small contractor, frequently working with his men, apparently escapes the resentment directed at large employers. By and large, however, industrialization results in larger units, unionization, and less opportunity for subcontracting, so that the areas of wage or cost inflation may be expected to grow as industrialization proceeds.

The persistence of small artisan shops, particularly in the metalworking and woodworking trades, has often been deplored by foreign writers. Such shops are, however, a natural consequence of wage inflation in the organized and presumably more "technical" companies in these fields. It has been alleged that small contractors exploit their men. But they can hardly be blamed for the low standard of living set by the disguised unemployed, and in reality their activities are helping to raise the general standard of living more than those that secure a relatively high wage for the few at the expense of more unemployment for the many.

In the kind of economies described here, one must constantly be on one's guard against an implicit and unwarranted assumption that the factors of production are fully employed in accordance with a pattern of demand and an allocation of resources that make sense, viewed as a rational and well-functioning economic organism. It is surprising how much of our reasoning must be modified when this assumption does not hold.

The Traditional State of Societies

Everett E. Hagen

7

The Impotence of the Peasant

To the peasant, life is a mystery in a profound sense in which it is not a mystery to modern man. There is favorable weather, and his crops flourish. Or drought or excessive rain comes, and they fail. Or storms destroy them. His cattle live, bringing moderate prosperity; or they die, bringing disaster. Above all, his wife and his children live or die for causes he cannot clearly understand (though he spins webs of explanation concerning all of these things). Half of the children he begets die before the age of five years; or, if he lives in a less favorable environment, half may die before the age of one. The birth rate of his society is close to the biological maximum except as poverty delays marriage, yet until the recent introduction from abroad of modern public health and medical measures barely two of his children survived through the years of parenthood to perpetuate the race. Before all of

From chapter 4, "The Traditional State of Societies," in *On the Theory of Social Change*, The Dorsey Press, Homewood, Illinois. Reprinted by permission of the author and publisher. The author is professor of economics, and senior staff member, Center for International Studies, Massachusetts Institute of Technology.

these events he is helpless unless he can induce the spirits to help him. To state that he feels impotent may give a wrong connotation, for it may imply that he feels that his position is not as it should be. He probably does not. He merely takes for granted that the phenomena of the world around him are arbitrary and not amenable to analysis, and that they control him unless the spiritual authorities which control them can be persuaded to favor him. The major aspects of his personality, and the relationships within his community, I hypothesize, are closely related to this sense of impotence.

Interpersonal Relationships in the Village

In such a world, in a nuclear family the number of children left as orphans by the death of their father would be large, for death strikes frequently at adults as well as at children. Hence the logical family unit is the extended family of several generations, in which all feel responsible for all. In the extreme form of the extended family the economic resources of the family are pooled and available to every member subject to the judgment of the family patriarch—constituting a rude but effective sort of social security. Such a thing as an individual business venture is virtually unknown. Every economic act is taken in the name of the family and the associates in economic activity are members of the family.

Even where the extended family does not exist in extreme form, the family group is usually larger than the nuclear family of husband, wife, and children and extends to kin of the several generations of living persons descended from the patriarch, breaking up into smaller groups only when the patriarch dies and each son becomes a head of his own group of descendants.[1]

The peasant depends for help against the hazards and difficulties of life not merely on the feudal relationship but also on a system of mutual self-help among members of the village or of the clan group in several villages. Members of the group help each other at planting time or harvest, or perhaps in maintaining irrigation ditches or paths, in some societies in house-building, usually at births, deaths, weddings, and other ceremonial occasions, almost

[1]But Yang noted in 1947 that even in China, where the diffuse family responsibilities and diffuse clan relationships pertain, at the time he wrote frictions sometimes caused families to separate before both parents of the oldest generation died. "Quarreling about dividing a large family is almost everyday news in the village." M.C. Yang, *A Chinese Village, Taitou, Shantung Province* (London: Kegan Paul, Trench, Trubner Co., Ltd., 1948), pp. 236-39. The quotation is from p. 239. This trend probably should be interpreted as a step in the breakup of peasant society.

Banfield noted that in a village in southern Italy which he studied the nuclear family prevails. If both parents or perhaps only the father dies before the children grow up, they usually become beggars. He suggests that the prevalence of the nuclear family may be due to the fact that before the feudal system broke up, the typical landholding had become so small that it would support only one nuclear family. See Edward C. Banfield and Laura Fasano Banfield, *The Moral Basis of a Backward Society* (Glencoe, Ill.: Free Press of Glencoe, Inc., 1958), pp. 153-54. This explanation is obviously incomplete, for there is as much land per person whether the family is patriarchal or nuclear. The explanation of the decay of traditional society which led to this situation (I assume that it did not pertain in the traditional society) must be complex.

everywhere whenever disaster strikes. The form of organization for the purposes and the scope of the reciprocal aid vary from society to society, as do the forms of organization for all of the functions described in this chapter. In Japan, the village is the unit of mutual aid; in China the clan within the village; in India an intervillage clan group; in Indonesia complex networks of voluntary associations for various purposes.[2] Life depends on this mutual help; many economic functions, and many religious ones of great emotional import, could not be carried out without it. No sanction of peasant social life is more compelling than the sanction of refusal of co-operation by the group to an individual who has violated the customary relationships.

The relationship among the members of the group is diffuse. Because no one has labor or goods to spare, there is indeed the most scrupulous observance of reciprocity in the exchanges of mutual help. The half-days of labor rendered, the number of cakes presented at a family occasion, are carefully noted in order that precise reciprocity may be rendered on occasion. But these are matters of building up a treasury of favors due; they are not a contractual exchange. In case of greater need, so that extra services are received, the family may feel an almost unbearable burden of obligation to the village, but the family is never sued. (Worse, however, if unco-operative it may be ostracized.)

One way to put the matter is that the obligations do indeed have the force of contract, but of a contract which is always renegotiable to prevent undue burden. Because the members of the village (or other group) must live in life-long intimate contact in the insecure world, the rigidity of the law and of contract is impossible. The enforcement of a rigid contract which turned out to bear harshly on a village member might endanger social relationships in the village throughout his life and even in coming generations. Similarly the application of rigid rules of civil or criminal law which in the name of uniformity worked inequity on a village member might endanger the structure of relationships on which the village life depends. Hence in the typical traditional society there is no contractual arrangement and there is no legal code. In many traditional societies each case of discontent with regard to an agreement among individuals and each grievance of one individual against another (whether civil or criminal in the Western frame of reference) is decided by the elders, not merely on grounds of equity but also with a keen sense of the relative power and social connections of the parties, the resentments aroused, and the implications for life in the village of the decisions reached. Equity enters primarily because a sense of unnecessary inequity will disturb future village relationships. When consensus has been reached concerning the action which best reconciles the interests involved,

---

[2] See John F. Embree, *Suye Mura: A Japanese Village* (Chicago: University of Chicago Press, 1939), concerning Japan; Yang concerning China; various chapters of McKimm Marriott (ed.), *Village India: Studies in the Little Community* (Chicago: University of Chicago Press, 1955), concerning India; and Clifford Geertz, "Form and Variation in Balinese Village Structure," *American Anthropologist*, Vol. LXI (December, 1959), concerning Indonesia.

the village head-man (or clan head) formulates the consensus as his decision, and his authority seals the decision.

It should not be supposed, however, that for the individual family, village interests have priority over its own. In many cultures the family submits to the common village good only if this is the way it can best get along. Village relations are everywhere carefully considered, but they are not everywhere idyllic. Perhaps they are hardly anywhere idyllic except to a casual observer. And in a few societies where the aggressiveness has become dominant, we have an atomistic dog-eat-dog existence with no pretense of group solidarity.[3] Even in cultures where the most scrupulous respect for interpersonal and interfamily relationships appear on the surface, the punctilious mutual considerateness may be a protection against jealousies and hostilities which are so dangerous that care must be taken to avoid giving any provocation. This seems to be the case in Japan; Japanese ritualized politeness is a protection against repressed aggressiveness. In Mexico the aggressiveness is slightly less carefully concealed. In Redfield's *Tepoztlan: A Mexican Village* one will find a description of near-idyllic village life; but in Oscar Lewis' account in *Life in a Mexican Village: Tepoztlan Restudied* one may note the hostility and rage seething through the same village; and there is little doubt that Lewis' more penetrating tools revealed a lower layer of truth. Sometimes the aggressiveness is still less concealed; consider Yang's picture of the degree to which a Chinese family observes village equities when dealing with other families of equal strength, but rides ruthlessly when it has the power....

We must conclude that aggressiveness is basic in personality; that the simple folk of most if not all traditional societies find satisfaction in being aggressive when they dare rather than merely resorting to aggression in case of necessity. All this of course may be unconscious. In the typical instance the villagers probably are not conscious that they have aggressive tendencies.

In such an environment the extended family is a close-knit defensive-offensive unit in other than economic ways. Each member is a representative of all. Each proper act of an individual casts credit on his family; each wrong act humiliates his family; and an act that offends the village will endanger his family.

The villager vents his aggression more freely outside the village than in it. Though he may feel a sense of national pride when a question of his nation versus others arises, his strong emotional tie is to his community, not his country. A person from outside the village or local group of villages is an alien. In many traditional societies, because he is an alien he is considered dangerous. As an alien he is fair prey for chicanery or robbery, and as a dangerous person he runs the risk of losing not only his property but also his life. This attitude prevailed in eighteenth

[3]See, for example, Banfield and Banfield, *The Moral Basis of a Backward Society.*

century England as well as in many societies which come to mind sooner when the term "traditional society" is used.[4] Since there are travelers' accounts of journeying unmolested through strange peasant lands, attacks on strangers are not universal, but the limited social horizon of which they are one type of manifestation is probably nearly so.

The Hierarchy

The extended family is a logical unit for reasons other than the advantages of solidarity.

In the midst of great unknown forces the longest experience is the best guide. Hence it is wise to depend upon the eldest members of the family group (and in matters stretching beyond the family, the elders of the village) for advice and decision.

The eldest man rules the family and advises it. He rules an age- and sex-based hierarchy. In probably all traditional societies after the years of infancy, children are expected to accommodate themselves to the convenience of adults to a degree that is not true in any Western society unless it is the German. In many traditional societies, also, sisters submit to brothers and younger boys submit to older ones and in turn dominate their juniors and sisters. This set of family rankings is the base of a hierarchy that extends upward to an apex of authority and status at the top of the society.

The individual's primary loyalty may be to his family (this is the general case); it may be to his clan, as in China; or it may go to the higher hierarchical levels, as in Japan or any ideal feudal system, so that the individual must do what will benefit his lord or emperor (and if his lord or emperor is in danger glories in doing so) even at cost to his family.[5] Even though his primary loyalty is to family or clan, generally the family or clan in turn acknowledges allegiance to persons who are higher in the hierarchy.

The loyalty is more than ceremonial. Between the peasant and his superior in the hierarchical relationship there exists a relationship of mutual obligation. The inferior owes certain obligations to the superior—obligations of rent or taxation, or work and perhaps military service, or of following the superior's guidance in public matters. The superior owes protection, advice, help in emergency, action as judge or magistrate in translocal matters, support of village festivals, and, not least, ritual services such as blessing of the annual festival, service as godfather, and appearance on ceremonial occasions and family occasions of emotional importance. Not all of these obligations hold in any one society, but many of them—and others—do in any society. These are

---

[4]T. S. Ashton, in *An Economic History of England: The 18th Century* (New York: Barnes and Noble, Inc., 1955), chap. i, notes that a stranger in England was apt to be stoned purely because he was a stranger.

[5]See Marion J. Levy, Jr., "Contrasting Factors in the Modernization of China and Japan," in S. S. Kuznets, W. Moore, and J. Spengler (eds.), *Economic Growth: Brazil, India, Japan* (Durham, N. C.: Duke University Press, 1955), pp. 496-536, for a discussion of contrasting cases in these two countries by Embree and Yang, respectively.

not quantitative exchanges whose magnitudes can be measured and contracted for but a much more diffuse obligational tie. In India this sort of relationship exists not so much between cultivator and landlord as between a member of the lower castes who is not a cultivator and some landlord who serves as his patron.

Rationality, Religion, and Magic

The dependence aspect of the hierarchy extends upward beyond the highest human to the spiritual forces that are seen to control the phenomena of nature. The peasant in the typical society is entirely "rational" insofar as "rationality" does him any good. He understands that there is a best time for planting, a best condition of the soil, the appropriate times and methods of irrigation, of cultivation, of harvesting, the best time and places to fish, the best design for a canoe. In all of these matters he exercises with craft, skill, and high rationality a learning accumulated throughout the generations.

But in other matters—storm, drought, the run of fish in the fishing grounds; death of his crops, his cattle, his kin—he knows that no direct actions of his will bring him security or save him from disaster. He knows that events have causes, and he attributes these events, whose causes are forces he cannot see, to the will of unseen forces. By magic or some equivalent he seeks to induce the spiritual forces to befriend rather than harm him. In some cultures great stress is placed on living in harmony with the universe so good may come; in others appeasement or bribing of the spirits is stressed. Whatever the precise approach, in every traditional (and primitive) society the relation to the spirits is important, and the attempt is made through that relationship to control uncertain events that are emotionally important.[6] The magic or equivalent does not control the event (except where the attitudes of the group have a causal influence), but it does serve the function of relieving the anxiety.

The Peasant View of the Social Structure

Just as it does not occur to the peasant that he can influence any of a wide range of phenomena of the physical world that are of great emotional importance to him, so it does not occur to him that the social

[6]Malinowski was the first to note clearly how primitive peoples operate with great skill and rationality in areas where experience teaches them that they can control events by their direct actions, and with magic where they cannot. Other anthropologists and sociologists made explicit that emotional importance of the result is an added condition for the appearance of magic, and Parsons noted carefully that the result will be magic *or its functional equivalent.* See Bronislaw Malinowski, "Magic, Science, and Religion," in Joseph Needham (ed.), *Science, Religion & Reality* (1925) (reprint; New York: George Braziller, Inc., 1955); Talcott Parsons, "The Theoretical Development of the Sociology of Religion," *Essays in Sociological Theory* (rev. ed.; Glencoe, Ill.: Free Press of Glencoe, Inc., 1954); and Robert K. Merton, *Social Theory and Social Structure* (rev. ed.; Glencoe, Ill.: Free Press of Glencoe, Inc., 1957), pp. 32-34.

structure is amenable to change. One should not conclude, however, that he is apathetic, despairing, and sullen. These he often is in the modern world, but the forces that bring him to this state are the forces that have disrupted his traditional society, not the circumstances of that society. In traditional society he seems to take both his physical environment and the social structure as data. Consciously, he neither grieves nor rejoices at them. They are simply there, and natural. He reveres the men who are learned concerning tradition and the invisible world—the humanistic-intellectual man and the religious functionary; honors the elders of his community and the representatives of indigenous national authority; sees the top elite as in a world far beyond his ken; and respects himself as a peasant. He looks on the statuses of these groups in his society as higher and lower, but also as not merely appropriate but proper. It never occurs to him to think that he might act so as to change things. The world is as it is. He thinks the concept of his trying to change it to be ridiculous, shocking, a little indecent, and immoral. . . .[7]

Class Relationships

The belief by the members of the traditional society in the essential superiority of the elite classes is one side of a coin. Its converse is belief by all classes in the nonimprovability of the simple folk and the fixity of their natural positions in life. Thus social classes are largely closed, and not necessarily by overt barriers. The member of each class simply knows of what class he is a member.

Though there is a certain amount of movement among peasant, artisan, and craftsman-shopkeeper occupations, and between them and the menials, the sons of each group normally expect to follow the occupations of their father. In the extreme cases, movement from any occupation to any other is interdicted.

Historically, this was true by legal decree in Japan and by social custom in the caste system of India and the feudal system of medieval Europe. Although similarly complete formal restrictions on occupational movement have not received as much historical note as these, they may have existed elsewhere as well.[8]

[7]Daniel Lerner comments as follows concerning interviews of Turkish villagers in 1950: "Late in the interview, after each respondent had named the greatest problem facing the Turkish people, Tosun asked what he would do about this problem if he were the president of Turkey. Most responded with stolid silence—the traditional way of handling 'projective questions' which require people to imagine themselves or things to be different from what they 'really are.' Some were shocked by the impropriety of the very question. 'My God! How can you say such a thing?' gasped the shepherd. 'How can I . . . I cannot . . . a poor villager . . . master of the whole world.' " *The Passing of Traditional Society* (Glencoe, Ill.: Free Press of Glencoe, Inc., 1958), p.24.

James C. Abegglen has reported in conversation the inability of many Japanese factory workers (interviewed in 1955 and 1956) to visualize themselves in any job other than the one they held.

[8]J. S. Furnivall in *Colonial Policy and Practice* (Cambridge, Eng.: The University Press, 1948), p. 15, notes such restrictions in pre-British Burma.

Yet almost everywhere in practice there were some exceptions. In Burma the king might marry a commoner girl who caught his eye, and with cunning and luck her son might become the next king. Receiving knighthood for some extraordinary service or deed of value might bring a rise in rank in medieval Europe, and adoption might do so in feudal Japan. And so on. In China it was possible for a peasant family which gained some wealth, perhaps through nonagricultural activity such as trading, to buy its way into the landed gentry, and some movement into and out of the gentry may have gone on at all times. In societies where landownership by peasants existed, or was possible *de facto* whatever the legal presumption, a number of lesser economic elite or superpeasants emerged. The kulaks of Russia, the individuals termed "big peasants" or "wealthy peasants" in Tokugawa Japan, and some of the yeomen of medieval England are examples. But it is doubtful that many individuals in any traditional society moved upward from these positions to become members of the true elite.

Historically, for individuals of either the elite or the simple folk who were deviant in personality there were special career channels. Thus a member of the nonelite classes, as well as a member of the elite, who possessed exceptional interest might become a monk or holy man, and if he also possessed exceptional capability and luck he might in other countries become a priest. (In Burma every young man spent a rainy season in a monastery, but this temporary acceptance of the role was quite different from permanent monkhood.) With the same qualities, he might possibly become a learned man; in many societies the career of learned man was one variety of career as monk or priest. In China, for the exceptional low-class individual who attracted such attention that a career of learning was made available to him, a civil service career was open. Entrance was based on erudition in the classic writings. These channels for variance or deviance, however, were not a bridge into the permanent elite. Typically, the careers in religious office implied celibacy; indeed, sexual deviance or variance was one of the characteristics which led an individual into such careers. In any case, they carried with them no inheritance of position.

Because his sense of identity depends so wholly on his position—because he sees no other evidence of his worth but his position in life—a member of the elite feels a deep moral imperative to preserve that position for himself and his family and next for his larger group. To preserve the status of his primary group, he may appropriate resources which according to Western values belong to the nation. The corruption and nepotism which the Westerner may criticize in a peasant society is the expression of this moral duty of the elite to his kin, his clan, and his class. The nepotism and corruption of the Chiang Kai-shek regime while it was in power in China, the corruption now being reported in the Congress party administration in India, the traditional financial performance of rulers in the Near East, the filching of the nation's wealth by the dictators or oligarchs of Latin America are all examples of this aspect of the culture of traditional society elite. They derive from the circumstances of the society as naturally as the more universalistic principles of Western society result from the conditions and history of the West.

The position of members of the elite is indeed frequently under some threat. Within the elite groups powerful individuals may not regard their place as fixed. The constraints on their aggressiveness are fewer than those which inhibit the simple folk, who must live in continuing face-to-face contact with each other. Elite aggressiveness therefore more often is unleashed; among the members of the elite there may be bitter competition for political and military power. Among the *daimyos* of Japan, the warlords of China, the feudal lords of medieval Europe, and probably the group possessing top economic and political power in most other peasant societies, conflict to force the allegiance of neighboring lords, enlarge one's territorial control, and ultimately gain national hegemony was frequent. When it was not occurring, it was always latent. Indeed, the national states of western Europe emerged as one or another lord was able to gain power ascendancy over all other lords (and became permanent as he gained not merely the acquiescence but also the loyalty of lesser nobles and the simple folk). In these struggles for power, or in measures by the dominant elite to prevent its displacement, might lie the seeds of social tensions that could lead to basic social change.

Recapitulation

In summary, societies in their traditional state are dual or in a sense triple societies; they consist of the peasantry and other simple folk, the elite classes, and, at one side, the trader-financiers.

The image of the world of the simple folk and elite classes alike includes a perception of uncontrollable forces around them that restrict and dominate their lives. The simple folk find protection from the material dangers in mutual aid within face-to-face groups and in dependence on elite individuals with whom they are related by material and symbolic bonds. The members of the elite find protection in their economic resources and their ability to levy (not necessarily by force) on the simple folk who owe allegiance to them. The lines of dependence extend upward to the spiritual powers, to whom the members of the society appeal for protection against the physical forces; in the appeal they gain relief from their anxieties.

The simple folk and the elite alike are aggressive. Interpersonal relationships whose nature is not clear are therefore dangerous; hence strangers are dangerous and may be attacked. Within the community the simple folk avoid the release of their aggression, which would endanger community life, by careful adherence to traditional relationships that provide for mutual accommodation. Moreover, each individual finds his place in the authoritarian hierarchy of human relationships. Conflict is obviated by submission to persons of superior status and domination of inferiors.

Domination over inferiors, like attack on aliens, also permits each individual to vent his aggressiveness. Even the lowliest peasant child may look forward to the exercise of dominance, increasing throughout his life as he attains the roles of older brother, father, and elder. Hence the simple folk find satisfaction in both submissiveness and domination; their personalities as well as those of the elite are authoritarian.

And members of both groups, fearing the world and fearing to attack its problems, preferring to avoid the issue of the rightness of solutions by letting them depend on authority, are by virtue of these characteristics uncreative.

In their values the members of the elite and the simple folk differ. The elite, needing to feel superior in essence to the simple folk to justify the privileged positions to which they are born, learn tastes which differentiate them from the simple folk, and in those tastes they see proof of their superiority. One element of these tastes is repugnance to manual labor, work with tools, or interest in the processes of the physical world, a repugnance which extends to all commercial and industrial work. Another is love of the landed life. They perceive also, as an element in their superior identities, the rightness of their greater authority. It follows that delegating authority, that is, sharing it with subordinates, is equivalent to sharing with them one's status, one's essential superiority. Thus in addition to their lack of creativity, the sense of identity of the elite creates peculiarly stubborn barriers to technological progress.

In these societies, except for struggles within the class of the elite itself, class relationships are fixed. Since the lower classes are of essence inferior, of course there is no way in which they can merit eliteness. But this class rigidity does not create a perception by the simple folk that they are bound or imposed upon, for they like both the avoidance of problems which the authoritarian hierarchy permits and the release of aggression which their own petty hierarchy of authorities permits. Traditional social structure persists because it is satisfying to all concerned. But some threat to its continuance lies in the struggles for power among the elite.

Population Control and Economic
Development

Goran Ohlin

8   A Turning Point in Population History?

The belief is spreading that economic development in the poor
countries of the world will never make much headway until their population
growth is slowed down. Many economists and demographers have long
believed this, but the acceleration of demographic growth in the developing
countries has accentuated the issue and made it seem that the remarkable
economic expansion which has been achieved in many of these countries
merely serves to keep larger populations at the same low levels of welfare.
The extraordinary projections of the future growth of population in the
world, and especially in the underdeveloped part of the world, have also
enormously enhanced the awareness of the population explosion. But above
all, those who in the developing countries have been given responsibility of

An excerpt from *Population Control and Economic Development*, Development
Centre of the Organization for Economic Cooperation and Development, Paris, 1967.
Reprinted by permission of the author and publisher. The author is at the Stockholm
School of Economics.

planning their economic and social advance have, by their experiences and their calculations, been forced to a realization of the burdens that population growth of 2-3 per cent a year imposes on their countries.[1] At such rates a population doubles in 25 years; this doubles the requirements of facilities they would like to provide in the form of schools, hospitals, and housing; conversely it cuts in half the benefits of what they might expect to provide in that time.

Until very recently, few people thought that anything could be done to stem the growth of population in a poor country, even if it were desirable to do so. Numerous pilot projects had attempted to introduce birth control in underdeveloped countries, and at least in India family planning had been national policy since the early 1950's. The results had been universally disappointing. It was widely assumed that a high degree of economic and social development must be awaited before birth rates could be expected to fall. Among those who feared that population growth itself would hold up such development for an indefinite period of time, this inspired a sense of defeat.

In the last few years, this situation has changed quite radically. A policy for population in developing countries has suddenly come to seem possible.

Many things have conspired to produce this change of perspective. The first was the realization that, contrary to many preconceived ideas, parents in underdeveloped countries do not want very large numbers of children. Ancient patterns of living have been moulded by a mortality that consumed one-half or one-third of all those born before they grew to survive their parents. Today, most of them survive, and in most of the countries in the developing world parents want smaller families.

Secondly, in the early 1960's a major breakthrough occurred in contraceptive technology. The oral and intra-uterine contraceptives have affected the prospects of fertility control the world over. In the underdeveloped countries, it is especially the intra-uterine device (IUD) that seems to have met the need for a cheap, effective, and acceptable method of contraception.

Thirdly, successful campaigns to make birth control methods available have at last been conducted in a few countries, stressing information rather than propaganda, and giving particular attention to problems of communication, motivation, and administration.

The full extent of this change became fully apparent only in 1965. In August that year, the First International Conference on Family Planning Programs in Geneva assembled some 200 family planning administrators, demographers, physicians, and sociologists. The proceedings of this conference provide a monumental record of developments which even a

[1]It is difficult even to those with much experience to realize intuitively the powers of compound interest, and as a more telling measure of the rate of growth, the doubling-time is often used, in analogy with the physicist's half-time. Growth at the rate of 1 per cent per annum results in doubling in about 70 years (rather than the 100 which arithmetic increases would imply), and other doubling-times are easily computed mentally by dividing the percentage rate into 70. At a growth rate of 2 per cent, the doubling time is 35; at 3 per cent it is 23 years, and so forth.

cautious observer must regard as quite spectacular.[2] Immediately thereafter, the Second World Population Conference in Belgrade demonstrated to what extent the problems of the developing world had moved into the centre of demographic attention, and among its contributed papers, a large number added further details on the recent experiences with population control and testified to the drastic change of mood that had occurred in the decade since the First World Population Conference in Rome in 1954.[3]

The year 1965 also brought other evidence of a heightened international awareness of the population problem. In the international organizations, in the Vatican Council, and in internal debates in all countries, developed or underdeveloped, the question of birth regulation received unprecedented attention. No single year had ever brought so much news of significant change in the field of population policy.

Many have suggested that this heralds a turning point in the growth of world population. At any rate it is clear that a new mood now surrounds the debate of the demographic prospects in developing countries. The following report was prompted by this sudden change which obviously has the greatest relevance for development strategy. If a policy of population control is possible, what are the economic implications? Is it possible to show that the economic benefits will outweigh the probable costs, and this by such a clear margin that such a policy has a strong claim on resources that could otherwise be devoted to more conventional programmes of economic development? The answer is not self-evident, but the result of the tentative examination in the following chapters is that population control seems to hold out enormous promise to governments willing to launch such an enterprise.

The term "population control" should not be taken to mean that governments are in a position to regulate the growth of population at wish. In the historical past, many governments have attempted to stimulate the growth of population by fiscal and other measures. There is no evidence that such efforts have ever had any effect. The policies now under consideration in underdeveloped countries have the modest aim of helping those who already wish to limit the size of their families but do not know how, and secondly to spread the notion of rational and responsible parenthood. Whether this is referred to as a policy of birth control, of family planning, or of family welfare, such efforts aim at one and the same thing: to keep the growth of families and thus of populations within limits where it is possible to provide more or less adequately for all "the guests at the banquet of life". The moral or theological aspects of such efforts will not be discussed in this report.

All experience suggests that the transition from high to low birth rates inevitably follows a change from high to low death rates as the process of modernization gains momentum. What is now being attempted is an

[2]*Family Planning and Population Programs. A Review of World Development*, ed. Bernard Berelson *et al.* (Chicago, 1966). In the following referred to as *FPPP*.

[3]The papers submitted to the World Population Conference were distributed in stenciled form and will be referred to as WPC followed by the number of the working paper.

acceleration of this transition, which is an effort both guided and aided by the course of history. It is, as the following pages will suggest, probably a matter of gaining a few decades. In the historical perspective this may seem trifling, but to thousands of millions it may make the difference between prospects of improvement now or only, at best, for the next generation.

To those who are already familiar with recent developments in population control the following attempt to survey and summarize them will convey nothing that is new. But these developments deserve to be more widely known. Inevitably, a progress report in this field must venture into many areas which are pertinent to population policy although they may seem remote from the usual problems of economic development. In reality they are not so remote, and no one seriously concerned about the prospects of progress in developing countries can today afford to remain ignorant of the possibilities of reducing their fertility.

Towards a Settled World: The Population Explosion and the Future

It is well known that the population of the world is increasing faster than ever before. What may be less widely realized is how soon, by any measure of historical time, this growth will have to cease or slow down. Man's conquest of the earth is very nearly completed. With the present trend of accelerating growth it would only take another hundred years for mankind to cover the inhabitable parts of the world with an average density greater than that of today's Holland. Science and technology may in the end make it possible to sustain an even more densely settled world than that, but even the most generous estimates of the ultimate carrying capacity of the world would be attained in less time than separates us from the European discovery of the rest of the world.

This dizzying perspective of being within reach of what seems like the end of history is a dramatic backdrop to present considerations of world population prospects. But the compelling reasons for concern are different. In those two-thirds of the world where the growth of population is most explosive, the present is the time of a new and urgent departure in history, a departure which may be jeopardized by this unprecedented growth. Before considering this problem, it is necessary to dwell briefly on the purely demographic aspects of the situation.

The Present

The population of the world in 1967 may be estimated at some 3.4 billion, and its annual rate of increase at 2 per cent. A generation ago, in the 1930's, it was slightly more than two billion (Table 1). At that time, a problem that caused acute concern in industrial countries was the prospect of the future population decline to which the falling birth rates in these countries pointed.

Table 1.   World Population, 1920-1960

	Population, in Billions		
Year	World	More Developed Regions	Developing Regions
1920	1.86	0.67	1.12
1930	2.07	0.76	1.31
1940	2.30	0.82	1.47
1950	2.52	0.86	1.66
1960	3.00	0.98	2.02
	Annual Rate of Growth (Per cent)		
Year	World	More Developed Regions	Developing Regions
1920-30	1.0	1.2	1.0
1930-40	1.0	0.8	1.2
1940-50	0.9	0.4	1.2
1950-60	1.8	1.3	2.0

Source: Population Division, United Nations, New York. More developed regions include North America, Temperate South America, Europe, Japan, Australia and New Zealand. Developing regions include Africa, East Asia (excluding Japan), South Asia, Latin America (excluding Temperate South America), Melanesia, Polynesia and Micronesia.

Today, those alarms seem to belong to another era. What is feared today is a continuation of the trends of the post-war years in which growth has steadily accelerated, especially in the underdeveloped countries. If these trends were continued, world population would in another generation, i.e. at the end of the century, be about 7.5 billion.

Individual populations in virtually unsettled territories have at times in the past grown at very high rates even by current standards. But the population of the world as a whole has, throughout most of human history grown very slowly. It probably reached its first billion only around 1800, and its second around 1930. The third was reached around 1960, and we are now well on our way to the fourth which will be reached before 1975.

Population is currently growing at a high rate in some of the industrial countries. In the United States and Canada, in Australia and New Zealand and in the USSR rates of growth are between 1.5 and 2 per cent per annum. But as Table 2 shows, much higher rates of growth prevailed in the underdeveloped countries in 1960-63, and in most of these regions they are rising. Any estimate of the average growth rate in the "developing regions" depends on the scope given to this definition, but on almost any count, in the mid-1960's this rate of growth seems to be at least 2.5 per cent. In some individual countries it is much higher. Many countries increased by more than 3 per cent annum already between 1950 and 1960, and a few smaller populations are growing at more than 4 per cent.

Declining Mortality

What has unleashed the great demographic acceleration in the underdeveloped countries has been a rather sudden and continued drop in mortality after World War II. Crude death rates are influenced by the age structure, and mortality is therefore better measured by the life expectancy at birth which expresses the average length of life of a new born infant under prevailing conditions of mortality. In the world of today this life expectancy ranges from 25-35 years in populations of high mortality, to about 75 years in the healthiest.[4]

Table 2. Rates of Growth and Crude Birth and
Death Rates by World Regions (Per thousand)

Region	Rate of Growth (1960-63)	Birth Rate (1958-63)	Death Rate (1958-63)
Africa	25	46	23
Northern America	16	24	9
Latin America	28	40	14
Japan	10	17	7
South Asia	24	42	20
Europe	9	19	10
Oceania	22	27	11
USSR	16	24	7

Source: United Nations, *Demographic Yearbook, 1964,* p.111.

In the Western world the increase in life expectancy was slow and irregular. Around the middle of the eighteenth century, European life expectancy was probably 30-35 years. In 1900 it was about 50 years and not until 1940 did it reach 65 years. Throughout this development the life span, i.e. the maximum age, did not change significantly, and there is probably an upper limit to life expectancy, which according to current opinion has almost been reached in the healthiest countries. Unless major breakthroughs are made in the understanding and treatment of degenerative diseases, life expectancy is not likely to be pushed much beyond 75 years.

However, all over the developing world remarkable and unanticipated increases in life expectancy have occurred in the last few decades. In Mexico life expectancy has risen from 36 years to 60 years between 1930 and 1964; in Mauritius it seems to have gone from 38 years in 1940 to 58 years in 1960. In Taiwan it increased from 45 years to 65 years in the same twenty-year period.[5]

[4]The life expectancies of men and women are significantly different: Women have smaller survival chances in poorer countries of high mortality but live longer than men in rich and healthy populations. For demographic purposes, the average is usually employed.

[5]J. Bourgeois-Pichat, *Population Growth and Development,* pp. 62 and 65.

In some underdeveloped countries, a slow decline in mortality was going on before the war; in others there was practically none. Now many of them have telescoped into a decade or two a development that took a century to achieve in the West. The causes of this extraordinary improvement are not universally agreed upon. Some observers attribute it to basic economic improvements. More efficient and regular distribution of food has averted food shortages and famines, and improved nutrition may account for much of the spectacular gain in infant mortality. On the other hand, post-war public health measures have been extremely effective in underdeveloped countries. The eradication of malaria by spraying with insecticides has had spectacular effects on mortality in some countries. In Ceylon, the first major antimalaria compaign with DDT coincided with a drop of the crude death rate from 20 to 14 between 1946 and 1947, and the average death rate for 1946-60 was about 12, while that of 1930-45 had been 22.[6] In Ceylon, as in most other countries where similar improvements have been recorded, economic conditions have also improved, but in Mauritius, where a sharp decline in the death rate has also been attributed to malaria eradication, this occurred in combination with a drastic deterioration of economic conditions.[7]

As a matter of fact, the decline in mortality seems to have been far more uniform than the gain in prosperity. Nor do the indisputable economic improvements in the developing countries seem so large compared to those which were reaped in Europe and North America in the nineteenth and twentieth centuries as to explain why mortality should now have declined so much more rapidly.

Public health measures have been of great variety. To analyse the effect of any one of them is an extremely difficult task, as illustrated by the finding that "both in Ceylon and in British Guinea, between four and five times as many deaths occurred because malaria was present as the deaths which were actually reported as due to malaria".[8] It is nevertheless difficult to resist the tentative conclusion that post-war public health measures with their arsenal of new insecticides and other techniques of controlling epidemics were and remain the chief agents of this reduction of mortality in the developing world, which does not seem to have depended very heavily on improvements in economic conditions.

The expectation of life at birth in the underdeveloped regions is probably now around 40-45 in Africa, 45-50 in Asia, and 55-60 in Latin America.[9] Thus, there remains a considerable margin for further improvement.

[6]Peter Newman, *Malaria Eradication and Population Growth* (1965), p. 14.

[7]R.M. Titmuss and B. Abel-Smith, *Social Policies and Population Growth in Mauritius* (London, 1961).

[8]Newman, *op. cit.*, p. 5.

[9]Bourgeois-Pichat, *op. cit.*, p.66.

Constant Fertility

In Western societies, the decline in mortality was eventually followed by decline in fertility. The response was not rapid. In most European countries there was a slow but fitfully accelerating decline in mortality throughout the nineteenth century, but it was not until the last quarter of that century that fertility began to follow suit. Until the Second World War, the records of these countries suggested a stage process of demographic evolution. At first mortality declined while fertility remained constant, which gave rise to an acceleration of growth. In the second stage, fertility declined rapidly enough to catch up with mortality, more or less.

In the overwhelming majority of underdeveloped countries this fertility decline has not even begun. In fact, crude birth rates in many of them have instead tended to increase, as illustrated in Table 3 which presents some recent estimates of birth rates in Latin America. Mortality in most Latin American countries has been declining longer than in other parts of the developing world, but only in Argentina, Chile, Cuba, and Uruguay, where European immigration was very heavy, has a fertility decline been observed. Improving health may stimulate fertility in many ways—by increasing fecundity, reducing the risk of miscarriage, and by reducing widowhood—and in societies where fertility varies among social groups high fertility groups may increasingly come to outnumber the others and raise the national average.[10]

Table 3. Estimated Birth Rates for
Latin American Countries

	1860-64	1900-04	1920-24	1940-44	1950-54	1955-59
Argentina	46.8	41.8	34.3	25.7	25.4	24.1
Bolivia				45.1	42.4	
Chile	46.9	44.7	42.2	38.3	37.0	37.6
Colombia		43.0	44.6	42.4	44.0	45.1
Costa Rica		46.9	44.9	42.8	45.0	45.3
Cuba		44.6	36.7	31.9	(30.0)	
Ecuador			47.7	46.0	46.4	46.5
El Salvador		43.8	46.6	45.2	47.9	47.9
Guatemala		45.8	48.3	45.2	50.9	49.0
Honduras			44.3	43.8	46.0	46.0
Mexico		46.5	45.3	43.8	45.0	45.8
Panama		40.3	40.0	39.5	38.5	40.5
Peru		40.3	40.0	44.5	45.5	46.2
Venezuela		41.8	41.2	41.5	44.2	44.3

Source: Andrew Collver, *Birth Rates in Latin America* (1965), p. 26.

About two-thirds of the underdeveloped countries thus have birth rates between 40 and 50 per thousand, while those of developed countries cluster around 20. At the present time fertility seems to provide a sharper criterion for distinguishing underdeveloped countries from developed ones than any

[10]Andrew Collver, *Birth Rates in Latin America* (1965), p. 56.

other social or economic variable.[11] This is equally true when fertility is measured by the gross reproduction rate, or the total fertility rate, measures which unlike the crude birth rate are independent of the age and sex distribution.[12] In underdeveloped countries, the gross reproduction rate clusters around 3, in developed ones around 1.5. Practically no developing countries fall below 2, and no developed countries have rates as high as that.

Fertility in underdeveloped countries is nowhere near the "biological maximum" although in societies where marriage is early and fertility unchecked it may come close to a "natural" level, with gross reproduction rates of 3.5-4 which corresponds to an average number of 7-8 births to women surviving to the age of 45. Actually, no major population in the world today has a gross reproduction rate above 3.5, and no one falls below 1.0.

Although fertility is not generally declining in underdeveloped countries, there are important exceptions. Some Latin American countries where this is the case have already been mentioned, and in addition it is true of a number of populations of Chinese origin. In Taiwan, Singapore and Hong Kong, where the rates of natural increase (apart from immigration) were about 3 percent at the beginning of the 1960's, birth rates have been declining slowly for some time, and in South Korea, which is growing at the same rate, such a decline seems to have started. . . .

The Projected Trends

The results of U.N. projections, in briefest summary, are presented in Table 4. (Table 5 shows the figures for major areas of the world; an abundant wealth of detail is of course available in the U.N. report.) It is enough to consider the figures for 1980 and 2000, as the trends are all rather smooth.

Table 4.   Summary of U.N. World Population
Projections, 1960-2000, in Billions

	1960	Constant Fertility		High Variant		Medium Variant		Low Variant	
		1980	2000	1980	2000	1980	2000	1980	2000
World	3.0	4.5	7.5	4.6	7.0	4.3	6.1	4.1	5.5
Developed regions	1.0	1.2	1.6	1.2	1.6	1.2	1.4	1.2	1.3
Developing regions	2.0	3.3	5.9	3.3	5.4	3.1	4.7	3.0	4.2

[11]*Population Bulletin* of the United Nations, No. 7, or United Nations, *World Population Prospects as Assessed in 1963*, Sales No. 66.XIII.2, forthcoming.

[12]The total fertility rate is the number of children born to a woman surviving to the end of the reproductive period, under the prevailing age-specific fertility pattern — in other words the sum of the age-specific fertility rates for all the years in the reproductive period. The gross reproduction rate is the number of *daughters* born in the same circumstance. On the average there are 105 boys to each 100 girls; the gross reproduction rate is thus the total fertility rate divided by 2.05.

Table 5.   Estimated World Population,
1960-2000, in Millions

	1960	Constant Fertility		High Variant		Medium Variant		Low Variant	
		1980	2000	1980	2000	1980	2000	1980	2000
World total	2,998	4,519	7,522	4,551	6,994	4,330	6,130	4,147	5,449
More developed areas:									
Europe	425	496	571	492	563	480	527	467	491
Soviet Union	214	295	402	296	403	278	353	269	316
Northern America	199	272	388	275	376	262	354	248	294
Oceania	16	22	33	23	35	23	32	22	28
Less developed areas:									
Mainland China	654	942	1,811	971	1,345	850	1,045	782	893
Japan	93	114	127	117	139	111	122	108	115
Other East Asia	47	87	175	83	139	80	120	76	110
South Asia	865	1,446	2,702	1,448	2,444	1,420	2,270	1,378	1,984
Africa	273	458	560	463	864	449	768	434	684
Latin America	212	387	736	383	686	378	638	362	532

The different projections move apart fairly slowly. For 1980 they range from 4.6 to 4.1 billion; the span between the highest and the lowest is of the order of 10 percent. For the year 2000, the gap is very much wider, ranging between 7.5 and 5.5 billion, or about 30 percent of the average between them. This illustrates what has been referred to as the long "braking distance"; even the rapid onset of low fertility would not make much difference by 1980.

The rates of increase over the projection period are of great interest as they bring out the net result of the race between declining mortality and fertility, such as it emerges from these projections. On the assumption of constant fertility at present levels, the rate of growth would gradually rise until toward the end of the century it had reached an approximate level of 2.8 per cent. In the less developed areas it would be about 3 per cent, but in Africa and Latin America it would be closer to 3.5. In the high variant, it is only after 1990 that any decline in the rate of growth would be registered. In the medium variant a drop would begin instantly but declines in fertility would on balance just barely outweigh the drop in mortality, and the rate of increase in the last decade of the century would not be much lower than in the 1960's. In the less developed areas, slight declines in Asian rates of growth would be offset by increases in Latin America and Africa. Only in the low variant would the rate of increase for the world as a whole point steadily downward. In all three variants, however, the situation at the end of the century would be distinctly different from the "constant fertility" case. The growth rate for world population would not be 2.8 but 1.9, 1.7 and 1.3 respectively —and these rates would be falling rather than increasing. The last point is particularly important for there is no reason to disregard entirely the years after 2000. ...

Food Pessimism

There is, as we shall see, abundant reason to be profoundly alarmed by the rapid growth of population in the underdeveloped world. But the "food pessimism", which is currently prominent in discussions of the population problem, seems warranted only when the case is put with great circumspection.

Nutritional levels in poor countries are poor, as they always have been. But, as a nutritionist well aware of the prevalence of malnutrition has emphasized,

> many of the worst nutritional scourges of mankind have been historically due as much to ignorance and to callousness as to lack of nutrients as such. Thousands of children die of protein deficiency in areas where the proteins which would save them do in fact exist and are often consumed in sufficient amounts in the very households where infants and toddlers die for their lack.[13]

The productivity of agriculture in developing countries is low, but opportunities of increasing labour intensity as population density increases have been found in the past and remain considerable. Reserves of land are large in many places and the low yields and high wastage represent an enormous potential for improvement. Self-sufficiency in food production for all countries is neither necessary nor desirable.

The immediate question, however, is not whether given a long time of adjustment, food production can be raised sufficiently, but whether it will be done rapidly enough. The future growth of food supply is sometimes thought to be limited by past trends, while demand will rise at an accelerated rate. But in this case the supply side cannot be disassociated from the demand side. So far, there is no firm ground for believing that there is a downward trend in nutritional conditions that should be linked to population growth. Per capita consumption and production have by and large remained stable, and food output has been correlated with population growth. Of all the possible consequences of the current population explosion, that of catastrophic food shortage seems the most remote. Occasional food crises in the developing countries must be expected in any case, as long as their levels of economic development are not signally raised, but they were far more frequent in the past when transportation was more inadequate.

On the other hand significant improvement, whether of food consumption levels or economic conditions generally, is rendered most unlikely by a high rate of population growth. In this sense, however, the population problem is not primarily a food problem but a general development problem. Although at present income levels in developing countries food is a dominant item in expenditure, nothing is gained by suggesting that the economic significance of population growth is

---

[13]Jean Mayer,"Food and Population: The Wrong Problem", *Daedalus*, Summer, 1964, pp. 838-839.

specifically related to food when the whole prospect of economic and social development is in jeopardy.[14]

It should be clear that this proposition is not intended to deny the urgency of present and future food relief in emergency situations. On the contrary, it is clearly of the essence that such aid should be forthcoming when in the short run no reallocation of available resources can make much difference.

But in the long run, the gravest prospect to be feared in the under-developed countries does not seem to be a failure to provide for continued support at present levels. One must face the more probable and equally far-reaching problem that excessive population growth will make the hopes of diminishing international inequalities futile. . . .

The Rate of Growth and the Age Distribution

The momentum of the growth of population in the developing world is considerable, and total population figures in the decades immediately ahead would not be very much affected even by fairly radical declines in fertility. The labour force will be even slower to react for the simple reason that those who will make up the active labour force in 1980 are already born. The task of increasing food production sufficiently and creating enough employment in the years to come will therefore not soon be reduced by an attrition of births.

This is not to say that the possible short-run benefits of population control are negligible. On the contrary, since they relate directly to the rate of growth, they make themselves felt rapidly.

Table 6. Population Growth with Unchanged and Declining Fertility

	Year	0	10	20	30	40	50	60
	Age							
(a)	0-14	434	616	870	1,261	1,840	2,655	3,848
	15-64	534	718	996	1,406	2,003	2,901	4,204
	65 +	32	43	43	90	132	180	245
	Total	1,000	1,377	1,931	2,757	3,975	5,736	8,297
(b)	0-14	434	567	637	676	783	901	994
	15-64	534	718	985	1,287	1,573	1,869	2,181
	65 +	32	43	65	90	132	180	245
	Total	1,000	1,328	1,687	2,053	2,488	2,950	3,420

Source: Ansley J. Coale, "Population and Economic Development", in Philip M. Hauser, ed., *The Population Dilemma*, Prentice-Hall, Englewood Cliffs, N.J., 1963. The model population has the following characteristics: initial birth and death rates 44 and 14 per thousand; life expectancy 53 years, rising over a period of thirty years to 70.

[14]Cf. Mogens Boserup, "The Economic Problem of the Demographic Explosion", WPC/WP/265.

A projection by Coale and Hoover may be used to illustrate the nature of these potential benefits.[15] Table 6 shows the growth of a population with the vital characteristics of most underdeveloped countries: high fertility and growth rates, low and declining mortality. The initial birth and death rates are 44 and 14 per thousand, and life expectancy is 53 years. Mortality is assumed to decline steadily until, after thirty years, life expectancy has reached 70. Two different assumptions are made about fertility: a) that it will remain unchanged; and b) that it will decline steadily over 25 years until fertility has been halved, whereupon it stabilises.

The two populations will differ in more than size: indeed the important difference that will assert itself first will be the change in the age distribution.[16] Even if output per head in the age group between 15 and 65 does not increase at all, this would suffice to increase per capita incomes to the population as a whole in the following way:[17]

Year	0	10	20	30	40	50	60
Income	100	104	113	123	125	125	125

During the first thirty years, this decline in the dependency burden will be a direct and major contribution. However, some of the resources which are released when the number of dependents decline will be channelled into savings and investment. The exact amounts will depend upon public policy and private thrift. As long as the labour force continues to grow at the same rate as in the high-fertility case, the stock of capital per worker will therefore increase somewhat faster. When the labour force begins to grow more slowly, a higher share of its output is devoted to investment, so the capital-labour ratio will continue to grow faster than in the high-fertility case.

Any estimate of the effect to be expected under this heading will require a considerable number of assumptions about savings behaviour, capital-output ratios, and policies with regard to outlays for education, health, and housing. The premises of the projection by Coale and Hoover implied that savings were essentially a function of per capita income, and that certain fractions of them were absorbed in non-productive welfare investments in proportion to the

[15] Ansley J. Coale and Edgard M. Hoover, *Population Growth and Economic Development in Low-income Countries* (Princeton, N.J., 1958) remains the most thorough exploration of the problem under review. For a summary presentation, see A.J. Coale, "Population and Economic Development", in Philip M. Hauser, ed., *The Population Dilemma* (Prentice-Hall, Englewood Cliffs, N. J., 1963), pp. 46-69.

[16] It is a common mistake to believe that a fall in infant and childhood mortality will have the effect of reducing the economic wastage involved in raising children who die before they reach productive age. If fertility does not fall, the fact that more children survive to become parents as well as workers will actually have the effect of raising the number of children more than the number of workers and thus, if anything, to raise the dependency burden. Age distribution in populations growing at a more or less steady rate is chiefly a function of the birth rate and is not much affected by the death rate.

[17] In a more elaborate analysis, account might be taken of the fact that children consume less than adults, and Coale and Hoover actually replaced income per capita by income per equivalent consumer. Their figures have been converted back to a per capita basis merely because this is the standard measure in most discussions of economic growth.

increases in population. The projection then yielded the following estimates of income relatives, i.e. per capita incomes in the low-fertility case compared to those in the high-fertility case:

Year	0	10	20	30	40	50	60
Income	100	104	120	150	179	205	232

As they are presented in relative form, these estimates of the probable effect of a reduction in fertility largely eschew the vexed question of the role of land scarcity and population density. Whether the pressure on scarce land and other resources is already such that marginal returns to labour are diminishing, or whether it will be in the future, has not been asked.

As Table 6 shows, after 60 years the population in the high fertility projection would be more than eight times as large as the initial one, and 2.5 times as large as on the low fertility assumption. In countries which are already densely populated, an eight-fold increase in 60 years might very well make it impossible to maintain self-sufficiency in food. But, as was stressed in the previous chapter, this is not the critical test in a world in which international trade very sharply reduces the consequences of the unequal distribution of extractive resources, whether agricultural or mineral. What matters is productivity, regardless of the specific activity in which it is found. Even so, it seems fair to assume that to most countries it will be an advantage if their population density in the future is not staggeringly large.

Whatever the possible benefits from checking the decline in the land-labour ratio, the figures above illustrate the least disputable and immediately relevant contributions of population control to economic development. On the particular assumptions made in this case, the growth rate of per capita income would be rapidly increased in the course of the first decades. The increase would be 0.4 percentage points in the first decade, 1.4 in the second, and 2.2 in the third decade, i.e., already twenty to thirty years after the onset of the fertility decline. This is more than the decline in the growth rate of the population, for one of the essential characteristics of the situation described is precisely that when less is spent on the rearing of children and more on capital equipment, while the labour force remains constant or grows slowly, a country that cuts its birth rate will produce a bigger total product, and this within a short time. In this particular projection, total output would, after thirty years, be 11 per cent higher than in the case of sustained high fertility, and this would be divided among a population 26 per cent smaller.[18]

[18]In the Coale-Hoover Projection, the assumption of a labour surplus is abandoned after the first thirty years. While increments to output before that date are related entirely to capital (with a capital-output ratio of about 3), in the following period they used a Cobb-Douglas production function in which the marginal returns to capital were only about half of what they had been taken to be previously, and in which the very much larger labour force in the high-fertility case begins to count. Therefore the gains in relative per capita income in the following decades gradually declined, the rate of growth of per capita income gradually declined, and eventually at the end of the sixty-year period, total output in the high fertility case caught up with that of the other population by virtue of its crushing superiority in numbers. Coale and Hoover, *op. cit.*, p. 321 ff.

The premise of the exercise was a fertility decline of 50 per cent in 25 years. A few years ago this would have seemed optimistic. Today, however, several countries have adopted more ambitious targets and hope to halve fertility in 10-15 years. It remains to be seen whether this is feasible, except in favourable circumstances, but it is obvious that on such assumptions the potential economic benefits would appear even greater than those illustrated here.

Part Two: Growth Theories

Economic Theory and
Development Policy

Hla Myint

9

Looking at a general development economist as a middleman between the tool makers and the tool users brings me face to face with the perennial controversy: how far are the existing tools of economic theory applicable to the underdeveloped countries? There are many distinguished economists[1] who would be impatient with my proposal to start from the existing theoretical framework and to try to improve its applicability to the underdeveloped countries in the light of accumulating experience and factual knowledge. They would say that the existing "Western" economic theory is so intimately bound up with the special conditions, problems and preconceptions of the industrially advanced countries that large portions of it have to be abandoned before we can come to grips with the problems of the underdeveloped countries.

Excerpted from a paper of the above title, delivered as an inaugural lecture at the London School of Economics and Political Science, December 1, 1966. Reprinted by permission of the author, the London School of Economics and Political Science, and G. Bell & Sons, Ltd. Hla Myint is professor of economics at the London School.

[1]For example, G. Myrdal, *Economic Theory and Underdeveloped Regions*, Duckworth, 1957; also his *An International Economy*, Routledge and Kegan Paul, 1956; D. Seers, "The Limitations of the Special Case", *Bulletin of Oxford Institute of Economics and Statistics*, May 1963.

These economists have advanced three main types of criticism against the existing economic theory.

First, they question the "realism" of trying to apply the standard models of theoretical analysis meant for the advanced countries to the different economic and institutional setting of the underdeveloped countries. I have no quarrel with this line of criticism. In fact I shall be giving illustrations of other types of lack of realism in applying economic theory to the underdeveloped countries which are not mentioned by the critics. But it seems to me that this is not an argument for abandoning existing economic theory but merely an argument for trying to improve its applicability.

Secondly, the critics question the "relevance" of the static neo-classical economics concerned with the problem of allocating given resources within an existing economic framework to the problem of promoting economic development in the underdeveloped countries, which are concerned with increasing the amount of available resources, improving techniques, and generally with the introduction of a dynamic self-sustaining process of economic change, disrupting the existing framework. Here again I agree that we do not possess a satisfactory dynamic theory for studying development problems. In fact, I would go further to say that the recent developments in dynamic economic theory in terms of growth models are not very relevant and are not meant to be relevant for the underdeveloped countries.[2] But I do not accept the conclusion which the critics have drawn: that the static theory of efficient allocation of given resources is irrelevant for the underdeveloped countries. I shall come back to this point in a moment.

Thirdly, the critics maintain that orthodox economic theory is inextricably bound up with preconceptions and biases in favour of orthodox economic policies of *laissez-faire,* free trade and conservative fiscal and monetary policies. They believe that these orthodox economic policies are generally inimical to rapid economic growth, which can be promoted only by large-scale government economic planning, widespread protection and import controls, and deficit financing of development programmes, if sufficient external aid is not available. Thus they propose that large chunks of existing economic theory, particularly the orthodox neo-classical theory, should be abandoned to pave the way for the adoption of these new development policies.

There are two questions here. The first is the general question whether the new policies are always more effective than the orthodox policies in promoting economic development in the underdeveloped countries. The second is the more specific question whether there is an unbreakable ideological link between orthodox economic theory and orthodox economic policies, so that if we wish to adopt the new development policies we must necessarily abandon large chunks of existing theory.

The underdeveloped countries vary widely among themselves and I, therefore, find it difficult to accept the general presumption that the new

[2]Cf. Sir John Hicks, *Capital and Growth*, Oxford University Press, 1965, p. 1.

policies will be always better for their economic development, whatever their particular individual situation. Later I shall give some examples where the orthodox type of economic policies have in fact been more effective in promoting economic development than the new-style development policies. However, I have chosen as the subject of my lecture today not the general debate on the rival merits of the orthodox and the new development policies, but the relation between economic theory and development policy. I have done this partly because I feel that such a general debate without reference to a concrete situation generates more heat than light, and partly also because it has been rapidly overtaken by events. Whether we like it or not, it is no longer an open question whether the underdeveloped countries should choose the orthodox or the new type of development policies. One after another they have already made their choice in favour of the new policies, which have now become a part of conventional economic wisdom. Accepting this as one of the facts of life the more immediately relevant question seems to be the second question, whether large chunks of the orthodox economic theory have now become obsolete because the underdeveloped countries wish to plan for rapid economic development.

I shall argue that this is not so; that on the contrary orthodox economic theory assumes a greater significance in the context of the new "progressive" development policies. I shall show that even if development planning is to be regarded as new and radical policy, the *theory* underlying development planning is, technically speaking, quite orthodox and conventional. Similarly, I shall show that the orthodox theory of international trade can be made to support more liberal and generous trade and aid policies towards the underdeveloped countries, if we choose to use it in this way. What I am saying is not new. It is merely a restatement of the familiar doctrine that economic theory is "ethically neutral" and can be made use of in the more efficient pursuit of the economic objectives to be chosen by the "value judgments" of the policy maker.

However, let us start by a closer look at the question of "realism" in applying existing economic theory to the underdeveloped countries. Some critics speak of "existing theory" as though it were contained in a modern textbook like Samuelson. Properly speaking, it should include the whole corpus of Western economic theory, offering a wide choice of theoretical models, ranging from those of the older economists writing at earlier stages of economic development to the highly complex and abstract models of contemporary economic theory. To my mind a very important cause of lack of realism arises from the wrong choice of theoretical models to be applied to the underdeveloped countries. Much in the same way as the governments of the underdeveloped countries succumb to the lure of the "steel mills" embodying the most advanced and capital-intensive type of Western technology, many development economists have succumbed to the lure of the intellectual "steel mills" represented by the latest and most sophisticated theoretical models. This is where, I believe, the greatest mischief has been done. This is why I have always maintained that a good development economist should also be something of an applied historian of economic thought.

If it is unrealistic to apply highly sophisticated theoretical models meant for the complex economic structures of advanced countries to the simpler economic structures of underdeveloped countries, has this been corrected by the new theories of development and underdevelopment which are specially meant for the underdeveloped countries? Looking at these new theories, which became popular during the 1950's, such as the "vicious circle", the "take-off" or the "big push", it does not seem to me that these have stood up to the test of realism any better. The weakness of these new theories is that they try to apply a composite model of the underdeveloped country, incorporating certain special features of some type of underdeveloped country, to all the underdeveloped countries. The "vicious circle" theory assumes poverty and stagnation caused by severe population pressure on resources; the "take-off" theory assumes the pre-existence of a fairly high level of development in the political, social and institutional framework; the "big push" theory assumes both and also an internal market large enough to support a domestic capital goods sector. By the time we have incorporated all these special features into a composite model, the number of the under-developed countries to which this model might apply becomes limited to one or two countries, such as India and possibly Pakistan.

The limitations of these new theories of development, particularly the "vicious circle" theory, can be illustrated by looking at the broad dimensions of the economic performance of underdeveloped countries during the decade 1950-60. During that decade, compared with the 4 per cent average annual growth rates for the advanced Western countries, the G.D.P. of under-developed countries as a group grew at the average annual rate of 4.4 per cent, giving them a growth in *per capita* incomes of a little over 2 per cent per annum.[3] This may or may not be very much, but the really interesting thing is that the G.D.P. of some underdeveloped countries was growing at a faster rate than the average, say between 5 per cent and 6 per cent, while that of other countries barely kept up with their population increase. Thus instead of the earlier *simpliste* view according to which all underdeveloped countries are caught up in a vicious circle of stagnation and population pressure, we are led to the question why some underdeveloped countries grow faster or slower than others.

When we try to answer this question, we become very aware of the differences between the underdeveloped countries, in size, in the degree of population pressure over natural resources, in the conditions of world demand for their exports and in their general level of economic development and political stability. These differences will by themselves explain quite a lot of the differences in the growth rate between different underdeveloped countries. If, in addition, we want to say something about development policy, we shall have to choose a fairly uniform group of

[3]United Nations, *World Economic Survey 1963*, Part I, p. 20.

countries where the basic social and economic differences are small enough for us to isolate the effect of economic policy.

To illustrate, let me take the concrete example of the post-war economic development of Southeast Asia. This will also serve to illustrate the dangers of generalising about development policies, particularly the danger of assuming that the new "progressive" development policies will always promote faster economic growth than the orthodox economic policies.

The five countries I have chosen, Burma, Thailand, the Philippines, Indonesia and Malaya, form a fairly homogenous group. In contrast to India or China, they are not only much smaller but also do not suffer from any great pressure of population. They do not have to contend with food shortage and have a much larger elbow-room of natural resources to allow for the working of economic incentives. They are also similar in the general level of social and economic development, and moreover have common exports such as rice, timber and rubber. Yet the rapid post-war economic development of Thailand, the Philippines and Malaya contrasts sharply with the economic stagnation of Burma and Indonesia. By 1960 both Thailand and the Philippines had doubled their pre-war G.N.P. in real terms, combined with a considerable growth in import-substituting industries; while the G.N.P. of Burma and Indonesia rose by a bare 11 per cent above the pre-war level, much slower than their population growth during that period. Malaya, starting at a somewhat higher *per capita* level than the others, has also enjoyed an economic prosperity which compares favourably, not only with Burma and Indonesia but also with Ceylon, to which her economic structure is similar in many aspects.

These larger differences in the rates of economic growth are closely related to the rate of expansion in the exports of the two groups of countries; since they have common exports sharing the same world market conditions, the differences in their export performance must be traced largely to the domestic economic policies which have affected the supply side of their exports. Here, broadly speaking, the first group of countries, with the faster rate of economic growth—Thailand, Malaya and the Philippines—have pursued the more orthodox type of economic policies with a greater reliance on market forces, private enterprise and an outward-looking attitude to foreign trade and enterprise; while Burma and Indonesia lean heavily on economic planning and large-scale state intervention in economic life, combined with an inward-looking and even hostile attitude towards foreign trade and enterprise.

More specifically: (i) Thailand and the Philippines have very successfully used market incentives to encourage their peasants to bring more land under cultivation and expand production both of export and domestic food crops, while the Burmese peasants have been depressed by the operation of the state agricultural marketing board, which has used peasant agriculture simply as a milch cow for government investment in state enterprises in manufacturing industry and social overhead capital. (ii) Thailand and the Philippines have encouraged their domestic entrepreneurs to set up new manufacturing industries through protection and subsidies, while Burma and Indonesia have tried to do this by state enterprises which have failed, amongst other reasons, because of a shortage of entrepreneurial ability among the civil servants. Here it may be noted that all these Southeast Asian countries suffer from the fear of being dominated by the Chinese or the Indian entrepreneurs who are or were prominent in small- or medium-scale enterprises in light manufacturing industries. Thus one may say that Burma and Indonesia have chosen to substitute Indian and Chinese private enterprise by indigenous state enterprise, while Thailand has absorbed the Chinese entrepreneurs into her own business class and the Philippines have successfully substituted in their place Filipino private entrepreneurs. This problem has yet to be solved in Malaya. (iii) Malaya, Thailand and the Philippines have offered a stable economic climate to Western enterprises both in the traditional plantation and mining sectors and in the new manufacturing sector, and have benefited from a considerable inflow of private foreign capital, while Burma and Indonesia have discouraged fresh inflow of private investment by nationalisation and other hostile policies. (iv) Malaya and Thailand have pursued conservative monetary and fiscal policies and their currencies have been very strong and stable, and the Philippines tackled her balance of payment disequilibrium successfully by devaluation in 1962. In contrast Burma and Indonesia have tried to solve their balance of payment problems, arising out of deficit financing and domestic inflation, through an intensification of inefficient and hurtful import controls, which combined with pervasive state interference at all levels of economic activity, have throttled most of the promising infant industries.[4]

It is not for me to judge the ultimate rightness or wrongness of the economic nationalism and the anti-Western attitude of Burma and Indonesia contrasted with the more pro-Western attitude of Malaya, Thailand and the Philippines. But at the conventional level at which economists judge development policies, it seems to me that in the case of Southeast Asia at least the orthodox types of economic policies have resulted in a more rapid rate of economic development during the post-war period than the newer "progressive" development policies. How far is the Southeast Asian experience applicable to other underdeveloped countries outside the region? I think that it may be of some relevance to the other smaller and less densely populated export economies, notably in West Africa. In that region also expansion in the exports of primary products still offers the most promising engine of economic development, both as a source of foreign exchange earnings to finance the new import-substituting industries, and even more importantly as the method of drawing the under-utilised natural resources of the subsistence sector into the money economy. But these conclusions in favour of the orthodox policies are likely to become weaker as we try to extend them to less similar types of country, particularly to large

[4]For a fuller treatment, see my paper "The Inward and the Outward Looking Countries of Southeast Asia and the Economic Future of the Region", Symposium Series II on *Japan's Future in Southeast Asia*, Kyoto University, 1966.

overpopulated countries like India. But conversely it would be equally unrealistic to try to apply the Indian model to the smaller export economies.

Let me now conclude my remarks on the "realism" of applying economic theory to the underdeveloped countries by drawing attention to the dangers of trying to be too different from the standard models of economic analysis. These arise from selecting the "queer cases" in the standard Western models of analysis, and in taking it for granted that these exceptions to the standard case must automatically apply to the underdeveloped countries because they are so different from the advanced countries in social values and attitudes and institutional setting. Such for instance is the famous case of the "backward sloping supply curve of labour" attributed to the underdeveloped countries by many writers, who also speak of the "demonstration effect" and "the revolution of rising expectations". Such too is the belief that the people of the underdeveloped countries, being more communally minded, will take more easily to co-operative forms of economic organization (while writers on the co-operative movement in the underdeveloped countries frequently complain about the lack of co-operative spirit and the excessive individualism of the people). Yet another example is the generalization that the people of the underdeveloped countries naturally lack entrepreneurial ability, irrespective of the economic policies followed by their governments. If one were to tell the politicians of the underdeveloped countries that their people are lazy, stupid, lacking in initiative and adaptability, one would be branded as an enemy; but if one were to rephrase these prejudices in another way and say that the people lack entrepreneurial capacity, one would be welcomed for giving "scientific" support for economic planning. To take just one more example, there is the hoary belief that peasants in the underdeveloped countries do not respond to economic incentives, while agricultural economists have been accumulating abundant evidence to show that peasants do respond to price changes by switching from one crop to another or by bringing more land under cultivation. The real problem is how to introduce new methods of cultivation which will raise productivity: this is a difficult practical problem, but in principle it is not all that different from, say, the problem of introducing new methods to raise productivity in British industry.

This is where I think that a closer co-operation between economics and other branches of social studies is likely to prove most useful, both in getting rid of questionable sociological generalizations and also in tackling the more intractable problems of analysing social and economic change . . . .

Let me now turn from the "realism" to the "relevance" of the existing economic theory to the underdeveloped countries. The problem of promoting rapid economic development in these countries may ultimately lie in the realm of social and economic dynamics of the sort we do not at present possess; and there is nothing in my argument to prevent anyone from launching into new dynamic theoretical approaches to the underdeveloped countries. But in the meantime, it is dangerously easy to underestimate the significance of the orthodox static theory of the allocation of given resources to the underdeveloped countries. The affluent Western economies with their steady rates of increase in productivity may be able to take a tolerant attitude towards misallocation of resources. But the underdeveloped countries are simply too poor to put up with preventable wasteful use of their given meagre economic resources. In particular, they can ill afford the well-recognised distortions of their price systems, such as the excessively high levels of wages and low levels of interest in their manufacturing and public sectors compared with those in the agricultural sector, and the overvaluation of their currencies at the official rates of exchange. Having to bear the brunt of low earnings and high interest rates discourages the expansion of agricultural output both for export and for domestic consumption and this in turn slows down the overall rate of growth of the economy. Higher wages attract a large number of people from the countryside to the towns, but only a small proportion of this influx can be absorbed because of the highly capital-intensive methods adopted in the modern import-substituting industries. This aggravates the problem of urban unemployment and the problem of shanty towns, which increases the requirements for investment for housing and social welfare. The scarce supply of capital tends to be wastefully used, both in government prestige projects and in private industry, because of the artificially low rates of interest. This is aggravated by the over-valuation of currencies and import controls in favour of capital goods, which positively encourage the businessmen who are fortunate enough to obtain import licences to buy the most expensive and capital-intensive type of machinery from abroad.

These then are some of the glaring sources of wastefulness which can be reduced by a better allocation of resources. Now I should point out that just because the orthodox neo-classical theory is concerned with the efficient allocation of *given* resources, it does not mean that it becomes unimportant in the context of aid policies to increase the volume of resources available to the underdeveloped countries. On the contrary, a country which cannot use its already available resources efficiently is not likely to be able to "absorb" additional resources from aid programmes and use them efficiently. That is to say, a country's absorptive capacity for aid must to a large extent depend on its ability to avoid serious misallocation of resources. A similar conclusion can be drawn about an underdeveloped country's ability to make effective use of its opportunities for international trade. If we find that a country is not making effective use of its already available trading opportunities, because of domestic policies discouraging its export production or raising the costs in the export sector, then we should not expect it to benefit in a dramatic way from the new trading opportunities to be obtained through international negotiations.

This is a part of the reason why I have suggested that orthodox economic theory, instead of becoming obsolete, has assumed a greater significance in the context of the new "progressive" policies for promoting economic development in the underdeveloped countries. Let me illustrate this argument further by examples from development planning theory and from recent discussions about the appropriate trade and aid policies.

I think that a great deal of confusion would have been avoided by clearly distinguishing the *policy* of development planning and the economic *theory* which underlies development planning, which is, as we shall see, only an application of the traditional theory of the optimum allocation of the *given* resources. This confusion was introduced during the 1950's when it was the fashion to try to make out the case for development planning mainly by attacking the orthodox equilibrium and optimum theory. At the macro-economic level, there were theories of deficit financing trying to show how economic development might be accelerated by forced saving and inflation, or by making use of "disguised unemployment" for capital formation. More generally, the theories of the "vicious circle", the "big push" or the "unbalanced growth" tried to show, in their different ways, the desirability of breaking out of the static equilibrium framework by deliberately introducing unbalances and disequilibria which would start the chain-reaction of cumulative movement towards self-sustained economic growth. Ironically enough, when the underdeveloped countries came to accept the need for development planning and to ask how this might be done efficiently, it turned out that the economic theory required for this purpose is basically nothing but the traditional equilibrium and optimum theory.

Thus according to the present-day textbooks on development planning,[5] the first task of the planner is to test the feasibility of the plan at the macro-economic level by making sure that the aggregate amount of resources required to carry out the plan does not exceed the aggregate amount of resources available. That is to say, deficit financing and inflation are to be avoided and this is to be checked at the sectoral level by ensuring that the projected rate of expansion of the services sector does not exceed the possible rate of expansion in the output of commodities by a certain critical margin. The next task of the planner is to test the consistency of the plan at the sectoral and micro-economic level to make sure that the demand and supply for particular commodities and services are equated to each other, and that there is an equilibrium relationship between the different arts of the economy, not only within any given year, but also between one year and another during the whole of the plan period. Finally, if the plan is found to be both feasible and consistent, the task of the planner is to find out whether the plan adopted is an optimum plan in the sense that there is no alternative way of reallocating the given resources more efficiently to satisfy the given objectives of the plan.

If this standard formulation of development planning is accepted, then there is no fundamental theoretical difference between those who aim to achieve the efficient allocation of the available resources through the market mechanism and those who aim to achieve it through the state mechanism. Both accept the optimum allocation of resources as their theoretical norm

---

[5]See particularly, *Development Planning*, by W. Arthur Lewis, Allen and Unwin, 1966: also, *Development Planning: Lessons of Experience*, by Albert Waterston, Oxford University Press, 1966 and W. B. Reddaway, *The Development of the Indian Economy*, Allen and Unwin, 1962.

and their disagreements are about the *practical* means of fulfilling this norm. In any given situation, they will disagree how far planning should be "indicative" or "imperative", that is to say, how far the task of allocating resources should be left to the decentralised decision-making of the market or to the centralised decision-making of the state. But technically speaking they are using the same type of economic theory—the extension of the orthodox neo-classical theory in the pursuit of their different practical policies.

From a theoretical point of view, the great divide is between those who believe that economic development of the underdeveloped countries can be promoted in *an orderly manner* by a more efficient allocation of the available resources, which are assumed to be steadily expanding between one period and another through good management of domestic savings and external aid, and those who believe that only sudden disruptive and *disorderly* changes such as social revolutions and technical innovations can bring about economic development. Now this second revolutionary approach to economic development may well be the correct approach for some underdeveloped countries. But it is difficult to see how this can be incorporated into the planning approach. Development planning is by definition an orderly approach: on the other hand, genuinely far-reaching and disruptive social changes cannot be turned on and turned off in a predictable way and incorporated into the planning framework. Those who advocate the necessity of breaking out of the static equilibrium framework by deliberately introducing unbalances and tensions, are in effect advocating at the same time the need to break out of the planning framework. Thus one may advocate social revolution now and planning later but not advocate social revolution and planning at the same time without getting into serious contradictions. Further, it should be pointed out that the revolutionary approach to economic development is by no means the monopoly of the critics of the private enterprise system. The case for *laissez-faire* can be made, not on grounds of static allocative efficiency, but on the ground that it imparts a "dynamism" to the economy by stimulating enterprise, innovation and savings. Schumpeter's picture of the disruption of the existing productive framework through a process of "creative destruction" by innovating private entrepreneurs, is a well-known illustration of this type of revolutionary approach to economic development.

Toward a Generalized Capital
Accumulation Approach to
Economic Development

Harry G. Johnson

10 The contemporary interest in the economics of education, and more broadly in the economics of all processes connected with the augmentation and application of knowledge, represents a confluence of interests derived from concerns with widely divergent problems. These problems include such matters as the economic value of education, the contribution of education to past economic development in advanced countries, and the role of education and expenditure on increased education in the planned development of underdeveloped countries.[1]

The title of this conference gives primary weight to one avenue of approach to concern with the economics of education, the potency of the amount of educational capital and knowledge embodied in the human

From a paper published in *The Residual Factor and Economic Growth*, Organization for Economic Cooperation and Development, Paris, 1964. Reprinted by permission of the author and publisher. Harry Johnson is professor of economics both at the University of Chicago and the London School of Economics.

[1]Cf. T.W. Schultz, editor, "Reflections on Investment in Man", *The Journal of Political Economy, Supplement*, Vol. LXX No. 5, part 2, October 1962, pp. 1-8.

population as a variable to explain that part of measured economic growth in the advanced countries—specifically the United States, where the bulk of the empirical research has been performed—that cannot be accounted for by increases in the inputs of labour and capital as conventionally measured. Concern with education, human capital, or the "quality" of labour inputs as an important determinant of the residual element of economic growth dovetails neatly with the apparent lessons of some fifteen years of experience with the planning of accelerated economic growth. This experience has strongly suggested that the early postwar emphasis on investment in material capital in the methodology of economic planning was seriously mistaken, and that economic development depends vitally on the creation of a labour force both equipped with the necessary technical skills for modern industrial production and imbued with a philosophy conducive to the acceptance and promotion of economic and technical change.

The formulation of concern with the economics of education (in a broad sense) in these particular terms, while appropriate to the current state of economic research and thinking, is for this very reason both restrictive in its implications and likely to appear before much more time has passed as a transient stage in the evolution towards a more comprehensive formulation of economic development problems in terms of a broadly conceived concept of capital accumulation. For one thing, progress in economics, and especially in those parts of economics of most direct relevance to policy-making, tends to proceed in a series of alternating phases of exaggerated concentration on one aspect of a problem to the denigration of others, the ascendancy of one approach eventually evoking insistence on the importance of factors neglected in that approach. Thus, in the general field of economic growth, concentration on the role of material capital and the shortcomings of this approach have led to a contrasting emphasis on the role of people, conceptualized in terms of an alternative type of capital, human capital.

Concentration on the role of human capital has already proceeded far enough to generate the beginnings of a counter-revolution. The general outlines of the counter-revolution are indeed already apparent. On the one hand, the recent emphasis on human capital formation in growth accountancy is based on the recognition that conventional measures of labour input fail to take account of improvements in the quality of labour and aims primarily at more accurate measurement of labour inputs. Application of the same criteria to inputs of capital suggests that the contribution of capital may also have been grossly underestimated, as a result both of understatement of the flow of capital services into production by the conventional equation of service flow with the depreciated value of capital stock, and of failure to measure accurately improvements in the performance characteristics ("quality") of capital equipment.[2] On the other hand, the evidence on rates of return to educational investment in the United States does not suggest that

[2]Cf. Zvi Griliches, "The Sources of Measured Productivity Growth: U.S. Agriculture, 1940-1960," *Journal of Political Economy*, Vol. LXXIV No. 4, August 1960.

there has been serious general underinvestment in education there, while both casual empirical observation of underdeveloped countries and some detailed research on the relative returns to investments in education and material capital in them[3] suggest that at least in some cases the proportion of resources devoted to human capital formation may be too high rather than too low.[4] A rehabilitation of investment in material capital as a potent source of economic growth may therefore be in prospect. What is more important, while the process of increasing economic knowledge proceeds in phases of exaggerated concentration on one or another aspect of a problem, both the effect and the intent are to arrive at a unified and more powerful synthesis of explanations of economic phenomena. The contemporary phase, in which the concepts of human capital and of investment in it figure as corrections of emphasis in a system of economic ideas dominated by material capital, is bound to merge into one in which human and non-human capital are treated as alternative forms of capital in general. The desirability of achieving such a synthesis is not merely a matter of scientific economy and elegance, it is also a prerequisite for rational discussion and formulation of policy for economic growth in both advanced and underdeveloped countries. The purpose of this paper, accordingly, is to sketch the outlines of such a synthesis, in the form of a generalised capital accumulation approach to economic development, and to discuss some of its implications of social and economic policy.

The essential elements of a generalised capital accumulation approach to economic development are already present in the literature of economics, and at least some applications of the approach (for example, the explanation of wage differentials) have been familiar to economists ever since economics became established as a separate subject of study. The foundations of it were explicitly laid in Irving Fisher's classic work on capital and income, and carried forward by F. H. Knight's work on the theory of capital; and the approach is exemplified, and its potency demonstrated, in the recent research of T. W. Schultz, Gary Becker, and others on human capital.[5] The essence of it is to regard "capital" as including anything that yields a stream of income over time, and income as the product of capital. From this point of view, as Fisher pointed out, all categories of income describe yields on various forms of capital, and can be expressed as rates of interest or return on the corresponding items of capital. Alternatively, all forms of income-yielding assets can be given an equivalent capital value by capitalising the income they yield at an appropriate rate of interest. By extension, the growth of income

[3]Cf. Arnold C. Harberger, *Investment in Man Versus Investment in Machines: The Case of India*, a paper prepared for the Conference on Education and Economic Development, University of Chicago, April 4-6, 1963. Harberger finds the rate of return on real investment in India to be substantially higher than the rate of return on investment in education.

[4]This proposition becomes almost a truism if the concept of investment in human capital formation is extended to include expenditures on improved health, whose effects on the rate of population increase constitute one of the major economic problems of underdeveloped countries.

[5]See T.W. Schultz, *op. cit.*

that defines economic development is necessarily the result of the accumulation of capital, or of "investment"; but "investment" in this context must be defined to include such diverse activities as adding to material capital, increasing the health, discipline, skill and education of the human population, moving labour into more productive occupations and locations, and applying existing knowledge or discovering and applying new knowledge to increase the efficiency of productive processes. All such activities involve incurring costs, in the form of use of current resources, and investment in them is socially worth while if the rate of return over cost exceeds the general rate of interest, or the capital value of the additional income they yield exceeds the cost of obtaining it. From the somewhat different perspective of planning economic development, efficient development involves allocation of investment resources according to priorities set by the relative rates of return on alternative investments.

The conception of economic growth as a process of accumulating capital, in all the manifold forms that the broad Fisherian concept of capital allows, is a potent simplification of the analytical problem of growth, and one which facilitates the discussion of problems of growth policy by emphasising the relative returns from alternative investments of currently available resources. The Fisherian concept of capital, however, and the approach to the analysis of production and distribution problems associated with it, are not as yet characteristic of the work and philosophical approach of the majority of economists, and to some the implications of the approach for policy with respect to human beings appear to be positively repugnant. Most economists instead employ a narrower concept of capital that identifies capital with material capital goods and equipment used in the production process, and distinguishes it sharply from labour.

This approach to the theory of production derives from English classical economics, which developed in response to the early stages of the industrial revolution, when a sharp distinction between capital goods and raw labour power made more sense than it does under modern industrial conditions, and when moreover the distinction between wages, profit and rent corresponded to a meaningful division of society into politico-economic classes. With the progress of technology, the replacement of brute human strength by mechanical power, and the increasing importance of skill and scientific knowledge on the part of labour force, the traditional distinction between labour as an original factor and capital as a produced factor has become increasingly unrealistic, while these developments together with the declining importance of rent consequent on technical progress in agriculture and the alteration of the relationship of property ownership to economic control consequent on the development of corporate enterprise have increasingly deprived the functional distribution of income of socio-political content. Nevertheless, the English neo-classical tradition continues to dominate the theory and policy of economic growth. Indeed, this tradition has been reinforced by the impact of Keynes' *General Theory*, with its emphasis on fixed capital investment as the key variable in the economic system and its assumption of a homogeneous labour force of a given quality, and by the subsequent conversion of the Keynesian short-run equilibrium model into the Harrod growth model.

As already mentioned, the limitations of accumulation of material capital as an explanation of a prescription for growth have prompted the contemporary interest in human capital formation, and suggest a generalisation of the concept of capital accumulation to include investment in all types of capital formation. An important obstacle to such a generalisation is that the treatment of human beings as a form of capital, even if only conceptually, seems offensive to some economists as being contrary to democratic political philosophy. This reaction, however, involves a confusion of analytical approach and normative recommendations unfortunately only too common in discussions of economic problems with policy connotations. To recognise that important areas of socio-economic policy involve decisions analytically identical with decisions about investing in machines is not at all to imply that people should be regarded as no different from machines; on the contrary, refusal to recognise the investment character of a problem because people are involved may result in people receiving worse treatment than machines. One might, indeed, hazard the generalisation that democratic free-enterprise economics tend to make wasteful use of their human resources, precisely because people are not sufficiently regarded as socially productive assets.

Conception of economic growth as a generalised process of capital accumulation provides a unifying principle for the statistical explanation of past growth and the formulation of policy for future growth or plans for economic development. It does not, however—and cannot be expected to—dispose of any real problems, though it does clarify understanding of them. Instead, it transforms these problems into problems of the special characteristics of particular types of capital, or of the specification of efficient investment programmes.

From the point of view of economically relevant differentiations, items of capital can be classified in a variety of ways. One fundamental distinction to be drawn relates to the nature of the yield or contribution to economic welfare—the distinction between consumption capital, which yields a flow of services enjoyed directly and therefore contributing to utility, and production capital, which yields a flow of goods the consumption of which yields utility. The returns from production capital are directly observable, and therefore more amenable to measurement than the returns on consumption capital.

Another fundamental distinction relates to the form in which capital is embodied—here it seems necessary not only to distinguish capital embodied in human beings from capital embodied in non-human material forms, but also to distinguish between capital embodied in both human and non-human physical forms and capital embodied in neither, the latter category comprising as such the state of the arts (the intellectual production capital of society) and the state of culture (the intellectual consumption capital of society). The significance of this distinction is closely related to a third distinction—one which is particularly relevant to policy problems—between types of capital according to whether the returns to investment in capital accumulation accrue to the investor or to others. Here it seems necessary to distinguish: (a) capital goods which render specific services to production or consumption by the owner; (b) human capital, the distinguishing characteristic of which is that, both inherently and by legal tradition, control over the use of the capital is vested in the individual embodying the capital, regardless of the source of finance of the investment in it; (c) social capital or collective capital the distinguishing characteristic of which is that for reasons of inherent necessity or administrative convenience its services to production or consumption are not charged to individual users but are paid for by taxation of the community at large; (d) intellectual capital or knowledge, the distinguishing characteristic of which is that, once created it is a free good, in the sense that use of it by one individual does not diminish its availability to others.

All forms of capital other than capital goods rendering specific services to production or consumption raise serious problems for economic analysis measurement and policy formation. The fusion of human capital with the personality of its owner raises among other things the problem of how far expenditure on the creation of human capital should be accounted as investment, and how far it should be classed as consumption; while the vesting of control over the use of the capital in the individual invested in, given the imperfection of markets for personal credit, poses the problem of how far education should be provided at public expense. The divergence of private and social costs and benefits inherent in free or subsidised education raises some particularly difficult policy problems in conjunction with the fact that educated people are especially mobile interregionally and internationally, so that resources devoted to education in poor countries may run substantially to waste in unilateral transfers of human capital to richer countries.[6] Social capital investment involves a similar separation of costs of investment from benefits, and a similar mixture of equity and efficiency considerations. Investment in knowledge raises the thorniest of all problems, since the zero marginal cost of knowledge to additional users implies that no system of recouping the cost of investment in knowledge-creation by charging for its use can be economically efficient. (The patent and copyright laws, as is well known, constitute a very inefficient compromise between encouraging investment in knowledge by rewarding the inventor and encouraging the use

[6]Brinley Thomas has emphasised the economic absurdity of the contemporary migration pattern between advanced and underdeveloped countries, in which the advanced countries cream off the professional talent of the underdeveloped countries by immigration and attempt to replace it by their own experts supplied at great expense as part of development aid. See Brinley Thomas, "International Factor Movements and Unequal Rates of Growth," *The Manchester School of Economic and Social Studies,* Vol. XXIX, No. 1, January 1961. The case of migration of educated people from under-developed countries, especially those in which English is the language of instruction, to advanced countries is a serious limitation on the potentialities of achieving economic development by educational investment and suggests the social desirability of devising means of obliging either the emigrants themselves or the countries receiving them to repay the social capital invested in them to their countries of origin.

of knowledge by making it freely available; in general, the more far-reaching an advance in knowledge the more does its creator have to be satisfied with the non-material rewards of intellectual accomplishment.)

The distinctions discussed above do not include a distinction between natural resources (natural capital) and man-made capital. For most economic purposes, such a distinction is unnecessary—natural resources, like capital goods, can be appropriated, transferred, and invested in. Natural resources do, however, raise two sorts of special problems. First, property rights in some range of natural resources are typically vested in society or the state: this poses the problem of ensuring efficient exploitation of these resources through appropriate accounting and charging for the use of the state's natural capital, a problem particularly inportant at the time when resources are first brought into use. Secondly, some kinds of natural resources, which are likely to be of particular importance to developing countries, are non-renewable, and pose the problems of efficient depletion and exhaustion—of efficient capital decumulation, rather than accumulation. The problems of achieving economic development through the exploitation of depleting natural resources become particularly acute and politically highly charged when such exploitation is dependent on the participation of foreign capital and enterprise.

Conception of economic development as a generalised process of capital accumulation, in conjunction with recognition of economically significant differences between various types of capital, has important implications for the efficient programming of investment of economic development. These implications centre on the relationships of complementarity and substitutability in both production and consumption that may exist between types of capital provided by different investment processes, and the consequent desirability of aiming at both balanced investment in the production of complementary types of capital and the selection of the most efficient combinations of types of capital in the light of the relative costs of different kinds of investment. The complementarity between modern equipment and technology, a skilled labour force, and social overhead capital in the transportation and distribution systems is by now sufficiently recognised for development planning to aim at producing integrated investment programmes comprising investment in education and vocational training (manpower programmes) as well as investment in industrial capital and social overheads. For such comprehensive development investment programmes to maximise the contribution of investment to economic growth, however, recognition of complementarity must be allied with recognition of substitutability and analysis of rates of return on the total investment of capital in alternative programmes involving investment in capital goods, human capital, social capital and the acquisition of new knowledge.

Much of the literature on economic development assumes far too easily that low-wage labour is necessarily cheap industrial labour, ignoring the magnitude of the investments in human and social capital that may have to be made to convert rural workers into skilled industrial labour, and the possibility that investment of the same capital in agricultural improvement might yield far higher returns. On the other hand, there is a strong possibility, exemplified by the successful development of exports of some technologically fairly advanced products from otherwise underdeveloped countries, that the greatest comparative advantage for such countries lies in skilled-labour-intensive products, for the reason that a generally low wage level makes the cost of investment in human capital low (especially foregone earnings and the cost of instruction and educational structures) by comparison with comparable costs in advanced countries. In addition, such countries may be able to catch up with the advanced countries far more rapidly in the accumulation of knowledge than in the accumulation of material capital.

Apart from its implications for planning for economic growth, a generalised capital accumulation approach to economic development points to the potential fruitfulness of research into and analysis of the efficiency of a wide range of processes and policies that involve the allocation of capital but are not usually thought of as concerned with investment. It has, for example, been amply demonstrated by empirical research that rates of return on investment in education vary widely between different levels of the education system; and there is good reason for doubting that existing educational systems are very efficient when considered as an industry producing extremely long-lived capital assets. The field of public health and medical care, viewed as an industry concerned with the repair and maintenance of human capital, also offers scope for economic analyses of rates of return on alternative investments. Institutional arrangements for supporting and rewarding fundamental and applied research, considered as an industry producing intellectual capital, provide an even greater challenge to economists. Within the traditional scope of economics, labour mobility, unemployment policy, and policy respecting the location of industry all demand the application of capital theory. Perhaps the most important area requiring rationalisation in terms of a broadened concept of capital accumulation, however, is the theory and practice of public finance. Not only do income tax systems typically make a very poor adjustment for the capital investment element in personal income, but the necessity of recouping by income and profits taxation the costs of investments in human capital customarily provided free or at a subsidised price to the people invested in creates disincentives to the efficient use and accumulation of capital of all kinds.

A Theory of Economic Development

Gustave Ranis
John C. H. Fei

11

This paper attempts to make a contribution towards the theory of growth by rigorously analyzing the transition process through which an underdeveloped economy hopes to move from a condition of stagnation to one of self-sustaining growth. Since the totality of economies bearing the "underdeveloped" label admittedly defies easy generalization, we shall be primarily concerned here with the labor-surplus, resource-poor variety in which the vast majority of the population is typically engaged in agriculture amidst widespread disguised unemployment and high rates of population growth. We hope to accomplish our task by drawing liberally on the stock of already accepted ideas and then proceeding to weave them into a general explanatory model of economic growth.

Our analysis begins with an economy's first departure from quasi-stagnation or the initiation of the so-called take-off process.[1] Rostow defines

An excerpt from an article in the *American Economic Review*, Papers and Proceedings, September 1961. Reprinted by permission of the authors and publisher. The authors are professors of economics at Yale University and Cornell University, respectively.

[1]This is not to understate the importance of a prior preconditioning period when potentially expansionary forces are being mobilized and render the system capable of a significantly positive response to a random stimulus.

this as a period of two or three decades during which the economy transforms itself in such a way that economic growth becomes, subsequently, more or less automatic; its characteristics are a reduction of the rural proportion of the population, a doubling of savings rates and the first marked and continuous flowering of industry stimulated by the availability of surplus labor. This well-known intuitive notion has been chosen as our point of departure. For our basic analytical tool-kit, however, we draw heavily on the work of Arthur Lewis.

In his celebrated articles Lewis presents a two-sector model and investigates the expansion of the capitalistic or industrial sector as it is nourished by supplies of cheap labor from the subsistence or agricultural sector.[2] Development consists of the re-allocation of surplus agricultural workers, whose contribution to output may have been zero or negligible, to industry where they become productive members of the labor force at a wage equal (or tied to) the institutional wage in agriculture. This process continues until the industrial labor supply curve begins to turn up.

Lewis, however, has failed to present a satisfactory analysis of the subsistence or agricultural sector. It seems clear that this sector must also grow if the mechanism he describes is not to grind to a premature halt. Pursuit of this notion of a required balance in growth then leads us to a logically consistent definition of the end of the take-off process.

Finally, the economy must be able to solve its Malthusian problem if the process of development along a balanced-growth path is to prove successful. Considerations of this nature have given rise to the so-called "critical minimum effort" theory, which deals with the size of the effort required to achieve a more-than-temporary departure from stagnation. We shall show, in the course of our analysis, that the concept of a critical minimum effort does not presuppose some absolute magnitude of effort to vary with the duration of the take-off process.

The contribution of this paper, then, is to construct a theory of economic growth of which the above ideas, rigorously formulated, constitute component parts. In Section I we present the basic structural assumptions of our model with emphasis on analysis of the role of the "neglected" agricultural sector. Section II generalizes the previously "static" analysis by admitting the possibility of a change of productivity in the agricultural sector . . . .

I. The Basic Assumptions

Our formal explanatory model is presented with the help of Diagram 1. Diagram 1.1 depicts the industrial sector and Diagrams 1.2 and 1.3 the

[2]We wish to underscore the absence of any necessary one-to-one relationship between the subsistence sector and agriculture, or between the capitalistic sector and industry in most less-developed economies. The existence of substantial islands of commercialized production in the primary sector and of sizable subsistence enclaves in the small-scale and service industries does not, however, bar Lewis, or us, from using this short-hand terminology.

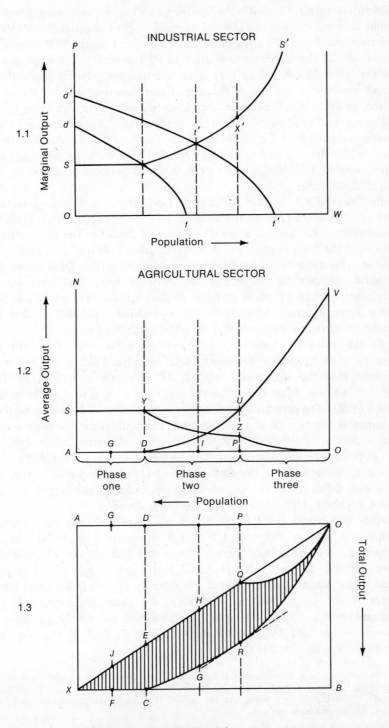

INDUSTRIAL SECTOR

1.1

Marginal Output →

Population →

AGRICULTURAL SECTOR

1.2

Average Output →

Population ←

Phase one · Phase two · Phase three

1.3

Total Output →

Diagram 1

agricultural sector. The first is the familiar Lewis diagram measuring industrial labor on the horizontal axis OW and its marginal physical productivity (MPP) on the vertical axis OP. The demand curve for labor (i.e., the MPP curve dtf), together with the supply curve of labor ($Stt'S'$), determines the employment of the industrial labor force (St). Since the marginal physical productivity curve depends on the size of the capital stock cooperating with the labor force, an increase in the capital stock leads to a shift of the MPP curve to the right, e.g. to $d't'f'$. Lewis' "unlimited" supply curve of labor is defined by the horizontal portion of the supply curve, i.e. St. When this supply curve turns up, unlimitedness comes to an end. Our first problem is to investigate the conditions of this turning point. This leads us to focus attention on the agricultural sector.

In Diagram 1.3 let the agricultural labor force be measured on the horizontal axis OA (reading from right to left), and let agricultural output be measured on the vertical axis OB (downward from O). The curve $ORCX$ describes the total physical productivity of labor (TPP) in the agricultural sector. This curve is assumed to have a concave portion ORC showing a gradually diminishing marginal productivity of agricultural labor and a horizontal portion XC where marginal product vanishes. The portion of any labor force in excess of OD may be considered redundant in that its withdrawal from agriculture would not affect agricultural output.

At the initial (or break-out) point let the entire labor force OA be committed to agriculture, producing a total agricultural output of AX. Let us assume that the agricultural output AX is totally consumed by the agricultural labor force OA. Then the real wage is equal to $AX//OA$ or the slope of OX. The persistence of this wage level is sustained by institutional or nonmarket forces since under competitive assumptions the real wage would fall to zero, at equality with MPP. We shall call this the institutional wage.

Let point R on the total output curve be the point at which the MPP equals the institutional wage, i.e. the dotted tangential line at R is parallel to OX. We can then define AP as the disguisedly unemployed agricultural labor force since, beyond P, MPP is less than the institutional wage.[3]

Note that Diagrams 1.1, 1.2, and 1.3 are "lined up." Any point on the horizontal axis of Diagrams 1.1 to 1.3 represents a particular way in which the total population or labor force OA is distributed between the two sectors; for example, at point P (Diagrams 1.2 and 1.3) the agricultural labor force is OP and the (already allocated) industrial labor force is AP. If, at the break-out point, the entire population, OA, is engaged in the agricultural sector, the allocation process during take-off can be represented by a series of points, A, G, D, I, P, etc., on OA, gradually moving towards O.[4]

---

[3]Redundancy is a technological phenomenon, i.e., determined by the production function. Disguised unemployment, on the other hand, depends upon the production function, the institutional wage, and the size of the agricultural population. In other work, it is an economic concept.

[4]The present assumption of an unchanging population will later be relaxed.

The important concepts of disguised unemployment, redundant labor force and institutional wage can be more clearly depicted with the aid of Diagram 1.2, in which agricultural output per worker is measured on the vertical axis *AN*. Let *ADUV* be the marginal physical productivity (MPP) curve of labor in the agricultural sector. Let the vertical distance *AS* equal the institutional wage (shown also as *PU*, equal to MPP of agricultural labor at *U*, lined up with *P* and *R* in Diagram 1.3). Three phases in the re-allocation process may now be distinguished: (1) Phase 1 is the range for which MPP = 0, i.e., the total productivity curve in Diagram 1.3 is horizontal. This phase marks off the redundant labor force, *AD*. (2) Phase 2 is the range for which a positive MPP is less than the institutional wage. Phases 1 and 2 together mark off the existence of the disguisedly unemployed labor force, *AP*. (3) Phase 3 is the range for which MPP is greater than the institutional wage rate assumed to prevail at the break-out point.

We assume that the institutional wage *AS* prevails during phases 1 and 2 and a wage rate equal to MPP prevails in phase 3. Only when the disguisedly unemployed have been absorbed, i.e. in phase 3, does the marginal contribution of labor to output become as great as or greater than the institutional real wage. As a result, it is then to the advantage of the landlord to bid actively for labor; the agricultural sector can be said to have become commercialized as the institutional wage is abandoned and competitive market forces yield the commonly accepted equilibrium conditions. Under these assumptions the agricultural real wage in terms of agricultural goods is defined by the curve *SUV* in Diagram 1.2, consisting of a horizontal portion *SU* and a rising portion, *UV*. This curve may be called the supply-price curve of agricultural labor. It indicates for each level of real wage the amount of labor that may be released from the agricultural sector.

The transition into phase 3 constitutes a major landmark in the development process. With the completion of the transfer of the disguisedly unemployed, there will occur a switch, forced by circumstance, in employer behavior, i.e. the advent of a fully commercialized agricultural sector. This landmark may be defined as the end of the take-off process. We know no other way to establish a nonarbitrary criterion for an economy reaching the threshold of so-called self-sustaining growth.[5]

Returning now to Diagram 1.3, we see that, as agricultural workers are withdrawn, a surplus of agricultural goods begins to appear. That portion of total agricultural output in excess of the consumption requirements of the agricultural labor force at the institutional wage is defined as the total

[5]Whether or not growth can ever really be "self-sustaining," in Rostow's phrase, is basically not a problem amenable to the tools of traditional economic analysis. The role of saving rates and per capita income levels in setting it in motion remains undefined. All we are saying here is that, after the turning point, the real wage in agriculture is determined by impersonal competitive market forces, a qualitative transformation which constitutes a necessary (if not sufficient) condition for growth to become automatic and routinized. It is this point which Lewis seems to have in mind when he speaks of "two different stages of economic development with two different sets of results" and describes the second stage as a situation in which "all the factors of production are scarce [and] . . . wages are no longer constant as accumulation proceeds."

agricultural surplus (TAS). The amount of TAS can be seen to be a function of the amount of labor reallocated at each stage. For example, if agricultural workers to the extent of AG are withdrawn in phase 1 and re-allocated, *JG* is required to feed the remaining agricultural workers and a TAS of size *JF* results. The TAS at each point of allocation in phases 1 and 2 is represented by the vertical distance between the straight line *OX* and the total physical productivity curve *ORCX*. (For phase 3, due to the rise of the wage rate, TAS is somewhat less than this vertical distance and equals the vertical distance between the curve *OQ* and the total productivity curve).

TAS may be viewed as agricultural resources released to the market through the re-allocation of agricultural workers. Such resources can be siphoned off by means of the investment activities of the landlord class and/or government tax policy and can be utilized in support of the new industrial arrivals.[6] The average agricultural surplus, or AAS, may now be defined as the total agricultural surplus available per head of allocated industrial workers.

The AAS curve is represented by curve *SYZO* in Diagram 1.2. In phase 1 as TAS increases linearly with the allocation of the redundant labor force from *A* to *D* we can picture each allocated worker as carrying his own subsistence bundle along with him. The AAS curve for phase 1 thus coincides with the institutional wage curve *SY*. In phase 2, however since the MPP in agriculture of the now allocated workers was positive there will not be sufficient agricultural output to feed all the new industrial arrivals at the institutional wage level. Thus, while TAS is still rising, AAS begins to fall.[7] It can, moreover, readily be seen that during phase 3 AAS declines even more rapidly (and TAS also declines) as the now commercialized wage in agriculture becomes operative.

We may now consider the derivation of the Lewis turning point in the agricultural sector. Lewis himself explains the turning point rather loosely as occurring when one of the following events puts an end to the horizontal supply curve of labor: (a) the worsening of the terms of trade for the industrial sector, and (b) the exhaustion of the labor surplus in the agricultural sector. But in our model any such explanation must take into account the basic determination of the entire industrial labor supply curve by the conditions postulated for the non-industrial sector.

The "worsening of the terms of trade" for the industrial sector occurs as the result of a relative shortage of agricultural commodities

[6]While it could easily be accommodated by the model, we neglect resource transfer costs as well as the possibility that it may be impossible to induce those left behind in agriculture to release the entire surplus.

[7]The following analogy with individual-firm analysis may be drawn to show more clearly the relationship between the marginal, total and average concepts involved. We may think of the total agricultural output curve *(ORCX)* and the total agricultural consumption curve *(OX)* in Diagram 1.3 as analogous to the total revenue curve and the total cost curve, respectively. Then the gap between these curves is the total curve which is equivalent to our TAS curve. The total profit curve reaches a maximum when marginal cost equals marginal revenue. This occurs at a point *U* in Diagram 1.2–because *SU* is the marginal cost curve and *ADUV* is the marginal revenue curve. The AAS curve in Diagram 1.2 is equivalent to an "average profit curve."

seeking exchange for industrial goods in the market. In our model, it will be recalled, this surplus is measured by total agricultural surplus (TAS) and, on a per-industrial-worker basis, average agricultural surplus (AAS). There is a tendency, then, for the industrial supply curve to turn up as phase 2 is entered because this is the time when there begins to appear a shortage of agricultural goods measured in AAS—causing a deterioration of the terms of trade of the industrial sector and a rise in the industrial real wage measured in terms of industrial goods. We thus see that the disappearance of the redundant labor force in the agricultural sector is a cause of the Lewis turning point.

The "exhaustion of the labor surplus" must be interpreted primarily as a market phenomenon rather than as a physical shortage of manpower; it is indicated by an increase in the real wage at the source of supply. If we assume that the real wage of the industrial worker is equal to the agricultural real wage,[8] then there is a tendency for the industrial supply curve of labor ($Stt'S'$ in Diagram 1.1) to turn upward when phase 3 is entered. With the disappearance of the disguisedly unemployed labor force and the commercialization of the agricultural sector, the agricultural real wage begins to rise (see Diagram 1.2). This leads to an increase in the industrial real wage level if the industrial employer is to compete successfully with the landlord for the use of the, by now "limited," supply of labor.

Putting the two factors (a and b) together, we can say that as labor is re-allocated from the agricultural to the industrial sector, the industrial supply curve turns up (i.e. the Lewis turning point occurs), in the first instance (at t), due to a shortage of agricultural goods traceable to the disappearance of the redundant agricultural labor force; and that this upward trend in the industrial real wage is later accentuated (at X') by the upward movement of the agricultural real wage traceable to the complete disappearance of the disguisedly unemployed labor force and the commercialization of the agricultural sector.

To facilitate our later analysis, let us refer to the boundary between phases 1 and 2 (i.e., point Y in Diagram 1.2) as the "shortage point" signifying the beginning of shortages of agricultural goods as indicated by the fact that AAS falls below the minimum wage; let us also refer to the boundary between phases 2 and 3 as the "commercialization point" signifying the beginning of equality between marginal productivity and the real wage in agriculture. The Lewis turning point thus

---

[8]"Governed by" may be a more realistic description. Lewis points out that urbanization, transfer costs, etc. may require an industrial real wage at a constant (he believes approximately 30 per cent) margin or "hill" above the institutional wage in agriculture; while, for simplicity of exposition, our model initially maintains strict quality between the two wage rates, this assumption is later relaxed. In his second article, Lewis also refers to certain "exogenous factors," including unionization and presumable other changes in the institutional milieu. Such a dynamically growing "hill" could also be accommodated by the model but has not been considered in this first approximation.

coincides with the shortage point and the upward movement of the industrial real wage is accentuated at the commercialization point.[9]

There are two factors which may lead to a postponement of the Lewis turning point: (1) increases in agricultural productivity, and (2) population growth. The fact that these two factors operate very differently—one, generally viewed as a blessing, by raising surplus agricultural output, the other, almost invariably considered a curse, by augmenting the supply of redundant labor, is intuitively obvious. We shall first examine the significance of an increase of agricultural productivity. The extension of our analysis to accommodate population growth will be undertaken later.

II. Changes in Agricultural Productivity

An increase in labor productivity in the agricultural sector can be described by an "upward" shift of the entire total physical productivity (TPP) curve of Diagram 1.3. Such productivity increases are depicted in Diagram 2.3 by a sequence of TPP curves marked *I, II, III* $\cdots$ etc. among which the *I*-curve is the initial TPP curve (as in Diagram 1.3) and *II, III* $\cdots$ represent the TPP curves after successive doses of agricultural investment. (For the present we assume no change in industrial productivity.)

Let us make the assumption that as agricultural productivity increases the institutional wage remains unchanged, i.e. *SA* in Diagram 2.2 equals the slope of *OX* in Diagrams 1.3 and 2.3 as determined by the initial TPP curve.[10] In Diagram 2.2 we may now plot the sequence of marginal physical productivity of labor curves marked *I, II, III* $\cdots$ (all containing the flat portion AS_1) and the sequence of average agricultural surplus curves marked *I, II, III* $\cdots$ corresponding to the total physical productivity curves *I, II, III* $\cdots$ in Diagram 2.3. According to the method already indicated, we can now determine the three phases for each level of productivity, i.e., the sequence of shortage points, $S_1, S_2, S_3 \cdots$ *and the sequence of commercialization points,* $R_1, R_2, R_3 \cdots$. Reference to these points will facilitate our analysis of the effects of an increase in agricultural productivity on the supply-price curve of agricultural labor and on the AAS curve.

[9]From a strictly logical standpoint the industrial supply curve of labor must be derived from the totality of conditions emerging from our analysis of the agricultural sector. The relevant conditions include (1) the agricultural real wage, (2) the AAS curve, and (3) a consumer preference map specifying preferences for agricultural vs. industrial goods. Space limitations prevent us from rendering a rigorous derivation of the industrial real wage at each point through the terms-of-trade mechanism.

[10]It is, of course, possible that the institutionally determined agricultural wage will be permitted to rise; but as the economy becomes increasingly capitalistic it seems highly doubtful that nonmarket forces in agriculture will be strengthened and thus prevent the closing of the artificial marginal productivity-wage gap. A second, and possibly more powerful, qualification arises from the fact that the institutional wage level in agriculture may be sufficiently close to caloric subsistence so that raising it may constitute a highly productive form of investment. We do not, however, consider this possibility in the context of the present model. Concerning the relative position of the industrial wage level see footnote 8.

INDUSTRIAL SECTOR

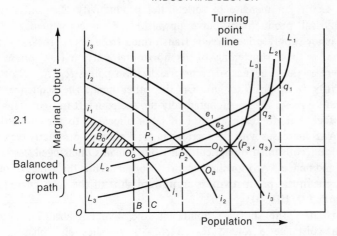

AGRICULTURAL SECTOR

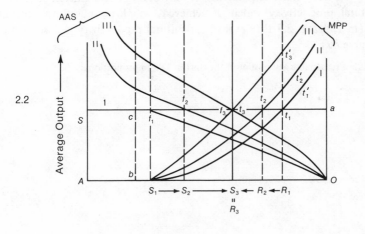

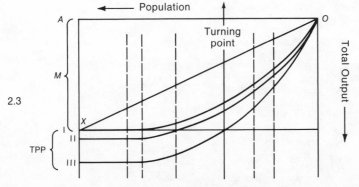

Diagram 2

As depicted in Diagram 2.2, for every amount of labor employed in the agricultural sector, an increase in agricultural productivity also shifts the marginal physical productivity curve upward.[11] As a consequence, the agricultural labor supply price curve is transformed from $St_1 t_1'$ to $St_2 t_2'$ to $St_3 t_3' \cdots$ etc. with a shortening of its horizontal portion (i.e., phase 3 arrives earlier) as the sequence of commercialization points $R_1, R_2, R_3 \ldots$ gradually shifts from right to left. On the other hand, the sequence of shortage points $S_1, S_2, S_3 \cdots$ etc. gradually moves from left to right. This is due to the fact that, for each amount of labor allocated to the industrial sector, the AAS increases with the increase in total physical productivity; the amount of food consumed by agricultural labor remains unchanged, leaving more TAS (and hence AAS) for the industrial workers. Thus the effect of our increase in agricultural productivity is an upward shift of the AAS curve (to positions marked II, III $\cdots$).

Sooner or later, the shortage point and the commercialization point coincide, the distance $S_1 R_1$, $S_2 R_2$, $S_3 R_3 \cdots$ vanishes and phase 2 is eliminated. In Diagram 2.2 such a point of coincidence is described by $R_3 = S_3$. We shall call this point the turning point. There exists one level of agricultural productivity which, if achieved, will bring about this turning point. (In Diagram 2.3 this level of agricultural productivity is described by TPP curve *III*).

[11]This is a reasonable assumption if the shift in TPP in proportional.

Theoretical Note on Time-Preference,
Productivity of Capital, Stagnation,
and Economic Growth

Wassily Leontief

12

Among the many factors which determine the growth
or stagnation—as the case may be—of a national economy, its rate of saving
out of current income and the subsequent increase in income resulting from
the investment of these savings play an important role. A relatively simple
method of graphic presentation and analysis makes it possible to articulate,
without explicit resource to algebra or calculus, the various effects which
different configurations of these two determinants can have on the state of
the economy and its development over time. Like any other purely
theoretical inquiry, this analysis only helps us to draw certain, possibly not
immediately obvious, conclusions from alternative sets of hypothetical
assumptions.

Figure 1 depicts the preferences of a given national economy between
present and future levels of consumption in terms of a conventional set of
social indifference curves. It deviates only in one respect from the graph used
by Irving Fisher in his classic exposition of his theory of interest. The
variables, Y and C, whose magnitudes are measured along the horizontal axis,
represent respectively the level of real income and the amount of goods
consumed in the present period. The variables Y' and C' measured vertically

From the *American Economic Review*, Papers and Proceedings, March 1958, pp.
105-111. Reprinted by permission of the author and publisher. The author is professor
of economics, Harvard University.

describe future income or consumption; "future," however, not in the sense of a single "second" period—as shown on Fisher's diagram—but in the sense of a steady, even flow which, beginning with the year following the present one, can be maintained in equal annual amounts in perpetuity.

Accordingly, every point between the coordinate axes in Figure 1 denotes a specific combination of a given present year's income (or consumption) level with a fixed level of annual income (or consumption) flow to be enjoyed in perpetuity from the next year on. Each indifference line represents a set of equally desirable combinations of present consumption levels and future consumption streams, the positions on higher indifference lines being naturally preferable to those on the lower.

The movement, from right to left, along any one of the negatively sloped straight lines, such as $P_1 P'_2$ or $P_2 P'_2$, accordingly describes an exchange of a batch of present goods for a constant stream of future goods or, in other words, the exchange of a capital sum for a perpetual series of equal annual interest payments. The (absolute) magnitude of the slope of each one of these exchange lines can consequently be interpreted as representing an annual real rate of interest. Given a free choice between alternative positions on a given exchange line, the income receivers would accordingly reach the highest attainable—under the given circumstances—level of welfare at tangency points, such as P'_1, P'_2 or P'_3.

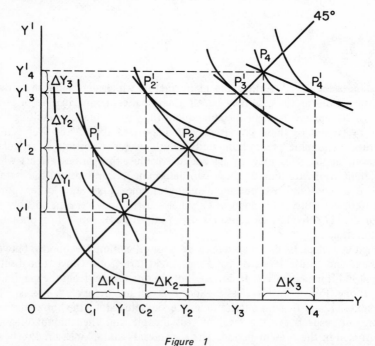

Figure 1

Any point, such as P_1, P_2 or P_3, situated on the 45° line drawn from the origin, describes a stationary position in which the present (Y) and the future

(Y') levels of income and consumption are identical. Actually faced with a choice between the maintenance of such a stationary state and a movement to some other position located along the exchange line which goes through it, income receivers will perpetuate the stationary state only if, as at P'_3, it happens also to be the point of tangency between the exchange line and the indifference curve which passes through that point. In other cases, they can improve their welfare by consuming less than their entire present income in order to secure a higher level of future income and consumption streams. Or, on the contrary, they might improve their situation by borrowing against the future, so as to allow the present consumption to exceed the rate of current revenue.

Thus, starting, for example, from the initial position P_1 and facing the exchange line which passes through that point, the representative independent income recipient or the central planning authority—whichever it may be—will move from P_1 to P'_1. It will allocate to immediate direct consumption that part of present income OY_1 which is measured by the distance from O to C_1; the rest of it, C_1Y_1, or $\triangle K_1$, will be saved and exchanged against future income. The rate of the potential income stream to be received in the next, and all later, years will be raised by $\triangle Y_1$ from OY'_1 to OY'_2, Point P_2, again located on the 45° line, thus represents the prospective position of the country in the second year.

Before pursuing further the sequence of given income, saving and increased income, let us turn to Figure 2 which describes the relationship between the total stock of capital invested and the net output (income) which it can produce on the basis of the existing technology in cooperation with the given supply of all other factors. Along the horizontal axis, we measure from right

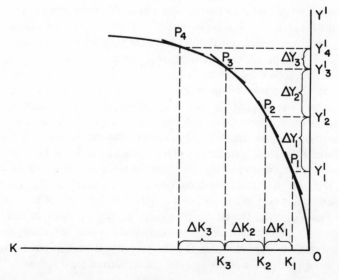

Figure 2

to left (in order to facilitate the subsequent comparison with Figure 1) the total stock of capital, and along the vertical axis the annual rate of net output, i.e., net income. The bending of the curve describes the well-known technical relationship between the stock of productive capital and the flow of output produced with its help. The slope of that curve at any point represents the marginal productivity of the particular amount of capital which corresponds to it.

Point P_1 in Figure 1 refers to the same state of the economic system as point P_1 in Figure 2. In this position, the total stock of capital amounts to K_1 and it produces a net income flow of Y_1 units per annum. The potential increase in output, which could be brought about by an increase in the existing stock of capital, can be read off Figure 2: Specifically, the ratio between the amount of invested savings and the resulting rise in future income flow is represented—at least for changes which are not very large—by the slope of the capital-output curve at point P_1. It is that slope which, when transferred to Figure 1, describes the real rate of interest, the ratio at which the present consumption can be foregone in favor of additional future income, or in other words, the slope of the line along which the country moves (see Figure 1) from P_1 to P'_1. The saving $\triangle K_1$, when added on Figure 2 to the original amount of capital, K_1, increases the total stock to K_2 and the corresponding annual rate of income flow—from Y'_1 to Y'_2. Measured on Figure 1 along the horizontal axes this is the increase from Y_1 to Y_2.

The income and consumption, represented by the position of point P_2 in Figures 1 and 2, could be maintained, as far as the country's productive power is concerned, from now on into the future without any further change. The combination of the marginal productivity of capital and time-preference, as shown at point P_2 in Figures 1 and 2, is, however, such that instead of consuming all of that increased income our developing economy will move on to point P'_2, i.e., save and invest again, increase its stock of capital from K_2 to K_3 and its income from Y_2 to Y_3. By the third year, it thus will find itself at P'_3. The slope of the indifference curve passing through that point in Figure 1 has been drawn so as to be equal to the slope of the capital-output curve at the corresponding point (P_3) in Figure 2. Hence the marginal productivity of capital is equated to marginal time-preference if the representative consumer, i.e., the country as a whole, chooses to consume neither more nor less than its entire current income. It is, in other words, an equilibrium position, a stationary state which can and will be maintained *ad infinitum* as long as no new factors enter the picture. Such a new factor might be a shift of the structural conditions, i.e., a change in the form of the production function in Figure 2 or a variation in the shape of the indifference curves in Figure 1. Or it might consist in the creation of new "initial conditions": sudden destruction—as the result of war—of some part of the existing stock of capital or, on the contrary, acquisition of additional capital from foreign sources, a developmental grant received from abroad.

On our graphs, the creation of such new initial conditions would be described, for example, as a shift from P'_3 to point P_2 or, say, to point P_4. In either case, if left to its own devices, the economy would return at once or by successive steps to its original position at P'_3. The difference between the movement from P_2 to P'_3 and from P_4 to P'_3 is that, in the latter case, having been pushed beyond the point of stable equilibrium, the system will come back to it through a process of capital consumption, i.e., by sacrificing some of the future income stream in order to be able to maintain during the transitory period a "present" level of consumption above its "current" income; while in the former case it would approach the stable equilibrium position, P'_3, from below, i.e., through a process of capital accumulation.

The economy of course does not necessarily find an equilibrium position. It might have none, or more than one, but in the latter case unstable as well as stable equilibria will necessarily be present. We call a state of unstable equilibrium one in which, in the absence of any change in its internal structure and without even the slightest variation in the initial conditions, the system would maintain itself *ad infinitum*, but from which it would tend to depart on the slightest provocation. It is analogous to the position of the proverbial egg, precariously balanced on its narrow end.

To work out in full the implications of the previous analysis, let us now turn to Figure 3. Along the horizontal axis, we measure the national income, Y. Of the two interlaced curves, *MP* represents the marginal productivity of capital, i.e., the slope of the capital-output line (Figure 2) as it gradually bends toward the horizontal with the increase in Y. *TP* measures the marginal time-preference, i.e., the slope of the indifference curves as they cross the 45° line in Figure 1 at various levels of income Y. The third curve below, identified by the letter D, represents the vertical distance (difference) between the first two (i.e., the excess of *TP* over *MP*); the points, a, b, and c, at which the D-curve crosses the zero axis mark those income levels at which the marginal productivity of capital is equal to the marginal time-preference when the country consumes exactly its entire income. They mark, in other words, the possible equilibrium positions of the system. The D-curve passes below the zero line at those income levels at which the marginal time-preference (or more precisely the slope of the indifference lines at point where they cross the 45° stationary income locus) is smaller than the corresponding marginal productivity of capital. As can be seen from Figure 1, in all such cases there will be some positive amount of saving. And as a result of it, the income will necessarily grow. Over all those intervals in which the D curve rises above the zero line, current consumption, on the contrary, will exceed net current output, the stock of capital will be diminished and income will consequently fall. The direction of the ensuing upward, or downward, change in income is indicated in Figure 3 by arrows.

To simplify the explanation of the interplay of the two sets of basic structural relationships represented, respectively, in Figures 1 and 2, the functioning of the economy has been viewed as if it had proceeded step by

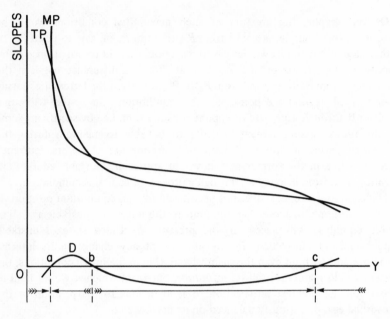

Figure 3

step. Such period analysis introduces, however, complications of its own which would be absent if the processes of production, consumption and investment were described in continuous terms. With due apology to the mathematically interested reader (who, however, should be able to work out all intermediate details himself), we will now interpret the curves in Figure 3 as if they reflected, as they well might, the properties of a continuous process. [The reader will note that the specific shapes of these curves do not actually correspond to those of the particular set of consumer-preference relationships and the production function depicted in the other graphs. While the combination of the structural relationships shown in Figures 1 and 2 yield only one equilibrium position (P'_3), Figure 3 shows the existence of three such positions, a, b, and c.]

Starting with a very small stock of capital and income inferior to that corresponding to the lowest equilibrium point, a, the system would proceed to expand toward a. If in its initial position the economy were located some place between a and b, it would also tend to move toward the former point. In this case, the process is a regressive one characterized by gradual diminution of the stock of productive capital, reduction in the rate of output (income) and incidentally—as the *MP* curve shows—an increase in the real rate of interest. Once a is reached in either way, the system would "stagnate" at that low but stable equilibrium position. When pushed to the left by the action of some outside force, such for example as an accidental loss of productive capital, it would move back again toward *a*, but not beyond. If, as beneficiary of a foreign loan or gift, it should find itself in the possession of some additional capital and correspondingly increased income, our country would at once proceed to "live above its means," i.e., consume its capital and gradually reduce its output until the stationary state at *a* would again be reached. Even a constant flow of foreign aid could, in such case, do no more than help the system to maintain its income and consumption at some point between *a* and *b*, without, however, releasing any tendency toward further growth.

These latter observations apply, however, only to gifts or loans not large enough to push the rate of output beyond *b*. Once on the other side of that unstable equilibrium position, the economy would begin to save, accumulate and increase its revenue; in short it would proceed to develop under its own power. According to the graph, a new stable equilibrium would be approached at the much higher income level, *c*. Had the structural conditions been such as to keep *MP* above *TP*, and thus the *D*-curve below the zero line, throughout its entire stretch to the right of *b*, the process of economic growth—once that threshold had been passed—would go on indefinitely.

By the way of a concluding observation, one might suggest, without detailed explanation, how the three graphs can also be used to trace through the possible effects of changes in the basic structural conditions of the economy. For instance technological advance, described as an upward shift of the capital-output curve in Figure 2, might—and most likely actually would—affect the shape of the *MP* and the *D*-curve in Figure 3. The equilibrium positions *a*, *b*, and *c* would shift. Depending on the magnitude and the nature of the change, some of these positions of stationary state might even disappear or new ones might be created.

To the extent to which a rise in the productivity of capital enables the economy to increase its income without any addition to its stock of capital, technological advance will shift the system at once to the right along the horizontal axis in Figure 3 from whatever position it had previously occupied. In fact, however, new technology as a rule requires a new type of equipment and different kinds of skills. That means that its introduction will depend itself on the current rate of saving and accumulation.

A further pursuit of these speculative arguments must clearly yield diminishing returns. The effort involved in construction and interpretation of more complicated graphs might better be spent on observation and explanation of the real world.

Allocative Efficiency vs.
"X-Efficiency"

Harvey Leibenstein

13

At the core of economics is the concept of efficiency. Microeconomic theory is concerned with allocative efficiency. Empirical evidence has been accumulating that suggests that the problem of allocative efficiency is trivial. Yet it is hard to escape the notion that efficiency in some broad sense is significant. In this paper I want to review the empirical evidence briefly and to consider some of the possible implications of the findings, especially as they relate to the theory of the firm and to the explanation of economic growth. The essence of the argument is that microeconomic theory focuses on allocative efficiency to the exclusion of other types of efficiencies that, in fact, are much more significant in many instances. Furthermore, improvement in "nonallocative efficiency" is an important aspect of the process of growth.

In Section I the empirical evidence on allocative efficiency is presented. In this section we also consider the reasons why allocation inefficiency is frequently of small magnitude. Most of the evidence on allocation inefficiency deals with either monopoly or international trade. However,

Excerpted from the *American Economic Review,* Papers and Proceedings, June 1966. Reprinted by permission of the author and publisher. The author is professor of economics at Harvard University.

monopoly and trade are not the focus of this paper. Our primary concern is with the broader issue of allocative efficiency versus an initially undefined type of efficiency that we shall refer to as "*X*-efficiency." The magnitude and nature of this type of efficiency are examined in Sections II and III. Although a major element of "*X*-efficiency" is motivation, it is not the only element, and hence the terms "motivation efficiency" or "incentive efficiency" have not been employed.

As he proceeds, the reader is especially invited to keep in mind the sharp contrast in the magnitudes involved between Tables 1 and 2.

I. Allocative Inefficiency: Empirical Evidence

The studies that are of interest in assessing the importance of allocative efficiency are summarized in Table 1. These are of two types. On the one side we have the studies of Harberger and Schwartzman on the "social welfare cost" of monopoly. On the other side we have a number of studies, among them those by Johnson, Scitovsky, Wemelsfelder, Janssen, and others, on the benefits of reducing or eliminating restrictions to trade. In both cases the computed benefits attributed to the reallocation of resources turn out to be exceedingly small.

Table 1.   Calculated "Welfare Loss" as Percentage of Gross or Net National Product Attributed to Misallocation of Resources

Study	Source	Country	Cause	Loss
A. C. Harberger	A.E.R. *1954*	*U.S.A. 1929*	*Monopoly*	*0.07. per cent*
D. Schwartzman	J.P.E. *1960*	*U.S.A. 1954*	*Monopoly*	*0.01 per cent*
T. Scitovsky	*(1)*	*Common Market 1952*	*Tariffs*	*0.05 per cent*
J. Wemelsfelder	E.J. *1960*	*Germany 1958*	*Tariffs*	*0.18 per cent*
L. H. Janssen	*(2)*	*Italy 1960*	*Tariffs*	*max. 0.1 per cent*
H. G. Johnson	Manchester School *1958*	*U.K. 1970*	*Tariffs*	*max. 1.0 per cent*
A. Singh	*(3)*	*Montevideo Treaty Countries*	*Tariffs*	*max. .0075 per cent*

Sources:
(1) [3].
(2) [6].
(3) Unpublished calculation made by A. Singh based on data found in A. A. Faraq, *Economic Integration: A Theoretical, Empirical Study,* University of Michigan, Ph.D. Thesis, 1963.

Let us look at some of the findings. In the original Harberger study [1]* the benefits for eliminating monopoly in the United States would raise income no more than 1/13 of 1 per cent. Schwartzman's [2] study which recomputes the benefits of eliminating monopoly by comparing Canadian monopolized industries as against counterpart competitive U.S. industries,

*Numbers in brackets identify the references listed at the end of the article.

and vice versa in order to determine the excess price attributable to monopoly, ends up with a similar result. Similarly, the benefits attributed to superior resource allocation as a consequence of the Common Market or a European Free Trade Area are also minute—usually much less than 1 per cent.

The calculations made by Scitovsky of the benefits to the Common Market (based on Verdoorn's data) led him to the conclusion that ". . . the most striking feature of these estimates is their smallness. In the one that is really important (for reasons to appear presently), the gain from increased specialization . . . is less than one-twentieth of one per cent of the gross social product of the countries involved. This is ridiculously small . . ." [3, p. 64]. J. Wemelsfelder [4, p. 100] had calculated that the welfare gain of reducing import duties and increasing imports and exports accordingly amounts to .18 of 1 per cent of national income. Harry Johnson in an article on England's gain in joining a Free Trade Area [5, pp. 247 ff.] calculates the net gain from trade at less than 1 per cent. That is, Johnson arrives at the conclusion that 1 per cent of the national income would be the absolute maximum gain for Britain from entering the European Free Trade Area.

A recent study by L. H. Janssen [6, p. 132] calculates that the gains from increased specialization for the different countries of the European Economic Community would be largest for Italy, but even here the amount is only 1/10 of 1 per cent of total production.[1] Janssen points out that, if the production gain for Italy due to specialization were calculated by Scitovsky's method, which he believes involves an overestimation, "the production gain in the most extreme case is still less than .4 per cent." Janssen concludes, as have others, that the welfare effects of a customs union based on the superior allocation of resources are likely to be trivial. He does, however, point to the possibility "that the mere prospect of the frontiers opening would infuse fresh energy into entrepreneurs." He recognizes that certain qualitative factors may be highly important and that the consequences of growth are certainly more significant than those of allocative welfare.

My research assistant, A. Singh, has calculated the gains from trade (following the Scitovsky method) for the Montevideo Treaty Countries[2] (Argentina, Brazil, Chile, Mexico, Paraguay, Peru, and Uruguay) and found it to be less than 1/150 of 1 per cent of their combined GNP. Even if we double or triple this result to allow for such factors as the effect of failing to take account of quantitative restrictions in the analysis, the outcome is still trivial.

[1]R. A. Mundell in a review of Janssen's book appears to reach a similar conclusion to the point made in this paper when he speculates that ". . . There have appeared in recent years studies purporting to demonstrate that the welfare loss due to monopoly is small, that the welfare importance of efficiency and production is exaggerated, and that gains from trade and the welfare gains from tariff reduction are almost negligible. Unless there is a thorough theoretical re-examination of the validity of the tools on which these studies are founded, and especially of the revitalized concepts of producers' and consumers' surplus, some one inevitably will draw the conclusion that economics has ceased to be important!" [7, p. 622].

[2]Based on data found in [7].

Harberger's study on Chile [1], which involves the reallocation of both labor and capital, yields a relatively large estimate. Harberger intends to obtain as large an estimate as possible of the consequences of reallocating resources by using what I believe to be (and what he admits to be) rather extreme assumptions in order to obtain maximum outer bounds. Despite this he comes up with a number that is between 9 and 15 per cent. However, no actual data are employed. What are used are outer-bound estimates based on personal impressions. I expect that a careful study similar to the Verdoorn-Scitovsky study would probably come up with numbers that would be no larger than 1 or 2 per cent.

The empirical evidence, while far from exhaustive, certainly suggests that the welfare gains that can be achieved by increasing *only* allocative efficiency are usually exceedingly small, at least in capitalist economies. In all but one of the cases considered all of the gains are likely to be made up in one month's growth. They hardly seem worth worrying about.

Let us see briefly why these gains are usually small. We cannot prove that we would expect them to be small on purely theoretical grounds. If we combine our theory with what we could agree are probably reasonable estimates of some of the basic magnitudes, then it appears likely that in many cases (but certainly not all *possible* cases) the welfare loss of allocative inefficiency is of trivial significance. The idea could be developed with the aid of the diagram employed by Harberger. (See Figure 1.) In Figure 1 we assume that costs are constant within the relevant range. D is the demand function. Under competition price and quantity are determined at the intersection C. The monopoly price is above the competitive price equal to AB in the figure. The monopoly output is determined at the point A. The welfare loss due to monopoly, which is the same as the welfare gain if we shifted to competition, is equal to the triangle ABC. We obtain an approximation to this amount by multiplying the price differential AB by the quantity differential BC, by

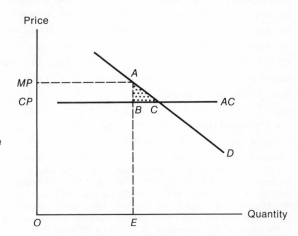

Price

MP = Monopoly Price
CP = Competitive Price

Figure 1

one-half, and multiplying this by the proportion of national income in industries involving the misallocation.

Let us play around with some numbers and see the kind of results we get as a consequence of this formulation. Suppose that half of the national output is produced in monopolized industries and that the price differential is 20 per cent and that the average elasticity of demand is 1.5. Now the outcome will turn out to be 1-1/2 per cent. But we really used enormous figures for the misallocation. And yet the result is small. Monopoly prices, according to estimates, appear to be only about 8 per cent on the average competitive prices. We can substitute some reason other than monopoly for the misallocation and still come out with similar results.[3]

Consider the cases of subsidized industries under some sort of governmental inducements to growth; and that of governmentally run industries. In the subsidy case the calculation would be similar. Suppose that as much as 50 per cent of the industries are subsidized to the extent of a 20 per cent difference in cost and that the output point on the demand function is where elasticity is unity. This last point may be reasonable since the operators of subsidized industries might want gross revenue to be as large as possible. If, on the other hand, we assume that they are profit maximizers and restrict output to a greater extent, then we might assume a price elasticity of two. This latter, however, is unlikely because monopoly profits are inconsistent with subsidized industries. Those who receive the subsidy would have the legitimate fear that the subsidy would be lowered if unusual profits were earned. Hence, behavior in the direction of revenue maximization appears reasonable and the calculated welfare loss is less than 2 per cent.

A similar result could be achieved in the case in which the government runs industries that affect 50 per cent of the national income of an economy. In all the cases we appear to be on the large side and the outcome is on the small side.

Of course, it is possible that the magnitude of allocative inefficiency would be large if there are large discontinuities in productivity between those industries where inputs are located and those industries to which the same inputs could be moved. This, in effect is the basic assumption that Harberger made in his study of Chile [1]. But if it turns out that there is a reasonable degree of continuity in productivity, and that the only way shifts could be made is by simultaneously increasing either social overhead capital or direct capital in order to make the shifts involved, then, of course, a great deal of the presumed gains would be eaten up by the capital costs and the net marginal gains would turn out to be rather small. My general impression is

[3]For the sake of completeness we should take the income effect into account in our estimation of consumer surplus. It may readily be seen that this magnitude is likely to be exceedingly small. Suppose that the initial effect of a superior allocation is 1 per cent; then the income effect for a noninferior good will be to shift the demand function to the right by 1 per cent on the average. Thus, the addition to consumers' surplus will be 1 per cent, and the consumers' surplus foregone will be roughly 1 per cent of 1 per cent. If we consider all consequent effects in a similar vein, then the estimated welfare loss will be .010101 . . . .0102. The actual magnitude will, of course, be smaller because the demand will shift to the left in the case of inferior goods. For an excellent discussion of these matters see A. P. Lerner [8].

that this is likely to be the case in a great many underdeveloped countries where differential productivities appear to exist between the agricultural sector and the industrial sector. One cannot go beyond stating vague impressions since there is a lack of hard statistical evidence on this matter.

Why are the welfare effects of reallocation so small? Allocational inefficiency involves only the net marginal effects. The basic assumption is that every firm *purchases and utilizes* all of its inputs "efficiently." Thus, what is left is simply the consequences of price and quantity distortions. While some specific price distortions might be large it seems unlikely that all relative price distortions are exceptionally large. This implies that most quantity distortions must also be relatively small since for a given aggregate output a significant distortion in one commodity will be counterbalanced by a large number of small distortions in the opposite direction in quantities elsewhere. While it is possible to *assume* relative price distortions and quantity distortions that would be exceedingly high, it would be difficult to believe that, without intent, the sum of such distortions should be high. However, it is not *necessarily* so on purely *a priori* grounds.

There is one important type of distortion that cannot easily be handled by existing microeconomic theory. This has to do with the allocation of managers. It is conceivable that in practice a situation would arise in which managers are exceedingly poor, that is, others are available who do not obtain management posts, and who would be very much superior. Managers determine not only their own productivity but the productivity of all cooperating units in the organization. It is therefore possible that the actual loss due to such a misallocation might be large. But the theory does not allow us to examine this matter because firms are presumed to exist as entities that make optimal input decisions, apart from the decisions of its managers. This is obviously a contradiction and therefore cannot be handled.

II. *X*-Efficiency: The Empirical Evidence

We have seen that the welfare loss due to allocational inefficiency is frequently no more than 1/10 of 1 per cent. Is it conceivable that the value of *X*-inefficiency would be larger than that? One way of looking at it is to return to the problem of the welfare loss due to monopoly. Suppose that one-third of the industries are in the monopolized sector. Is it possible that the lack of competitive pressure of operating in monopolized industries would lead to cost 3/10 of a per cent higher than would be the case under competition? This magnitude seems to be very small, and hence it certainly seems to be a possibility. The question, essentially, is whether we can visualize managers bestirring themselves sufficiently, if the environment forced them to do so, in order to reduce costs by more than 3/10 of 1 per cent. Some of the empirical evidence available suggests that not only is this a possibility, but that the magnitudes involved are very much larger. As we shall see, the spotty evidence on this subject does not prove the case but it does seem to be sufficiently persuasive to suggest the possibility that X-efficiency exists, and that it frequently is much more significant than allocational efficiency.

Professor Eric Lundberg in his studies of Swedish industries points to the case of the steel plant at Horndal that was left to operate without any new capital investment or *technological change,* and furthermore maintenance and replacement were kept at a minimum, and yet output per man hour rose by 2 per cent per annum. Professor Lundberg asserts that according to his interviews with industrialists and technicians "sub-optimal disequilibrium in regard to technology and utilization of existing capital stock is a profoundly important aspect of the situation at any time." (This according to Gorin Ohlin's summary of Lundberg's findings [9].) If a suboptimal disequilibrium exists at any time, then it would seem reasonable that under the proper motivations managers and workers could bestir themselves to produce closer to optimality, and that under other conditions they may be motivated to move farther away from optimality.

Frederick Harbison reports visiting two petroleum refineries in Egypt less than one-half mile apart. "The labor productivity of one had been nearly double that in the other for many years. But recently, under completely new management, the inefficient refinery was beginning to make quite spectacular improvements in efficiency with the same labor force" [10, p. 373]. We may inquire why the management was changed only recently whereas the difference in labor productivity existed for many years. It is quite possible that had the motivation existed in sufficient strength, this change could have taken place earlier.

In a recent book on the firm, Neil Chamberlain [11, p. 341] visualizes his firms reacting to variances between forcasted revenues and expenditures and actual. He quotes from the president of a corporation: "Actual sales revenue for the fiscal year varied one per cent from the original forecast. Expenditures varied 30 per cent. The reasons were practically entirely due to manufacturing problems of inefficiency and quality .... The only actions specifically taken were in attempted changes in methods of production ... [and] the use of an engineering consulting firm ...." One would have thought that the cost-reducing activities mentioned could be carried out irrespective of the variance. Nevertheless, the quotation clearly implies that, in fact, they would not have been motivated to attempt the changes were it not that they were stimulated by the variance.

Before proceeding to present more empirical evidence on the possible magnitude of X-efficiency it is of importance to say something about the nature of the data. The empirical evidence does not present many unambiguous cases. Most of the evidence has to do with specific firms, or, at best, industries, and not with the economy as a whole. In the evidence presented on allocative efficiency the entire economy was considered. It is quite possible that the cases considered are entirely atypical and could not be duplicated in large segments of the economy. In addition, the cases do not always deal with *X*-efficiency in a pure sense. Some additional inputs or reallocations are sometimes involved. Also uncertainty elements and accidental variations play a role. Nevertheless, it seems that the magnitudes involved are so large that they suggest that the conjecture that *X*-efficiency is frequently more significant than allocative efficiency must be taken seriously.

Now let us turn to Tables 1 and 2. In contrast to Table 1 where the misallocation effects are small, we see in Table 2 that the *X*-efficiency effects, at least for specific firms, are usually large. Table 2 abstracts (in the interest of conserving space) from a much more comprehensive table developed by Kilby [12] that summarizes the results of a number of ILO productivity missions. (I usually picked for each country the first three and the last items contained in Kilby's table.) It is to be observed that the cost-reducing methods used do not involve additional capital nor, as far as one can tell, any increase in depreciation of obsolescence of existing capital. The methods usually involve some simple reorganizations of the production process, e.g., plant-layout reorganization, materials handling, waste controls, work methods, and payments by results. It is of interest that the cost reductions are frequently above 25 per cent and that this result is true for a technically advanced country such as Israel as well as for the developing countries considered in other parts of the table. If the firms and/or operations considered are representative, then it would appear that the contrast in significance between *X*-efficiency and allocative efficiency is indeed startling. Representativeness has not been established. However, the reports of the productivity missions do not suggest that they went out of their way to work only on cases where large savings in costs could be obtained. By comparative standards (with other productivity missions) some of the results were modest, and in some cases Kilby reports that when some members of the missions returned to some of the firms they had worked on previously (e.g., in Pakistan) they found a reversion to previous methods and productivities.

There are of course a number of other studies, in addition to those by Lundberg and Harbison just mentioned which present results similar to the ILO reports. L. Rostas in his study of comparative productivity in British and American industry [13] points to the finding that differences in amount and quality of machinery per worker and the rates of utilization and replacement do not account for the entire difference in output per worker in the two countries. He further states that ". . . in a number of industries (or firms) where the equipment is very largely identical in the U.S. and U.K., (eggs, boots and shoes, tobacco, strip steel) or in firms producing both in the U.K. and U.S. . . . , there are still substantial differences in output per worker in the U.K. and the U.S." Clearly there is more to the determination of output than the obviously observable inputs. The nature of the management, the environment in which it operates, and the incentives employed are significant.

That changes in incentives will change productivity per man (and cost per unit of output) is demonstrated clearly by a wide variety of studies on the effects of introducing payments by results schemes. Davison, Florence,

Table 2.   ILO Productivity Mission Results

Factory or Operation	Method[1]	Increase in Labor Productivity %	Impact on the Firm (Unit Cost Reduction)	
			Labor Savings %	Capital[2] Savings %
India				
Seven textile mills	n.a.	5-to-250	5-71	5-71
Engineering firms				
All operations	F, B	102	50	50
One operation	F	385	79	79
One operation	F	500	83	83
Burma				
Molding railroad brake shoes	A, F, B	100	50	50
Smithy	A	40	29	29
Chair assembly	A, B	100	50	50
Match manufacture	A, F	24	19	—
Indonesia				
Knitting	A, B	15	13	—
Radio assembly	A, F	40	29	29
Printing	A, F	30	23	—
Enamel ware	F	30	23	—
Malaya				
Furniture	A, D	10	9	9
Engineering workshop	A, D	10	9	9
Pottery	A, B	20	17	17
Thailand				
Locomotive maintenance	A, F	44	31	31
Saucepan polishing	E, D	50	33	—
Saucepan assembly	B, F	42	30	—
Cigarettes	A, B	5	5	—
Pakistan				
Textile plants	C, H, G			
Weaving		50	33	33
Weaving		10	9	9
Bleaching		59	37	37
Weaving		141	29	29
Israel				
Locomotive repair	F, B, G	30	23	23
Diamond cutting and polishing	C, B, G	45	31	—
Refrigerator assembly	F, B, G	75	43	43
Orange picking	F	91	47	—

[1]A=plant layout reorganized   E=waste control
B=machine utilization and flow   F=work method
C=simple technical alterations   G=payment by results
D=materials handling   H=workers' training and supervision

[2]Limited to plant and equipment, excluding increased depreciation costs.

Source: P. Kilby [12, p. 305].

Gray, and Ross [14, p. 203] review the literature in this area for British industry, survey the results for a number of manufacturing operations, and present illustrative examples of their findings from a number of firms. The summary of their findings follows: "The change in output per worker was found to vary among the different operations all the way from an increase of

7.5 per cent to one of 291 per cent, about half the cases falling between 43 per cent and 76 per cent. Such increases in output, most of them large, from our 'first-line' case histories, and from additional evidence, were found not to be just a 'flash in the pan' but were sustained over the whole period of study."

Roughly similar findings were obtained for the consequences of introducing payments by results in Australia, Belgium, India, the Netherlands, and the United States [15]. In Victoria it was found that "soundly designed and properly operated incentive plans have in practice increased production rate in the reporting firms from 20 to 50 per cent." In the Netherlands labor efficiency increases of 36.5 per cent were reported. It seems clear that with the same type of equipment the working tempo varies considerably both between different workers and different departments. Appropriate incentives can obviously change such tempos considerably and reduce costs, without any changes in purchasable inputs per unit.

The now-famous Hawthorne Studies [16] suggest that the mere fact that management shows a special interest in a certain group of workers can increase output. That is, management's greater interest in the group on whom the experiments were tried, both when working conditions were improved and when they were worsened, created a positive motivation among the workers. (The magnitudes were from 13 to 30 per cent [17].) In one of the ILO missions to Pakistan an improvement in labor relations in a textile mill in Lyallpur resulted in a productivity increase of 30 per cent. Nothing else was changed except that labor turnover was reduced by one-fifth [18] [19].

Individual variations in worker proficiency are probably larger than plant differences. Frequently the variation between the best to poorest worker is as much as four to one. Certainly improved worker selection could improve productivity at the plant level. To the extent that people are not working at what they are most proficient at, productivity should rise as a consequence of superior selection methods [20, p. 147].

Although there is a large literature on the importance of psychological factors on productivity, it is usually quite difficult to assess this literature because many psychologists work on the basis of high- and low-productivity groups but do not report the actual numerical differences. In general, it seems that some of the psychological factors studied in terms of small-group theory can account for differences in productivity of from 7 to 18 per cent. The discoveries include such findings as (1) up to a point smaller working units are more productive than larger ones; (2) working units made up of friends are more productive than those made up of nonfriends; (3) units that are generally supervised are more efficient than those that are closely supervised [21]; and (4) units that are given more information about the importance of their work are more proficient than those given less information [22]. A partial reason for these observed differences is probably the likelihood that individual motivation towards work is differently affected under the different circumstances mentioned.

The shorter-hours movement in Western Europe and in the United States, especially up to World War I, has some interesting lessons for productivity differentials without capital changes. Economists frequently assume that for a given capital stock and quality of work force, output will be proportional to number of hours worked. Experiments during World War I and later showed that not only was the proportionality law untrue, but that frequently *absolute* output actually increased with reductions in hours—say from a ten-hour day to an eight-hour day.[4] It was also found that with longer hours a disproportionate amount of time was lost from increased absenteeism, industrial accidents, and so on. In many cases it would obviously have been to a firm's interest to reduce hours below that of the rest of the industry. Firms could have investigated these relations and taken advantage of the findings. For the most part, governments sponsored the necessary research on the economics of fatigue and unrest under the stimulus of the war effort, when productivity in some sectors of the economy was believed to be crucial. The actual reduction of hours that took place was a consequence of the pressure of labor unions and national legislation . . . .

III. The Residual and *X*-Efficiency:
An Interpretation

The main burden of these findings is that *X*-inefficiency exists, and that improvement in *X*-efficiency is a significant source of increased output. In general, we may specify three elements as significant in determining what we have called *X*-efficiency: (1) intra-plant motivational efficiency, (2) external motivational efficiency, and (3) nonmarket input efficiency.

The simple fact is that neither individuals nor firms work as hard, nor do they search for information as effectively, as they could. The importance of motivation and its association with degree of effort and search arises because the relation between inputs and outputs is *not* a determinate one. There are four reasons why given inputs cannot be transformed into predetermined outputs: (a) contracts for labor are incomplete, (b) not all factors of production are marketed, (c) the production function is not completely specified or known, and (d) interdependence and uncertainty lead competing firms to cooperate tacitly with each other in some respects, and to imitate each other with respect to technique, to some degree.

The conventional theoretical assumption, although it is rarely stated, is that inputs have a fixed specification and yield a fixed performance. This ignores other likely possibilities. Inputs may have a fixed specification that yields a variable performance, or they may be of a variable specification and yield a variable performance. Some types of complex machinery may have fixed specifications, but their performance may be variable depending on the exact

[4]The empirical findings and experimental literature are reviewed in a number of places. For a brief review of the literature see [*18*]. See page 5 for bibliography of major works in the area.

nature of their employment. The most common case is that of labor services of various kinds that have variable specifications and variable performance—although markets sometimes operate as if much of the labor of a given class has a fixed specification. Moreover, it is exceedingly rare for all elements of performance in a labor contract to be spelled out. A good deal is left to custom, authority, and whatever motivational techniques are available to management as well as to individual discretion and judgement.

Similarly, the production function is neither completely specified nor known. There is always an experimental element involved so that something may be known about the current state; say the existing relation between inputs and outputs, but not what will happen given changes in the input ratios. In addition, important inputs are frequently not marketed or, if they are traded, they are not equally accessible (or accessible on equal terms) to all potential buyers. This is especially true of management knowledge. In many areas of the world managers may not be available in well-organized markets. But even when they are available, their capacities may not be known. One of the important capacities of management may be the degree to which managers can obtain factors of production that in fact are not marketed in well-organized markets or on a universalistic basis. In underdeveloped countries the capacity to obtain finance may depend on family connections. Trustworthiness may be similarly determined. Some types of market information may be available to some individuals but not purchasable in the market. For these and other reasons it seems clear that it is one thing to purchase or hire inputs in a given combination: it is something else to get a predetermined output out of them.

Another possible interpretation of the data presented is in connection with the "residual" in economic growth analysis. The residual manifests itself in three basic ways: (1) through cost reduction in the production of existing commodities without inventions or innovations; (2) the introduction of innovations in processes of production; and (3) the introduction of new commodities or, what is the same thing, quality improvements in consumer goods or inputs. We have ignored the introduction of new commodities, but the other two elements are pertinent here. The data suggest that cost reduction that is essentially a result of improvement in X-efficiency is likely to be an important component of the observed residual in economic growth. In addition, there is no doubt that, in some of the cases of reduced cost, new knowledge was conveyed to the firms involved, and this too is part of the residual. It is of special interest that such new knowledge involves knowledge dissemination rather than invention. The detailed studies suggest that the magnitudes are large, and hence a significant part of the residual does not depend on the types of considerations that have been prominent in the literature in recent years, such as those that are *embodied* in capital accumulation or in invention. We have considered the problem in terms of decreasing real costs per unit of output. It is clear that for a given set of resources, if real costs per unit of output are decreased, then total output will grow, and output per unit of input will also rise. Such efforts to reduce cost are part of the contribution of the residual to economic growth. . . . .

References

1. A. Harberger, "Using the Resources at Hand More Effectively," *Am. Econ. Rev.*, Proc., May 1959, *59*, 134-47.
2. D. Schwartzman, "The Burden of Monopoly," *Jour. Pol. Econ.*, December 1960, *68*, 727-29.
3. T. Scitovsky, *Economic Theory and Western European Integration*, Stanford, 1958.
4. J. Wemelsfelder, "The Short-Term Effect of Lowering Import Duties in Germany," *Econ. Jour.*, March 1960, *60*, 94-104.
5. H. Johnson, "The Gains from Freer Trade with Europe: An Estimate," *Man. School Econ. Stud.*, September 1958, *26*, 247-55.
6. L. H. Jannssen, *Free Trade, Protection and Customs Union*, Leiden, 1961, 132.
7. R. A. Mundell, review of L. H. Janssen, "Free Trade, Protection and Customs Union," *Am. Econ. Rev.*, June 1962, *52*, 621-22.
8. A. P. Lerner, "Consumer Surplus and Micro-Macro," *Jour. Pol. Econ.*, February 1963, *71*, 76 ff.
9. G. Ohlin, review of E. Lundberg, "Productivity and Profitability: Studies of the Role of Profit in the Swedish Economy," *Am. Econ. Rev.*, September 1962, *52*, 827-29.
10. F. Harbison, "Entrepreneurial Organization as a Factor in Economic Development," *Quar. Jour. Econ.*, August 1956, *70*, 364-79.
11. N. Chamberlain, *The Firm: Micro Economic Planning and Action*, New York, 1962.
12. P. Kilby, "Organization and Productivity in Backward Economies," *Quar. Jour. Econ.*, May 1962, *76*, 303-10.
13. L. Rostas, *Comparative Productivity in British and American Industry*, Nat. Inst. Econ. Soc. Research Paper 13, Cambridge (England), 1964, 64 ff.
14. J. P. Davison, P. S. Florence, B. Gray, and N. Ross, *Productivity and Economic Incentives*, London, 1958.
15. International Labor Organization, "Payment by Results," ILO Studies and Reports, New Ser. No. 27, Geneva, 1951.
16. F. T. Roethlisberger and W. J. Dickson, *Management and the Worker*, Cambridge, 1939.
17. H. A. Landsberger, *Hawthorne Revisited*, Ithaca, 1958, 13ff.
18. International Labor Organization, "ILO Productivity Missions to Underdeveloped Countries," Part 1, *Inter. Lab. Rev.*, July 1957, *76*, 1-29.
19. —————"ILO Productivity Missions to Underdeveloped Countries," Part 2, *Inter. Lab. Rev.*, August 1957, *76*, 139-66.
20. E. E. Ghiselli and C. W. Brown, *Personnel and Industrial Psychology*, New York, 1948.
21. M. Argyle, G. Gardner, and F. Cioffi, "Supervisory Methods Related to Productivity, Absenteeism, and Labor Turnover," *Human Relations*, 1958, *10*, 13-29.
22. T. Tomekovic, "Levels of Knowledge of Requirements as a Motivational Factor in the Work Situation," *Human Relations*, 1962, *15*, 197-216.

Notes on the Theory of the "Big Push"

P. N. Rosenstein-Rodan

14

I. Methodology

"There is a minimum level of resources that must be devoted to . . . a development program if it is to have any chance of success. Launching a country into self-sustaining growth is a little like getting an airplane off the ground. There is a critical ground speed which must be passed before the craft can become airborne . . . ."[1] Proceeding "bit by bit" will not add up in its effects to the sum total of the single bits. A minimum quantum of investment is a necessary, though not sufficient, condition of success. This, in a nutshell, is the contention of the theory of the big push.

From *Economic Development for Latin America,* edited by H. S. Ellis, IEA Proceedings (London: Macmillan & Company Ltd., 1951), pp. 57-66. Reprinted with the permission of Dr. P. N. Rosenstein-Rodan, The International Economic Association, St. Martin's Press Inc., The Macmillan Company of Canada, Ltd., and Macmillan & Company Ltd. The author is professor of economics, Center for International Studies, Massachusetts Institute of Technology.

[1]Massachusetts Institute of Technology, Center for International Studies, *The Objectives of United States Economic Assistance Programs* (Washington, 1957) p. 70.

This theory seems to contradict the conclusions of the traditional static equilibrium theory and to reverse its famous motto, *natura non facit saltun.* It does so for three reasons. First, it is based on a set of more realistic assumptions of certain indivisibilities and "non-appropriabilities" in the production functions even on the level of static equilibrium theory. These indivisibilities give rise to increasing returns and to technological external economies. Second, in dealing with problems of growth this theory examines the path towards equilibrium, not the conditions at a point of equilibrium only. At a point of static equilibrium net investment is zero. The theory of growth is very largely a theory of investment. Moreover, the allocation of investment—unlike the allocation of given stocks of consumer goods (equilibrium of consumption), or of producers' goods (equilibrium of production)—necessarily occurs in an imperfect market, that is, a market on which prices do not signal all the information required for an optimum solution.[2] Given an imperfect investment market, pecuniary external economies have the same effect on the theory of growth as technological external economies. They are a cause of a possible divergence between the private and the social marginal net product.[3] Since pecuniary, unlike technological, external economies are all-pervading and frequent, the price mechanism does not necessarily put the economy on an optimum path. Therefore, additional signalling devices apart from market prices are required.[4] Many economists, including the author, believe that these additional signals can be provided by programming. Third, in addition to the risk phenomena and imperfections characterizing the investment equilibrium, markets in underdeveloped

[2]See P. N. Rosenstein-Rodan, "Programming in Theory and in Italian Practice," in Massachusetts Institute of Technology, Center for International Studies, *Investment Criteria and Economic Growth* (Cambridge, Massachusetts, 1955).

[3]T. Scitovsky, "Two Concepts of External Economies," *Journal of Political Economy,* April 1954.

[4]Futures markets and futures prices could perhaps provide such signalling devices. It is a moot point whether perfect futures markets for all goods can exist. The author's suspicion (without proof) is that they cannot exist for the same reasons for which foresight is impossible. In reality they certainly do not exist.

"In an economy in which economic decisions are decentralized, a system of communications is needed to enable each person who makes economic decisions to learn about the economic decisions of others and co-ordinate his decisions with theirs. In the market economy, prices are the signalling device that informs each person of other people's economic decisions; and the merit of perfect competition is that it would cause prices to transmit information reliably and people to respond to this information properly. Market prices, however, reflect the economic situation as it is and not as it will be. For this reason, they are more useful for co-ordinating current production decisions which are immediately effective and guided by short-run considerations than they are for co-ordinating investment decisions which have a delayed effect and—looking ahead to a long future period—should be governed not by what the present economic situation is but by what the future economic situation is expected to be. The proper co-ordination of investment decisions, therefore, would require a signalling device to transmit information about present plans and future conditions as they are determined by present plans; and the pricing system fails to provide this." T. Scitovsky, *op. cit.* p. 150.

countries are even more imperfect than in developed countries. The price mechanism in such imperfect markets does not provide the signals which guide a perfectly competitive economy towards an optimum position.

II. Terminology

Indivisibilities and external economies are portmanteau expressions which are loosely used. Fortunately, recent publications have clarified the concepts.[5] Not all indivisibilities give rise to external economies and not all external economies are due to indivisibilities. Some external economies are due to the impossibility of appropriating a factor—even if divisible. Pecuniary external economies are an almost superfluous concept in static equilibrium theory. They refer to those inter-industry relations which are due to the fact that production functions of different industries are not linear[6] and homogeneous. Their true function in the theory of static equilibrium is to mark a place for a concept which will become important in the theory of growth. Technological external economies are rare in a static competitive economy with one important exception, the training of labour[7] and education. In the theory of growth, however, external economies abound. Given the inherent imperfection of the investment market, as well as imperfect knowledge and risks, pecuniary and technological external economies have a similarly disturbing effect on the path towards equilibrium. While the distinction between pecuniary and technological external economies becomes practically irrelevant in the theory of growth, three different kinds of indivisibilities and external economies may be distinguished.

First, there is indivisibility in the production function, especially indivisibility in the supply of social overhead capital (lumpiness of capital) which is

---

[5]See H. W. Arndt, "External Economics in Economic Growth," *Economic Record*, November 1955; T. Scitovsky, *op. cit.*; F. M. Bator, *Capital, Growth and Welfare: Essays on the Theory of Allocation*, a doctoral dissertation submitted at Massachusetts Institute of Technology, 1956, Part III; L. Lefeber, *External Economies and Transportation in the General Equilibrium System*, a doctoral dissertation submitted at Massachusetts Institute of Technology, 1957, Part K; M. Fleming, "External Economies and the Doctrine of Balanced Growth," *Economic Journal*, June 1955, confines his analysis to conditions of a static equilibrium.

[6]This is almost but not quite the same as saying that there are indivisibilities in the production functions. There can be continuous though non-linear production functions where, for instance, inputs and outputs are non-linearly linked. The decisive criterion is non-convexity of production possibility curves. In most cases that is due to indivisibilities.

[7]In a slave economy, investment in training slave workers may pay. In a non-slave economy in which mortgages on workers do not exist, a trained worker may contract at a higher wage rate with another firm which did not invest in his training. The supply of training facilities in a competitive economy will therefore be normally below optimum. The best way of training workers is probably on the job. Industrial workers in towns with many establishments and industries acquire skill by working, by talking to each other, exchanging experiences and changing jobs, much more quickly than isolated peasants. This fact alone, apart from better division of labour, is a source of increasing returns to the industrial system as a whole and a differential advantage of industrialization.

discussed in Section III. Second, there is indivisibility of demand (complementarity of demand), discussed in Section IV. Third, there is indivisibility (kink) in the supply of saving, discussed in Section VI.

In one way the first indivisibility is fundamental. If it did not exist, the others would not arise. Linear homogeneous production functions are basic in this sense, but they are completely unrealistic. They imply no economies of scale or of agglomeration, no entrepreneurship, no phenomenon of minimum quantum or threshold, so that they threaten to obscure the nature of the economic process and the risks involved rather than throwing light on it. In reality there are indivisibilities in the production function. They create not only non-constant returns but also risks of investment and imperfect markets which give rise to the indivisibility (complementarity) of demand.

III.   Indivisibility in the Production Function (Lumpiness of Capital)

Indivisibilities of inputs, processes, or outputs give rise to increasing returns, that is, economies of scale, and may require a high optimum size of a firm. This is not a very important obstacle to development since with some exceptions (for instance in Central America) there is usually sufficient demand, even in small, poor countries, for at least one optimum scale firm in many industries. There may be room, however, only for one or a few firms with the obvious danger of monopolistic markets.

As Allyn Young pointed out, increasing returns accrue to a firm not only with the growth of its size but with the growth of the industry and with the growth of the industrial system as a whole. Greater specialization and better use of resources become possible when growth helps to overcome indivisibilities generating pecuniary external economies. The range of increasing returns seems to be very wide indeed.[8]

Social overhead capital is the most important instance of indivisibility and hence of external economies on the supply side. Its services are indirectly productive and become available only after long gestation periods. Its most important products are investment opportunities created in other industries. Social overhead capital comprises all those basic industries like power, transport, or communications which must precede the more quickly yielding, directly productive investments and which constitute the framework or infrastructure and the overhead costs of the economy as a whole. Its installations are characterized by a sizeable initial lump and low variable costs. Since the minimum size in these basic industries is large, excess

---

[8]The capital-output ratio in the United States has fallen over the last eighty years from around 4:1 to around 3:1, while income per head, wage-rates, and the relative importance of heavy industry were rising. This is due to technical progress (change in production functions), increasing returns on balance (increasing returns prevailing over decreasing returns), and to the rising demand for labour-intensive services characteristic of high-income economies. It is my conviction that increasing returns played a considerable part in it.

capacity will be unavoidable over the initial period in underdeveloped countries.[9] In addition, there is also an irreducible minimum industry mix of different public utilities, so that an underdeveloped country will have to invest between 30-40 per cent of its total investment in these channels. Since overall vision is required as well as a correct appraisal of future development, programming is undoubtedly required in this lumpy field. Normal market mechanisms will not provide an optimum supply.

Social overhead capital is characterized by four indivisibilities. First, it is indivisible (irreversible) in time. It must precede other directly productive investments. Second, its equipment has high minimum durability. Lesser durability is either technically impossible or much less efficient. For this and other reasons it is very lumpy. Third, it has long gestation periods. Fourth, an irreducible minimum social overhead capital industry mix is a condition for getting off the dead-end.

Because of these indivisibilities and because services of social overhead capital cannot be imported, a high initial investment in social overhead capital must either precede or be known to be certainly available in order to pave the way for additional more quickly yielding directly productive investments. This indivisibility of social overhead capital constitutes one of the main obstacles to development of underdeveloped countries.

IV.   Indivisibility of Demand
(Complementarity of Demand)

Relatively few investments are made in the small market of an underdeveloped country. If all investment projects were independent (which they are not) and if their number grew, the risk of each investment project would decline by simple actuarial rules. The lower marginal risk of each investment dose (or project) would thus constitute internal economies. In reality, however, various investment decisions are not independent. Investment projects have high risks because of uncertainty as to whether their products will find a market.

Let us restate our old example,[10] at first for a closed economy.[11] If a hundred workers who were previously in disguised unemployment[12] (so that

[9]We may distinguish in fact between the development social overhead capital which provides for a hoped for but uncertain future demand and the rehabilitation social overhead capital which caters to an unsatisfied demand of the past. The first with its excess capacity will necessarily have a big sectoral capital-output ratio ($10-15:1$); the second, through breaking bottlenecks, has a certain high indirect productivity and a much lower capital-output ratio.

[10]See P. N. Rosenstein-Rodan, "Problems of Industrialization of Eastern and South-Eastern Europe," *Economic Journal,* June-September 1943; R. Nurske, *Problems of Capital Formation in Underdeveloped Countries* (Oxford, 1953).

[11]The assumption of a closed economy will be dropped in Section V.

[12]On the concept and measurement of disguised unemployment see P. N. Rosenstein-Rodan, *Notes on Disguised Unemployment,* Massachusetts Institute of Technology, Center for International Studies (Cambridge, Massachusetts, 1956), Part I.

the marginal productivity of their labour was equal to zero) in an underdeveloped country are put into a shoe factory, their wages will constitute additional income. If the newly employed workers spend all of their additional income on the shoes they produce, the shoe factory will find a market and will succeed. In fact, however, they will not spend all of their additional income on shoes. There is no easy solution of creating an additional market in this way.[13] The risk of not finding a market reduces the incentive to invest, and the shoe factory investment project will probably be abandoned. Let us vary the example. Instead of putting a hundred previously unemployed workers in one shoe factory, let us put ten thousand workers in one hundred factories and farms which between them will produce the bulk of the wage-goods on which the newly employed workers will spend their wages. What was not true in the case of one single shoe factory will become true for the complementary system of one hundred factories and farms. The new producers will be each other's customers and will verify Say's Law by creating an additional market. The complementarity of demand will reduce the risk of not finding a market. Reducing such interdependent risks naturally increases the incentive to invest.

If one unit of any wage-good could be produced as efficiently as many units, that is to say, if there were no indivisibilities in the production functions of wage-goods, a relatively small investment might suffice to produce a mix which would satisfy, and create, the additional market. Indivisibilities make the minimum investment much larger.

The risk of any single investment in any one industry is increased by the fact that various goods are highly imperfect substitutes for each other in low income underdeveloped countries. The southwest corner of the indifference map shows very high degrees of convexity. Demand for most goods will therefore be highly inelastic. Low elasticities of demand make it much more difficult to fit supplies to demands. The difficulty of fitting demand to supply on a small scale constitutes a risk which is higher in a small than in a large and growing market. Complementarity of demand will reduce the marginal risk of growing and diversified investments but will be below a *minimum sensible* for small doses of investment. There is therefore a minimum threshold at which the complementarity of demand manifests itself. The discontinuity in the complementarity of demand may therefore, be called indivisibility of demand.

A minimum quantum of investment is required to produce the bulk of additional wage-goods on which additionally employed workers will spend their additional income. Unless it is probable that other investments will take place, many single investment projects may be too risky to be undertaken. The mobilization of sufficient investment to provide this minimum quantum is the first hurdle which underdeveloped countries must overcome, but it is not the only one. Even if saving and investment sufficient to provide a

---

[13]In an open economy the output of the shoe factory may replace former shoe imports, or may find export markets, although this too is uncertain. See Section V below.

minimum quantum of wage-goods were forthcoming, the previous creation of a minimum quantum of social overhead capital constitutes a second hurdle which must be overcome. While the first minimum quantum of investment in wage-goods may amount to say \$20 million, the minimum quantum of investment in social overhead capital may amount to \$60 to \$80 million. The effective minimum of total investment may thus amount to, and require a big push of, from \$80 to \$100 million.

V. International Trade Reduces the Size of the Minimum Push

Complementarity of demand was examined in Section IV above under the assumption of a closed economy. In an open economy a shoe factory may replace former imports or may be efficient enough to find export markets. The world market can be a substitute for the additional domestic market required in a closed economy. Can the world market provide enough continuity to obviate the need for a minimum quantum of investment? It is submitted that the mobility of products is in reality an imperfect substitute for the mobility of factors. International trade undoubtedly reduces the size of the minimum push required, so that not *all* the wage-goods need be produced in the developing country, but it does not eliminate it.

The great expansion of international trade in the nineteenth century led neither to an equalization nor even to a reduction in the inequality of factor rewards. Theoretically this fact may be due to three reasons:[14] first, transport costs as impediments to the mobility of factors; second, complete rather than partial specialization of production; and third, different production functions in different countries.

The fact that transport costs have been sharply reduced during the last 150 years should have led to a growing equalization of factor rewards. The increasing importance of partial, as opposed to complete, specialization of production should also have worked in this direction. The English Industrial Revolution may, indeed, have increased the share of complete specialization of production. In England during that period, export-gaining industries expanded more than import-saving industries. Nevertheless, subsequent industrial revolutions, for example, the industrial revolution in Germany, showed a greater expansion of import-saving than of export-gaining production, although exact statistical information does not seem to exist.[15]

Therefore, the main explanation of why this tendency to a growing equalization of factor rewards did not materialize—why, in fact, labour

[14]See P. A. Samuelson, " International Trade and the Equalisation of Factor Prices," *Economic Journal,* June 1948, and "International Factor-Price Equalisation Once Again," *Ibid.,* June 1949.

[15]Much depends, of course, on the definition of the *same* or *similar* products in various countries.

rewards tended to become more unequal[16]—must rest on the assumption that production functions are different in various parts of the world. "The laws of nature may be the same everywhere, but the laws of nature and the economically relevant production function relating maximum output obtainable from specified concrete inputs are two quite different things. Effective knowledge ('know-how') is probably as important a variable in understanding economic history and geography as is specific factor endowment. . . . The 'effective' organization is different."[17] There is no doubt that differences in effectiveness of organization do exist in different countries and that effective knowledge cannot be acquired by reading a book or by editorial exhortation. It can be acquired, however, on the job! This possibility is a major source of increasing returns to the industrial system as a whole. Perhaps the most important yield of development is a cumulative increase in effective knowledge! The growth of international trade during the last 150 years has not reduced the inequality in this field.

We may conclude that international trade would not eliminate—although it would reduce—the indivisibility of demand, even if markets, other than the investment market, were more or less perfect. In reality, of course, markets are imperfect; and those in underdeveloped countries are probably more imperfect than those in the developed countries. International trade does much to reduce the danger of monopolies. It also effectively reduces the size of the minimum quantum of investment. But it does not dispense with the need for a big push.

VI. Indivisibility in the Supply of Savings

A high minimum quantum of investment requires a high volume of savings, which is difficult to achieve in low income, underdeveloped countries. There is a way out of this vicious circle. In the first stage when income is increased due to an increase in investment which mobilizes additional latent resources, mechanisms must be provided which assure that in the second stage the marginal rate of saving is very much higher than the average rate of saving. Adam Smith's dictum that frugality is a virtue and prodigality a vice has to be adapted to a situation of growing income. Economic history does not show that the English Industrial Revolution was preceded by a period of falling consumption. It only shows that the proportion saved from the increase in income was higher than the previous average rate of saving.

A zero (or very low) price elasticity of the supply of saving and a high income elasticity of saving thus constitute the third indivisibility.

---

[16]This was not due to a differentially higher increase in population in the underdeveloped countries. On the contrary, their increase in population was smaller than that of developed countries.

[17]P. A. Samuelson, *op. cit.* (1948), p. 181.

These three indivisibilities and the external economies to which they give rise, plus the external economies of training labour, form the characteristic pattern of models of growth of underdeveloped countries.

VII. Psychological Indivisibility of the Development Drive

The economic factors discussed so far give only the necessary, but not the sufficient, conditions of growth. A big push seems to be required to jump over the economic obstacles[18] to development. There may be finally a phenomenon of indivisibility in the vigour and drive required for the successful development policy. Isolated and small efforts may not add up to a sufficient impact on growth. An atmosphere of development may only arise with a minimum speed or size of investment. Our knowledge of psychology is far too deficient to theorize about this phenomenon. This does not make it a less important factor. It may well constitute the difference between necessary and sufficient conditions for success. . . .

[18]The extent and relative importance of the three indivisibilities and external economies is greater in underdeveloped than in developed countries. The same applies to the degree of imperfect knowledge and of imperfect competition.

Unbalanced Growth: An Espousal

Albert O. Hirschman

15

Is Balance in Supply Required?

[Previously] ... we criticized the idea that development must take place simultaneously in many activities to provide the element of "mutual support" that alone will make it possible to clear the market of the newly produced goods. Having discarded this "pure" theory of balanced growth we must still consider a far less rigorous version, one that insists that if growth is not to be stunted the various sectors of an economy will have to grow jointly in some (not necessarily identical) proportion; no sector should get too far out of line, not because of demand but because of supply of "structural" considerations. For instance, if secondary industry grows, the food and raw material input needed by the workers and the machines will go up; if some of these requirements are imported, then an increase in exports is necessary, etc., etc.

In this form, the balanced growth theory is essentially an exercise in retrospective comparative statics. If we look at an economy that has

From *The Strategy of Economic Development* (New Haven: Yale University Press, 1958), pp. 62-65. The author is professor of economics, Columbia University.

experienced growth at two different points in time, we will of course find that a great many parts of it have pushed ahead: industry and agriculture, capital goods and consumer goods industries, cars on the road and highway mileage—each at its own average annual rate of increase. But surely the individual components of the economy will not actually have grown at these rates throughout the period under review. Just as on the demand side the market can absorb "unbalanced" advances in output because of cost-reducing innovations, new products, and import substitution, so we can have isolated forward thrusts on the supply side as inputs are redistributed among users through price changes, and at the cost of some temporary shortages and disequilibria in the balance of payments or elsewhere. In fact, development has of course proceeded in this way, with growth being communicated from the leading sectors of the economy to the followers, from one industry to another, from one firm to another. In other words, the balanced growth that is revealed by the two still photographs taken at two different points in time is the end result of a series of uneven advances of one sector followed by the catching-up of other sectors. If the catching-up overreaches its goal, as it often does, then the stage is set for further advances elsewhere. The advantage of this kind of seesaw advance over "balanced growth," where every activity expands perfectly in step with every other, is that it leaves considerable scope to *induced* investment decisions and therefore economizes our principal scarce resource, namely, genuine decision-making.

Classical economics, while not taking so positive a view of the imbalances of the growth process, at least was never particularly concerned about them because it relied on prices to signal, and on the profit motive to eliminate rapidly and reliably, any structural disequilibria that might arise in the course of growth. The critics of classical economics, on the other hand, have always pointed to cases in which these "market forces" would not act with adequate strength and speed. Having thus convinced themselves that the adjustment mechanism is beset with virtually insuperable obstacles, some of the critics naturally enough took the defeatist view that growth has to be balanced from the start or cannot take place at all.

This counsel of perfection is not only impractical but also uneconomical. We need not sacrifice the valuable development mechanisms brought into play by unbalanced growth, especially if we go beyond the overly narrow view of the adjustment process that has long dominated economic literature.

Tradition seems to require that economists argue forever about the question whether, in any disequilibrium situation, *market forces acting alone* are likely to restore equilibrium. Now this is certainly an interesting question. But as social scientists we surely must address ourselves also to the broader question: is the disequilibrium situation likely to be corrected at all, by market or nonmarket forces, or by both acting jointly? *It is our contention that nonmarket forces are not necessarily less "automatic" than market forces.* Certainly the almost monotonous regularity with which interventionist economists have come forward—and with which authorities have acted—when the market forces did not adequately perform their task testifies to the fact that we do not have to rely exclusively on price signals and profit-maximizers to save us from trouble.[1]

The case of unbalanced growth provides a good illustration. When supply difficulties arise in the course of uneven progress in sectors—such as education and public utilities—where private enterprise is not operating, strong pressures are felt by public authorities to "do something"; and since the desire for political survival is at least as strong a motive force as the desire to realize a profit, we may ordinarily expect some corrective action to be taken.[2]

There is no implication here that any disequilibrium whatsoever will be resolved by some combination of market and nonmarket forces. But if a community cannot generate the "induced" decisions and actions needed to deal with the supply disequilibria that arise in the course of uneven growth, then I can see little reason for believing that it will be able to take the set of "autonomous" decisions required by balanced growth. In other words, if the adjustment mechanism breaks down altogether, this is a sign that the community rejects economic growth as an overriding objective.

The inclusion of probable reactions of nonmarket forces not only serves to make economic analysis more realistic. It also protects us against a fallacious chain of reasoning that is fairly common in development economics and of which the doctrine of balanced growth is itself an excellent illustration. In this reasoning, one first selects some objective of economic policy that seems desirable enough; then one proves that the objective cannot be attained through the operation of market forces; and one concludes that state action surely will bring the objective about. But this conclusion is clearly a non sequitur. The fact that private entrepreneurs will be unable or unwilling to do certain jobs which we would like to see done does not in itself ensure that the government can handle them. We must examine whether these jobs are likely to be performed satisfactorily by public authorities, which function after all in the same society as the entrepreneurs . . .

---

[1]Some traditional equilibrium mechanisms were unable to dispense entirely with help from agents outside the market. Thus, the restoration of balance-of-payments equilibrium and the damping of the business cycle was, for a long time, made to depend on correct manipulation by the central bank of the rate of interest, in reaction to developing disequilibria. But this role of the central banker has usually been rationalized as an exception to the rule; and in the minds of many economists, the central banker became a sort of honorary member of the market forces.

[2]Sectoral imbalances have of course been a conspicuous feature of Russian economic development. The resulting difficulties have been described in Soviet literature as "nonantagonistic contradictions" which are not only admitted to exist but apparently considered to perform a useful signaling and corrective function: "The characteristic trait of our difficulties and contradictions consists precisely in that they themselves indicate to us the basis and the means for their solution." V. Kozlovskii, *Antagonisticheskie i neantagonisticheskie protivorechiia* (Moscow, Moskovskii, Rabochii, 1954), p. 70. These "nonantagonistic" contradictions which are successfully overcome by administrative action of the Communist party and the government are then opposed to the "antagonistic" contradictions which are said to afflict capitalism and which can be resolved only by revolution.

Investment Choices and Strategies

Albert O. Hirschman

16

Efficient Sequences versus Investment Criteria

We can now begin to consider one of the most crucial problems in development theory and policy: that of investment choices.

Development requires the undertaking of a series of projects producing favorable effects on the flow of income, in a wide variety of fields: public administration, education, health, transportation, power, agriculture, industry, urban development, etc. The limitation of resources, be they savings available for investment or our "ability to invest," compels a choice among these projects. In traditional economics, the market performs this function by equating the productivities of the various projects at the margin. It is recognized, however, that in any economy a substantial proportion of funds must be devoted to projects (in education, health, some public utilities, etc.) whose output has no readily assigned or fully recoverable market value. Moreover, underdeveloped economies tend to exhibit certain systematic

From *The Strategy of Economic Development* (New Haven: Yale University Press, 1958), pp. 76–83.

discrepancies between private costs and social costs, and in such cases reliance on the market would lead to misallocation of resources.[1]

These considerations and the practical needs of development planners have led to the elaboration of *investment criteria*. The problem that has been discussed in this connection can be formulated as follows: given a limited amount of investment resources and a series of proposed investment projects whose total cost exceeds the available resources, how do we pick out the projects that will make the greatest contribution relative to their cost? In answering this question, economists have ordinarily interpreted "contribution" as *direct contribution to output* once the project has been completed. This is only natural if growth is visualized as depending exclusively on aggregate output and income which, via the propensity to save, secretes the means for further growth. On these premises, the measurement of what has been called the "social marginal productivity" (SMP) of different projects—essentially a more or less sophisticated benefit-cost ratio—becomes the instrument that should in theory permit us to rank different projects in the order of their expected contribution to output and therefore to further growth.[2]

Recently, a far more elaborate concept has been proposed by Leibenstein: In addition to the output stream, investment criteria ought to take account also of the differential effects of the proposed ventures on the supply of entrepreneurship and of savings, on consumption habits, population increases, and a variety of other factors affecting further growth.[3] Leibenstein admits that a criterion embodying all these repercussions (in addition to SMP proper) would be of unusually difficult application.[4] In practice, his criticism seems likely to result in an agnostic "it all depends" attitude since it seriously impairs the usefulness of the SMP criterion without replacing it by a manageable new instrument.

In attempting a different approach, we shall first draw a distinction between substitution choices and postponement choices. Consider any choice between project *A* and project *B*: If the decision favors *A* this may mean either that *B* is *discarded permanently* or that it is *postponed*. In the former case, the choice is between technical substitutes such as alternative means of providing a city with power or water supply. Many important choices are of this kind. They relate to the best means of attaining a given end or to the best design of a project whose output itself is needed beyond question. In deciding

[1] There are at least three important areas in which such systematic discrepancies are apt to occur: the wage rate (because of disguised unemployment), the exchange rate (because of overvaluation of the currency), and the interest rate (because of rationing of loan funds on the part of the banks). See J. Tinbergen, *The Design of Development* (Baltimore, 1958), pp. 39 ff.

[2] A. E. Kahn, "Investment Criteria in Development," *Quarterly Journal of Economics*, 55 (Feb. 1951), 38-61; H. B. Chenery, "The Application of Investment Criteria," *Quarterly Journal of Economics*, 57 (Feb. 1953), 76-96; J. Ahumanda, "Preparación y evaluación de proyectos de desarrollo económico," *El trimestre económico*, 22 (July-Sept. 1955), 265-96.

[3] Leibenstein, *Economic Backwardness and Economic Growth*, Ch. 15.

[4] *Ibid.*, p. 268.

such choices, the usual investment criteria retain considerable usefulness. Nevertheless, we feel that in underdeveloped countries additional considerations must be introduced and we will do so in Chapter 8.

Let us suppose for the time being that all substitution choices have been made and that we have before us a series of useful projects which are ideally designed to accomplish their respective purposes. In this situation, we are only faced with postponement choices.[5] We no longer choose A instead of B; rather, we choose the sequence AB instead of the sequence BA. What is the possible rationale for such a choice? If we suppose that our goal is to have both A and B, but that "now" we can undertake only either A or B, leaving B or A, respectively, for "later," then it is clear that the only conceivable reason for preferring AB to BA is that B will be possible sooner once A is in place than vice versa. In other words, our choice depends entirely on the pressure that the existence of A exerts toward the coming into existence of B as compared to the corresponding pressure that would emanate from B toward A. Once the problem is formulated in this way it becomes quite clear that the comparative productivity of A and B which will both have to be undertaken is likely to be a rather minor factor in the decision assigning the priority.

Although our reasoning has been drastically simplified, it takes hold of an important aspect of the development problem. Essential tasks always abound in underdeveloped countries since backwardness has so many different interrelated facets. From this interrelatedness we do not draw the balanced growth conclusion that a simultaneous attack is essential. But what might be called a sequential or chain solution is indeed required. In other words, isolated progress in one area is possible, but only for a limited period; if it is not to be choked off, it must be followed by progress elsewhere. Therefore to compare the productivity increases that result from two projects in, e.g., education and transportation, is an insoluble problem not only in practice but conceptually. Such comparisons must be made on the *ceteris paribus* assumption that progress is being achieved in only one of the areas; and on this assumption the longer-term productivity of both undertakings is simply *zero* since the improved transportation facilities will serve little purpose and will fast deteriorate if education is not also improved in due course and vice versa. Therefore, the question of priority must be resolved on the basis of a comparative appraisal of

[5]In an earlier paper, "Economics and Investment Planning: Reflections Based on Experience in Colombia" in Investment Criteria and Economic Growth, ed. M. F. Millikan (Cambridge, Mass., M.I.T., 1955, multilithed), I argued essentially that economists ought to confine themselves to the making of substitution choices. I still believe that the most urgent task of development planners usually consists in arriving at correct substitution choices; but I realize now that postponement choices cannot be evaded. They must be made at two different stages of the process of development planning: first before it is decided in which sector or sectors substitution choices are to be studied, for the decision seriously to study alternative means of fulfilling a given need usually already implies a decision to give priority to this need; and secondly, after substitution choices have been completed in several different sectors.

the strength with which progress in one of these areas will induce progress in the other.[6] In these basic types of development decisions, it is therefore not sufficient to supplement, qualify, and otherwise refine the usual investment criteria. We must evolve entirely new aids to thought and action in this largely uncharted territory of efficient sequences and optimal development strategies.

There is no doubt that the task that we have set ourselves is extremely complex. Let us suppose that we know which are the n steps that need to be taken to, say, double a country's per capita income. Then there exist in principle $n!$ possible sequential arrangements of these n steps! Of course, there can be no question of neatly deducing, through a series of syllogisms, *the* most efficient sequence. Rather, we will strive to "suboptimize"[7] and to develop a few guideposts, principles, and illustrative models.

To begin with, there was a great deal of exaggeration in our statement that there exist $n!$ sequences in which the n steps may be undertaken. Many sequences are unavoidably "one-way" for purely technical reasons (a road must be built before it can be paved); one also feels that other one-way sequences are imposed not because they are technically determined but because they are necessary if development is to be properly planned, i.e., is to proceed in an "orderly" fashion. But here there may be some doubt as to how far it is advisable to go. Observation tells us that rapid growth of countries, cities, industries, and individual firms hardly ever proceeds in a completely orderly fashion, but that an excess of disorderliness may exert an inhibiting and demoralizing influence on further growth. Can we then perhaps define an optimum degree of orderliness in development? To illustrate this problem, let $A, B, C,$ and D in Figure 1 represent a group of development steps we wish to take and that ought to be taken in this order if ideal "orderliness" is to be achieved. Let us also suppose that step A *must* be realized before B, C or D can possibly be undertaken, but that with A accomplished the sequence is no longer imposed. In the absence of limiting factors, the sequence $ABCD$ would be chosen because it provides the smoothest transition from state A to state $ABCD$. But we now introduce a limited resource, such as decision-making or organizational ability, or simply time, and assume that different amounts of this resource are spent in going from one point to another. We want to minimize the use of this resource. If, say, ten units of this resource are spent in going from A to B, from B to C

---

[6]It may be objected that indivisibility could not be such as to prevent us from investing our resources partly in education and partly in transportation. However, the point we are making does not depend on indivisibility in the sense of "lumpiness." Let us assume that we have identified n essential and interrelated projects, costing 200 million dollars, but that we have only 100 million dollars at hand. Suppose that out of the n projects we can put together various collections of $m < n$ projects costing 100 million dollars. Then again the criterion for picking any particular collection of m projects would be the strength with which their execution would induce the remaining projects. Thus indivisibility is assumed only in the trivial sense that some projects will necessarily be undertaken ahead of others.

[7]Charles Hitch, "Sub-optimization in Operations Problems," *Journal of Operations Research Society of America,* 1 (May 1953), 87-99.

and from C to D, then it is natural to think that to go from A directly to C will take a somewhat larger (say 12 units) and from A to D, perhaps a much larger amount (say 25 units), because of the absence of the intermediate preparatory stages. On the other hand, less than ten units (say 5) should be needed to "fill in" B or C after C or D, respectively, because once the later steps have been realized the lack of the intermediary ones makes itself felt in so pressing a manner that the decision to undertake them requires far smaller quantities of the scarce ability or time than when they represented genuine forward steps.

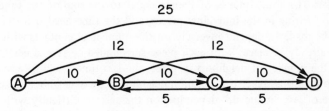

Figure 1.   The Optimum Disorderliness Model

If we apply the foregoing illustrative figures, then the expenditure of our scarce resource that is involved in the various possible sequences is as follows:

A to B to C to D	$30\,(10 + 10 + 10)$
A jump to C then fill in B, then D	$27\,(12 + \ 5 + 10)$
A to B then jump to D, then fill in C	$27\,(10 + 12 + \ 5)$
A jump to D, then fill in B and C	$35\,(25 + \ 5 + \ 5)$

In this example the figures have been selected so as to show that a limited amount of "putting the cart before the horse" may be efficient as compared to both maximum orderliness and maximum disorderliness.

It may be helpful to attempt a translation of this model into more familiar terminology. Let us assume two ventures, m and n, which require equal amount of capital and have a yield of 10 percent and 8 percent respectively. At the beginning of period 1 the interest rate stands at 9 percent, hence only venture m is undertaken. At the beginning of period 2, with venture m in existence, the expected yield of venture n has risen to 10 percent and is now also launched. But we are free to suppose that, if n were undertaken first, m would be urgently required and that its expected yield would rise to 14 percent at the beginning of period 2. In this eventuality, investors would maximize income by selecting in period 1 the investment with the lower yield! Besides they would do everything to rush m to completion. Such strange results are avoided in traditional theory by the implicit assumption which we chose to discard here, that the profitability of different ventures is invariant with respect to the order in which they are undertaken.

The preceding examples are highly artificial as they imply that development proceeds along a single path. Nevertheless, they embody a number of

concepts that are recurring throughout this essay: the difference between
"permissive" and "compulsive" sequences, the possible rationality of
violating "first things first" norms and the fact that the difficulty of taking a
development decision is not necessarily proportional to the amount of capital
it requires.

A more complex and perhaps more realistic model would be to consider
development as the putting together of a jigsaw puzzle. The fitting in of
individual pieces would represent the taking of discrete development steps.
The problem would again be to minimize the time needed to put the puzzle
together. The total time is of course equal to the sum of the time periods
spent on fitting in the individual pieces, and the time needed for each piece
could be made to depend inversely on the number of contacts with adjacent
pieces already in place: with each piece surrounded by several neighbors, the
larger the number of neighbors in place, the less time it will take to find and
fit into its proper place the common neighbor of these neighbors. Each fitting
is more or less "induced," depending on the ease or difficulty with which it
may be made.[8] An efficient sequence for putting the puzzle together could
be found by trial and error once we have information about the varying
amounts of time needed for fitting in individual pieces. For instance, if the
time needed fell rapidly toward zero the larger the number of neighbors
already in place, then the efficient sequence would turn out to be completely
different from the one that would be optimal if the increase in the facility
with which pieces may be fitted in were subject to decreasing returns as the
number of neighbors increased.

Up to this point, we have considered that the difficulty of taking any
development steps (i.e., the fitting in of the individual jigsaw pieces) depends
exclusively on the number of neighbors already in place. We can bring our
model one step closer to reality by supposing that the taking of the different
steps varies in intrinsic difficulty *besides* being affected by the number of
neighbors. If this is the case, then the putting together of the puzzle becomes
far more determinate than before: for now we would aim at surrounding by
"neighbors" those pieces that are intrinsically most difficult to fit in, securing
thereby far greater economies of effort than if we surrounded those pieces
that are intrinsically of average or less-than-average difficulty.

These fanciful digressions may illustrate the kind of models in terms of
which a general theory of "efficient sequences" might be built. I doubt,

---

[8]In the usual jigsaw puzzle the task of fitting in a piece also becomes progressively
easier as the game progresses and the number of remaining loose pieces declines. Although this feature of a jigsaw puzzle could be related to the "takeoff" concept and to
Simon's learning model, it is rather a disturbing element from the point of view of the
problem which we wish to illustrate at this juncture. To eliminate it, we may imagine
that the jigsaw puzzle goes on forever: only a limited number of loose pieces can be
chosen from at any point of time, but as soon as one piece is fitted, a new one is mixed
in among the loose pieces on the table. Such a representation of our model is consistent
with the view that the growth process is an infinite one, but that at any one point of
time only a limited number of steps-to-be-taken is within the horizon of the decision-
makers.

however, that it is useful to go very far in this direction. Our short discussion had primarily the purpose:

1. to make the concept of efficient sequence a little more palpable; and

2. to show that efficient sequences will necessarily vary widely from region to region and from country to country depending on the location and stubbornness of the principal development difficulties . . . .

Balanced Thought and Economic Growth

Warren Frederick Ilchman
Ravindra C. Bhargava

> In framing an ideal we may assume what we wish,
> but should avoid impossibilities.
>
> —Aristotle, *Politics*

17 In no field does orthodoxy seem to last less long than in development economics. Today's general strategy for economic growth becomes tomorrow's barrier. A factor considered crucial in one schema becomes a highly dependent variable in another. Often the whole strategy is premised on a tautology: to develop economically, a nation must develop economically. The attempts to discover basic psychological sources of the process, such as motivational patterns in a society, have pushed the answers back to deviant minority groups and the *leit-motifs* of children's fairy tales.[1] For the economic strategist in a low-income country, these latter studies,

From *Economic Development and Cultural Change*, July 1966, pp. 385-399, by permission of The University of Chicago Press. The authors are at Williams College and the Planning Department, Government of Uttar Pradesh, India, respectively.

[1]Everett E. Hagen, *On the Theory of Social Change* (Homewood, 1962); David C. McClelland, *The Achieving Society* (Princeton, 1961).

while important and interesting, are as useful in guiding his investment decisions as the studies by Max Weber.

But are the more exclusively economic strategies of greater value? It is the contention of this article that the major strategies so far advanced by economists are relevant operationally only in highly specific situations. These situations, furthermore, are not defined by economic factors alone. They are determined by crucial political, sociological, and administrative factors as well. A further contention of this article is that the only operational strategies for "development" are the products of a cross-disciplinary social science perspective with a strong contribution from political scientists.

To prove this contention, the authors have analyzed several major theorists concerned with three potentially operational strategies—"Big Push" balanced growth, unbalanced growth, and capital formation through unlimited supplies of labor.[2] These theories are not assessed in terms of their economic merits. Instead, they are analyzed in terms of the major social problems that might arise from undertaking them and the political regime and administrative systems they presuppose.[3] In other words, these strategies are analyzed in terms of what they assume about the rest of the social system. Among the

[2]"Big Push" balance growth—P. N. Rosenstein-Rodan, "Problems of Industrialization of Eastern and South-Eastern Europe," in A. N. Agarwala and S. P. Singh, *The Economics of Underdevelopment* (New York, 1963), pp. 145-55; Ragnar Nurkse, *Problems of Capital Formation in Underdeveloped Countries* (New York, 1960), Ch. 1; Unbalanced growth—Albert O. Hirschman, *The Strategy of Economic Development* (New Haven, 1958); Capital formation through unlimited supplies of labor—W. Arthur Lewis, "Economic Development with Unlimited Supplies of Labour," in Agarwala and Singh, *op. cit.*, pp. 400-49; Nurkse, *op. cit.*, Ch. 2.

[3]Certain assumptions are made in this article about the social system and its response to economic change. First, the population is increasingly "mobilized," i.e., a population shifting to wages and a more complex division of labor, exposed to mass media and increasing education, and more easily susceptible to new forms of organization. See Karl W. Deutsch, "Social Mobilization and Political Development," *American Political Science Review* (September 1961), 493-514. Second, extreme inequalities of income, inflation over a long period of time without redistribution, and accelerated urbanization without adequate social overhead expenditures and provision for the maintenance of primary group relationships or acceptable alternatives, are destabilizing to a social system. See, for example, Bert F. Hoselitz, "Urbanization and Economic Growth in Asia, *"Economic Development and Cultural Change* (October 1957), 42-54; Neil J. Smelser, "Mechanisms of Change and Adjustment to Change," in Bert F. Hoselitz and Wilbert E. Moore, eds., *Industrialization and Society* (UNESCO, The Hague, 1963), pp. 32-54; Philip M. Hauser, "The Social, Economic, and Technological Problems of Rapid Urbanization," in *ibid.*, pp. 199-217; Richard D. Robinson, "Turkey's Agrarian Revolution and the Problem of Urbanization," *Public Opinion Quarterly* XXII (Fall 1958), 397-405; Joseph A. Kahl, "Some Social Concomitants of Industrialization and Urbanization," *Human Organization* (Summer 1959), 53-74 (especially bibliographical section). An act is destabilizing when it threatens the legitimacy of the institutions of civil authority and their means of handling conflict and distribution. See, for example, Seymour Martin Lipset, *Political Man, The Social Bases of Politics* (Garden City, New York, 1960), Ch. 3; Ronald C. Ricker, "Discontent and Economic Growth," *Economic Development and Cultural Change*, XI (October 1962), 1-15. For the authors' general approach to the social system and its subsystems, see Marion J. Levy, Jr., *The Structure of Society* (Princeton, 1953); S. N. Eisenstadt, *Essays on the Sociological Aspects of Political and Economic Development* (The Hague, 1961); David E. Apter, "System, Process and the Politics of Economic Development," in Hoselitz and Moore, *op. cit.*, pp. 135-58.

questions asked are: What is the character and membership of the elite? What is the degree of organization of two of the affected sectors—the urban working force and the peasantry? How responsive is the political system to group demands? What is the expected role of government in the strategy? How many civil servants will be required, and to what extent and in what way must they be trained? How much and what types of data are required? Detailed answers to these questions, of course, cannot be given in an article of this length. But, despite the necessary abstractions, a clear idea will be given of the "non-economic" criterion by which these strategies must be judged before they can be considered operational.

Balanced Growth

The "Big Push" balanced growth strategy for the development of underdeveloped countries may be attributed to Ragnar Nurkse and Paul Rosenstein-Rodan. In general, the strategy argues that the low per capita incomes which prevail in underdeveloped countries are a consequence of the low levels of productivity and that substantial increases in productivity require increased capital formation. However, another consequence of the low levels of income is that the demand for most manufactured goods is small, most of the income being utilized for subsistence. This limitation to the extent of the market implies that no enterpreneur can profitably, even with a monopoly, set up a modern factory, as the indivisibilities of capital result in the unit being of such a size that, at its low levels of operation, the costs of production are too high. Consequently, capital formation in manufacturing is not feasible, productivity does not increase, and poverty continues. To break this vicious circle, the balanced growth theorists suggest that in a country a whole set of complementary investments should be made, such that factories themselves, as well as the workers in them, can buy up all the produce either as intermediate goods or for final consumption. This will then render all the investments profitable. Thus, it is proposed to solve the demand problem by means of investment itself. In this way, capital formation will be made possible and vicious circles broken.

The most striking feature of the "Big Push" strategy is that, whereas investments in general are not profitable in the economy, there are combinations of investments,[4] which if implemented simultaneously, will prove profitable. To achieve these "right" bundles of investments, qualitatively and quantitatively, together with the time schedule for execution, is not easy. It involves planning substantial changes in production patterns with little assistance from the market mechanism and requires anticipating the market requirements once these changes have been made. In a scheme of balanced growth, every component must be at the right place at the right

[4]The probability of formulating alternative combinations of investments in under-developed countries is small. Indeed, at present, it is rare even to find alternative projects to choose from. See, for example, Government of Pakistan, Planning Commission, *Final Report of the Committee on Review of On-going Schemes* (Karachi, 1961), pp. 3-16.

time in the right quantity. The entire effort is based on the capability of a country to organize its relevant sectors, enact the proper controls and incentives, and acquire and submit to the best technical judgments on the combinations of investments for balanced growth.

The capital required for the "Big Push" will come from two sources— domestic and foreign savings. For domestic savings, taxation, higher profits, and inflation will be the chief means. However, with the large requirements of the strategy, domestic savings, even under the best of circumstances, will not be adequate, and foreign capital inflows will have to be substantial. The inflow would be in the form of government grants and loans and direct private investment.

What are the so-called "non-economic factors" which might enable an underdeveloped country to adopt successfully this strategy? Above all, there must exist in the country some authority or institutional arrangement capable of planning and implementing the combination of investments. This presupposes a political ruling elite with considerable unanimity of purpose and agreement on measures that may be taken to achieve this goal, a political system supportive, in the short and at least medium run, of the resulting programs, and an administrative system capable of bearing the technical burden of preparing and implementing the strategy.

Two ruling elites are possible. They are distinguished by their membership, especially private sector representation, and the role they conceive for government to play. The first is a modernizing elite made up largely of intellectuals, the military, and civil servants. It would be, in varying degrees, distrustful of the private sector. For this elite, the government is the obvious agent for balanced growth. Any role for the private sector, if allowed at all, would have to be subject to extensive controls. Reliance on incentives and indirect controls to secure the massive complementarity of investment would contain too much uncertainty. Government ownership and operation would be preferable for this elite.[5]

The membership of a second possible ruling elite would be distinguished by heavy representation from the business sector. This elite would have to be particularly small and closely knit to achieve the cooperation necessary to plan and organize the establishment of a whole complex of industries in the balanced growth pattern. Active government help and encouragement to provide the necessary incentives and business conditions would also be required. Taxes on industries and the elite must be low (or subventions high); high profits and monopolies permitted; infrastructure investments and technical assistance provided; trade union activity controlled; and internal security maintained. Indeed, it is unnecessary to distinguish between government and the private sector; they are virtually the same.[6]

---

[5] See Zbigniew Brzezinski, "The Politics of Underdevelopment," *World Politics,* IX (October 1956), 55-75; Alexander Eckstein, "Individualism and the Role of the State in Economic Growth," *Economic Development and Cultural Change,* VI (January 1958), 81-87.

[6] The "Big Push" strategy can also be formulated by differing proportions of authoritarian and oligarchical rule, but authoritarian and/or oligarchical, nonetheless.

Both ruling elites will have to be narrow in membership. A broadly based nationalist elite, drawing from several social sectors, such as the urban working force, would be too susceptible to the demands of its members, and this would impede the success of the strategy. This narrow base presupposes either a quiescent population, no political opposition of a formal or informal sort, heavy expenditures on coercion, or all three.[7] This is, of course, another way to describe an authoritarian situation, for it must be apparent that the "Big Push" cannot be undertaken unless the ruling elite can effectively restrict access by the broad mass of the public to the substance of the strategy. Furthermore, ideally, the technical considerations in the "Big Push" even subordinate the elite's judgment to that of the engineers and the economists.

Therefore, for the length of time required to break the "vicious circle of poverty," the political system cannot be sensitive to group demands. But in the "Big Push," this is highly unlikely for several reasons. First, the strategy requires that within a short period of time a country will find itself with a large industrial sector superimposed on an economically primitive base. Industrialization, and attendant urbanization, means the influx of large numbers of people from the rural areas into an entirely different set of social conditions. These people would find their values and ways of life unsuited to the new environment and would need considerable readjustment to be absorbed into industry and to attain stability. Their problems would be aggravated by the fact that it would be unlikely that adequate arrangements for housing, sanitation, medical attention, recreation, etc., would exist, since the numbers involved would be so large and the capital available for these purposes inadequate. Because of the nature and objectives of either ruling elite, trade union activity would be restricted and any liberal labor legislation unimplemented. All claims for redistribution would be unacceptable. This would tend to produce a restless and dissatisfied mass of people, who will have little to say in the political system and will constitute a constant threat to the social system, necessitating an elaborate coercive apparatus. It is true that the problems of adjusting the rural population to the modern sector always create tensions and difficulties, but in the "Big Push" strategy, the magnitudes would be much larger. Industrialization would not be arriving gradually, but would be more in the nature of a "once-and-for-all" process.

Second, the problems of regional disparities would constantly press for redress. The "Big Push" strategy, however, permits this only insofar as the redress fulfills a role in the total combination of investments. Probably, the dictates of location economics, and the possible bias of the ruling elite, would lead to the concentration of economic activity in certain areas, to the neglect of other regions. The experience in several countries, Pakistan, India, and

---

[7]A fourth possibility is a population almost unanimous in its commitment to economic development. This is relevant, in the authors' view, to no country now in existence. Even when a large proportion of the "effective" population has economic development as *one* of its top priorities—even its top priority—the interpretations of what "development" means, who is to sacrifice, what is to be foregone, and who is to prosper are legion, and the view of the economic strategist, or the ruling elites, is never accepted as definitive.

Nigeria among them, has shown how serious a situation may result from this.

Third, the financing of the strategy renders it vulnerable to group demands. On one hand, major reliance on foreign capital would be unacceptable to nations which have recently won, and intend to sustain, freedom from foreign controls. Any restriction on their use of foreign capital, whether borrowed or granted, is considered compromising to their independence. Prohibitions against foreign capital imports, restrictions on the use of foreign capital, the universal condemnation of "strings" on foreign aid, the demands for trade rather than aid, the popularity of nationalization through confiscation are common manifestations of this.[8] Under these conditions, the capital-exporting and aid-giving countries will hardly be encouraged to fill the capital needs. And to remove these impediments requires a regime unmenaced by an opposition able to exploit this sensitive issue. On the other hand, the burden of domestic saving from taxation and inflation would be borne by the non-profit-earning classes—the urban working force, the middle class, the service professions, and the rural sector. At the same time, particularly in a predominantly private sector strategy, there will be increasing disparities of income. The public in all regimes tolerate the above condition to a certain degree. But if the destabilization produced by massive foreign capital is to be avoided, or if the required capital is not available, increased reliance will be placed on mobilizing domestic savings. For the authority of a regime (and consequently the strategy) to remain unaffected in this case presupposes the existence of a long-suffering and tranquil non-profit-earning class or the existence of a widely effective coercive apparatus, whose costs the "Big Push" strategist externalizes. In reality, the demands for redistribution would be great and fully exploitable by any opposition in low income countries.

Thus, at a time when social harmony is an essential and assumed part of the strategy for economic development, it is that same strategy that is least likely to produce it.

Administratively, the "Big Push" necessitates, in the public and/or private sector, an extensive and highly skilled bureaucracy. This would have to be in addition to the existing civil service, for retraining a civil service for development objectives is a long-term process, and the needs of "law and order" would undoubtedly increase greatly under the pressure of the "Big Push." These personnel would be needed for both the formulation and execution of the strategy. New skills of many kinds and in great quantities would be called for—managerial and technical skills for operating the new enterprises, organizational and administrative skills for over-all coordination and the various forms of controls, including coercion. The experience with the execution of comparative modest development programs in several countries has revealed the shortcomings in these fields. Furthermore,

[8]See, for example, Donald Hindley, "Foreign Aid to Indonesia: Its Political Implications," *Pacific Affairs*, XXXVI (Summer 1963), 107-19; M. Bronfenbrenner, "The Appeal of Confiscation in Economic Development," *Economic Development and Cultural Change*, III (1954), 201-18.

formulating the strategy requires a large quantity of reliable data, not only of economic variables like elasticities of demand, income distribution, price changes, and technologies, but also of non-economic variables like changes in taste, motivations, and values. The data-gathering and processing machinery will, therefore, have to be widespread and able—far more than what exists at present in any underdeveloped country.[9]

Unbalanced Growth

Albert Hirschman developed his theory of unbalanced growth in response to the "Big Push" idea. The different kinds of resources required for the "Big Push," he contended, are ones which low income countries have in short supply. Indeed, that is why they are underdeveloped. He also insists that development is a gradual process, and it is unrealistic to think in terms of superimposing a large modern sector on a traditional economy. But the greatest shortage, according to his analysis, is the ability to perceive and take investment decisions, even when opportunities exist. The strategy of unbalanced growth seeks to remedy this shortage by creating situations in which people are forced to take investment decisions. Such situations are achieved by deliberately "unbalancing" different sectors of the economy. If certain parts of the economy are made to grow, the shortages in the complementary parts will create pressures for their growth also forcing investments to be made. The areas which lead the development should be so selected that investments in the complementary areas are really compulsive rather than permissive.

The most important field of application of this strategy is to governmental decisions regarding investments in economic and social overhead capital. The role of government is usually defined to include the function of providing this infrastructure, in order that entrepreneurs may make profitable investments of a directly productive nature. Hirschman, however, points out that investments in infrastructure are basically permissive of directly productive investments. They do not create any compelling situation for the latter to be made. Consequently, infrastructure investments are often uneconomic, insofar as they remain under-utilized for long periods. A better sequence would be for the government to provide only the barest minimum of infrastructure and to encourage entrepreneurs through incentives, such as tariff protection and subsidies, to invest in directly productive activities. As more of these investments are made, the deficiencies of overhead facilities become marked and increase the cost of production. Entrepreneurs would then press for provision of these services. This pressure would be an indicator to government for the more rational allocation of infrastructure investments.

[9]See, for example, Albert Waterston, " 'Planning the Planning' Under the Alliance for Progress," in Irving Swerdlow, *Development Administration, Concepts and Problems* (Syracuse, 1963), pp. 141-62; "Progress in Planning in Latin America," *Economic Bulletin for Latin America,* VIII (October 1963), 129-46; John P. Lewis, *Quiet Crisis in India* (Garden City, New York, 1964), pp. 129-40.

Thus, by having infrastructure lag behind productive activities, development would be quicker, and better use would be made of the available resources.

Hirschman applies this technique to other matters, such as the choice of investments, selection of technology, and ensuring maintenance of capital. To ensure the continuance of productive investments being made, he suggests that the initial activity chosen should be one that maximizes the backward and forward linkages. Instead of starting industrial efforts by making finished goods, the investments should be made in activities which are near the middle of a triangularly arranged input-output matrix. In choosing the technology, an attempt should be made to adopt "machine-paced" operations that compel labor to work at a predetermined rate, despite such a technique being more capital-intensive. Hirschman recommends that underdeveloped countries should choose complicated techniques, where the consequence of a breakdown would be more serious and hence compel adequate maintenance.

Finally, Hirschman does not favor central planning, for it tends to internalize both the external economies and diseconomies.[10] He believes that the net effect would not necessarily be positive, and more rapid growth can be achieved by encouraging aggressive entrepreneurship in the 19th century fashion. He would also favor a certain amount of inflation in the interest of forcing savings and making investments more profitable.

Although Professor Hirschman has insights into the problems facing at least some of the underdeveloped countries, his strategy ignores important political, social, and administrative factors. What sort of regime is necessary for adopting the strategy of unbalanced growth? Dominant power in the country, needless to say, would be exercised by one group—the business class. A regime totally sympathetic to private sector development and serving its interests would be required. There would be no governmental responsibility for comprehensive central planning and execution, and government would best fulfill its functions by providing the right social overheads at the right time and maintaining law and order. This latter task will be particularly difficult, as the urban working force and the middle class will be subject to inflation, low wages, and increasing disparities of income. At the same time, the government will be observed to tax the businessman inadequately and even to grant him subsidies to swell his profits. To compound this problem, the urban working force will be subject to the destabilizing effects of inadequate social overhead investments—in housing, education, and welfare programs. In addition, the adoption of machine-paced and capital-intensive operations would increase, or at least fail to reduce, unemployment. This would come at a time when trade union activity would be discouraged or completely curtailed by the state. Furthermore, the regime cannot be disturbed by any political objections to foreign business activity in the country. Nor would the demands of regional balance be permitted to affect

[10]Professor Hirschman has since modified his position. See Albert O. Hirschman, "Economics and Investment Planning: Reflections Based on Experience in Colombia," *Investment Criteria and Economic Growth* (Bombay, 1961), pp. 38-39. This modification, however, does not affect this article's analysis.

the "unbalancing" decisions. This, of course, presupposes a high degree of national unity.

What regimes are excluded from adopting the strategy of unbalanced growth? Socialist regimes are, of course. So are those in which businessmen are held in low repute, and only a few businessmen, if any, are part of the core elite guiding decisions. Regimes are excluded in which trade union activity is strong and the political mechanisms sensitive to claims for redistribution. Finally, a regime which invested in social overhead for any reason other than on demonstrated need by directly productive activities would be considered hopelessly inefficient.

Administratively, the demands of the strategy, though less than those of the "Big Push," will nevertheless be considerable. The skill for taking profitable investment decisions is not the same as skills required to organize and operate enterprise. Government must gather data for rationally deciding between alternative infrastructure investments. Also, it will have to select the sectors and areas where activity is to be promoted on the basis of comparative advantage and the likely trends in the demand function. Determination of a suitable system of subsidies and sources of revenue will be necessary. Decisions, it might be added, on purely economic grounds would be difficult, owing to the differing degrees of political power various business interests would possess. Lastly, the administrative requirements for coercion would be considerable.

Capital Formation with Unlimited Supplies of Labor

W. Arthur Lewis believes that in several underdeveloped countries there are virtually unlimited supplies of labor which can be used for capital formation. Disguised unemployment in the agricultural sector, large numbers in domestic service, population growth at a rate faster than the rate of growth of productive employment, and women who can work if opportunities arise—these are the main sources.

The development of the economy takes place by the increase of the sector using reproducible capital—the capitalist sector. This sector has a higher level of productivity than the remaining part of the economy, which is at subsistence level. As development takes place, the capitalist sector expands, while the subsistence sector grows smaller. Lewis also assumes that the capitalist class, which owns the reproducible capital, has a propensity to save and reinvest a large proportion of its profits. Hence, for the growth of the capitalist sector, it is necessary for profits to grow. It is immaterial to the argument whether the state itself is the capitalist.

The capitalist sector has to hire labor to work the capital it owns. As the sector expands, the requirements for labor keep increasing. Since the model assumes virtually unlimited supplies of labor, the process of growth cannot stop because of lack of workers, at least until all the surplus labor has been absorbed. Moreover, as capital accumulates, it causes labor productivity to rise, while technological innovations have the effect of increasing the productivity of both labor and capital. Consequently, the volume of profits, and possibly the profit rate also would keep rising, assuming other factors remain unchanged, and the process of growth would continue. However, growth can be slowed, or even stopped, if the wages increase at such a rate that, despite increases in productivity, the volume of profits falls. This will lead to a decrease in savings and investments. Thus, for the success of this model, keeping wages in check is essential.

The wages paid by the capitalist sector are determined by the wages and the average product of workers in the subsistence sector. To attract workers away from the farms and the villages, the capitalist has to offer an adequate incentive in the form of higher wages. As workers are drawn away from the subsistence sector in quantities large enough to decrease the absolute numbers, the average product rises, and hence the capitalist wages also have to rise in order to maintain the differential. An even more important cause for wages to rise in the capitalist sector would be the relative increase in the price of foodstuffs, as compared with the price of industrial products. The process of drawing workers into the capitalist sector would raise real incomes and increase the demand for food, necessitating larger supplies of food being brought to the market by the farmers. If this does not happen, owing to output being inelastic, food prices would rise, and hence the wages of the capitalist sector workers must rise correspondingly. Further, as the real wages in the subsistence sector would also be increasing, the maintenance of the differential would mean a rise in the capitalist wages. However, if food output does continue to increase, wages would still have to keep rising to keep pace with the average product of the subsistence sector. The solution is twofold: increasing the output of food and, by drawing away the surplus in the form of a land tax, preventing the farmer from taking advantage of this increase. If this can be successfully done, capital formation would continue until all the surplus labor was absorbed and the productivity of the two sectors raised to a high and almost equal level.

Nurkse has a somewhat similar model. He also proposes to utilize the disguised unemployed to form productive capital, i.e., roads, dams, irrigation canals. To minimize the cost of this operation, he intends that these workers be fed from the existing food production by keeping unchanged the consumption of those remaining on the farms. This will be accomplished by the imposition of a land tax or by compulsory requisitioning of food. Nurkse realizes that the workers transferred from the farms need to be given some small increase in consumption. He also recognizes the necessity of making all the surplus population work to avoid the "demonstration effect" inducing people to return to the villages.

As with other strategies of development, these models also appear to require a specific set of conditions. Lewis's model can work either with complete state ownership of the means of production, or with a government dominated by a business elite. In either case, the rural population and the industrial working force will not be in a position to influence the allocation of resources or the distribution of income and wealth. The government has to follow a policy of keeping the wages of the subsistence sector and the industrial workers at the minimum possible level. The tools for this will largely be heavy doses of land taxation, control of the activities of organized labor, non-implementation of any liberal labor legislation, and coercion. If the industries are being developed by private entrepreneurs, the economy will have to be geared to maximize their profits, to encourage investments. Accordingly, monopolies will presumably be allowed and taxes on business and high incomes kept at low levels. The state would provide the infrastructure investments, credit facilities, and other institutional arrangements to enable entrepreneurs to make investments. Consequently, the state will have few resources to invest in general welfare activities. In any case, income transfers to the working class would not be in accordance with the logic of the model.

The model assumes that the rural and urban working population will either be docile enough to accept this situation or the state able to coerce a condition of stability. But growing income disparities, regressive taxation, and suppression of the right of organization are policies which are difficult to adhere to for long. Nurkse's model has the added complication of labor conscription to make it operational. Finally, the social problems of adjustment, arising from industrialization and accentuated by the living conditions which the industrialists are likely to provide, would be as acute as in the balanced and unbalanced growth theories. Few underdeveloped countries today could undertake this strategy.

Administratively, the major task would be the maintenance of internal stability, coercion of the working class, and prevention of expressions of disaffection. An elaborate and reliable machinery for the collection of land tax would be required—a machinery not prone to leakages through corruption. In countries where land holdings are small, this problem would be even more difficult. Further, the success of the model demands rapid increase in food output. While imposing and collecting land taxes, the government would also have to embark upon an extensive program of agricultural extension. Experience in several countries has shown in recent years that this is not an easy matter and calls for high technical, administrative, and organizational skills. This has been true even where the farmers were generally cooperative, and the frictions of high taxes were not present.[11] Another task requiring substantial and advanced skills is the planning and implementing of a consistent program. If the state participated in the productive investments, the additional problem of making public enterprise efficient will have to be solved.

[11]See, for example, Government of India, Planning Commission, *Reports of the Programme Evaluation Organization,* especially nos. 6 and 7; Kusum Nair, *Blossoms in the Dust* (London, 1961), *passim.*

The three strategies analyzed claim that their implementation will probably lead to economic growth. No demands are made explicitly on the regime undertaking them, except, by implication, that the regime follow generally the prescribed program. From a social scientist's and a planner's point of view, however, certain questions need to be asked of these and other strategies.

1. What type of regime is required for undertaking the strategy? To what extent are a regime's values or the ruling elites' composition limitations? Must there be separate strategies for economic growth for "liberal" regimes, "radical" regimes, "tutelary democracies," pro-business regimes, anti-business regimes, regimes in which labor and/or small landholders are important components of the ruling elite, regimes in which taxes cannot be effectively collected, or where there is a low tolerance for bilateral foreign assistance or foreign private investment? Is a moratorium on politics necessary for the period during which the strategy is being implemented? Can there be permitted opposition parties which might try to exploit grievances against the regime and its new policies?
2. How does the strategy affect various social and economic sectors? Will substantial disorganization result for many existing economic and social institutions and functions? How long must this disorganization be endured before "growth" provides new institutions and articulates new functions? Is the strategy profligate of a society's integrative institutions, values, and beliefs? What have been or might be some of the unintended consequences of implementing the strategy? An increase in the number of landless laborers? Greater urban unemployment because of increasing capital intensiveness of investment and advancing requirements for skills?
3. What is implicit in the strategy for the distribution of wealth? Will this "formula" change? If so, how and when will it change? What new demands might be made on the political system as a consequence of implementing the strategy? Will there be greater demands for welfare expenditures and urban amenities? Does the strategy allow for them? Does the strategy "internalize" their costs?
4. To what degree is the strategy dependent on coercion? Persuasion? What, from the experience of other regimes, might be the short-term economic costs of coercion? Are they internalized in the strategy? What might be the long-term economic and social costs of a policy of coercion? Are social deviancy, anomie, and extremist movements likely "prices" to pay?
5. What does the strategy demand of the administrative system? Will more personnel and new skills be needed? Will the needs of the strategy for administrators in one sector starve the other sectors in their needs?[12] Will existing machinery for supervision and coordination be adequate? Are new data, and hence data-gathering machinery, required? Are these costs internalized in the strategy?

[12]See Joseph LaPalombara, "Bureaucracy and Political Development: Notes, Queries, and Dilemmas," in Joseph LaPalombara, ed., *Bureaucracy and Political Development* (Princeton, 1963), pp. 34-61.

The authors of these strategies might insist that models are necessarily abstract and that implementation must be moderated to meet each country's particular situation. At this point, the relevant political, social, and administrative information is added. But this answer will not do. First, the authors of the strategies were inspired by the process of economic growth in specific countries. In each instance, this process took place in a socio-political context from which the process acquired effectiveness and without which it would be virtually meaningless. Professor Nurkse's balanced growth strategy found many precedents in the Soviet Union, Professor Hirschman's proposals in a composite of occurrences in Latin America, and the advocates of capital formation through unlimited supplies of labor in Japanese and, less enthusiastically, Soviet experience.[13] Answers to the questions posed previously are also part of the record. Advice, hence, could also be given on the political, social, and administrative prerequisites, requisites, and consequences. Important costs can be calculated. Whether or not the strategy is relevant, with the addition of the appropriate information, can be assessed. Only then, the strategy for economic growth really becomes a strategy for social, political, and administrative change as well. Second, the strategies are, in different ways, unsusceptible to moderation in economic terms. Balanced growth requires a massive complementarity of supply and demand. Anything short of a total package of investments would fail in the "Big Push." Although most countries have unbalanced growth all the time, a substantially moderated "unbalance" will probably fail to achieve Professor Hirschman's objectives. Also, most conscious efforts in this direction, despite moderated intensity, might still be destabilizing to civil authority. Any moderation in the capital formation through the use of unlimited supplies of labor strategy would be difficult, because of the small size of the profit-making sector and the declared rate of economic growth of most underdeveloped countries. For these countries, moderating any one of the three strategies really means abandoning it. Finally, the strategies might tend, if followed only "moderately," toward self-justification. For example, failure to achieve high rates of capital formation through the Lewis and Nurkse models would set up pressures to remove the political and social barriers to "efficiency." Judgment on the strategy's effectiveness would have to be postponed until a country's social and political system approximated the strategy's "hidden" requirements.

One major reason for the difficulties inherent in implementing the economic strategies is that they were constructed by tools developed for nations with different problems and needs. While this assertion is not novel, it has usually been argued within the terms of economic analysis. Part of the justification for the allegation here is in an interpretation of the history of ideas. The key problems confronting underdeveloped countries are the

---

[13]Nurkse, *op. cit.*, pp. 15-16, 43, 76, 90-91, 143, 148-50; Hirschman, *op. cit.*, pp. 14, 112-13; see also Albert O. Hirschman, *Journeys Toward Progress* (New York, 1963), *passim.;* Lewis, *op. cit.*, pp. 422-23, 434. The experiences of other nations were also relevant, but this does not alter the argument.

survival of the centralized polity and the existing regime. Neither can claim the likelihood of permanence. The centralized polity, often the rather recent creation of a former colonial power, has institutions too new or too dubious to be accorded deference and legitimacy by various elites in the country. Even the nation's existence is menaced from many sources: threats of and attempts at secession; over-weening neighbors, allies, and would-be allies; and retreats into regional and village loyalties and consequent starving of resources and support for the central government's objectives.[14] The existing regime is always a changing coalition, resting in varying proportions on charisma, promises, and coercion. Each of these has built-in limitations— limitations insofar as many demands are exclusive of others in their fulfillment, limitations to the endurance of coercion and restraints by various groups, limitations in resources (which are much more than economic resources) to meet promises, limitations to the mystique of the nationalist movement, "the hero of Independence," the popular military figure. Much of modern economic analysis, however, was developed for an economic sub-system in a larger social system in which the political problems confronted by most underdeveloped countries had been largely solved or the pace of industrialization had not raised them as starkly. The centralized polity's existence could be assumed, and the ruling regime was expected primarily to help make the market mechanism more efficient and more authoritative.[15] This assumed virtual autonomy of the economic sphere was and is theoretically more acceptable for, say, Great Britain or the United States than it can be in the foreseeable future for underdeveloped countries. In the latter, the initial political prerequisites for a functioning national market are not yet met, and it is, furthermore, the intention of most of the regimes to rely (optimistically, of course) on the political marketplace in the first instance as the authoritative allocator of resources and power.

There are other reasons as well for the difficulty inherent in implementing these economic strategies. One is the extreme division of labor and consequent assumptions dominant in the social sciences.[16] Each discipline has staked out a process, defined perhaps too sharply the relevant variables, developed intrinsic indices, and tended to erect boundaries against trespassing from the other social sciences. When representatives of other social sciences have, nevertheless, successfully crossed the boundaries, the "host" social science incorporates a previously exogenous variable into its system. But

[14]See, for example, Reinhard Bendix, "Public Authority in a Developing Political Community: the Case of India," *Archives Européennes de Sociologie,* IV (1963), 39-85; Selig S. Harrison, *India: the Most Dangerous Decades* (Princeton, 1960).

[15]This point cannot be adequately developed in an article of this length. Indirectly, a similar argument can be inferred from: Joseph A. Schumpeter, *History of Economic Analysis* (New York, 1954), pp. 143-208; Bert F. Hoselitz, "The Scope and History of Theories of Economic Growth," *Revista de Economía Política,* V (May 1953), 9-28; William Letwin, *The Origins of Scientific Economics* (London, 1963), *passim.;* Karl Polanyi, *The Great Transformation* (New York, 1944), Chs. 10 and 19.

[16]See also Fred W. Riggs, *Administration in Developing Countries: The Theory of Prismatic Society* (Boston, 1964), pp. 19-31.

there is seldom a cross-disciplinary attempt to penetrate the interrelationship of "each discipline's variables" in terms of the social system as a whole.[17] The three economic strategies analyzed in this article are premised on an essentially autonomous economic sphere in which government and/or private persons make decisions about directly productive activities and related social overhead. The strategies accept as evidence of success, among other economic indicators, an increase in gross national product or a decrease in the incremental capital/output ratio. But these decisions subsume other crucial decisions and judgments. The major judgment is simply that there *will be* a long run for which the short-term sacrifice in consumption is made. This judgment, which is more explicit in underdeveloped countries than can be imagined by analysts from politically well established nations, is the product of other judgments and decisions: a nation's laws will be honored; social conflict can be contained in the institutions of the state; the administrative apparatus is adequate and predictable enough to make just and rapid decisions; material productivity is a "good;" the present distribution of privilege, power, and resources is desirable and/or sufficiently supported, etc. As can easily be seen, the underlying judgments are narrowly social and political in character. The relevant data are not simply economic and cannot be viewed so restrictively.

Another reason stems from a misunderstanding of the mandate given by rulers of underdeveloped countries. The mandate is never a *carte blanche* for development in the most efficient way. In addition to the usual limitations on productive factors, economic development programs are limited by the character and intentions of the existing political regime and social system. The concept of "rising expectations" refers to different sectors (social and economic) and their differing demands, not a unanimous "general will" in this direction.[18] Phrases like "Arab Socialism," "communocracy," and "socialist pattern of society" may imply a "general will," but they must always be interpreted in terms of the elites endorsing these phrases. Furthermore, no nation has ever had or could have an exclusive, secular goal of economic development to which all others must be subordinated. The elites and mobilized publics of every nation, rich and poor, have many objectives for public policy: national survival, national grandeur, distributive-welfare goals, political stability, maximum public choice, maintaining a particular elite combination in power, and the "higher life" among them.[19] While it is true that economic development is necessary for some of these goals, it is also true that economic development is not sufficient. In other

[17]An obvious "heroic" exception is Talcott Parsons and Neil J. Smelser, *Economy and Society* (London, 1956).

[18]An interesting study of a nation's sectors and their demands in Myron Weiner, *The Politics of Scarcity, Public Pressure and Political Response in India* (Bombay, 1963).

[19]See, for example, Rupert Emerson, "Nationalism and Political Development," *Journal of Politics,* XXII (February 1960), 3-28.

goals, it is dysfunctional.[20] In most cases, the other public goals and economic development are mutually necessary. Ignoring this, some economic strategists complain about "prestige" expenditures and concentration on "unproductive" activities. These complaints, heard often from professional economists in underdeveloped countries, place a great burden on the political system. Trained as they and their Western counterparts are in a discipline concerned with the most productive use of scarce resources, they are uncomfortable in the face of politics and the ambiguities of social structure and cultural values.[21] There is a growing feeling among these people that anything short of exclusive concentration on the goal of economic growth is treason by the politicians. A political system able to arbitrate many claims and move toward many common goals cannot long bear this alienation.

How would a more integrated social science be of greater relevance for the problems of underdeveloped countries? Basically, a new question must replace the "economic growth" question. Rather than "How should a nation allocate its scarce resources to achieve economic growth?" the question should be, "How should a government allocate its scarce resources to modernize?" This permits the social scientist and the policy-maker to look at a total social system and its institutions and puts economic growth where it belongs, as part of a broader process—the process of modernization. Modernization can be defined generally as a process of improving the capability of a nation's institutions and value system to meet increasing and different demands.[22] Theoretically, a modern nation is one in which the institutions and values are able to meet or adequately handle the increasing and different demands made on them. Political modernization, for example, involves improving the capability of the political system. The general modernization process is dependent on securing a centralized polity, its penetration into the various spheres of life, and obtaining for the polity free-floating resources, unattached to any ascriptive group, to pursue further

20See, for example, Bert F. Hoselita and Myron Weiner, "Economic Development and Political Stability in India," *Dissent*, VIII (Spring 1961), 172-84.

21For an example of an economist handling the political preconditions of economic development in terms of an autonomous (i.e., less subject to the influence of the political sub-system) economic system and the consequent role for the state to play, see Joseph J. Spengler, "Economic Development: Political Preconditions and Political Consequences," *Journal of Politics*, XXII (August 1960), 387-416. Among other things, Professor Spengler argues, "Only a well-entrenched party, or a pair of parties strongly committed to economic development, is likely to be able to keep the ideology of development effectively alive, to impose the necessary costs of development on the population, and yet to remain in office long enough to get economic growth effectively underway. A dictatorship might find itself in somewhat similar position, given that it sought to promote economic growth and had fairly widespread support . . . a multi-party system is not compatible with economic growth; it is too likely to give in to ever-present demands for "liberal" welfare-state provisions." In other words, a moratorium must be called on politics to achieve the optimum product of a nation's scarce resources.

22See S. N. Eisenstadt, "Modernization: Growth and Diversity," *India Quarterly*, XX (January-March 1964), 17-24; S. N. Eisenstadt, *The Political Systems of Empires* (New York, 1963), pp. 3-32.

modernizing goals. It is also dependent on changing certain values: acquiring a new time perspective, a different valuation of the objectives of the state, a changed allegiance from particularistic to broader, more functionally specific associations and institutions, and, finally, new assessments of human activity and achievement. Developing the capability to meet changing and increasing demands is by no means a settled achievement of the underdeveloped nations.[23]

How do "modernization" and "economic growth" differ? The latter becomes part of the former. As a process, modernization is social and political as well as economic. Indeed, to separate the activities is to suggest a divisible character of the phenomena which does not exist. Although economic growth is one way of increasing the stock of free-floating resources to meet demands, it is not exhaustive. The range of demands includes claims for prestige, status, and power; these demands may or may not require economic resources. But like economic growth, modernization must be planned and, above all, invested in as rationally as in the too narrowly conceived directly productive activities and social overhead capital.

Viewed from the perspective of modernization, the concept of social overhead becomes useful in formulating strategy. Social overhead or "infrastructure" permits thinking about essential conditions for building a modernized nation. In doing so, it makes more explicit the character of the social system and, particularly, the role of the state. Society must be seen in terms of developing within it new structures and sanctioning different values: institutions to integrate the members of society, who were forced to leave traditional institutions and values, into new, more materially productive relationships, values to justify modernization as a process. These, too, constitute infrastructure—social infrastructure. Likewise, a modernization strategy casts the state into a more realistic role. The state becomes more than a "fomenter" or the best instrument for capital formation, as it is for the economic development strategies; it becomes the authoritative allocator of society's scarce values and resources—even when the authoritative decision is in favor of the private sector. For the objectives of public policy, the state becomes the arbiter of claims—economic, social, ideological, and philosophical—made by the sectors of society. To fulfill these functions, particularly as they expand in later phases of modernization, a solid political infrastructure must be built: institutions to contain conflict; institutions to aggregate and simplify claims; value systems which accept the legitimacy of the state's authoritative allocations. Just such institutions and values preceded and became more implicit in the modernization of the West and were subsumed in the development of modern economic thought. Finally, an administrative infrastructure is needed. This the economic development strategists also recognize. But the modernization perspective does not allow

[23]See the excellent study by Lucian W. Pye, *Politics, Personality and Nations Building: Burma's Search for Identity* (New Haven, 1962), pp. 3 ff. See also Herbert Feith, *Decline of Constitutional Democracy in Indonesia* (Ithaca, 1962).

the glib suggestion that administration must switch from "law-and-order values" to development values! Modernization brings in its wake intensified social problems for which increased expenditures on law-and-order institutions and values are required. At the same time, the administrative infrastructure must be expanded in new directions, with emphasis on values of expedition in non-law-and-order fields; on skills—economic, sociological, and managerial—to comprehend the wider range of relevant phenomena and activity; and on institutions designed to cope with the needs for coordination. Infrastructure, hence, is too inadequately conceived by strategists for economic development. The viable modernized state which would have as a major activity economic development requires conscious and rational investments in social, political, and administrative infrastructure as well.

Perhaps the concept of modernized values needs further explanation. How does a state encourage in its citizens the longer time perspective, the revised valuation on the objectives of the state, the shifting allegiance from particularistic to more universalistic associations and the new assessments of human activity and achievements? The answer is: in terms of rational, planned investments. One difference, however, is that the concept of resources for investment, as understood by economic development strategists, must be expanded. Resources, as used here, include coercion, threats of coercion, economic resources, power to command resources, prestige, and security. These "factors" are brought together in different proportions for the major investments to obtain the needed value changes.[24]

Three major types of investments can be thought of for modernization of the state: stability investments, legitimacy investments, and solidarity investments. The contents, proportions, and amount of resources for each differ. Stability investments are allocations aimed at reducing potential and probable opposition to civil authority. Opposition, in this case, might take the form of secessionist groups, radical trade unions, or an urban mob of unemployed. In content, the "investment" would mainly include coercion, threats of coercion, and economic resources. By proportion and amount,

[24] An increasing example of how the economist is now widening his concept of investment in the sphere of education. The usual practice, when projecting future demand and production patterns, by means of input-output models or linear programming models, has been to treat the labor inputs as given, along with the capital inputs. However, it is obvious that labor is no homogeneous input, which is given like any natural resource. Investments have to be made to create the skills required for different productive activities. The amounts of such investments are dependent on the level and nature of these activities. Therefore, if in a linear programming model, an attempt is being made to obtain the optimal allocation of all available resources, the activity by which human skills are created should also be included along with the other activities, and not as a primary input. Only in this way can the economically optimal allocation be approximated. If, however, the investments in creating skills are treated as exogenous, to be determined on the basis of the optimal investment pattern, it is unlikely to obtain the "optimal results." For if the costs of creating the skills were attributed to different activities, the model would in all likelihood give a different pattern. This is a fact which economists are only realizing now. This article's contention is that there are other activities in which resources have to be invested, even if the only goal is the maximization of output.

there would be a heavy emphasis on coercion and meeting demands with economic resources. Legitimacy investments are very similar to stability investments, but go farther. They are investments aimed at inculcating acceptance of civil authority as right and correct, at discouraging in the public any feeling that they have a right to make authoritative allocations except through civil authorities. These investments, made for instance in educational programs, are comprised of coercion, threats of coercion, power to command economic resources, and economic resources. But the proportion of resources and coercion decreases. The decrease in coercion is primarily due to the fact that the state can rely on the traditional acceptance of authority by most citizens, and the threat of coercion, usually handled in terms of consequences resulting from the deprivation of authority, is adequate. Legitimacy investments can also be made by sharing the power to command economic resources—hitherto reserved by the central government—with local governments. Panchayati Raj is conferring legitimacy on the Indian state and its authoritative acts by sharing power with local governments.

But this last example could easily be used to illustrate the third investment level—solidarity investments. These investments are aimed at securing emotional commitments to the state and a willingness to sacrifice personal resources and forego demands for it. Coercion and threats of coercion are absent in these investments, except insofar as they define people outside the state. Prestige, security, power to command economic resources—all are involved. Identifying a sector (such as private business) as patriotically useful, an important role at the United Nations, safeguarding the population against the "enemy," participation through representative bodies, and allocations of resources for "regional balance," stadia, national air lines—all conduce to integration into the structures and values of a modernized state. In all three types of investment, the size of each decreases over time, though reduced recurrent expenditures continue.

Free primary education might be useful in illustrating this concept. Some economic development strategists are increasingly finding free primary education a luxury consumption expenditure and argue for greater expenditures in higher and more technical education or more directly productive activities.[25] On the other hand, a modernization strategy might use free primary education in several ways. As a stability investment, it might be useful as a way of pacifying dissident groups, as part of a *quid pro quo* for civil obedience. Or, in the context of a rapidly modernizing society, the denial of free primary education might be destabilizing to large numbers of status-conscious parents. But free primary education is mostly relevant as an investment in legitimacy and solidarity. Not only does this means of human

[25]See, for example, Sixto K. Roxas, "Investment in Education: The Philippine Experience," *The Philippine Economy Bulletin,* II (September-October 1963), 32-38. The authors are not including in the above statement the excellent recent work of Professors Harbison and Myers, although their "human resource development orientation" is concerned essentially with skills, not values. See Frederick Harbison and Charles A. Myers, *Education, Manpower, and Economic Growth* (New York, 1964).

improvement (status and income) come from the state, but it provides an opportunity to teach "the rules of the game" to a modernizing nation's young citizens. As a solidarity investment, it provides a common experience for citizenship, avoids the extremes of education and the resulting social friction, provides an opportunity to stress the importance of the state, modernization, and all its other values. As an economic investment, the arguments for free primary education are obvious.

Most economic development strategists do not recognize these social and political investments. They make little room for them in their writings and calculations. When these investments are made, as they will be, the strategists label them "compromises," "politically motivated," "prestige items," and "unproductive." Yet, these investments provide the basis for subsequent investments in directly productive activities. Without these prior investments, "correct decisions" will not be made or maintained. These are investments in modernization values. And, if understood from a modernization perspective, they can be made with greater rationality and efficiency. Indeed, many of these investments would be acceptable as sound under the stricter criterion of economic development strategy.

If the appropriate question is "modernization" and not "economic growth," then social scientists must work on strategies jointly. For data, they have the tools and findings of survey research, the growing compilations of political and social quantitative indicators, and the record of modernizing activities of, among many others, Napoleon, Bismarck, the Bolsheviks, the Congress Party of India, Mexico's PRI, Nasser, and Mao Tse-Tung. Much needs to be known about the character of social change; greater precision must be achieved in defining problems and seeking relationships of variables within the wider social system. Indeed, it might be suggested that modernization first begin in the social sciences.

Part Three: Land and the Peasants

Communism and the Peasants

David Mitrany

18

The most effective side of the Communist advance, and the least understood, has been the association between Communists and peasants in eastern Europe and in Asia.

Marxism was a doctrine for the industrial proletariat, and a movement by the proletariat for taking over the most advanced strongholds of industrial capitalism. In fact, Communism has so far nowhere come within reach of power in Western industrial countries; it has secured power only in undeveloped peasant countries. In every instance, from 1917 in Russia to 1949 in China, Communism has risen to victory on the back of disaffected peasantries. So far, it has always been a proletarian revolution without a proletariat, a matter of Communist management of peasant discontent. But while this shows that in the countries where this happened the peasants were ripe for revolt, it does not show that they inclined to Communism. As regards eastern Europe, at any rate, the evidence is all the other way.

From *The Annals of the American Academy of Political and Social Science,* July 1951. Reprinted by permission. The author was, until his retirement, William Allen Nielson Research Professor at Smith College.

Marxist View of Peasants

That actual association between Communists and peasants rests on a double paradox. Neither side expected or wanted the alliance. All Marxists, whether Socialists or Communists, have for the past century refused to have anything to do with the peasants politically, or to help the peasants in any way socially. As early as 1848, in the *Communist Manifesto*, Marx declared the peasants to be an anachronism and moribund as a class. To Marx and Engels, concentration in ownership and especially in production was the mark of economic advance. In *Das Kapital* Marx simply assumed that agriculture, like industry, must develop into ever larger units of production. He therefore laid it down as the goal of socialist policy to have a relatively small number of very large farm units which would be farmed with "armies of laborers."

That doctrine remained a sacred prescription with Marxists everywhere. Even the British Labor party, which has always been more Fabian than Marxist, insisted on the need to nationalize the land and agriculture right up to 1945; that is, until it came to power. As regards political action, Marx also looked upon the peasants as merely the least stupid among the beasts of the farmyard, and therefore as quite incapable of any revolutionary action. He even found it in him to praise capitalism for having rescued, as he said, large numbers of people from the idiocy of rural life. At no time did Socialists or Communists try to work out a political program of common action with the peasants, nor did they ever mitigate the demand for the dictatorship of the proletariat, even in the eastern countries where the peasants formed the bulk of the population.

Peasants' View of Marxism

As for the peasants, they never had any use for the ideas and policy of Marxism. To them, the traditional peasant homestead was not merely a means of living but a way of life. They were inclined to be devout, and found the harsh materialism of Marxist doctrine repugnant. Everywhere they had a tradition of mutual self-help, but not of class. All of them, rich and poor, disliked the economic and cultural domination of the towns, and had little understanding for the abstract revolutionary creed of Marxism or liking for its idea of a centralized planned economy. All they wanted was more land and a decent administration, and everywhere they seemed to prefer to get that by normal political action and to pay for it.

There is no instance of any substantial peasant group joining politically with Socialists or Communists. In western Europe the peasants formerly struggled together with the radical townspeople and the workers against autocracy and aristocratic privileges, but the rise of Marxist Socialism drove them rather into the arms of Conservative parties and groups. In central and eastern Europe, where peasants were numerous and workers few, peasants formed strong and progressive democratic parties of their own.

Leninist Adaptation

No one, therefore, could have foreseen that the peasants of eastern Europe and of Asia would become the instrument for the victory of Communist regimes. That was made possible by two things, one positive and one negative. On the one side there was the remarkably astute insight of Lenin; on the other, the curious indifference of the West. After the collapse of the rising of 1905, Lenin realized that revolution could not succeed in Russia unless it had the support of the peasant masses. From that moment he worked assiduously in his writings and in his actions to bring about at the crucial moment the possibility of joint action between Communists and peasants; and to that end he modified, against severe criticism from purer Marxists, the ideas and prescription of Marx on the agrarian problem.

Lenin did not give up the central idea of an economic system based on industrial development and on centralized control, or the idea of the necessary dictatorship of the proletariat so as to lead the revolution to an effective conclusion. But he insisted that when the revolution occurred, land would have to be given to the mass of the peasants, in small equal holdings of the kind which the peasants thought to be fair. Secondly, he believed and taught that the ultimate aim of a collectivized agriculture could be achieved only by converting the peasants to voluntary acceptance of the idea, and that it would therefore be a long, gradual process. It was, indeed, the handing over of the land to the peasants at once, without restriction and without compensation, that made possible the Bolshevik victory in October 1917.

Western Indifference

Western liberals never adapted their ideas and actions in a similar way to the realities of the democratic problem in eastern Europe and elsewhere. They took a deep interest in the struggle of the eastern people for national liberation, and in general infused a more liberal content into international relations. Yet it was the same liberal trend, concerned as it was above all with democratic political forms, that showed little sense that independence would not mean much to those people unless it brought them social improvement, and that the core of the social problem in the East was the fate of the peasants. Western Socialists added to an equal indifference a positive dislike of the peasants, in the true Marxist tradition.

When, at the end of the first World War, the empires of central and eastern Europe collapsed, the liberal peacemakers at Versailles showed concern only for national self-determination; in spite of the Russian Revolution, they ignored the social implications of that collapse, while the Socialists blundered into trying to set up in Munich and Vienna and Budapest Socialist regimes in the midst of a peasant countryside. One English Socialist, at least, later realized the mistake. He wrote:

To the Balkan peoples the indissoluble connection between national unity, individual liberty and peasant proprietorship seemed as self-evident as it did to Tom Paine; to Western industrial workers it had no sort of significance; to the Communists it was an outworn ideology which must be ruthlessly crushed. Once again as in 1848 the democratic revolution failed to reach completion, but this time the Western democrats failed to show any concern over its failure.

It is still more strange that, in spite of the swelling totalitarian current, Western liberals and Socialists in general did not change their attitude during the interwar period and during the Second World War. In central and eastern Europe, outside Russia, an impressive peasant movement sprang up after 1919. Without exception, those Peasant parties were progressive and democratic, they stood firmly for international peace, and while they all supported a policy of friendly relations with the Soviet Union, they would have nothing to do with Communism as such. They were out to secure better government and a better life for the masses in their respective countries, and for that very reason they became the butt of persecution and violence on the part of the old landed and privileged groups in those countries. The cry was always against the Communist wolf, but it was the peasant shepherds that were imprisoned or murdered or ostracized.

In no instance, however, did a Western government protest against that violence, in the way that those governments have repeatedly protested against the denial of free elections in those parts since 1945. Though the Peasant parties and movement were clearly the only safe bulwark against totalitarianism from either Left or Right, the Western governments showed no hesitation in working with the oppressive and brittle dictatorial regimes of Marshal Pilsudski and Admiral Horthy, of Prince Paul and King Boris and King Carol.

The Cost

Western liberalism and Socialists in general were to pay heavily for such neglect of the peasants. During the Second World War, when the support of the peasants was vital, their political leaders were given prominent positions in all the Eastern governments in exile. But when the war ended with the victorious Soviet advance, the Western governments were unable to secure for the peasants equal standing in the so-called governments of popular union which, under strong Communist pressure, were set up in the countries of eastern Europe. With great difficulty they secured a place for Mikolajczyk in the Polish government, but he soon found himself checked in his work and had to flee the country to save himself. In Rumania, in Hungary, in Bulgaria, in Yugoslavia, the old Peasant leaders were imprisoned or hanged unless they were able to escape, so the chief of them went into exile, this time in Washington, where they set up an International Peasant Union. Dictatorship from the Left thus continued and completed the work of destroying the democratic Peasant movement which dictatorship from the Right had started in central and eastern Europe.

As for the Socialists, they not only found themselves as Marxists impotent to resist Communist pressure and tactics; they actually shared in the undermining of the Peasant groups, only to be themselves destroyed as separate political groups. Indeed, throughout the eastern half of Europe the democratic Socialists have been wiped out even more thoroughly than have the Peasant groups.

Communist Use of Peasants

The curious side, and the significant lesson, of those events is that while the Socialists tried to remain good Marxists, the Communists only cared to remain good Leninists. To them the only goal that mattered was power, and to that end their tactics were as adaptable as their policy was un-Marxist.

The position was very different from that in 1917. Then the Bolsheviks had been faced with a widespread peasant revolution, and the only thing they could do was to go along with it. In 1945, the Soviet armies and Communist groups were in control throughout the eastern half of Europe, and they would have found it easy to impose the nationalization of the land and the collectivization of agriculture, which in the meantime had been completed in Russia. Instead, they did the very opposite. While they destroyed the political peasant movement, socially they applied the full peasant program. Large estates and farms, and even the holdings of the richer peasants, were broken up and distributed in very small lots to the mass of poor peasants. This was done even in the Soviet zone of Germany, and everywhere quickly, without any preparation or plan, mostly through local peasant committees, and inevitably with serious if temporary detriment to agricultural production.

The picture is completed by the skillful and effective way in which the Chinese Communists used the long sufferings and the land hunger of the peasants to open up for themselves the road to power. The land problem is, if anything, more acute in the countries of Asia than it ever was in eastern Europe. Not long ago an American writer, Mr. Erich Jacoby, showed in a careful study how in the past decades peasant subsistence farming had been pressed back by commercial farming for export; production had risen, but not the "level of living." When opening the Indian National Commission for Cooperation with UNESCO, in the spring of 1949, Mr. Nehru told the assembly that "the agrarian problem is naturally the most important problem in Asia, and a body connected with UNESCO must have full appreciation of this."

Hence, in China as in eastern Europe, land reform was the first and most important reform carried out when Communists took charge anywhere. The attitude of the Communists did not mean, however, that they had abandoned Communism and that they had come to love the peasants. It only meant, as Stalin has more than once explained, that they had learned to turn the peasants, during the revolutionary struggle, from a possible reserve of the bourgeoisie into an active reserve of the proletariat. That was indeed the lesson which the Soviet leaders passed on to their lieutenants in every place where peasants still formed a powerful section of the working population. Not only in eastern Europe and in Asia, but in Italy and France and elsewhere, the Communists work hard to gain access to the countryside, and to that end do not hesitate to leave their Marxism at home.

Un-Marxist Action

There is, indeed, a very interesting theoretical side to this story. From the point of view of Marxist theory and practice, the whole Communist action is as un-Marxist as it could well be. It is true that in the meantime in Russia, and to some extent in the eastern countries of Europe, the policy has been reversed and agriculture has been or is being collectivized. But this does not happen in the Marxian way. To Marx, growing concentration in production was simply a law of economic nature. Hence he assumed and prescribed it as the only possible trend for Socialist society. Yet, unlike the growth in industry, in agriculture such concentration has nowhere come to pass as part of the natural evolution of economic life under capitalism. As for the Communist system, concentration in agriculture has had to be imposed by force and maintained by force.

In a genial moment, during one of their wartime meetings, Marshal Stalin confided to Mr. Winston Churchill that collectivization had been a "second revolution," and one tougher and more dangerous than the first. The Marshal did not complete the picture by explaining that that second revolution was directed not against feudal landlords and bourgeois capitalists, but against the hardest-working section of the working class. But that no doubt explains why, fully a generation after the Communist triumph in Russia and with Russian collectivization completed, at the moment of their great military and political victory the Soviets in 1945 nowhere tried to apply their Marxist program, but instead applied an extreme peasant program.

The political consequence of this is also bound to be highly un-Marxist. No doubt, wherever they have the chance, the Communists will try to revert, as they have done in Russia, to the agrarian formula of Marxism. But given the nature of the countries in which they have come to power, they can do so only insofar as they can build up a large industry and in the process also a large proletarian class. To that end they must impose prolonged and heavy sacrifices upon the mass of the peasant population. The probability therefore is that, as in Russia, the policy of forced economic development will go hand in hand with a long period of uncompromising political dictatorship.

Marxist Theory Disproved

In the light of the erstwhile socialist ideal, the upshot is certainly strange. Through a combination of undialectical circumstances, the Communists have come to power, from 1917 in Russia to 1949 in China, only as leaders of peasant-agrarian revolutions. Because of that, the agrarian side of Marxist theory, with its "scientific" claims, is the only side which so far has been tested in practice. In the process, that theory has been proved wrong in every respect. Marx's analysis of the evolution of agriculture has nowhere been proved right; his prescription for the organization of agricultural production has never come to be practiced as part of a normal economic evolution.

The Marxist view of the backwardness and political incapacity of the peasants has been made ridiculous by the dependence of the Communist advance on the peasants' political temper and stamina; but the expectation of a natural revolutionary alliance between proletariat and poor peasants through class division in the village, in spite of much Communist effort and propaganda, has never materialized. In no instance has communism as such been supported consciously and deliberately by the peasants, and in no instance has the victory of the Communists been simply the success of their own efforts and program. In every instance the Marxist agrarian idea, when tried, has had to be applied by force and to rely on force for its survival; while the Socialist groups which wanted to remain democratic have in every instance had to abandon it altogether.

The historical reality of the whole revolutionary episode since 1917 is therefore a vast peasant uprising over half of Europe and most of Asia, the final demolition of feudal conditions on the land. Marxism has had nothing to contribute to that, whether as a theory or as a movement. The Communist part in that great historical upheaval was accidental and has remained artificial. Insofar as it has been successful politically, it has been the very negation of Marxist doctrine. The Communist advance has been a series of tactical victories. It would have had little chance had not the Western liberal movement of the new middle class, and the social movement of the new working class, been afflicted with an introverted urbanism which caused them to remain as indifferent to as they were ignorant of the tremendous social and political implications of the peasant problem in eastern Europe and in Asia.

Stages in Agricultural Development

Clifton R. Wharton, Jr.

19

Agricultural economists have not been immune to the current vogue [Hoselitz[1]] of "staging" agricultural development employing historical analogies. Three models that attempt to classify the agricultural developmental process have recently been put forward: Perkins-Witt,[2] Johnston-Mellor,[3] and Hill-Mosher.[4]

The Perkins-Witt classification of stages is based upon the process of agricultural and general development. Their main focus is upon the process of capital formation and capital allocation:

> *Stage I*   A large subsistence sector in agriculture and unused agricultural resources which can be used for output

Excerpt from *Research on Agricultural Development in Southeast Asia,* a publication of the Agricultural Development Council. Reprinted by permission. The author is Vice-President of the Agricultural Development Council.

[1]B. F. Hoselitz, "Theories of Stages of Economic Growth", in *Theories of Economic Growth*, B. F. Hoselitz, ed. (The Free Press, Glencoe, Illinois, 1960).

[2]Maurice Perkins and Laurence Witt, "Capital Formation, Past and Present", *Journal of Farm Economics,* May 1961.

[3]J. W. Mellor, "The Use and Productivity of Farm Family Labor in Early Stages of Agricultural Development", *Journal of Farm Economics,* August 1963.

[4]F. F. Hill and A. T. Mosher, *Organizing for Agricultural Development*, Monograph for U.N. Conference on Application of Science and Technology, Geneva, February 1963.

increases without technological change. Capital formation is through investment of surplus labor.

Stage II   No unused agricultural resources remain and increases in output can only take place through technological changes. Social overhead capital investments become important as do education, training programs, research and extension.

Stage III   The subsistence sector disappears, capital substitution for labor becomes profitable, and a technologically advanced and commercial agriculture has developed.

The Johnston-Mellor stages are focused primarily on agriculture as a whole and are defined as:

Stage I   "Providing agricultural development preconditions."
A phase which is technologically stagnant, but during which changes occur in attitudes and institutions required for later technological advance. Some change or increase in production is possible with traditional techniques and inputs, but the magnitudes are not impressive, and technology is static.

Stage II   "Rising agricultural production—low-capital, labor-intensive technology."
A phase when dynamic development begins, characterized by a continuing rate of increase which is initially the result of a few "large-return" innovations but later the result of a larger number of changes with smaller individual response, although with large aggregate impact. This phase witnesses a gradual reduction in agriculture's share of national production and a rise in labor-saving machinery (or a rise in the capital-labor ratio). The emphasis here is on technological advance and reapportioning of factors of production.

Stage III   "Rising agricultural production—high-capital, labor-saving technology."
A phase where man-land ratios have fallen due to the substitution of labor-saving machinery, which has resulted from a rise in the productivity of labor (higher opportunity costs), and where agriculture occupies a much smaller proportion of the economy.

The Hill-Mosher taxonomy is very similar to the Johnston-Mellor one although the terminology differs and the focus is upon the characteristics of the individual farm:

Stage I   "Traditional"
Techniques of production are traditional; family labor is primarily used, and farm production is mainly or entirely consumed by the family. The farm-home complex is a self-contained unit and a very few factor inputs are purchased which are produced in the non-farm sector.

Stage II   "Transitional"
This phase is characterized by an increased use of purchased inputs for both farm and home, by a larger fraction of farm production sold, and by a greater degree of specialization in production. This phase also involves a change from tradition to choice-making agriculture.

Stage III   "Commercial"
Commercialization is virtually complete, i.e. nearly all factor inputs and farm production go through the market process. Decision-making is more oriented toward costs and receipts than toward family consumption needs.

Despite slight differences in emphasis, Stages I and II in all three models are essentially the same. If one were to synthesize the three models into one, there are ten elements which can be discerned upon which attention is focused:

1. General values, attitudes and motivations.
2. Goals of production.
3. Nature of decision-making process.
4. Technology or state of arts.
5. Degree of commercialization of production.
6. Degree of commercialization of farm inputs.
7. Factor proportions and rates of return.
8. Infrastructure institutions affecting or serving agriculture.
9. Availability of unused agricultural resources.
10. Share of agricultural sector in total economy.

Chart 1 is an attempt to present a synthesis of the three models in a somewhat more systematic form, and views the ten elements as though each operates in a separate spectrum. Stage I is essentially viewed as a "static" or "backward" period; Stage II as the "transitional" or change-over period; and Stage III, as the "dynamic" or advanced period.

The taxonomers who have developed these models recognize that the models are generalized approximations of reality. Countries, like people, are not homogeneous and each maintains its individuality and special character. Thus a country may have six of the elements fall into Stage I and four fall into Stage II.[5]

Whenever considering "staging models," I am always tempted to view the process as a continuous curve which looks like an adoption curve or cumulative probability curve, and would prefer to divide the process up into just two stages. Stage I would then be that portion of the curve up to the mid-point and Stage II would be the portion beyond the mid-point. The "take-off" point into self-sustained growth is then merely the point of inflection or a very narrow range around the mid-point.

[5]This point has been stressed by my colleague, Dr. H. W. Beers.

Chart 1. A Diagrammatic Summary of Ten Major
Characteristics of Agricultural Development
from Stage I through Stage II and into Stage III[a]

		Stage I	Stage II.	Stage III
General Character		Static ——→	Transitional ——→	Dynamic
1.	General values, attitudes, motivations (orientation to change)	Negative or resistant		Positive or receptive
2.	Goals of production	Family consumption and survival		Income and net profit
3.	Nature of decision-making process	Irrational or traditional		Rational or "choice-making"
4.	Technology or state of arts	Static or traditional with no or slow innovation		Dynamic or rapid innovation
5.	Degree of commercialization of farm production	Subsistence or semi-subsistence		Commercial
6.	Degree of commercialization of farm inputs	Family labor and farm produced		Commercial
7.	Factor proportions and rates of return	High labor/capital ratio; low labor return		Low labor/capital ratio; high labor return
8.	Infrastructure institutions affecting or serving agriculture	Deficient and imperfect		Efficient and well developed
9.	Availability of unused agricultural resources	Available		Unavailable
10.	Share of agricultural sector in total economy	Large		Small

[a]The chart is an attempt to synthesize the three models of Perkins-Witt, Johnston-Mellor, and Hill-Mosher.

Not all ten elements have either analytical or program significance. Each of the ten elements can be approached from either a descriptive or analytical standpoint. One can either describe the attitudes of farm people in Stage I or one can analyze the role of such attitudes as inhibitors or stimulators of the development process. Although infrequently done, such research might also inquire what are the implications, if any, of these descriptive realities for programs designed to stimulate agricultural development.

If we consider agriculture development to be a desirable goal and if the conditions obtaining for agriculture in Stage III are considered characteristics of goal achievement, then what is desired from any research effort is information useful for getting a country from Stage I to Stage III. Research then takes on a rather special character which seeks the answers to two kinds of questions: (1) What keeps a country's agriculture in Stage I, or what prevents a country from entering Stage II? (2) What makes a country's agriculture enter Stage II and proceed to Stage III? In other words, the goal of research in such a context is not merely to know what the social phenomena studied look like, but rather to discover what impels, motivates, causes, and stimulates the desired change.

I must admit a certain disenchantment with those who approach economic or agricultural development with a "staging" model, since by and large their efforts are directed at categorizing the *descriptive* characteristics of a nation or country in each of the three stages rather than the *analytical* relevance of these characteristics.[6] Knowing that agriculture is the dominant sector of an economy in terms of gross national product, labor force and exports is certainly not as important as knowing what implications this fact has for differential rates of growth between agricultural and non-agricultural sectors. Too frequently, describing the stages has led to a false sense of security that, by knowing the characteristics of the stages, we thereby automatically know what to do to induce the necessary changes. Knowing that a Malayan padi farmer uses a small hand knife to harvest instead of a sickle tells us that he is Stage I and not Stage II, but it does not tell us why he prefers the *tuai* or what real economic effect this has on his yields or how we can get him to change.

However, the ten elements which I have used to synthesize the three models are useful as a "check list" to judge the extent to which information is or is not available on the analytical components, as opposed to the descriptive components, of each stage. Out of such an exercise, I would hope that we could develop a set of research priorities useful for understanding and promoting the process of agricultural development. . . .

[6]This is a point I have made elsewhere. "The only fault which one finds with the 'taxonomers' is that, once their taxonomy is complete, little of analytical or predictable vigor emerges. *Why* is a nation in stage one or stage three? And *what* does a nation have to *do* to go from stage one to stage two? Or, if a nation is now tradition-directed what national policy should the government adopt and what programs should it inaugurate to move from tradition to science as the orientation mechanism?" Clifton R. Wharton, Jr., "Economic and Non-economic Factors in the Agricultural Development of Southeast Asia: Some Research Priorities", Agricultural Development Council paper, August 1962. For more practical and analytic use of stages, see J. W. Mellor, "Increasing Agricultural Production in Early Stages . . . ", *Indian Jour. of Agric. Econ.,* Vol. 17, No. 2 (April-June 1962).

Agricultural Economics and
Agricultural Development

Arthur T. Mosher

20

Agriculture ... means the manipulation of biologic growth, on farms, to produce products useful to man.

... It embraces a great variety of enterprises. It includes farms producing single crops like rice, rubber, and tea. It includes farms of all sizes, each producing many different field crops and livestock products. It includes vegetable farms and fruit orchards. It includes farms devoted exclusively to the production of poultry or of milk. It includes many different combinations of all of these. And these myriad combinations of enterprises on many sizes of farms are not the result of capricious choice; they represent realistic managerial adjustments to differing resources, markets, states of technology, and complementary and supplementary relationships among various crop and livestock enterprises.

From *The Role of Agricultural Economics in Agricultural Development,* a paper of the Agricultural Development Council. This paper was presented at a conference on the teaching of agricultural economics held at the University of Malaya, Kuala Lumpur, in May 1967. Reprinted by permission. The author is Executive Director of the Agricultural Development Council.

... A *farm* ... [is] the basic managerial unit by which agriculture is carried on. As we shall see in discussing agricultural development, managerial decisions on a farm are influenced both by the nature of the resources it can command and by a large number of conditions and influences imposed upon it by the human environment within which it operates. But it is this basic managerial unit that we mean by a farm. The land used by a farm may be owned, or rented, or both. The fields of any one farm may be in one continuous block or they may be at some distance from each other. The physical labor utilized may be that of the manager himself, or the unpaid labor of members of his family, or hired labor, or any combination of these. The "manager" of the farm may be an individual owner or renter, or a joint family, or an employed manager. The activities carried on may be the cultivation of fields, orchards, or gardens, or the husbandry of livestock, or any combination of these. A farm may be an isolated subsistence unit or a corporate estate covering thousands of hectares. What makes any of these a farm is its unity of management. The responsibility of the farm manager may be very broad in a society characterized by strong individualism and by wide availability of land, labor, and credit. Or it may be very narrow, due either to strong traditional influences on what a farm operator may and may not do, or due to rigid governmental regulations. In any case, a *farm* as the term is used in this paper, means the basic managerial unit by which agriculture is carried on.

This concept of the farm is of central importance when we turn our attention to agricultural development. For agricultural economics makes its contributions to agricultural development at the points of *decision-making*. There are two large groups of these decisions. One is the group of decisions about production and marketing made by the operator, the manager, of each farm. The other group of decisions that, taken together, determine the complex environment of laws, prices, markets, transportation, research, and education within which all farms of any given region must operate. Agricultural economics has a contribution to make to both of these groups of decisions, and neither group can be neglected if agricultural development is to be accelerated.

Agricultural Development

By agricultural development I mean a process, over time, through which farms become more productive. This "more productive" may take either or both of two forms. It may be an increase in farm production, or it may be the production of a given value of output at decreasing cost. The first of these is a matter of securing development by achieving full use of available resources at a given level of agricultural technology in practice on farms. It occurs wherever resources previously unused, or used for less productive purposes, are brought into agricultural use either on existing farms or on new farms, thereby increasing agricultural production. The second—raising the level of output or securing any given level of output at decreasing cost by changing the agricultural technology in practice on farms—is the other form of agricultural development and is the more important of the two in the long run. Agricultural economics has a role to play in both, but our discussion in this paper will be chiefly about its role in the latter: agricultural development through changing agricultural technology.

The reason I use the phrase "a process through which *farms* become more productive" instead of saying "a process through which agriculture becomes more productive" in my definition of agricultural development is because it is of the highest importance that we keep the *farm* constantly in mind in all of our thinking about agricultural development. We think more realistically when we think of agriculture not as rice plus corn plus eggs plus papayas in national aggregates but as many, many farms of diverse types, with many joint products and joint costs, and with complementary, supplementary, and competing enterprises. If we are interested in agricultural development we must never forget that the crucial management decisions are made by individual farm managers or operators to maximize utility, or net income, or a combination of these. While we much too frequently forget it, one of the most important responsibilities of agricultural economists to agricultural development is constantly to bear witness to the fact that agriculture is farms.

Before leaving this definition of agricultural development I want to make two comments about it.

My colleague, Dr. A. B. Lewis, in criticizing the first draft of this paper, said: "To me, development is the unfolding of the potentialities of the people who produce goods and services through the use of resources."

There is considerable merit in this definition. Farm practices do not change; they are changed by persons. New fertilizers do not occur by spontaneous generation; they are developed by persons. Crop and livestock enterprises do not arrange themselves; they are arranged by persons. So another way to define agricultural development is to say that it is what happens to farms when people grow in understanding of biological, engineering, and economic relationships and when they increasingly concern themselves about, and grow in skills with respect to manipulating biologic growth, on farms, to produce products useful to man.

Some of these persons who must develop, whose potentialities must come to fruition if farms are to become more productive, are farm managers and farm laborers. Others, as we shall see, are bankers, and merchants, and editors, and statesmen. In this context, the question we are reviewing in this paper is: what is the role of agricultural economics with respect to the development of the people on whom the productivity of farms depends?

My second comment is closely related to this. It is that there are two kinds of resources for agricultural development: economic and self-generating.

It is when we are thinking of agricultural production at a given level of technology that we speak of the necessity of *economizing* in the use of land, capital, and labor. Capital is always scarce, so careful choices must be made between different uses of it to achieve maximum returns from it. Land is usually scarce in this part of the world, so again we must economize in its use. Labor, in the sense of physical manpower to perform specific agricultural tasks, is scarce at least intermittently, usually at seed-time and harvest. Consequently, physical manpower also must be allocated in such a way as to produce maximum returns.

But physical manpower is neither a homogeneous factor in agricultural production nor is it a separate resource; it is always part of a package: the whole person. And each person has other attributes equally important to agricultural development. One of these is his mind; the other is his attitudes and values.

Each man's physical energy can be increased by appropriate nutrition and health practices. How effectively he uses this energy in agricultural production is a matter of skill and dexterity, both subject to training, whether in guiding a plow, tapping a rubber tree, or operating a tractor.

Health, physical vigor, and training in the skills of farm labor are important to agricultural development. Of greater importance, however, is the transformation that can take place in a person's mind, both in his powers of thought and analysis and in his store of knowledge. And equally important to agricultural development are each person's attitudes and values, for it is these that motivate him, urging him to creative thought and action or confirming him in acceptance of his present circumstances.

It is these human powers of mind and these human attitudes and values which constitute important *self-generating* resources for agricultural development. They may be called self-generating because they are cumulative and mutually reinforcing. They are not consumed but are augmented by being used; therefore they need not be economized. The confidence engendered in a farmer by successful adoption of one changed practice makes him more ready to try another. The discovery that one recommendation of an agricultural economist, or of any other expert, is realistic and dependable makes a farmer more ready to listen and to act on other recommendations. As these changed attitudes in individual farmers become more widespread they result in changed social attitudes until a point is reached where change, innovation, and experimentation constitute commendable behavior. This further strengthens the forces making for agricultural development and hence constitutes an important resource in itself.

To repeat, agricultural development is the process by which farms become more productive. This process proceeds by steps, each of which is an additional or a changed practice. Many of these practice changes must be made by the decision of each farm manager or operator. Others must be made by bankers, merchants, all citizens (both rural and urban), and by statesmen, since these decisions determine the legal, commercial, and social environment within which farmers must operate.

There are resources of land, physical labor, and capital that must be economized if agricultural development is to take place. Central to all agricultural development, however, are changes in the human beings involved: increases in manual skills, changes leading to greater capacity for understanding agricultural processes and for making economic choices, and changes in attitudes and values leading to confidence in the possibility of increased agricultural production, confidence in farmers as managers, and confidence in the agencies, both official and non-official, seeking to service and to accelerate agricultural development.

The Role of Agricultural Economics

Agricultural economics is the study of alternatives or of choices within agriculture, and within the national culture but affecting agriculture, with respect to the impact of these alternatives or choices on farm production.

What, then, is the role of this field of study with respect to agricultural development?

To examine this question effectively we must ask it separately about each of a considerable number of the components of agricultural development. What are some of these, and what is the role of agricultural economics with respect to each?

1. *Agricultural development requires an increase in the efficiency of plants and animals in converting soil nutrients and feeds into economic products.*

Throughout the earlier stages of agricultural development this is accomplished by observant farmers through selection and controlled reproduction of the most productive individual plants and animals. One of the earliest contributions of the field of farm management was to study the comparative efficiency of different plants and animals in common use among farmers in relation to farm earnings, and to pass the results of their studies on to other farmers.

In later stages of agricultural development the biological phase of this task of increasing the efficiency of plants and animals is shared by farmers with research workers in the plant and animal sciences. Here, also, the same economic problem arises: How does the adoption of the new strain affect farm earnings?

2. *Agricultural development requires increasing control of diseases and pests of plants and animals.*

The development of techniques for such controls is primarily the responsibility of pathologists and entomologists, but, again, the critical question is this: how do the financial benefits to be secured from the use of these control measures compare with the costs of buying them, applying them, and meeting the other production costs of the increased yields to which they lead? Examples of control measures which lead to increases in output but which cost more than they are worth are not at all uncommon.

3. Agricultural development involves increasing use of fertilizers, and increasing attention to the residual fertility effects of cropping systems.

We all know of examples of unqualified recommendations of particular fertilizers without careful attention having been given to what amounts of the fertilizer to apply to what types of soil, and without prior calculation of the optimum amount of fertilizer to apply from the standpoint of unit costs of the fertilizer and of the value of marginal returns in crop product at different rates of fertilizer application.

Similarly, the problem of whether or not, and to what extent, to leave fields fallow, and the problem of what crops to plant in what sequence from the standpoint of residual soil fertility, are problems requiring analysis in terms of cost, current income, and the value of residual fertility.

The same is true of the question of combinations and quantities of feeds to be fed to livestock.

At the same time (and this point is as good as any other at which to mention it) we must guard against the idea that professional agricultural economists should have a monopoly on cost analysis. Farms and fields vary so enormously in present fertility, and costs of fertilizer vary so much due to transportation costs, and in many regions the extent of homogeneous soils is so restricted relative to the costs of economic analysis of fertilizer responses by professional agricultural economists, that much of this analysis of how much fertilizer to use at what cost on which fields must be left to farmers. Consequently, teaching farmers to read, to calculate, to think about agricultural problems so that they can make their own adaptations of meager research results to local conditions is an important phase of agricultural development.

4. Agricultural development requires an increase in the efficiency of power sources in converting fuel or feed into applied power, and of implements in converting applied power (human, animal, or mechanical) into completed farm operations.

Farmer-inventors, both in the past and at the present time, play a major role in this. Four months ago, in a remote valley of Central Java, I was taken to see a homemade cassava-shredder which greatly reduces the labor involved in a monotonous task. Water-lifts in Egypt, India, and Japan, the Persian wheel, portable hand-powered threshers in Taiwan, and numerous other developments in the field of power and implements are the products of alert and ingenious farmers. Even quite complicated farm machinery is being developed now, as in the past, by skilled and ingenious farmers.

Wherever power sources or implements are purchased rather than home-made in a farmer's spare time, whether developed by farmers or by professional engineers, the advisability of employing any specific power source or implement on a particular farm depends on its cost per unit of performance, with adjustment for any influence on either the quantity or the quality of the product.

5. *Agricultural development requires increasing access to markets for farm products, and increasing efficiency of the marketing process.*

Physical access to markets is primarily a matter of highways and of transportation facilities. With limited governmental revenues where should highways be built or improved, and in what order of priority? It is not up to agricultural economists to build highways, but they do have a contribution to make in calculating the value of highway access to agricultural producers and in establishing priorities for road construction. The recent study of *The Value of Rural Roads in the Philippines,* by the College of Agriculture of the University of the Philippines, is an excellent example of such a contribution.

The efficiency of the marketing process, whether through independent wholesalers and jobbers, or through cooperative societies, or through state agencies, is another field for economic analysis. After they have made such studies, agricultural economists can also be of help in setting up and in administering public marketing agencies to handle agricultural products and to distribute agricultural requisites.

6. *Agricultural development necessitates increasing efficiency in forecasting economic demand and supply of each major agricultural commodity and the probable future trend of specific major costs of producing each.*

As agricultural development proceeds, farm operators have to learn to live more and more in a world of market trends. No longer can a farm operator follow a set pattern of production to provide for a level of home consumption which remains the same from year to year or which changes only in ways he can predict because of his knowledge of his own family's needs. Increasingly he now produces for the market or, more accurately, for a variety of markets, each subject to its own price fluctuations determined by forces of supply and demand and, in many cases, by governmental regulations as well.

Moreover, the production period in agriculture varies from perhaps 80 days in the case of broilers to 12 to 15 months in the case of sugar cane and even longer in the case of certain other agricultural products. Consequently, efficient farm operation requires dependable estimates of markets and costs far in advance. This very large task of collecting and analyzing data with respect to price and market trends is a special responsibility of agricultural economists.

7. Agricultural development involves increasingly widespread use and analysis of farm accounts.

As agriculture becomes more and more commercial, efficiency on the farm requires increasing attention to costs and returns. Even though many operators of wholly commercial farms still do not keep careful financial records even in the most advanced economies, some sort of farm accounting can almost always contribute to more efficient management. Moreover, it is the analysis of such accounts by competent agricultural economists that identifies many of the management practices that lead to more profitable farming.

At the same time, we do well to remind ourselves that many significant facts about efficient farm management do not show up in most types of farm accounts. Consequently, let us go on to recognize that—

8. Agricultural development can be accelerated by continuous study of the effect of different farm practices on farm production and on farm earnings.

In an early stage of agricultural development, farms grow crops and livestock from seeds and young stock produced on the farm. Few, if any, fertilizers, or implements, or feeds, or fuels are purchased. Crop and livestock enterprises are usually determined primarily by consumption needs of the farm family. The chief concern of farm management at this stage of agricultural development is the *utility in home consumption* of grains, tubers, fruits, fibers, and animal products.

At a considerably later stage of agricultural development farms are operated primarily as business "firms," using many materials such as seeds, fuels, feeds, insecticides, implements, etc. purchased in the market either for cash or on credit. Practically all of the products of such farms are sold in the market. The chief concern of farm management at this stage is not utility in home consumption but the margin of total income from agricultural products sold over total production expenses of the farm business (after due allowance for the net value of productive resources on hand at the beginning and at the end of the accounting periods).

Much of the agriculture of Southeast Asia has progressed considerably beyond the self-sufficient "early" stage, but only on numerous vegetable farms near the larger cities and on some large commercial estates has the much later stage of farms as business firms been reached as yet.

In the earlier stages of agricultural development each farmer has choices which affect the volume of production (for which market prices nearly always exist) but which do not involve costs for which a monetary value can be established with any accuracy or even reality. He has a choice as to how thoroughly he destroys weeds in a seed-bed before sowing. He has choices as to how frequently and how thoroughly he weeds his crop after sowing. He has choices as to how and when he will select seed to be sown the following year and as to how he will store that seed. He has choices as to whether he will grow the same crop in a field year after year or whether he will rotate crops in a manner which maintains the field's fertility. He has choices as to whether he will use all of the grain his family produces as human food or whether he will feed part of it to livestock to produce animal products for human consumption and manure for his fields. He has choices as to whether he will allow promiscuous breeding of livestock or will breed only to the best sires. In other words, he has choices in farm *management* that will affect the volume and the nature of physical production within the limits of the resources available to him.

Historically, this is where the study of farm management began. It began by observing the association between specific farm practices, to many of which no monetary cost could be assigned, and total farm production and earning. Invariably, in every country where they have been undertaken, studies of this type have revealed wide variations in the physical volume of production secured by different farm operators from virtually the same "supply" of factors of production. And it has been possible, by identifying the farm practices associated with these variations in production, and by making knowledge of these available to other farmers, to secure substantial increases in total production without purchasing additional resources in the market. Consequently, even in the early stage of agricultural development there is a substantial contribution to be made by the study of farm management even though many of the practices affecting farm production and earnings cannot be expressed in financial terms.

Later on, with more and more requisites of agricultural production being purchased, and with their costs being reflected in financial accounts of farm businesses, we are prone to begin omitting farm practices having no monetary supply cost from our studies of farm management. *Some* of the farm practices conducive to higher production on wholly commercial farms involve easily discernible cash costs. Other practices, such as a choice between two seeds or between two tractors with the same purchase price but fitting into different total farm production plans leading to produce with differing market values, have differing values not reflected in market prices.

In other words, it is *how resources are utilized on the farm* as well as how much they cost in the market that affects net farm earnings. This remains true no matter how far agriculture advances. Consequently, on the *cost* side, farm management must always deal with nonmonetary management practices as well as with market prices even in wholly "commercial" agriculture.

The only way to do this is by continually making studies of the various farm practices associated with different levels of farm production and earnings, whether or not these involve specific monetary costs.

Making such studies, and bringing the results of these studies to the attention of farmers, can be a very important contribution of agricultural economists to agricultural development in Southeast Asia today and in the years to come.

9. *Agricultural development requires enlarged and increasingly appropriate credit facilities for financing agricultural production.*

Here, as in the case of marketing, how much responsibility agricultural economists must take depends on how much actually gets done by others. At the very least, it is agricultural economists who should assess both the amount and the periodicity of the needs of the farmers in particular regions for production credit and who should suggest realistic terms and timing of repayment. Whenever cooperative societies or state credit agencies are involved the role of agricultural economists is much more extensive than this. And if the experience of the United States is any guide, increasing numbers of agricultural economists will be employed by banks, both private and public, to administer their agricultural credit programs as agricultural development proceeds.

10. *Agricultural development necessitates increasing flexibility in shifting lands from less productive to more productive uses.*

The earliest form of this, at a relatively early stage of agricultural development, is land development through clearing, drainage, and irrigation. Very substantial economic problems are involved in this. For what types of agricultural production will a particular tract of land be appropriate after initial development? How does the probable production of the land after development compare with the probable costs of development? Should there be any limitation on the size of farms? If so, what sizes of farms are likely to be most efficient? What credit and marketing facilities will be necessary and how are these to be provided?

At much later stages of agricultural development quite different but equally complex problems keep arising. New findings in the plant and animal sciences make new breeds, varieties, and strains more profitable than the old. Changes in food habits and new industrial processes alter the demands for various agricultural products. Changes in power sources and in implements and in labor rates result in new optimum sizes of farms.

It is the responsibility of the agricultural economist to analyze these trends. While he is advising farm operators, on the one hand, as to the impact on farm efficiency of different choices within the current setting of land use possibilities, he should be advising citizens and governments, on the other, with respect to changes in laws and policies necessary to increasing flexibility in land use to take advantage of emerging technical advances within agriculture.

11. *Agricultural development requires evolution of a pattern of land tenancy and tenure conducive to continuous agricultural development.*

This complicated problem involves social and political values in addition to its effect on agricultural production and efficiency. These other considerations are valid, and certainly we should not suggest that decisions with respect to land tenancy and tenure be left to economic analysis alone.

What each country does need from agricultural economics with respect to this problem is a sound analysis of what effect different systems of tenancy and tenure are likely to have on the rate of agricultural development. I suggest that agricultural economists should ask at least four questions about any proposal in this field:

a. Does the proposal combine the possibility of security of tenure with freedom of entry and exit, so that those now farming may quit if they choose and those not inheriting land may become farmers if they wish?
b. Will the proposed system stimulate productive investments in the land?
c. Will the proposed system be one that provides adequate incentives to the farmer to increase current production?
d. Does the proposed system make adequate provision for changes in the size of farms as agricultural technology and the demand for various agricultural products change?

These are criteria for economic analysis with the results being considered together with social and political factors in making the final decision.

12. *Agricultural development depends in part on a conscious, continuous re-examination of government policies from the standpoint of their impact on agricultural development.*

This is another of the points at which many considerations other than that of agricultural development must be taken into account, but certainly an analysis of general policies from the standpoint of agricultural development should be among the factors considered in determining general public policies. Where governments regulate food prices they face a conflict between the desire to hold down urban living costs and the desire to provide farmers with price incentives for greater production. Policies with respect to degree of national self-sufficiency and degree in international trade have repercussions on opportunities, costs, and markets for agriculture. The allocation of government investments in public works and services as between cities and different rural areas affects agricultural development. Among the responsibilities of agricultural economists is that of analyzing the impact of such general public policies on agricultural production and efficiency and of stating agriculture's case in public forums.

Consideration of these twelve examples of the many specific essentials for agricultural development reminds us of the very substantial role to be played by agricultural economists. It reminds us also that we can do only a fraction of what must be done. The plant and animal sciences, engineering, pathology, and entomology make essential contributions; merchants, bankers, transport agencies, and government policy-makers all have distinctive roles to play; above all, farm operators are the ones who not only do most of the work and much of the innovation, but who must make the vital final decisions about what is to be produced and how. In the last analysis it is their decisions and their managerial skill that determine the rate of agricultural development.

We must guard against a feeling of frustration and confusion when we set the paucity of our numbers against the myriad responsibilities of agricultural economics with respect to agricultural development. What we must do, instead, is to think very hard about the pertinence and priorities of the research projects we undertake, and about the content of the courses in agricultural economics which we teach to young men. Let us make those courses so basic in what we present, so pertinent to the urgent problems of agricultural development in each of our countries, and so challenging in the glimpse they give of unsolved problems awaiting study by dedicated agricultural economists that our numbers may be rapidly increased by many young men more competent than we.

Conclusion

... Throughout, ... I have spoken of agricultural economics, and only seldom of agricultural economists. Agricultural economics is a field of study, and it is the relationship between that field of study and agricultural development that is our topic today. Agricultural economists, on the other hand, are, or ought to be, people. They are called agricultural economists because they are assumed to be and try to be competent in the field of study called agricultural economics.

Surely, however, the interrelationships I have mentioned between agricultural economics and the plant and animal sciences, engineering, the psychology of motivation, and political science are sufficient to demonstrate that as persons agricultural economists need to be very broadly trained and widely interested citizens even to be competent within the field of agricultural economics. In considering problems of land tenure and tenancy, for example, the fact that many relevant considerations are social and political rather than economic does not mean that the person who undertakes the economic analysis should leave the analysis of these entirely to someone else. The more he understands about them the better, and the more likely he is to be able to see the economic aspects in perspective.

As a matter of fact, it is my conviction that narrowly trained agricultural economists are a menace to agricultural development. Agricultural development is far more than, and probably not most fundamentally, an economic problem, although it has many economic aspects. Consequently, we need agricultural economists in every country who are such broadly trained and widely interested men that they can submit the product of whatever economic analysis they engage in before the judgement bar of their own deep and general human wisdom.

Whatever other formal training agricultural economists should have, certainly they should be thoroughly grounded in the practices of farming and in the applied agricultural sciences. Unless they study and ponder the peculiarities and particularities of agriculture as in industry they are likely to go astray in their decisions as to what is pertinent and useful from the toolroom of general economics, but with such understanding they are more likely to come up with analyses and recommendations useful in the real world of farms and of public policy.

The Agricultural Revolution in Asia

Lester R. Brown

21 For those whose thinking of Asia is conditioned by the food crises of 1965 and 1966, the news of an agricultural revolution may come as a surprise. But the change and ferment now evident in the Asian countryside stretching from Turkey to the Philippines, and including the pivotal countries of India and Pakistan, cannot be described as anything less. This rural revolution, largely obscured in its early years by the two consecutive failures of the monsoon, is further advanced in some countries— Pakistan, the Philippines and India—than in others, but there is little prospect that it will abort, so powerful and pervasive are the forces behind it.

That the agricultural revolution of the less developed world began in Asia is fortunate, since it is both densely populated and has a rapid rate of population growth. In this respect, Asia is unique among the world's major geographic regions. Western Europe is heavily populated but its population grows slowly; Latin America's population is expanding rapidly but as yet most of the region is sparsely populated. Fifty-six percent of the world's 3.3 billion people live in Asia; one-third of the world's population, an estimated

Reprinted by special permission from *Foreign Affairs,* July 1968. Copyright by the Council on Foreign Relations, Inc., New York. The author is administrator of the International Agricultural Development Service in the U.S. Department of Agriculture.

1.1 billion, live in Asia outside China. It is this part of the world and this third of mankind that this article deals with.

Historically, as Asia's population increased, it was supported by traditional agriculture on an ever-expanding area of cropland. As the postwar population explosion gained momentum in the late 1950s and early 1960s, the supply of new land was used up, but the productivity of land under cultivation increased little. The result was a slowdown in the rate of gain in food production and a growing concern that population growth and food production were on a collision course.

The gravity of the situation came into focus as the monsoon on the Indian subcontinent failed two years running, in 1965 and 1966. The United States responded by shipping the equivalent of nearly one-fifth of its wheat harvest, feeding sixty million Indians for nearly two years. This record shipment, the largest ever between two countries, was sufficient to stave off famine.

As of mid-1968, both the food situation and food production prospects in Asia have changed almost beyond belief. The Philippines is self-sufficient in its staple food, rice, for the first time since 1903. Iran, with a substantial expansion in wheat acreage, is actually a net exporter of wheat this year. Ceylon's rice harvest climbed 13 percent above the previous record, as it both expanded the area under cultivation and raised yields.

Pakistan's wheat crop, harvested in April and May, is estimated to be 30 percent above the previous record. So is India's. The total Indian foodgrain crop, officially estimated at 100 million tons, is up 32 percent from last year's drought-depressed levels and, more importantly, up 12 percent from the previous record. Good weather has helped boost the harvest on the Indian subcontinent this year, but increases above the previous record are largely the results of solid technological progress—more efficient varieties, more fertilizer and better farm practices.

What has caused this remarkable turnabout? One factor is new political commitments at the top in several countries. Short-changing agriculture is no longer either feasible or fashionable. This new political climate has led to firm allocations of budgetary and foreign-exchange resources. India, for example, increased its budget for agricultural development by one-third in 1966-67; it is now using the equivalent of nearly one-fifth of its foreign-exchange earnings to import fertilizer and raw materials for manufacturing fertilizer. Turkey's imports of fertilizer may make up the largest single item in overall imports this year, exceeding for the first time petroleum and petroleum products. The availability of fertilizer in Pakistan is twice that of two years ago and several times that of 1960; it is expected at least to double again by 1970.

Many governments which heretofore neglected agriculture have been encouraged to give agriculture a higher priority by the "short-tether" policy of the United States, whereby food-aid agreements are of short duration and renewal depends on local effort and performance. The overall scarcity of foodgrains, particularly rice, in many Asian countries increased prices to the point where it suddenly became very profitable for large numbers of farmers to use fertilizer and other modern inputs.

While some factors contributing to the takeoff in agriculture are of recent origin, others have been long in the making. The agricultural infrastructure is capable of supporting current advances because of several years of AID investment in farm-to-market roads, in irrigation projects and in agricultural research and training. Investment in irrigation systems over the years provides a vast acreage of well-watered land, much of it well suited to the intensive use of modern farm technology. Adequate supplies of water and fertilizer are needed to attain high yields. The training of some 4,000 Asian agriculturists over the past decade, sponsored jointly by AID, the U. S. Department of Agriculture, and the Land Grant Universities, contributes to a corps of trained professionals capable of adapting and disseminating new technology.

The availability of fertilizer has increased severalfold over the past decade, partly as a result of expanding indigenous production and partly because of steadily rising imports. The financing of fertilizer imports is now a major AID activity, requiring a sizable portion of the agency's budget. Investment by fertilizer manufacturers and other supporting industries has helped to fuel the takeoff in agricultural production. Countries in which U.S. firms have built or are building fertilizer plants include South Korea, the Philippines, Taiwan, India, Iran and Malaysia. Fertilizer produced in these plants could increase the region's annual food-producing capability by an estimated 25 million tons of grain. Other agrobusiness activities such as the manufacture of pesticides and farm equipment are also contributing to the rapid growth in food production.

Perhaps the most exciting development is the rapid spread of new, high-yielding varieties of cereals. The Mexican wheats now proving so adaptable throughout Asia are the product of more than twenty years of work by the Rockefeller Foundation. Efficient new rice varieties are coming principally from the International Rice Research Institute in the Philippines, an institution founded jointly by the Rockefeller and Ford Foundations in 1962 and devoted solely to the improvement of rice production in the tropics and subtropics. Work on high-yielding varieties of corn, sorghum and millet is concentrated in India, where the Rockefeller Foundation is providing leadership for the program. Areas planted to the new varieties went from a few hundred acres in 1964–65 to about 23,000 acres in 1965–66, nearly four million acres in 1966–67 and over twenty million acres during 1967–68, the crop year just ended. Plans and expectations indicate a further expansion of up to forty million acres in 1968-1969.

Several factors are responsible for this rapid gain in acreage. The new varieties often double yields of traditional varieties; their superiority is so obvious that farmers are quickly persuaded of their merits. This contrasts sharply with improved varieties made available in the past, which were only marginally superior to varieties being used. Another reason is the degree to which the high yields attained on the experimental plots are transferable to field conditions. There are reports of instances in which farmers actually attained higher yields under field conditions with large acreages than researchers did on experimental plots.

The availability of these new seeds has enabled many Asian countries to shorten materially the agricultural development process. The importing of numerous varieties in small quantities for testing purposes was in itself an effort to achieve a shortcut; food-deficit countries availed themselves of the results of plant-breeding work undertaken elsewhere. But they did not stop there. Once it was demonstrated that a given high-yielding variety was adapted to local growing conditions, large tonnages of seed were imported, thus eliminating the several years required to multiply and accumulate sufficient supplies of seed locally.

Pakistan imported 42,000 tons of seed wheat from Mexico during 1967, enough to plant 1.5 million acres. As a result, Pakistan now has enough seed to plant its entire wheat acreage to Mexican wheats. India imported 18,000 tons of Mexican wheats in 1966. This, coupled with indigenous multiplication of seed from the initial introduction of the same varieties, enabled Indian farmers to plant 8 million acres this year—the target acreage for 1970–71, and more than double the target of 3.5 million acres for the current year. Turkey, starting later than India or Pakistan but determined to catch up, imported 21,000 tons of high-yielding wheat, including some U.S. varieties, for use on a much smaller acreage. Both the import of samples of the new varieties initially, and the larger shipments later, represent a massive infusion of a new technology at a nominal cost, with potentially widespread application. They constitute a windfall gain in food production for many of the less developed countries.

The new varieties possess several distinctive characteristics. They are almost all short-stemmed, so they can absorb large quantities of fertilizer without lodging (becoming top-heavy and falling down); they are much more responsive to fertilizer at all levels of application. A given amount of fertilizer produces a much greater increase in yield than with the older varieties of grain. And unlike high-yielding varieties of cereals developed in the United States or Japan for rather specific growing conditions, these varieties are adapted to a much broader range of latitudes.

The new varieties of rice are early maturing, ripening in 120 to 125 days compared with 150 to 180 days for the older varieties. They are also rather insensitive to the length of daylight and thus can be planted at any time of the year if the prevailing temperature and water supply permit. With adequate water, some farmers in the Philippines and India are harvesting two or even three crops each year. Where water supplies are not sufficient to grow rice during the dry season, farmers grow high-yielding hybrid grain sorghums or hybrid corn. Triple-cropping of rice, or rice in combination with sorghum or corn, is resulting in yields under field conditions as high as 8 tons of grain per acre per calendar year. This contrasts with average yearly rice yields in Japan of just over 2 tons per acre and wheat yields in Europe of less than 2 tons per acre. The introduction of the early-maturing Mexican wheats in northern India and Pakistan is permitting the double-cropping of wheat and corn, with wheat grown during the *rabi* (winter) season and corn during the *kharif* (summer) season.

Introduction of the new varieties is changing not only the technology of production but also the economics. The potentially far-reaching economic implications of the agricultural revolution are only now becoming clear. Projected demand for agricultural inputs such as fertilizer, pesticides, water and irrigation equipment must be recalculated. Many of the assumptions underlying current strategies of agricultural development must also be reexamined. For example, in the short run, the profitability of using fertilizer will increase demand above what it would otherwise have been. Over the longer run, however, the demand for fertilizer may be lower than would otherwise be the case since a smaller amount of fertilizer will be required on the more responsive varieties to reach a given level of production.

High rates of return on investments in production inputs, reflecting a more favorable economic climate due to better prices for farm products and more efficient new technologies, are mobilizing rural savings not previously available for production purposes. Investment is on the rise not only in those things which increase output in the short run, such as fertilizer, but also in those which boost food-producing capability over the long run, such as tubewells, and irrigation pumps. Over the course of five years, Pakistan farmers in the cotton and rice-growing areas of the former Punjab, where the water table is quite near the surface, have installed some 32,000 private tubewells, costing from $1,000 to $2,500 each. The value of the supplementary irrigation made possible by these wells is such that farmers characteristically have paid for them in two years. A large proportion were installed without government assistance or subsidy of any kind. The number of low-lift pumps installed in East Pakistan, totaling 2,200 in 1965, is expected to increase to 14,000 by 1969, greatly increasing the potential for double-cropping rice during the dry season. Similar high rates of return on small-scale irrigation investments are reported in India, where the number of wells is also climbing at an astronomical rate.

Early-maturing varieties of rice which ripen during the monsoon require mechanical drying before storage, since the time-honored method of spreading rice in the roadside to dry is not feasible. The demand for grain-drying equipment, now climbing rapidly, was not anticipated. Similarly, the use of pesticides, often uneconomic when average rice yields were 1,000 to 1,500 pounds of milled rice per acre, is suddenly very profitable on the new varieties, averaging 3,000 to 4,000 pounds. Growth in demand for both pesticides and application equipment such as knapsack sprayers and dusters will be closely associated with the spread of the improved seed.

The new varieties, with their potential for multiple-cropping, place a premium on fast preparation of the seedbed. Farmers planning to double-crop or triple-crop their land may no longer have several weeks to prepare the ground with bullocks or water buffalo; they may have to use power-driven farm equipment to prepare the seedbed quickly and plant the next crop. Even in some countries where new varieties are not yet widely spread, the profitability and feasibility of farm mechanization are being increasingly recognized. In Thailand, where the movement of goods from farm to market is largely by canal or river, rice fields are prepared principally by water buffalo. Under these circumstances, farmers are discovering it is more economical to hire someone with a tractor to plow the rice fields for a few dollars per acre than to feed and care for a team of water buffalo all year just to use them during a few weeks at plowing time. Some 20,000 to 25,000 imported tractors plowed an estimated one-fourth of the rice acreage this past year, mostly on a custom-hire basis—not unlike the way in which wheat is harvested in the Great Plains of the United States.

The more intensive farming methods associated with the new technology require more farm labor. The new varieties will not respond to the traditional practice of planting the crop and then virtually forgetting it until harvest time. Substantial amounts of additional labor must be invested in applying fertilizer, weeding and the like. Expansion of the area that can be multiple-cropped is also resulting in a more effective use of the rural labor supply, particularly during the dry season. In Asia, where underemployed labor constitutes one of the world's largest underutilized resources, this promises a major economic gain. For the first time, there is the possibility of significant labor scarcities in localized rural areas.

Changes associated with the new farm technology have a social as well as an economic impact. The exciting new cereal varieties are so superior to the traditional varieties and so dramatic in their impact that they are becoming "engines of change" wherever used. They may be to the agricultural revolution in Asia what the steam engine was to the industrial revolution in Europe.

Successful adoption of the new seed requires the simultaneous adoption of new cultural practices and the use of modern inputs. The seasonal rhythm of rural activity, once determined largely by the monsoon, is changing as farmers begin to double-crop and to introduce new combinations of crops. Farmers taking advantage of the new technology must enter the market; they cannot remain subsistence farmers. Rural Asians will change and innovate—when it is to their advantage to do so. Significantly, there may be some spin-off from this breakthrough in agriculture, this initial break with tradition. Family planners should take heart. As farmers learn that they can indeed influence their destiny, they may become much more susceptible to family planning and other equally "radical" departures.

Not all changes wrought by the new technology are desirable. In some areas, tenants are being reduced to farm laborers as landowners discover the profitability of the new technology in the current economic setting. Even though income to the landless may rise, the socioeconomic gap between the landowners and the landless may widen. Dissidents among the landless group in some states in India now form the nucleus of the opposition parties. Among those who own land, the income gap between those owning fertile, well-watered land and those with marginal land is also likely to widen. While many of the former may easily triple or quadruple output, the latter may not be able to employ the new technology at all. Those who can, and are thus permitted to enter the market, are likely to become more vocal and more interested in influencing the economic policies affecting their fortunes in the marketplace. Political activization of rural populations is an expected concomitant of the agricultural revolution now under way.

The leadership in most Asian countries is not unaware of the political implications of recent changes in rural areas. Prime Minister Demirel of Turkey feels strongly enough about the crash program in wheat production, initiated at his behest less than two years ago, to have it directed and monitored from his office. Some observers think President Marcos of the Philippines, who has brought his country to self-sufficiency in rice by emphasizing rural development, may be the first President of the Philippines ever to be reelected to office. Former Prime Minister Maiwandwal of Afghanistan was so impressed with the production potential of the Mexican wheats and with the urgent need to arrest Afghanistan's growing dependence on imported wheat that he assessed each of the Ministries 2.5 percent of its current year's development budget to create a fund to launch an accelerated wheat-production program. Two years later, the Afghans appear to be progressing toward their goal of self-sufficiency in wheat. President Ayub of Pakistan shows a deep personal interest in the agricultural programs under way in his country and follows their progress on an almost daily basis. India's progressive C. Subramaniam, former Food and Agriculture Minister, took advantage of the food crisis to mobilize support for and launch the accelerated food-production effort responsible for much of India's gains.

Recent agricultural progress should not give cause for complacency. Many difficult problems lie ahead, especially in the fields of farm credit, water development, plant disease, foreign-exchange availability, marketing and price incentives.

Purchases of farm inputs are often concentrated initially among the larger farmers who are able to finance their own purchases. The rate at which small farmers adopt new technologies is frequently determined by the availability of farm credit on reasonable terms. If, like the great majority of Asian farmers, they are dependent on the local moneylender for credit, often at interest rates ranging from 20 to 100 percent per year, they may not find it profitable to use modern inputs such as fertilizer. Available evidence indicates that fertilizer distribution in some parts of India and West Pakistan is beginning to slow because of a lack of credit.

Intensive cultivation of the new high-yielding varieties requires, in addition to an adequate supply of water, a far more sophisticated system of water control and management. At present not more than one-third of Asia's rice land is considered suitable for the new, short-stemmed rice varieties. Excessive and erratic flooding during the monsoon or rainy season is not conducive to the intensive cultivation of rice, which requires hand-weeding and the use of fertilizer and pesticides. Either too little or too much water can be damaging.

Associated with the massive introduction of exogenous varieties is the risk that some local insect or disease could suddenly wipe out the entire acreage, thus creating possible famine not unlike that occurring in Ireland more than a century ago. The worst of this threat may have passed, however, for the number of new varieties has already reduced dependence on any single one. Each year that passes should make the threat less dangerous.

Rice production during the dry season, once limited by the lack of varieties adapted to the off season, is now limited by a lack of water. This can be remedied either by developing underground water resources, which are quite abundant in some areas, or by using pumps to lift water from the numerous rivers and canals that flow through many of the rice-growing areas during the dry season. The exploitation of unused water resources will expand the acreage suitable for planting the high-yielding rices. Few, if any, developing countries are endowed with all the raw materials needed for manufacture of chemical fertilizers—phosphate rock, potash, sulfur and natural gas or naphtha. As the use of fertilizer expands, many countries, chronically faced with a scarcity of foreign exchange, are hard pressed to find enough hard currency for the required imports. For some individual countries, such as India, this scarcity of foreign exchange could effectively reduce the rate of agricultural progress.

Frustrating though these problems may be, the dominant constraint on agricultural growth is likely to be inadequate marketing systems and an overall lack of markets. The recent emphasis on agricultural development has been concentrated on the expansion of production; marketing has been largely neglected, with the result that some of the promising gains made in production may be negated. Over the past decade many of Asia's large coastal cities—Karachi, Bombay, Madras, Calcutta, Colombo and Djakarta—have become increasingly dependent on imported foodgrains. To become self-sufficient requires not only producing a surplus in the countryside sufficient to feed these cities, but also having a marketing system capable of moving rural surpluses to the cities when needed. This means farm-to-market roads, storage facilities and a market-intelligence system to rationalize the movement of commodities.

Several Asian countries, such as Pakistan, the Philippines and Turkey, could produce exportable surpluses of grain within the next few years, joining Thailand and Burma. If they do, they must develop the transport and storage facilities needed to move potentially large surpluses of grain from often remote rural areas into world markets. If exportable surpluses develop, there will be mounting pressure on Japan and the EEC countries—where cereal production is often subsidized at prices double the world market price—to reduce subsidies and permit imports.

Problem areas notwithstanding, an agricultural revolution is under way in Asia. The new cereal varieties provide a means for tapping some of the vast, but as yet largely unrealized, food-producing potential of the tropics and subtropics, putting them on a more competitive footing with the temperate-zone cereal producers. The agricultural breakthrough occurring in several major Asian countries can be repeated in Latin America and Africa. Mexico, which once depended on imports for nearly half its wheat needs, is now exporting small quantities of both wheat and corn. Kenya, until recently a food-aid recipient, has produced an exportable surplus of corn, its food staple. Tunisia and Morocco are introducing the Mexican wheats. Much of the technology now being applied in Asia will also be applied in both Latin America and Africa, if the necessary top-level political support and proper combination of economic policies are forth-coming.

The farm sector now constitutes from one-third to one-half of most Asian economies. It is conceivable that the 2 percent rate of increase in food production prevailing during the early and mid-1960s could accelerate to 4 or 5 percent yearly over the next few years, provided markets can absorb the additional output. The additional purchasing power thus generated for both production and consumer goods will stimulate a more rapid rate of growth in the non-farm sector. The net effect should be a much more rapid rate of overall economic growth than would otherwise have prevailed. If the Asian agricultural revolution continues, it could well become the most significant world economic development since the economic rebirth of Europe following World War II.

This agricultural revolution is not the ultimate solution to the food-population problem, but it does buy some much needed additional time in which to mount effective family-planning programs. If food scarcity lessens as anticipated in some of the major food-deficit countries, governments recently preoccupied with real or impending food crises can again turn their attention to the business of development. Although the need for food aid is likely to lessen sharply within the next few years, capital needed for investment in the agricultural infrastructure is certain to increase. The need for technical assistance seems likely to rise as the problems generated by dynamic movement in agriculture increase. The need for foreign private investment in agrobusiness will also rise sharply as farmers clamor for the inputs they need to take full advantage of the new genetic potentials available to them.

The positive economic effects of an agricultural takeoff in Asian countries are quite evident. What is not so readily realized is that it will bolster the confidence of national leaders in their ability to handle other seemingly insoluble problems. It may also strengthen their faith in modern technology and its potential for improving the well-being of their people.

Part Four: International Trade and Economic Growth

Comparative Advantage and
Development Policy[1]

Hollis B. Chenery

22

In the great revival of interest in economic development that has marked the past decade, attention has centered on two main questions: first, what determines the over-all rate of economic advance? second, what is the optimal allocation of given resources to promote growth? Analysis of the growth rate has relied mainly on the Keynesian tools and has produced a multiplicity of aggregate growth models. The second question, however, reopens more ancient economic issues, and their analysis must start from the classical and neoclassical solutions. Only very recently have the two types of discussion tended to come together in the more comprehensive framework of general equilibrium analysis.

In the field of resource allocation, controversy centers around the implications of the classical principle of comparative advantage, according to which growth is promoted by specialization. The defenders of this principle

From the *American Economic Review,* Papers and Proceedings, March 1961, pp. 18-51. The author is presently the Director of the Program Review and Coordination Staff, Agency for International Development.

[1]I am indebted to Moses Abramovitz, Bela Balassa, and Lawrence Krause for helpful comments. Research for this article was undertaken at the Cowles Foundation for Research in Economics under Task NR 047-006, Office of Naval Research. [This is the third in a series of survey articles for which the Rockefeller Foundation has provided support.—*Editor.*]

draw their inspiration from David Ricardo, J. S. Mill and Alfred Marshall, while the lines of attack stem from Friedrich List, J. A. Schumpeter, A. A. Young and J. H. Williams. The chief criticism is that comparative advantage is essentially a static concept which ignores a variety of dynamic elements.

This issue is of great practical importance to the governments of underdeveloped countries, most of which take an active part in allocating investment funds and other scarce resources. The main purpose of the discussion has therefore been to discover workable principles for the formulation of development policy. The classical approach derives these principles from international trade theory, while its critics base their analysis on modern growth theory. Elements of a dynamic, general-equilibrium theory are needed to resolve the differences between the two approaches. The more general analysis is of very limited value, however, unless its empirical implications can be ascertained.

The present paper discusses the analysis of resource allocation in less developed economies from three points of view. Section I tries to ascertain the extent to which the allocation principles derived from trade theory and from growth can be reconciled with each other without losing their operational significance. Section II compares various approaches to the measurement of optimal resource allocation in terms of their logical consistency and their applicability to different conditions. Section III examines some of the practical procedures followed in setting investment policy in underdeveloped countries in the light of the earlier discussion. Finally, some of the theoretical issues are re-examined to indicate their practical importance.

I. Conflicts between Trade Theory and Growth Theory

The main contradictions between comparative advantage and other principles of resource allocation derive from their different orientation and assumptions. The classical analysis focuses on long-run tendencies and equilibrium conditions, while modern theories of growth are concerned with the interaction among producing and consuming units in a dynamic system. Since both approaches are familiar, I shall only try to identify the differences in assumptions and emphasis that lead to different policy conclusions.

A. The Implications of Comparative Advantage for Resource Allocation

The modern version of the comparative cost doctrine [20] * is essentially a simplified form of static general equilibrium theory.[2] The optimum pattern

---

*Numbers in brackets identify the references listed at the end of the article.

[2]An excellent discussion and synthesis of the several versions of trade theory is given by Caves [7]. The terms "comparative advantage" and "comparative cost" are used interchangeably in most discussions.

of production and trade for a country is determined from a comparison of the opportunity cost of producing a given commodity with the price at which the commodity can be imported or exported. In equilibrium, no commodity is produced which could be imported at lower cost, and exports are expanded until marginal revenue equals marginal cost. Under the assumptions of full employment and perfect competition, the opportunity cost of a commodity, which is the value of the factors used to produce it in their best alternative employment, is equal to its market value. Market prices of factors and commodities can therefore be used to determine comparative advantage under competitive conditions. Long-term changes are not ignored, but they are assumed to be reflected in current market prices.

The Heckscher-Ohlin version of the comparative cost doctrine has been widely recommended as a basis for development policy because it provides a measure of comparative advantage that does not depend on the existence of perfect competition and initial equilibrium. This version states that a country will benefit from trade by producing commodities that use more of its relatively abundant factors of production. It will export these commodities and import commodities using more of its relatively scarce factors unless its pattern of domestic demand happens to be biased toward commodities using domestic factors. The critical assumptions in this analysis are that factors of production are comparable among countries and that production functions are the same. These assumptions are not required by classical trade theory.

The applicability of the comparative cost doctrine to present-day conditions in underdeveloped countries has been re-examined by Viner and its validity has been reaffirmed with some modifications. Viner criticizes the Heckscher-Ohlin version because its assumption of comparable factors does not allow for observable differences in their quality [63, p. 16]. In his recent answer to critics of the comparative cost approach [64], however, Viner admits the necessity of interpreting comparative advantage in a dynamic setting in which the efficiency of production may change over time, external economies may exist, and the market prices of commodities and factors may differ from their opportunity cost. As Nurkse points out [64, p. 76], these modifications rob the original doctrine of much of its practical value. It is now necessary to have an explicit analysis of the growth process itself before it is possible to determine, even theoretically, where comparative advantage lies; market prices and current opportunity costs are no longer sufficient.

B. Implications of Growth Theory
Resource Allocation

Modern growth theory is concerned with the interactions over time among producers, consumers, and investors in interrelated sectors of the economy. In the writings of such economists as Rosenstein-Rodan [43], Lewis [29], Nurkse [36], Myrdal [34], Rostow [44], Dobb [12], and Hirschman [23], there is much more emphasis on the sequence of expansion of production and factor use by sector than on the conditions of general equilibrium. Growth theory either ignores comparative advantage and the possibilities of trade completely, or it considers mainly the dynamic aspects, such as the stimulus that an increase in exports provides to the development of related sectors or the function of imports as a carrier of new products and advanced technology. With this different point of view, growth theorists often suggest investment criteria that are quite contradictory to those derived from considerations of comparative advantage.

The conflicts between these two approaches to resource allocation may be traced either to differences in assumptions or to the inclusion of factors in one theory that are omitted from the other. Growth theory contains at least four basic assumptions about underdeveloped economies that differ strongly from those underlying the comparative cost doctrine: (1) factor prices do not necessarily reflect opportunity costs with any accuracy; (2) the quantity and quality of factors of production may change substantially over time, in part as a result of the production process itself; (3) economies of scale relative to the size of existing markets are important in a number of sectors of production; (4) complementarity among commodities is dominant in both producer and consumer demand.

Some of the implications of these factors are developed by Rosenstein-Rodan [43] and Nurkse [36] as arguments for "balanced growth," by which is meant simultaneous expansion of a number of sectors of production.[3] Assuming an elastic supply of either capital or labor, these authors show that investment will be more profitable in related sectors, because of horizontal and vertical interdependence, than in the same sectors considered separately. Market forces will not necessarily lead to optimal investment decisions because present prices do not reflect the cost and demand conditions that will exist in the future. This effect of investment in one sector on the profitability of investment in another sector, via increased demand or reduced costs, has been called by Scitovsky [47] a "dynamic external economy." The imputation of these economies to the originating sectors may seriously affect the estimate of comparative advantage.

If we assume fixed investment resources instead of an elastic supply, the same set of factors provide an argument for concentrated or unbalanced growth [48] [50]. In order to achieve economies of scale in one sector, it may be necessary to devote a large fraction of the available investment funds to that sector and to supply increased requirements in other sectors from imports (or to curtail them temporarily). The optimal pattern of investment will then be one which concentrates first on one sector and then on another, with balance being approached only in the long run. Streeten [53] has developed further dynamic arguments for unbalanced growth from the fact that technological progress may be more rapid if increases in production are concentrated in a few sectors, while Hirschman [23] argues for imbalance to economize on entrepreneurial ability.

The historical significance of the balanced growth argument has been examined by Gerschenkron [18], Rostow [44], and Ohlin [38], in the

---

[3]The term "balanced growth" has been given a variety of meanings, but the idea of simultaneous expansion on several fronts is common to all of them.

context of nineteenth-century industrial development in Europe. They show that vertical interdependence has been important in stimulating the growth of related industrial sectors, although the nature and origin of these complexes differ from country to country. In one case they may be related to exports, in another to expansion for the domestic market. The importance of inter-dependence among producers emerges fairly clearly from these historical studies.

The net effect of the discussion of dynamic interdependence and balanced vs. unbalanced growth is to destroy the presumption that perfect compe-tition, even if it could be achieved, would lead to the optimum allocation of resources over time. Since the doctrine of comparative advantage in its conventional form is a corollary of general equilibrium theory, the theoretical qualifications that apply to the latter also apply to the former. If, then, the doctrine of comparative advantage is to be useful for development policy, the essential elements of the growth analysis must be combined with it.

C. Dynamic Modifications of Comparative Advantage

Classical trade theory does not exclude changes in the supply of factors and other data over time, but it does insist that under perfect competition the effects of such changes will be reflected in the market mechanism. If, on the other hand, we take comparative advantage as a principle of planning rather than as a result of market forces, we can include any foreseeable exogenous changes in technology, tastes, or other data without going beyond the framework of comparative statics.

Some of the modifications suggested by growth theory are dynamic in a more essential way, in that a particular change depends not only on the passage of time but on other variables in the system. For example, the rate of increase in the productivity of labor in an industry may depend on an increasing level of production in that industry. Some of these dynamic elements can also be analyzed by methods of comparative statics if our purpose is only to choose among alternative courses of action.

The four assumptions of growth theory discussed above (Section B) lead to the following requirements for the analytical framework to be used in determining comparative advantage in a growing economy:[4] (1) recognition of the possibility of structural disequilibrium in factor markets; (2) the inclusion of indirect (market and nonmarket) effects of expanding a given type of production; (3) simultaneous determination of levels of consumption, imports, and production in interrelated sectors over time when decreasing costs result from the expansion of output; and (4) allowance for variation in the demand for exports and other data over time.

[4]Some of these criticisms of static analysis were made years ago by Williams [66], and a number of the elements were, of course, recognized by the classical economists themselves. I am not concerned with explicit criticism of the classical analysis, but with the possibility of reconciling it with growth theory.

These changes destroy the simplicity of the classical system, in which allocation decisions can be based on a partial analysis because adjustments in the rest of the economy are reflected in equilibrium market prices. In the dynamic analysis, it may not be possible to state that a country has a comparative advantage in producing steel without specifying also the levels of production of iron ore, coat and metal-working over time. In short, we are forced to compare alternative patterns of growth rather than separate sectors, and we cannot expect to find simple generalizations of the Heckscher-Ohlin type concerning the characteristics of individual lines of production.

Since there is no well-developed body of theory concerning the formal properties of the system just outlined,[5] I shall only try to indicate in a general way the modifications that some of these elements of growth theory will produce in the analysis of comparative advantage.

Factor costs. It is generally agreed that costs of labor and capital in underdeveloped countries do not reflect their opportunity costs with any accuracy because of market imperfections, but there is wide disagreement as to the extent of the typical discrepancies. Some types of labor may be overvalued while particular skills are undervalued. Factor costs may also change markedly over time as a result of economic development, so that an advantage based on cheap labor may prove quite limited in duration. As Lewis [29] and Hagen [21] show, the effects on comparative advantage of correcting for disequilibrium factor prices are often very substantial. (The effects of disequilibrium in factor markets are discussed further in Part II.)

Export markets. Two of the main arguments against the trade pattern produced by market forces concern (1) the fluctuating nature and (2) the low income and price elasticities of the demand for primary products. The existence of cyclical fluctuation is well established, but the income and price elasticities vary considerably among primary commodities. Their net effect on the terms of trade of primary producers over time is a matter of dispute [64]. These characteristics are often used as an argument for reducing specialization in underdeveloped countries and for expanding industry for local consumption rather than expanding primary exports [41] [51].

These factors can be admitted without seriously modifying the principle of comparative advantage. The market value of the stream of export earnings should be reduced to reflect the drawbacks to the economy resulting from its variable characteristics, and this social value should be used in comparing investment in primary exports to other alternatives. When export demand has a low elasticity, marginal revenue should be used in place of average revenue. Since it is quite likely that the market evaluation of the attractiveness of an investment in exports will differ from this social evaluation, some form of government intervention may be warranted. It is wrong, however, to conclude from this analysis that continued specialization in primary exports may

[5]In his survey of modern trade theory, Caves [7] shows that attempts to introduce dynamic elements have been concerned with particular aspects and have led not to new principles, but rather to extensions of static results.

not be the best policy, because even the corrected return on exports may be greater than that on alternative investments. The supply of foreign investment may also be greater for export production.

Productivity change. The possibility of rising efficiency as labor and management acquire increasing experience in actual production has long been recognized [66] and forms the basis for the infant industry argument. This argument has been generalized to include the effects of increasing production in any industry on the supply of skilled labor and management available to other industries. Since manufacturing is thought to have more important training effects than primary production [33] [41], the fact that improvements in factor supply are not reflected in the market mechanism may introduce a bias against manufacturing. The empirical basis for this argument has been questioned by several economists [46],] 63], who assert that there is often as much scope for technological improvement in agriculture as in industry. Without trying to settle the empirical question that has been raised, it may be concluded that productivity change is an important factor and therefore that comparative advantage should be measured over time. It cannot be said, however, that allowance for this factor will always favor manufacturing.

Dynamic external economies. As indicated above, dynamic external economies are received by an industry from cost reductions or demand increases in other sectors. Cost reductions may result from economies of scale, productivity increases, or new technology. The customary analysis of comparative advantage on a sector-by-sector basis would require that the cost reduction from simultaneously developing interrelated sectors be allocated separately to each. However, if a group of investments will only be profitable when they are undertaken together, comparative advantage can only be determined for alternative combinations of investments. As shown in [11], not only do market prices fail to produce the best investment allocation in this situation, but any structure of equilibrium prices may also be an inadequate guide in the presence of economies of scale.

There is considerable evidence that external economies are more important in the industrial sectors than in primary production because of internal economies of scale, training effects, and high demand elasticities. Their omission from the market mechanism is therefore likely to bias resource allocation against manufacturing. The quantitative significance of this factor is very hard to determine, however, since it involves simultaneous changes in a number of sectors.

Uncertainty and flexibility. The limited ability of policy-makers to foresee changes in demand and supply conditions puts a premium on flexibility in the choice of a development strategy. This factor not only argues against specialization in one or two export commodities but it also favors the development of a diversified economic structure which will enable the economy to shift to new types of exports or import substitutes when changing trade conditions may require them. Kindleberger [26] sees this factor as the main explanation for his finding that the terms of trade have favored developed countries although they have not favored countries exporting manufactured goods in general.[6] The argument is similar to that of Stigler [52] concerning the optimum choice of techniques in a manufacturing plant. The optimum design for a changing market is likely to differ from the optimum under static conditions because in the former case the proper criterion is lowest-cost production for varying operating levels and with changes in product design. Similarly optimum development policy should result in a pattern of resource allocation that allows for unforeseen changes in supply and demand conditions even at the cost of some loss of short-term efficiency.

II. The Measurement of Optimum Resource Allocation

The development of an adequate theory is only the first step in formulating economic policy. In order to reach practical conclusions, it is also necessary to specify the environment in which the policy-maker functions. Relevant aspects of a particular society include its general objectives, the policy instruments to be considered, and the information available. The theory must then be combined with these elements in such a way as to yield guides to action or "decision rules" for particular stiuations.

Although the growing science of operations research is concerned with the development of decision rules for business and military operations, less progress has been made in developing an operational approach to long-run economic policy. Tinbergen [55] and Frisch [15] have outlined a general framework for policy analysis, but it has had relatively little impact on the discussion of the development of underdeveloped countries. In this field the failure to specify adequately the decision-making environment and to distinguish between decision rules and the corollaries of pure theory has led to great confusion.

Since the information needed for over-all economic analysis is available to a very limited extent in underdeveloped countries, there has been a considerable effort to derive decision rules or "investment criteria" that can be based on partial analysis. I shall group the various suggestions into three categories: (1) factor-intensity criteria; (2) productivity criteria; (3) programming criteria based on accounting prices. Although these various approaches often lead to contradictory results, each has some merit as a form of decision rule if properly qualified. In general, the theoretically more valid formulations require more information and must be replaced by cruder approximations when adequate data are not available. Since a major part of the literature in the development field has been devoted to the discussion of investment criteria, it is important to identify the sources of conflict among them and to

[6]This argument is also discussed by Caves [7, pp. 264–66].

specify the circumstances under which each may be approximately correct.

In economic theory, capital and labor are assumed to be separately allocated in single units to different uses. In national planning, however, it is more convenient to consider the decision to install a given productive process or plant, representing the allocation of a group of inputs in specified quantities, as the basic choice. Investment criteria are customarily formulated for "projects" of this sort, since they form the basis for the decisions of planning authorities. This procedure recognizes that very small productive units are uneconomical, and it permits a consideration of different scales of output. The choice of techniques can be considered as a choice among projects producing the same output from different input combinations. In this way the allocation procedure can be divided into two steps: the choice of the best technique for a given type of product, and the decision whether to produce the commodity at all. The principle of comparative advantage is more directly relevant to the second type of choice, but the two cannot be separated entirely.

A. Factor-Intensity Criteria

The simplest approach to any allocation problem is to concentrate on the scarcest resource. Since this is often capital in underdeveloped countries, it seems reasonable to choose the technique that uses the least capital to produce a given output. The same logic is applied to the choice of sectors of production: an underdeveloped country is advised to produce and export commodities that use relatively less capital per unit of output and to import items requiring more capital. Statements of this type occur in many economic writings of the past fifteen years. Buchanan [5] was among the first to state this criterion for investment in underdeveloped countries and to base policy recommendations upon it.

The "minimum capital-output ratio" criterion is only valid under the following restrictive conditions:[7] (1) Either capital is the only scarce factor in the system, or other inputs are so abundant relative to capital that the latter is the dominant element in determining cost differences. (2) Either the same output is produced by each investment alternative, or the market values used to compare the different products coincide with their social values. (3) Production takes place under constant costs.

The use of the capital-output ratio theoretically requires a measurement of the total capital used in producing a given commodity, including the capital used in producing all materials and services purchased. Alternatively, the indirect use of capital can be allowed for by subtracting the cost of purchased inputs from the value of output and expressing the criterion as the ratio of capital to value added. This procedure requires

[7]A rigorous analysis of the validity of marginal and average factor-output ratios as indicators of optimum allocation in a two-factor system is given by Bator [4].

the further assumption that market prices correctly reflect the use of capital in the rest of the economy.

A closely related allocation criterion is the capital intensity: the ratio of capital to labor. This test is derived directly from the Heckscher-Ohlin version of the comparative cost doctrine. If the same production functions exist in all countries and if capital is scarce relative to labor in the underdeveloped countries, comparative advantage in the latter can be identified by low capital-labor ratios. This approach does not assume that labor has zero opportunity cost, as does use of the capital-output ratio, but only that the ratio of labor cost to capital cost is lower than in the country's trading partners. To allow for differences in the quality of labor among countries, it is sometimes suggested that the assessment of relative labor cost should be made for labor units of equal efficiency—e.g., the labor required in each country to perform a given type of operation with the same capital goods and organization.

A principal criticism of the use of both these ratios is that they ignore the existence of other factors of production, such as natural resources. If either labor or natural resources has a significant opportunity cost, the capital-output measure must be replaced by the more general marginal productivity of capital criterion, which is discussed in the next section.

To judge comparative advantage by the capital-labor ratio is to assume either that this ratio will be the same for the same industry in all countries, or that capital is equally substitutable for labor in producing all the commodities traded. Deviations from these assumptions, along with the omission of other inputs and variations in efficiency by sector, make the capital-labor criterion a very crude approximation indeed to a proper estimate of comparative advantage.

B.   Marginal Productivity Criteria[8]

A more comprehensive allocation criterion is the social marginal product of a given unit of resources in a given use. Where the factor-intensity criteria are at best only correlated with the increase in national income produced by a project, the productivity criteria try to measure the increase. The marginal productivity test is in turn less general than the over-all programming approach, because it is based on a partial equilibrium analysis that is only valid for relatively small changes in the economic structure.

The several forms of marginal productivity criterion that have been proposed differ in the assumptions made about the social welfare function and in the extent to which allowance is made for the indirect effects of a given allocation. All versions are alike in assuming that the government controls, directly or indirectly, a certain fraction of the investible resources of the country and wishes to allocate them in such a way as to maximize future welfare.

[8]Surveys of these and other investment criteria are given by Castellino [6], Vaidyanathan [62], and the United Nations [61].

Since the productivity criteria are usually applied to investment projects rather than to single units of capital, they are "marginal" only in the sense that a project normally constitutes a small fraction of the total capital invested in a given year. For very large projects a breakdown into smaller units would be more appropriate.

The static SMP criterion. As proposed by Kahn [25], the social marginal product (SMP) is a general equilibrium concept which is conventionally defined as the net contribution of a marginal unit (project) to the national product.[9] The related decision rule is to rank investment projects by their SMP and to go down the list until the funds to be allocated are exhausted. Alternatively, any project having an SMP above a given level can be approved.

Kahn uses the SMP criterion to show the fallacies in the factor-intensity measures that had been advocated by Buchanan [5], Polak [40], and other writers. He points out that: "The existence of a particular natural resource, specialized skills, particular climatic conditions, or the importance of a particular product or service may make the SMP of capital higher in a line which is more capital intensive than in another which is less so" [25, p. 40]. He also argues that even when there is substantial rural unemployment, a considerable amount of capital and other inputs are required to transport, train, and house the workers who are to be employed elsewhere. Kahn's arguments against the simple capital-intensity criteria appear to have been generally accepted, although he admits that a lower capital-output ratio may be a useful guide when other information is lacking.

Some modifications in the SMP criterion were suggested by the present author [8] to allow for artificial elements in the price system (tariffs, subsidies, etc.) and to provide for the evaluation of labor and foreign exchange at opportunity cost rather than at market value. Further allowances for the difference between market price and social value can be made by estimating the benefits to be provided to other sectors in the form of external economies, and by including overhead costs in the estimate of the cost of labor. All of these elements are included in Eckstein's synthesis and extension of the productivity approach [14].[10]

The SMP criterion is entirely consistent with the general programming approach discussed below, which derives opportunity costs from an explicit analysis of total factor use. In the absence of such an over-all analysis, the corrections suggested for the calculation of the productivity of investment are likely to be quite approximate. There is no logical conflict between the results of the SMP analysis and the dictates of comparative advantage because each is a corollary of a general equilibrium solution over a given time period.

[9]To be more accurate, cost and output streams should be discounted to the present, but I shall not be concerned with differences in the time pattern of output of different projects.

[10]Eckstein points out that the assumption of capital rationing implies a social judgment as to both the amount of investment in the current period and the discount to be applied to future outputs, since the market rate of interest is rejected for both purposes.

The marginal reinvestment criterion. A sharp criticism of the SMP criterion was made by Galenson and Leibenstein [17], who challenge some of its basic premises. They would substitute a different social welfare function in which the aim is to maximize per capita income at some time in the distant future rather than to maximize a discounted stream of income over time. They also assume severe restrictions on the policy instruments available to the government, and in particular deny its ability to affect the rate of saving by fiscal measures. Under these assumptions, it is necessary to take account of the division of income resulting from a project between profits and wages, since savings from the former are higher.

To maximize the total output at some distant future time, Galenson and Leibenstein easily show that the most "productive" project is not necessarily the one which maximizes national income in the near future but the one which leads to the highest savings. Since it is assumed that neither voluntary savings nor taxes can be extracted from wages, the most productive project will be the one with the highest profit rate per unit of capital invested.[11] The assumption that profits are saved and reinvested leads to the "marginal reinvestment quotient" as a decision-rule to be applied in place of the SMP.

Galenson and Leibenstein push their argument one step further and identify the most profitable project as the one with the highest capital-labor ratio. This result leads them to the paradoxical conclusion that the factor-intensity rule should be reversed: countries should prefer the most capital-intensive rather than the least capital-intensive techniques in order to promote savings and future growth. This conclusion involves an implicit assumption about the nature of production functions: that increasing the capital intensity will necessarily raise the average return to capital in each sector of production. This is obviously not true in general and is not necessarily true of existing productive techniques. The savings effect of a given project should therefore be measured directly and not assumed to vary in proportion to the capital-labor ratio.

Galenson and Leibenstein have been widely criticized for their extreme assumptions [4] [14] [24] [35], in particular for the use of a social welfare function in which the starvation of half the population in the near future would appear to be a matter of indifference and for the assumption that limitations on fiscal policy make a lower income preferable to a much higher one if the former has a higher savings component. Their analysis has nevertheless been useful in emphasizing that other effects of an investment besides its immediate contribution to the national product should be included in the productivity criterion.[12]

The marginal growth contribution. Eckstein [14] has successfully reconciled the conflict between the Kahn-Chenery SMP approach and the

[11]I omit the possibility of an effect on population growth, which leads Galenson and Leibenstein to state the criterion on a per capita basis.

[12]In [28], Leibenstein restates in more restrained form his arguments for including labor training, savings, population growth, and other indirect effects in a comprehensive productivity measure.

Galenson-Leibenstein reinvestment approach, and in so doing he has provided a considerable generalization of each. First, he assumes that the social objective is to maximize the present value of the future consumption stream. With a zero discount rate, this objective approximates the long-term income objective of Galenson and Leibenstein, while with a high discount of future consumption it leads to the maximization of income in the short term. Second, Eckstein assumes that there is a different savings (reinvestment) coefficient associated with each project, but he allows for any savings rate out of wages and profits. From these assumptions, he derives a measure of the "marginal growth contribution" of a given project that consists of two parts: (1) an *efficiency term,* consisting of the present value of the consumption stream; and (2) a *growth term,* consisting of the additional consumption to be achieved by reinvesting savings.

The relative importance of the two terms depends largely on the rate of discount that is applied to future consumption. Even with a low rate of discount, the significance of the second term depends on how much variation there is in the fraction of income saved among different projects. If the savings ratio is not related to the form of income generated, then, as Bator [4] shows, there is no conflict between maximizing income in the short run and in the longer run. Eckstein's formula provides for all possible intermediate assumptions between the two extreme views of the determinants of savings.[13]

In principle, one might include other indirect dynamic effects, such as the value of the labor training provided, in the measurement of the total productivity of a given project. There is a danger of double counting if partial-equilibrium analysis is extended too far, however, and most indirect effects can be more readily evaluated in the more general programming framework considered below.

C. Programming Criteria and Accounting Prices

The allocation rules discussed up to now are based on the existing structure and are strictly applicable only for relatively small changes in it. Although it may in many instances be necessary to rely primarily on these marginal criteria for lack of data on the rest of the economy, it is important to have some way of testing larger changes and of evaluating the errors that are introduced by the marginal procedure. Furthermore, without a more comprehensive analysis it is impossible to reconcile fully the conflicting policy implications of comparative advantage and growth theory.

The difficulties of partial analysis increase with the number of modifications that have to be applied to market prices in order to arrive at social value. Both the factor-intensity ratios and the partial productivity measures assume that there is one principal restriction on the system, the scarcity of

[13]Sen [49] independently formulated a more general investment criterion that is very similar to Eckstein's, in which the SMP and reinvestment criteria are shown to be limiting cases.

capital. They do not allow for the fact that in allocating capital according to any one of these rules some other restriction on the system, such as the supply of foreign exchange, of skilled labor, or of a particular commodity, may be exceeded.

The programming approach to resource allocation begins with the problem of balancing supply and demand for different commodities and factors of production. Until quite recently, practical programming methods have been more concerned with ensuring the consistency of a given allocation of resources with certain targets than with testing the efficiency with which resources are used. Historically speaking, the programming approach is thus the operational counterpart of the theory of balanced growth, from which much of its conceptual framework is derived.

One of the earliest attempts at formulating a comprehensive development program for an underdeveloped area was Mandelbaum's illustrative model for Southeastern Europe, undertaken during the war [31]. He starts, as many subsequent programs have done, from an estimate of the increase in national income required to absorb a prospective increment in the labor force. The allocation of capital and labor is made initially from demand estimates and by analogy to the structure of more advanced countries. The principle of comparative advantage is only introduced intuitively in modifying the initial projection. The main test of resource allocation is the balance of demand and supply for each sector and factor of production.

The development of mathematical programming methods makes it possible to carry out this type of analysis in a much more precise way. In several countries, consistent development programs have been formulated by using input-output analysis, as in the studies of the Economic Commission for Latin America [58] [59] [60]. It is only with the development of linear programming, however, that it is possible to reconcile the consistency criteria and the productivity criteria in a systematic way.

A link between the test of consistency (feasibility) in resource allocation and the test of productivity (efficiency) is provided by a consideration of the price implications of a given allocation. Assume that a set of production levels has been worked out so as to be consistent with the available supplies of labor, capital and natural resources, given the structure of consumer demand and the country's trading possibilities. These sector production and trade levels constitute a "feasible program." Any such program implies a unique set of commodity and factor prices if the economy is in equilibrium. If production activities are assumed to operate at constant cost, linear programming provides a method of calculating the "shadow prices" corresponding to the equilibrium conditions, in which the price of each commodity is equal to its cost of production.[14] Prices are determined by the solution to the following set of simultaneous equations, one for production activity included in the program:

[14]The assumptions of linear programming and methods of finding solutions to programming models have been discussed in a number of recent publications, such as [13].

$$(1) \qquad a_{1j}P_1 + a_{2j}P_2 + \ldots + a_{nj}P_n = 0 \qquad (j = 1 \ldots n)$$

where a_{ij} is the input or output of commodity or factor i by activity j, and P_i is the shadow price of commodity or factor i. The input coefficients may be measured at existing prices or in other convenient units. In an open economy, activities of importing and exporting are also included in the system, and the price solution contains the equilibrium price of foreign exchange. An example of this calculation is given in Table 1, which will be explained shortly.

The use of shadow or "accounting" prices in evaluating investment projects has been suggested by Tinbergen [54] [56], Frisch [15] [16], and Chenery [9] [10]. Although Tinbergen does not use a linear programming framework, his accounting prices for factors have the same meaning as shadow prices: the opportunity cost implied by a given resources allocation.[15] He suggests computing the costs associated with a project by using accounting prices; any project that shows a positive net return over cost (including capital cost) should be approved. This test is equivalent to the SMP criterion, as shown below.

The general linear programming problem is to maximize the value of a linear objective function subject to linear constraints. In development programs, the principal constraints are that the demands for commodities and factors should not exceed their supplies; the function to be maximized is usually taken as the national income. Alternatively, the objective may be the achievement of a given increase in output at minimum cost in investment (including foreign investment). Other social objectives, such as a minimum employment level or a specific degree of regional balance, can be included as additional restrictions on the program. The instrument variables can also be constrained to fall within specific limits, as in the models of Frisch.[16]

To illustrate the meaning and use of shadow prices in evaluating investment projects, I shall take up a very simplified programming model that is worked out in more detail elsewhere [11]. The truncated system given in Table 1 covers only a small part of the economy, but it will serve to illustrate the way in which interdependence influences investment decisions and the effect of having more than one scarce factor.

[15]Tinbergen [56, p. 39] defines accounting prices as those "that would prevail if (i) the investment pattern under discussion were actually out, and (ii) equilibrium existed on the markets just mentioned" [i.e., labor, capital, foreign exchange markets]. The relation between accounting and shadow prices is discussed in Chenery [10] and Qayum [42].

[16]Frisch is one of the strongest advocates of the use of linear programming for development planning, as indicated in the preface to a recent methodological study: "In the beginning of 1959, during my work as a United Nations expert in Cairo, I was confronted with the problem of working out a methodology for *optimal investment programming* in a rapidly expanding underdeveloped country. I have always believed—and my Cairo experiences have confirmed it—that such a method must be formulated in terms which ultimately make the problem amenable to linear programming. Otherwise one is practically certain to be taken by surprise afterwards in unexpected balance of payments difficulties and other troubles" [16, p. 1].

Table 1. Evaluation of Production and Import Activities by Accounting Prices[1]

Commodities and Factors	Production Activities				Import Activities			Accounting Prices				Restrictions (12)
	X_1 (1)	X_2 (2)	X_3 (3)	X_4 (4)	M_1 (5)	M_2 (6)	M_3 (7)	Trial A (8)	Trial B (9)	Trial C (10)	Trial D (11)	
1. Metal Products	1.00 (3.41)				1.00 (3.41)			2.55	3.42	3.41	2.26	1000
2. Iron and Steel	-0.22 (-0.89)	1.00 (4.03)				1.00 (4.03)		3.60	4.82	4.03	3.50	1000
3. Iron Ore		-0.08 (-0.25)	1.00 (3.12)				1.00 (3.12)	3.30	4.42	3.12	2.19	0
4. Foreign Exchange				1.00 (4.01)	-0.85 (-3.41)	-1.20 (-4.81)	-1.10 (-4.41)	3.00	4.02	4.01	2.92	0
5. Other Inputs	-0.20 (-0.62)	-0.25 (-0.78)	-0.70 (-2.17)	-0.10 (-0.31)				3.00	3.20	3.10	2.20	—
6. Labor	-0.70 (-1.05)	-0.20 (-0.30)	-0.30 (-0.45)	-1.00 (-1.50)				1.50	1.50	1.50	0.50	—
7. Capital	-0.70 (-0.70)	-2.70 (-2.70)	-0.50 (-0.50)	-2.20 (-2.20)				1.00	1.00	1.00	1.00	—
Social Profitability[2]												
Trial A	-0.59	-0.41	+0.25	-1.00	0	0	0					
Trial B	-0.03	+0.37	+1.23	0	0	0	0					
Trial C	+0.15	0	0	0	0	-0.78	-1.29					
Trial D	0	-0.03	0	0	-0.22	0	-1.02					
Production and Import Levels												
Trial A	0	0	0	2050	1000	1000	0					
Trial B	0	1000	80	850	1000	0	0					
Trial C	1000	1200	98	0	0	0	0					
Trial D	1000	0	0	1464	0	1220	0					

[1] Based on Chenery [11], Table 1. Prices satisfy equation (1) except for P_4 in Trial A. Figures in parentheses are $(a_{ij}P_i)$ for Trial C.

[2] Calculated from equation (4).

The model contains four production activities (X_1, X_2, X_3, X_4) and three import activities (M_1, M_2, M_3). Each activity is represented in Table 1 by a column of coefficients a_{ij}, showing the amount of input $(-)$ or output $(+)$ of commodity i when the activity is operated at unit level. (These coefficients are the boldface figures in columns 1 to 7.) The net output is taken as unity in all cases. The production activity X_1, for example, represents the production of one unit of metal products from .22 units of iron and steel, .20 units of "other inputs," .70 units of labor, and .70 units of capital. The import activity M_1 provides an alternative way of supplying a unit of metal products by an expenditure (input) of .85 units of foreign exchange. A similar choice is provided between X_2 and M_2 (iron and steel) and between X_3 and M_3 (iron ore). The fourth production activity shows the resources used in the marginal export sector to provide a unit of foreign exchange.

In a complete programming model, the amounts of all commodities required for final use at a given level of income would be entered as restrictions on the solution. Similarly, the amounts of available capital and labor of different types would be specified. In this limited illustration, the problem is to supply requirements of 1000 each for metal products and iron and steel at minimum cost. Iron ore and foreign exchange are therefore taken to be intermediate goods having no net outside demand. "Other inputs," labor and capital are supplied from outside the model at prices reflecting their opportunity costs in the rest of the economy. The main difference in principle between this submodel and a complete programming system is that the prices of only the first four commodities are determined in the model in the present case, while in general all prices are so determined.

The four restrictions in the model consist of equations stating that the supply of each of the first four inputs must be equal to the specified demand:[17]

$$X_1 + M_1 = 1000$$
$$-.22X_1 + X_2 + M_2 = 1000$$
(2) $$\qquad -.08X_2 + X_3 + M_3 = 0$$
$$X_4 - .85M_1 - 1.20M_2 - 1.10M_3 = 0$$

The objective is to minimize the amount of capital required to supply the given final demands, with the use of labor and "other inputs" valued at their opportunity costs in terms of capital. This is the same as supplying each commodity at minimum unit cost, since the amount of each to be supplied is fixed.

A feasible solution to the model contains either a production or an import activity for each of the three commodities plus the export activity for foreign exchange. The corresponding activity levels can be determined from equations (2) and are shown at the bottom of Table 1. The amounts of the outside factors (F_i)—labor, capital, and "other inputs"—required by each solution can then be determined from the following equations:

[17] I omit the possibility of overfulfilling demands, since there are no joint products in the present case.

$$\text{Other inputs: } F_5 = .20X_1 + \ \ .25X_2 + .70X_3 + \ \ .10X_4$$

(3)   Labor: $F_6 = .70X_1 + \ \ .20X_2 + .30X_3 + 1.00X_4$

$$\text{Capital: } \quad F_7 = .70X_1 + 2.70X_2 + .50X_3 + 2.20X_4$$

The programming model thus contains two types of equations: price equations of the type of (1), and equations for the supply and demand of commodities and outside factors, (2) and (3). As outlined in [10], the general procedure for solving a programming model of this type involves three steps: (a) finding a feasible program or set of activity levels that satisfies the supply-demand restrictions; (b) calculating the shadow prices associated with the given program; (c) using these prices to determine whether any improvement in the initial program is possible. This procedure is repeated as long as any further improvements can be made.

The programming criterion used to compare projects or activities is the social profitability of each as measured from the shadow prices. Any profitable activity should be included in the program. It is the recalculation of prices that distinguishes this procedure from the partial programming approach suggested by Tinbergen. In either case, however, the test of social profitability of activity j can be expressed as:

$$(4) \qquad\qquad \pi_j = \sum_i a_{ij} P_i$$

By definition, the activities that were used in determining the shadow prices will have a profitability of zero. The optimum solution is identified by the condition that all other activities have zero or negative profitability.

Some idea of the type of adjustment that results from moving from partial toward general equilibrium analysis may be given by determining solutions to the model in Table 1 under four different procedures: (a) the use of market prices; (b) correcting for the overvaluation of foreign exchange; (c) finding the optimum solution for the submodel alone; (d) finding the optimum solution for the submodel with changes in the opportunity costs of labor and other inputs determined from a general programming model. The accounting prices corresponding to each assumption are shown in columns 8 to 11 of Table 1. The calculation of social profitability of each activity, given the accounting prices, is illustrated in the table for trial C by giving cost and revenue figures in parentheses in columns 1 to 7.

Trial A. Assume that market prices are based on the cost of importing and are determined by setting profits on the import activities equal to zero, with a given foreign exchange cost of 3.00. The exchange rate is assumed to be overvalued, so that the price of foreign exchange is less than the cost of securing it through expanded exports. At these market prices, only activity X_3 (iron ore) is profitable, but there is no domestic demand for iron ore unless steel is also produced (the export price is lower than that of imports because of transport costs). The use of market prices therefore leads to imports of steel and metal products, since the opportunity cost of expanding exports is not taken into account. The corresponding activity levels are shown at the bottom of the table.

Trial B. Assume now that we correct for the existing structural equilibrium by setting the price of foreign exchange equal to its opportunity cost of 4.02 as determined from the export activity X_4. Allowance is also made for a rise in the accounting price of "other inputs," some of which are imported. A new set of accounting prices for commodities 1–3 is determined from the cost of imports. Substituting these prices into equation (4) shows that X_2 and X_3 are both profitable ($\pi_2 = .37$, $\pi_3 = 1.23$). Investment should therefore take place in steel, iron ore, and exports on this test.

Trial C. To find the optimum solution to the submodel by linear programming, we can start from trial B and recalculate the shadow prices from the activities that are included: X_2 X_3 X_4 M_1. The four shadow prices P_1 to P_4 are determined by applying equation (1), taking the prices of the outputs (P_5, P_6, P_7) as given. The elimination of excess profits from the prices of iron ore and steel lowers the cost of producing metal products, providing an example of pecuniary external economies. Instead of a loss, activity X_1 now shows a profit of .15 and should be substituted for the import activity M_1. With the original prices for labor and capital, the optimum solution to the submodel is therefore to produce all three commodities and import nothing, since all import activities are unprofitable.

Trial D. If a similar analysis is carried out for the economy as a whole, it is likely that the initial estimate of the opportunity cost of labor (equal to its market price) will be revised. Assume that the shadow price of labor (equal to its marginal product in the rest of the economy) is only a third of its market price, or .5 units of capital. This lower labor cost will reduce the costs of production in different activities in proportion to their use of labor. Since exports are cheapened more than steel production by this calculation, it now becomes socially profitable to import steel and produce metal products. The optimality of this solution is shown by the prices in trial D, in which there is a loss of $-.03$ on X_3. The optimum quantity solution is shown at the bottom of the table. Valuing other inputs and labor at their accounting prices, it has a capital cost of 5760, compared to 8200, 7470, and 7290 in trials A, B, and C.

The programming approach of trials C and D adds two elements to the analysis of accounting prices. The first is the inclusion of repercussions on input prices from investment in supplying sectors. This is one of the main types of dynamic external economies which are omitted from partial analysis. It is much more significant when there are economies of scale. The second element is the revision of the initial estimate of the opportunity costs of labor, capital, and foreign exchange. This revision is determined by the relation between supply and demand for these factors and thus takes into account the requirements of feasibility.[18]

The profitability criterion (usually called the "simplex" criterion) that is used in linear programming is logically equivalent to the SMP test if the same prices are used in both. The two can be put in a comparable form as follows:

[18]An example in which these successive adjustments are calculated in detail is given in [10]. Frisch has outlined a computational procedure for handling large numbers of investment projects without going beyond the capacity of simple calculating equipment [16].

(4a)   Social profit on activity j: $\pi_j = \sum a_{ij}P_i - k_j$

(5)   SMP of investment in activity j: $(SMP)_j = \dfrac{\sum\limits_i a_{ij}P_i}{k_j} = \dfrac{\pi_j}{k_j} + 1$

where $-k_j$ is used for the capital input coefficient instead of a_{7j}. An activity having a positive social profit in equation (4a) will have an SMP of greater than 1.0 in (5), and the same projects would be accepted by either test. If the prices used are not the equilibrium prices, however, the project rankings by the two formulae will not necessarily be the same.

Although the example given here contained only one technique of production for each commodity, linear programming methods readily encompass alternative techniques. In a trial application of linear programming to Indian planning, Sandee [45] includes three alternative ways of increasing agricultural output—increased use of fertilizer, irrigation, and extension services—which are substitutes over a limited range. The four alternative techniques for producing textiles cited by Galenson and Leibenstein [17] could also be more properly evaluated in a programming model in which the cost variation associated with their different requirements for materials, maintenance, and skilled labor could be included. However, it is only necessary to include alternative techniques in a programming model when the choice between them depends on the outcome of the solution. Probably in most cases the range of shadow prices can be foreseen accurately enough to determine in advance which technique is more efficient for a given country. The initial assumption can always be verified after the analysis has been completed by using the resulting prices.

Linear programming can be extended to include many of the indirect effects of investment that are suggested by growth theory. The production of trained labor, the effect on savings, or other indirect benefits can be considered as joint outputs whose value can be specified in the objective function. Similarly, indirect costs of production, such as the provision of housing to urban workers, can be included as additional inputs. The shadow prices computed from such an expanded system will therefore reflect nonmarket as well as market interdependence to the extent that it can be specified in quantitative form.

In formal terms, it is also quite easy to extend the programming model in time and to compute future prices for commodities and factors. The measurement of social profitability could then be made against a pattern of changing future prices. Given the degree of uncertainty attached to all future economic magnitudes, however, this is not likely to be a very useful procedure beyond the customary five-year planning period except in the most general terms. It would, however, be desirable to estimate the change in the equilibrium prices of foreign exchange and labor over a longer period of time, since these are the most important variables in choosing among investment projects.

D. Investment Criteria and
Comparative Advantage

The linear programming approach provides a convenient link to the principle of comparative advantage because the optimal pattern of trade is determined simultaneously with the optimum allocation of investment. The model is considerably more general than that of market equilibrium because it allows for different social objectives and takes account of costs and benefits other than those entering the market. The limitations to the programming model are of two sorts: the form of the restrictions that are specified, and the omission of relationships that cannot be expressed in quantitative form.

The introduction of inelastic demands or increasing costs does not create any more theoretical difficulty in a programming model than in the corresponding general equilibrium system, although the computational aspects of such models have not been widely explored. The accounting prices perform the same function as guides to proper allocation, but the test of social profitability must be applied in marginal rather than average terms. In development programs, this modification is particularly important in the case of exports, where the price elasticity of demand is often rather low.[19] As Nurkse [37] points out, marginal comparative advantage for the under-developed countries may for this reason be quite different from that inferred from the average costs and prices of primary exports.

The existence of increasing returns creates the same problem for the programming model as it does for equilibrium theory. Marginal-cost pricing is not sufficient to determine whether an investment should be undertaken, and the total cost of alternative solutions must also be considered. Although practical methods of solving programming models containing decreasing costs are now being developed, they do not give allocation criteria that rely only on accounting prices. It is approximately correct to say that beyond a certain output level country A has a comparative advantage in the production of steel, but the precise determination of the break-even point depends on the level of output in other sectors also.[20]

The most serious theoretical qualification to the principle of comparative advantage comes from the type of nonquantitative interdependence among sectors that is assumed by Hirschman [23]. If, as he supposes, one growth sequence is more effective than another because it economizes on decision-making ability or provides a greater incentive to political action, a set of criteria having little or nothing to do with comparative advantage is implied. The empirical significance of these psychological and sociological factors remains to be established, but they lead to a conflict that cannot be resolved in economic terms.

[19]A programming model including this feature is given in Chenery [9].

[20]The nature of solutions to this type of problem is considered in [11], from which the data in Table 1 were taken. In this situation of decreasing average cost, the programming model may provide a greater improvement over the solution using partial criteria.

When the practical limitations on information and analysis are recognized, the possibilities of conflict between comparative advantage and growth theory are greatly increased, and Wiles [65] suggests that marginal efficiency calculations may be less important. An aversion to risk-taking may be a valid reason for limiting the extent of specialization in the export of primary products beyond the amount that would be optimum in the light of more accurate information. An inability to measure the extent of economies of scale, labor training, and other sources of external economies also makes possible a continuing disagreement as to their magnitude. . . .

IV. Conclusions

This paper has considered development policy from the standpoint of economic theory, as a problem in operations research, and as it is actually carried on by governments. Much of the confusion in the field stems from a failure to distinguish these different levels of analysis. Theorists are prone to suggest decision rules that omit some of the relevant institutional limits, while economists who have been working in particular areas often arrive at conclusions that do not fit other cases. As in other fields of economics, most of the disagreement can be traced to implicit differences in assumptions.

There are a number of contradictions between the implications of trade theory and growth theory. To make the two theories consistent, it is necessary to discard the assumption of equilibrium in factor markets, to allow for changes in the quantity and quality of factors of production over time, and to take account of internal and external economies of scale. Although under these assumptions market forces do not necessarily lead to efficient resource allocation, a pattern of production and trade can be determined that maximizes income over time. The commodities to be produced and traded cannot be determined by a simple ranking procedure along the lines of classical comparative advantage because of the interdependence among sectors. At best, it may be possible to say, for example, that a country has a comparative advantage in steel production for a specified set of production levels in supplying and using sectors. In advanced countries, this qualification may be unimportant, but in the less developed ones it is crucial in a number of industries.

Much of the attack on the use of comparative advantage is based on its omission of various nonmarket elements. It is assumed that the inclusion of the latter favors the development of industry, and special benefits are often attributed to capital goods and heavy industry. The intangible benefits stemming from trade in the form of new products, improved technology, and technical assistance tend to be overlooked in this discussion. Although I support the critics who wish to include more of growth theory in determining the desirability of specialization, I doubt that this extension will favor balanced growth to the extent that they suppose.

The other main theoretical attack on comparative advantage is aimed at its supposed support for continued specialization in primary exports. Granting the low elasticity of demand for many primary products, it is wrong to conclude that comparative advantage is thereby superseded by principles of balanced growth. The increasing shortage of foreign exchange makes it even more important to economize on its use and to seek efficient ways for increasing its supply. The comparison of domestic to foreign sources of supply that is implied by comparative advantage is no less relevant to this situation than to the case in which investment is more evenly divided between exports and import substitutes.

The aspects of growth theory which do not seem to be reconcilable with the notion of comparative advantage are the sociological and political effects of choosing one production pattern instead of another. While the concept of opportunity cost can be extended to include a number of non-market phenomena, such as labor training and overhead facilities, it can hardly be stretched to cover differences in fertility rates or political attitudes. So far as I can see, in the present state of knowledge of social phenomena, considerations such as these may be used to modify the results of economic analysis but cannot be directly incorporated into it.

At the level of operations research, the search for simple decision rules for investment in low-income countries seems to have been useful mainly in exposing the fallacies in some of the common rules of thumb. One can specify conditions under which ratios such as the capital intensity or the effect on the balance of payments would be a valid indicator of the desirability of an investment, but the apparent gain in simplicity is offset by the danger of applying the test in inappropriate circumstances. A more fruitful approach to partial equilibrium analysis is provided by the use of accounting prices to compute the social profitability of a given use of resources. This method allows simultaneously for several overvalued or undervalued inputs, and it can include whatever elements of general equilibrium analysis are available.

Since market forces cannot be relied on to balance supply and demand under conditions of initial disequilibrium and accelerated growth, a principal concern of development policy is to ensure the consistency of production levels with commodity demands and factor supplies. The technique of linear programming is designed to combine the test of consistency with the test of the social profitability of a given resource use. Although it cannot be applied very extensively in underdeveloped countries, as yet, the programming methodology serves as a guide to improved practical measures.

To most economists, a survey of the procedures actually followed in designing development policy would probably suggest that balance is over-emphasized and that the potential gains from trade are often neglected. This emphasis may be partly justified by the greater uncertainties attached to trade and by an aversion to risk that is greater than seems warranted to the outside observer. Better understanding of the working of the underdeveloped economies and better information for planning is needed to redress the balance and enable countries to secure the potential gains from trade without conflict with measures for domestic development.

References

1. B. A. Balassa, *The Hungarian Experience in Economic Planning.* New Haven 1959.
2. W. Baer, "Puerto Rico: An Evaluation of a Successful Development Program," *Quart. Jour. Econ.,* Nov. 1959, *73,* 645-71.
3. Bank of Israel, *Annual Report, 1959.* Jerusalem 1960.
4. F. M. Bator, "On Capital Productivity, Input Allocation, and Growth," *Quart. Jour. Econ.,* Feb. 1957, *71,* 85−106.
5. N. S. Buchanan, *International Investment and Domestic Welfare.* New York 1945.
6. O. Castellino, "La Scelta degli Investimenti nei Programmi di Sviluppo Economico," *L'Industria,* 1959, No. 1, 60−76.
7. R. E. Caves, *Trade and Economic Structure.* Cambridge 1960.
8. H. B. Chenery, "The Application of Investment Criteria," *Quart. Jour. Econ.,* Feb. 1953, *67,* 76−96.
9. ————, "The Role of Industrialization in Development Programs," *Am. Econ. Rev., Proc.,* May 1955, *45,* 40−57.
10. ————, "Development Policies and Programmes"; *Econ. Bull. for Latin America,* Mar. 1958, *3,* 51−77.
11. ————, "The Interdependence of Investment Decisions," in Abramovitz *et al., The Allocation of Economic Resources.* Stanford 1959.
12. M. Dobb, *An Essay on Economic Growth and Planning.* London 1960.
13. R. Dorfman, P. A. Samuelson, and R. M. Solow, *Linear Programming and Economic Analysis.* New York 1958.
14. O. Eckstein, "Investment Criteria for Economic Development and the Theory of Intertemporal Welfare Economics," *Quart. Jour. Econ.,* Feb. 1957, *71,* 56−85.
15. R. Frisch, *A Method of Working out a Macroeconomic Plan Frame with Particular Reference to the Evaluation of Development Projects, Foreign Trade and Employment.* Oslo 1959 (mimeo.).
16. ————, *A Powerful Method of Approximation in Optimum Investment Computations of the Normal Type.* Oslo 1959 (mimeo.).
17. W. Galenson and H. Leibenstein, "Investment Criteria, Productivity, and Economic Development," *Quart. Jour. Econ.,* Aug. 1955, *69,* 343−70.
18. A. Gerschenkron, "Economic Backwardness in Historical Perspective," in B. Hoselitz, ed., *The Progress of Underdeveloped Areas.* Chicago 1952.
19. Government of India Planning Commission, *The Third Five Year Plan.* New Delhi 1960.
20. G. Haberler, "Some Problems in the Pure Theory of International Trade," *Econ. Jour.,* June 1950, *60,* 223−40.
21. E. Hagen, "An Economic Justification of Protectionism," *Quart. Jour. Econ.,* Nov. 1958, *72,* 496−514.

22. B. Higgins, *Economic Development.* New York 1958.
23. A. O. Hirschman, *The Strategy of Economic Development.* New Haven 1958.
24. ————, "Investment Criteria and Capital Intensity Once Again," *Quart. Jour. Econ.,* Aug. 1958, *72,* 469—71.
25. A. E. Kahn, "Investment Criteria in Development Programs," *Quart. Jour. Econ.,* Feb. 1951, *65,* 38—61.
26. C. P. Kindleberger, *The Terms of Trade: A European Case Study.* New York 1956.
27. R. Komiya, "A Note on Professor Mahalanobis' Model of Indian Economic Planning," *Rev. Econ. Stat.,* Feb. 1959, *41,* 29—35.
28. H. Leibenstein, "Why Do We Disagree on Investment Policies for Development?" *Indian Econ. Jour.,* Apr. 1958, *5,* 369—86.
29. W. A. Lewis, "Economic Development with Unlimited Supplies of Labor," *Manchester School,* May 1954.
30. P. C. Mahalanobis, "The Approach of Operational Research to Planning in India," *Sankhya,* Dec. 1955, *16,* 3—131.
31. K. Mandelbaum, *The Industrialization of Backward Areas.* Oxford 1945.
32. J. M. Montias, "Planning with Material Balances in Soviet-type Economies," *Am. Econ. Rev.,* Dec. 1959, *49,* 963-85.
33. H. Myint, "The Classical Theory of International Trade and the Underdeveloped Countries," *Econ. Jour.,* June 1958, *68,* 317-37.
34. G. Myrdal, *Economic Theory and Underdeveloped Regions.* London 1957.
35. H. Neisser, "Investment Criteria, Productivity and Economic Development," *Quart. Jour. Econ.,* Nov. 1956, *70,* 644—47.
36. R. Nurkse, *Problems of Capital Formation in Underdeveloped Countries.* Oxford 1953.
37. ————, *Patterns of Trade and Development.* Stockholm 1959.
38. P. G. Ohlin, "Balanced Economic Growth in History," *Am. Econ. Rev., Proc.,* May 1959, *49,* 338—53.
39. The Philippines National Economic Council, *The Five-Year Economic and Social Development Program for Fiscal Years 1957—1961.* Manila 1957.
40. J. J. Polak, "Balance of Payments Problems of Countries Reconstructing with the Help of Foreign Loans," *Quart. Jour. Econ.,* Feb. 1943, *57,* 208—40.
41. R. Prebisch, "Commercial Policy in the Underdeveloped Countries," *Am. Econ. Rev., Proc.,* May 1959, *49,* 251—73.
42. A. Qayum, *Theory and Policy of Accounting Prices.* Amsterdam 1959.
43. R. Rosenstein-Rodan, "Problems of Industrialization of Eastern and South-Eastern Europe," *Econ. Jour.,* June-Sept. 1943, *53,* 205—16.
44. W. W. Rostow, "The Take-Off into Self-Sustained Growth," *Econ. Jour.,* Mar. 1956, *66,* 25—48.
45. J. Sandee, *A Long-Term Planning Model for India.* United Nations pub. New York 1959.
46. T. W. Schultz, "Latin American Economic Policy Lessons," *Am. Econ. Rev., Proc.,* May 1956, *46,* 425—32.
47. T. Scitovsky, "Two Concepts of External Economies," *Jour. Pol. Econ.,* April 1954, *62,* 143—51.
48. ————, "Growth-Balanced or Unbalanced," in M. Abramowitz *et al., The Allocation of Economic Resources* Stanford 1959.

49. A. K. Sen, "Some Notes on the Choice of Capital Intensity in Development Planning," *Quart. Jour. Econ.,* Nov. 1957, *71,* 561–84.

50. J. Sheahan, "International Specialization and the Concept of Balanced Growth," *Quart. Jour. Econ.,* May 1958, *72,* 183-97.

51. H. W. Singer, "The Distribution of Gains Between Investing and Borrowing Countries," *Amer. Econ. Rev., Proc.,* May 1950, *40,* 473–85.

52. G. Stigler, "Production and Distribution in the Short Run," reprinted in Am. Econ. Assoc., *Readings in the Theory of Income Distribution.* Philadelphia 1946.

53. P. Streeten, "Unbalanced Growth," *Oxford Econ. Papers,* June 1959, *11,* 167–91.

54. J. Tinbergen, "The Relevance of Theoretical Criteria in the Selection of Investment Plans," in M. Millikan, ed., *Investment Criteria and Economic Growth.* Cambridge 1955.

55. ———, *Economic Policy: Principles and Design.* Amsterdam 1956.

56. ———, *The Design of Development.* Baltimore 1958.

57. United Nations, Department of Economic and Social Affairs, *Analyses and Projections of Economic Development.* New York 1955.

58. ———, *Analyses and Projections of Economic Development.* III. *The Economic Development of Colombia.* Geneva 1957.

59. ———, *Analyses and Projections of Economic Development.* V. *The Economic Development of Argentina.* Mexico City 1960.

60. ———, *Analyses and Projections of Economic Development.* VI. *The Industrial Development of Peru.* Mexico City 1959.

61. United Nations, *Manual of Economic Development Projects.* New York 1959.

62. A. Vaidyanathan, "A Survey of the Literature on Investment Criteria and Development of Underdeveloped Countries," *Ind. Econ. Jour.,* Oct. 1956, *4,* 122–44.

63. J. Viner, *International Trade and Economic Development.* Oxford 1953.

64. ———, "Stability and Progress: The Poorer Countries' Problem," in D. Hague, ed., *Stability and Progress in the World Economy.* London 1958 (with comment by R. Nurkse).

65. P. Wiles, "Growth versus Choice," *Econ. Jour.,* June 1956, *66,* 244–55.

66. J. H. Williams, "The Theory of International Trade Reconsidered," *Econ. Jour.,* June 1929, *39,* 195–209. Reprinted in Am. Econ. Assoc., *Readings in the Theory of International Trade.* Philadelphia 1949.

The Distribution of Gains between Investing and Borrowing Countries

Hans W. Singer

How the Importance of Foreign Trade
to Underdeveloped Countries
Has Been Obscured

23

International trade is of very considerable importance to underdeveloped countries, and the benefits which they derive from trade and any variations in their trade affect their national incomes very deeply. The opposite view, which is frequent among economists, namely that trade is less important to the underdeveloped countries than it is to industrialized countries, may be said to derive from a logical confusion—very easy to slip into—between the absolute amount of foreign trade, which is known to be an increasing function of national income, and the ratio of foreign trade to national income. Foreign trade tends to be proportionately most important when incomes are lowest. Second, fluctuations in the volume and value of

From the *American Economic Review,* Papers and Proceedings, May 1950. Reprinted by permission of the author and publisher. The author is a member of the Economic Secretariat, United Nations.

foreign trade tend to be proportionately more violent in trade of under-developed countries and therefore *a fortiori* also more important in relation to national income. Third, and *a fortissimo*, fluctuations in foreign trade tend to be immensely more important for underdeveloped countries in relation to that small margin of income over subsistence needs which forms the source of capital formation, for which they often depend on export surpluses over consumption goods required from abroad.

In addition to the logical confusion mentioned above, the great importance of foreign trade to underdeveloped countries may also have been obscured by the great discrepancy in the productivity of labor in the underdeveloped countries as between the industries and occupations catering for export and those catering for domestic production. The export industries in underdeveloped countries—metal mines, plantations, etc.—are often highly capital-intensive industries supported by a great deal of imported foreign technology. By contrast, production for do-mestic use, especially of food and clothing, is often of a very primitive subsistence nature. Thus the economy of the underdeveloped countries often presents the spectacle of a dualistic economic structure: a high-productivity sector producing for export coexisting with a low-productivity sector producing for the domestic market. Employment statistics in underdeveloped countries do not adequately reflect the importance of foreign trade, since the productivity of each person employed in the export sector tends to be a multiple of that of each person employed in the domestic sector. Since, however, employment statistics for underdeveloped countries are notoriously easier to compile than national income statistics, it is again easy to slip from the fact that the proportion of persons employed in export trade is often lower in underdeveloped countries than in industrialized countries to the conclusion that foreign trade is less important to them. This conclusion is fallacious, since it implicitly assumes rough equivalence of produc-tivity in the export and domestic sectors. This equivalence may be safely assumed in the industrialized countries but not in the under-developed countries.

A third factor which has contributed to the view that foreign trade is unimportant in underdeveloped countries is the indisputable fact that in many underdeveloped countries there are large self-contained groups which are outside the monetary economy altogether and are therefore not affected by any changes in foreign trade. In industrialized countries, by contrast, it is true that repercussions from changes in foreign trade are more widely spread; but they are also more thinly spread.[1]

---

[1]A more statistical factor might be mentioned. Some underdeveloped countries—Iran would be an illustration—exclude important parts of their exports and imports from their foreign trade statistics insofar as the transactions of foreign companies operating in the underdeveloped country are concerned. This is a tangible recognition of the fact that these pieces of foreign investments and their doings are not an integral part of the underdeveloped economy.

The Drain on the Benefits of Investment

The previously mentioned higher productivity of the foreign trade sector in underdeveloped countries might, at first sight, be considered as a cogent argument in favor of the view that foreign trade has been particularly beneficial to underdeveloped countries in raising their general standards of productivity, changing their economies in the direction of a monetary economy, and spreading knowledge of more capital-intensive methods of production and modern technology. That, however, is much less clearly established than might be thought. The question of ownership as well as of opportunity costs enters at this point. The facilities for producing export goods in underdeveloped countries are often foreign-owned as a result of previous investment in these countries. Again we must beware of hasty conclusions. Our first reaction would be to argue that this fact further enhances the importance and benefits of trade to underdeveloped countries, since trade has also led to foreign investment in those countries and has promoted capital formation with its cumulative and multiplier effects. This is also how the matter is looked at in the economic textbooks—certainly those written by nonsocialist economists of the industrialized countries. That view, however, has never been really accepted by the more articulate economists in the underdeveloped countries themselves, not to mention popular opinion in those countries; and it seems to the present writer that there is much more in their view than is allowed for by the economic textbooks.

Can it be possible that we economists have become slaves to the geographers? Could it not be that in many cases the productive facilities for export from underdeveloped countries, which were so largely a result of foreign investment, never became a part of the internal economic structure of those underdeveloped countries themselves except in the purely geographical and physical sense? Economically speaking, they were really an outpost of the economies of the more developed investing countries. The main secondary multiplier effects, which the textbooks tell us to expect from investment, took place not where the investment was physically or geographically located but (to the extent that the results of these investments returned directly home) where the investment came from.[2] I would suggest that if the proper economic test of investment is the multiplier effect in the form of cumulative additions to income, employment, capital, technical knowledge, and growth of external economies, then a good deal of the investment in underdeveloped countries which we used to consider as "foreign" should in fact be considered as domestic investment on the part of the industrialized countries.

Where the purpose and effect of the investments were to open up new sources of food for the people and for the machines of industrialized countries, we have strictly domestic investment in the relevant economic

[2]Often underdeveloped countries had the chance to use royalties or other income from foreign investment judiciously for the transformation of their internal economic structure—a chance more often missed than caught by the forelock!

sense, although for reasons of physical geography, climate, etc., it had to be made overseas. Thus the fact that the opening up of underdeveloped countries for trade has led to or been made possible by foreign investment in those countries does not seem a generally valid proof that this combination has been of particular benefit to those countries. The very differential in productivity between the export sectors and the domestic sectors of the underdeveloped countries, previously mentioned as an indication of the importance of foreign trade to underdeveloped countries, is also itself an indication that the more productive export sectors—often foreign-owned—have not become a real part of the economies of underdeveloped countries.

The Nonprogressive Nature of Traditional Investment

We may go even further. If we apply the principle of opportunity costs to the development of nations, the import of capital into underdeveloped countries for the purpose of making them into providers of food and raw materials for the industrialized countries may have been not only rather ineffective in giving them the normal benefits of investment and trade but positively harmful. The tea plantations of Ceylon, the oil wells of Iran, the copper mines of Chile, and the cocoa industry of the Gold Coast may all be more productive than domestic agriculture in these countries; but they may well be less productive than domestic industries in those countries which might have developed if those countries had not become as specialized as they now are in the export of food and raw materials, thus providing the means of producing manufactured goods elsewhere with superior efficiency. Admittedly, it is a matter of speculation whether, in the absence of such highly specialized "export" development, any other kind of development would have taken its place. But the possibility cannot be assumed away. Could it be that the export development has absorbed what little entrepreneurial initiative and domestic investment there was, and even tempted domestic savings abroad? We must compare, not what is with what was, but what is with what would have been otherwise—a tantalizingly inconclusive business. All we can say is that the process of traditional investment taken by itself seems to have been insufficient to initiate domestic development unless it appeared in the form of migration of persons.

The principle of specialization along the lines of static comparative advantages has never been generally accepted in the underdeveloped countries, and it has not even been generally intellectually accepted in the industrialized countries themselves. Again it is difficult not to feel that there is more to be said on the subject than most of the textbooks will admit. In the economic life of a country and in its economic history, a most important element is the mechanism by which "one thing leads to another," and the most important contribution of an industry is not its immediate product (as is perforce assumed by economists and statisticians) and not even its effect on other industries and immediate social benefits (thus far economists have been led to go by Marshall and Pigo) but perhaps beyond this its effect on the general level of education, skill, way of life, inventiveness, habits, store of technology, creation of new demand, etc. And this is perhaps precisely the reason why manufacturing industries are so universally desired by underdeveloped countries: they provide the growing points for increased technical knowledge, urban education, and the dynamism and resilience that goes with urban civilization, as well as the direct Marshallian external economies. No doubt under different circumstances commerce, farming, and plantation agriculture have proved capable of being such growing points, but manufacturing industry is unmatched in our present age.

By specializing on exports of food and raw materials and thus making the underdeveloped countries further contribute to the concentration of industry in the already industrialized countries, foreign trade and the foreign investment which went with it may have spread present static benefits fairly over both. They may have had very different effects if we think from the point of view, not of static comparative advantages, but of the flow of history of a country. Of this latter school of thought the "infant" argument for protection is but a sickly and often illegitimate offspring.

To summarize, then, the position reached thus far, the specialization of underdeveloped countries on export of food and raw materials to industrialized countries, largely as a result of investment by the latter, has been unfortunate for the underdeveloped countries for two reasons: (1) it removed most of the secondary and cumulative effects of investment from the country in which the investment took place to the investing country; and (2) it diverted the underdeveloped countries into types of activity offering less scope for technical progress, internal and external economies taken by themselves, and withheld from the course of their economic history a central factor of dynamic radiation which has revolutionized society in the industrialized countries. But there is a third factor of perhaps even greater importance which has reduced the benefits to underdeveloped countries of foreign trade-*cum*-investment based on export specialization in food and raw materials. This third factor relates to terms of trade.

It is a matter of historical fact that ever since the seventies the trend of prices has been heavily against sellers of food and raw materials and in favor of the sellers of manufactured articles. The statistics are open to doubt and to objection in detail, but the general story which they tell is unmistakable.[3] What is the meaning of these changing price relations?

The Meaning of Unfavorable Price Relations

The possibility that these changing price relations simply reflect changes in the real costs of the manufactured exports of the industrialized countries relative to those of the food and primary materials of the underdeveloped

[3]See *Relative Prices of Exports and Imports of Under-developed Countries,* United Nations, Department of Economic Affairs, Sales No. 1949 II.B.3.

countries can be dismissed. All the evidence is that productivity has increased if anything less fast in the production of food and raw materials, even in the industrialized countries[4] but most certainly in the underdeveloped countries, than has productivity in the manufacturing industries of the industrialized countries. The possibility that changing price relations could merely reflect relative trends in productivity may be considered as disposed of by the very fact that standards of living in industrialized countries (largely governed by productivity in manufacturing industries) have risen demonstrably faster than standards of living in underdeveloped countries (generally governed by productivity in agriculture and primary production) over the last sixty or seventy years. However important foreign trade may be to underdeveloped countries, had deteriorated terms of trade (from the point of view of the underdeveloped countries) reflected relative trends of productivity, this could most assuredly not have failed to show in relative levels of internal real incomes as well.

Dismissing, then, changes in productivity as a governing factor in changing terms of trade, the following explanation presents itself: The fruits of technical progress may be distributed either to producers (in the form of rising incomes) or to consumers (in the form of lower prices). In the case of manufactured commodities produced in more developed countries, the former method, i.e., distribution to producers through higher incomes, was much more important than the second method, while the second method prevailed more in the case of food and raw-material production in the underdeveloped countries. Generalizing, we may say that technical progress in manufacturing industries showed in a rise in incomes, while technical progress in the production of food and raw materials in underdeveloped countries showed in a fall in prices. Now, in the general case, there is no reason why one or the other method should be generally preferable. There may, indeed, be different employment, monetary, or distributive effects of the two methods; but this is not a matter which concerns us in the present argument where we are not concerned with internal income distribution. In a closed economy the general body of producers and the general body of consumers can be considered as identical, and the two methods of distributing the fruits of technical progress appear merely as two formally different ways of increasing real incomes.

When we consider foreign trade, however, the picture is fundamentally changed. The producers and the consumers can no longer be considered as the same body of people. The producers are at home; the consumers are abroad.

[4]According to data of the WPA research project, output per wage earner in a sample of fifty-four manufacturing industries increased by 57 per cent during the twenty years 1919-1939; over the same period, agriculture increased only by 23 per cent, anthracite coal mining by 15 per cent, and bituminous coal mining by 35 per cent. In the various fields of mineral mining, however, progress was as fast as in manufacturing. According to data of the National Bureau of Economic Research, the rate of increase in output per worker was 1.8 per cent per annum in manufacturing industries (1899-1939) but only 1.6 per cent in agriculture (1890-1940) and in mining, excluding petroleum (1902-1939). In petroleum production, however, it was faster than in manufacturing.

Rising incomes of home producers to the extent that they are in excess of increased productivity are an absolute burden on the foreign consumer. Even if the rise in the income of home producers is offset by increases in productivity so that prices remain constant or even fall by less than the gain in productivity, this is still a relative burden on foreign consumers, in the sense that they lose part or all of the potential fruits of technical progress in the form of lower prices. On the other hand, where the fruits of technical progress are passed on by reduced prices, the foreign consumer benefits along with the home consumer. Nor can it be said, in view of the notorious inelasticity of demand for primary commodities, that the fall in their relative prices has been compensated by total revenue effects.

Other factors have also contributed to the falling long-term trend of prices of primary products in terms of manufactures, apart from the absence of pressure of producers for higher incomes. Technical progress, while it operates unequivocally in favor of manufactures—since the rise in real incomes generates a more than proportionate increase in the demand for manufactures—has not the same effect on the demand for food and raw materials. In the case of food, demand is not very sensitive to rises in real income, and in the case of raw materials, technical progress in manufacturing actually largely consists of a reduction in the amount of raw materials used per unit of output, which may compensate or even overcompensate the increase in the volume of manufacturing output. This lack of an automatic multiplication in demand, coupled with the low price elasticity of demand for both raw materials and food, results in large price falls, not only cyclical but also structural.

The End Result: Maldistribution of Gains

Thus it may be said that foreign investment of the traditional type which sought its repayment in the direct stimulation of exports of primary commodities, either to the investing country directly or indirectly through multilateral relations, had its beneficial cumulative effects in the investing country; and the people of the latter, in their capacity as consumers, also enjoyed the fruits of technical progress in the manufacture of primary commodities thus stimulated and at the same time, in their capacity as producers, enjoyed the fruits of technical progress in the production of manufactured commodities. The industrialized countries have had the best of both worlds, both as consumers of primary commodities and as producers of manufactured articles; the underdeveloped countries have had the worst of both worlds, as consumers of manufactures and as producers of raw materials. This perhaps is the legitimate germ of truth in the charge that foreign investment of the traditional type formed part of a system of "economic imperialism" and of "exploitation."

Even if we disregard the theory of deliberately sinister machinations, there may be legitimate grounds in the arguments set out above for maintaining that the benefits of foreign trade and investment have not been equally shared between the two groups of countries. The capital-exporting countries have received their repayment many times over in the following five forms: (1) possibility of building up exports of manufactures and thus transferring their population from low-productivity occupations to high-productivity occupations; (2) enjoyment of the internal economies of expanded manufacturing industries; (3) enjoyment of the general dynamic impulse radiating from industries in a progressive society; (4) enjoyment of the fruits of technical progress in primary production as main consumers of primary commodities; (5) enjoyment of a contribution from foreign consumers of manufactured articles, representing as it were their contribution to the rising incomes of the producers of manufactured articles.

By contrast, what the underdeveloped countries have to show cannot compare with this formidable list of benefits derived by the industrialized countries from the traditional trade-*cum*-investment system. Perhaps the widespread though inarticulate feeling in the underdeveloped countries that the dice have been loaded against them is not so devoid of foundation after all, as the pure theory of exchange might have led one to believe.

It is, of course, true that there are transfer difficulties on the part of the underdeveloped countries which are avoided by production for export directly to the investing countries, but the above analysis may perhaps make a contribution to understanding why this traditional investment system broke down so rapidly and so irreparably in 1929 and 1930. The industrialized countries had already received real repayment from their foreign investments in the five forms described above, and in these ways they may have collected a pretty good return on their investments. When, on top of the returns received in those five forms, they also tried to "get their money back," they may perhaps have been asking (in the economic though not in the legal sense) for double payment; they may have been trying to get a quart out of a pint bottle. . . .

Potential Consequences of This Analysis

Rather than end on a wild historical speculation, it may be useful to summarize the type of economic measures and economic policies which would result from the analysis presented in this paper. The first conclusion would be that in the interest of the underdeveloped countries, of world national income, and perhaps ultimately of the industrialized countries themselves, the purposes of foreign investment and foreign trade ought perhaps to be redefined as producing gradual changes in the structure of comparative advantages and of the comparative endowment of the different countries rather than developing a world trading system based on existing comparative advantages and existing distribution of endowments. This, perhaps, is the real significance of the present movement toward giving technical assistance to underdeveloped countries not necessarily linked with actual trade or investment. The emphasis on technical assistance may be interpreted as a recognition that the present structure of comparative advantages and endowments is not such that it should be considered as a permanent basis for a future international division of labor.

Insofar as the underdeveloped countries continue to be the source of food and primary materials and insofar as trade, investment, and technical assistance are working in that direction by expanding primary production, the main requirement of underdeveloped countries would seem to be to provide for some method of income absorption to ensure that the results of technical progress are retained in the underdeveloped countries in a manner analogous to what occurs in the industrialized countries. Perhaps the most important measure required in this field is the reinvestment of profits in the underdeveloped countries themselves, or else the absorption of profits by fiscal measures and their utilization for the finance of economic development, and the absorption of rising productivity in primary production in rising real wages and other real incomes, provided that the increment is utilized for an increase in domestic savings and the growth of markets of a kind suitable for the development of domestic industries. Perhaps this last argument, namely the necessity of some form of domestic absorption of the fruits of technical progress in primary production, provides the rationale for the concern which the underdeveloped countries show for the introduction of progressive social legislation. Higher standards of wages and social welfare, however, are not a highly commendable cure for bad terms of trade except where the increment leads to domestic savings and investment. Where higher wages and social services are prematurely introduced and indiscriminately applied to export and domestic industries, they may in the end turn out to be a retarding factor in economic development and undermine the international bargaining strength of the primary producers. Absorption of the fruits of technical progress in primary production is not enough; what is wanted is absorption for reinvestment.

Finally, the argument put forward in this paper would point the lesson that a flow of international investment into the underdeveloped countries will contribute to their economic development only if it is absorbed into their economic system, i.e., if a good deal of complementary domestic investment is generated and the requisite domestic resources are found.

Trends in Terms of Trade, and Their
Repercussions on Primary Producers

Theodore Morgan

24

I. Concepts of the Terms of Trade

With one exception, we will in this paper use the simplest and most available concept of the terms of trade:

1. The ratio between the prices of two commodities, or of two groups of commodities, that may be exchanged against each other. This is often called the *commodity terms of trade*; Taussig called it the 'net barter terms of trade'.
2. The classical concept is different. It looked to the real quantity of factors exchanged for each other through the intermediation of commodities—in Marshall, the labour in G-bales exchanged for the

Excerpted from a paper of the above name in Roy Harrod and Douglas Hague, eds., *International Trade Theory in a Developing World*, Macmillan and Co., Ltd., London, and St. Martin's Press, Inc., New York, 1963. The author is professor of economics, University of Wisconsin.

labour in E-bales. The classical concept is thus *the double factoral terms of trade*, or the commodity terms of trade times the reciprocal of changes in technical coefficients for exports and imports.

These two concepts amount to the same thing if there are constant proportions among the factors used in each of two countries trading, and constant returns to scale. Conversely, they diverge to the extent there are technological improvements and/or diminishing returns due to limited supply of one of the factors.

The classical concept therefore immediately indicates a limitation on the significance of the commodity terms of international trade: a change in the latter might be offset, in its effect on factor real earnings, by an inverse change in factor productivity. A further qualification lies in possible effects on distribution of income, including the remission abroad of earnings on foreign investment and for immigrant labour services, as an offset to export surpluses. Such surpluses may be a fourth or more of the total value of exports, so that the question of the proportion in which export earnings are shared may be as important for local people as the terms of .trade. A third qualification is that real prices received by primary producers can differ from export and import (border) prices to the extent that there are export or import tariffs, price divergences due to exchange control or quota restrictions on imports, and, of course, domestic transportation and handling costs.[1] Fourth and finally, the terms of trade ignore favourable or unfavourable effects from the check or stimulus they can give to growth and/or business cycle cumulative processes of expansion or contraction.[2]

At least five other terms-of-trade concepts have been suggested, of which three can be calculated, and may be useful for special purposes.

3. One of these, *the income terms of trade*, is used below. It is the index of the value for exports divided by the index of the price for imports, and so shows the imports obtainable in exchange for the exports actually sent out.[3]

[1]Cf. H. Myint: 'The Gains from International Trade and the Backward Countries', *Rev. of Econ. Stud.*, Vol. XXII (2), 1954-55, pp. 131, 132.

[2]Haberler feels that the possible distribution and business cycle effects of trade and terms-of-trade changes give 'such an unreal air [to the basic analysis] that there is little point in pursuing [it] further'. *The Theory of International Trade,* New York, Macmillan, 1937, p. 166.

[3]Or, alternatively, the income terms of trade weights the commodity terms of trade in proportion to shifts in the volume of exports. The two statements are algebraically identical. The income of trade are, by definition,

$$\frac{Px_i}{Px_o} \frac{Qx_i}{Qx_o} \cdot \frac{1}{\dfrac{Pm_i}{Pm_o}},$$

where P is price, Q is quantity, x stands for exports, m for imports, and i for the given year, o for the base year. The formula can be presented instead as: (continued)

4. A fourth terms-of-trade concept is Taussig's 'gross barter terms of trade', or the ratio of real values of exports to real values of imports (*International Trade*, New York, 1927, p. 113). This, he judges, should be used whenever a country's balance of payments contains unilateral payments, that is, more than goods and services only. (Cf. Haberler's criticism of the concept, *op. cit.* p. 164.)

5. The 'single factoral terms of trade' is a modification of the classical double factoral concept 2 above. It measures the quantity of imports bought by a unit of factors; that is, the commodity terms of trade corrected for changes in productivity in producing exports.

6. Viner suggests that a closer approximation to the real gain from trade can be obtained by multiplying 5, the single factoral terms of trade, by the 'disutility co-efficient' of the factor inputs used in the export commodities.

7. A still closer approximation, Viner continues, is logically obtainable through multiplying 6 by an index of the average relative marginal utility per unit of imported commodities, and of home commodities that would have been produced had resources not been shifted to producing for exports.

Concepts 6 and 7 are hardly calculable, even given much statistical coverage, while 2 and 5 require almost as much coverage, as soon as we move away from a world in which there is only one factor. But 1, 3 and 4 are plain going.[4]

II.   Importance of the Terms of Trade

A chorus of opinion from economists who in other respects have held very different views attests to the importance of the (commodity) terms of trade. In 1912, the late Lord Keynes estimated at £37 million the extent to which Britain was worse off because of falling terms of trade between 1900 and 1911.[5] D. H. Robertson in 1915 spoke of the trend of the terms of trade as 'perhaps the most significant economic fact in the world today'.[6] The UN Committee authors of *Commodity Trade and Economic Development*

$$\frac{Px_i/Px_o}{Pm_i/Pm_o} \cdot \frac{Qx_i}{Qx_o} .$$

See G. S. Dorrance, 'The Income Terms of Trade', *Review of Economic Studies*, 1948–49, pp. 50-6.

[4]Cf. Viner, *Studies in the Theory of International Trade*, pp. 558-65; Haberler, *International Trade*, 159-66; C. Iversen, *International Capital Movements*, Copenhagen and London (Oxford Press), 1936, pp. 337-42; W. W. Rostow, 'The Terms of Trade in Theory and Practice', *The Economic History Review*, 2nd series, Vol. iii, No. 1, 1950, pp. 1-15.

[5]*Economic Journal*, 1912, 'Official Papers, "Return of Estimated Value of Foreign Trade of United Kingdom at Prices of 1900" ', p. 630. Quoted in W. W. Rostow, 'The Terms of Trade in Theory and Practice', *The Economic History Review*, 2nd series, Vol. iii, No. 1, 1950, p. 14.

[6]*Industrial Fluctuations*, King, London, 1915 (reprinted London School of Economics, 1948), p. 169 n.

stressed the basic policy implications of terms-of-trade changes.[7] Myrdal and Kindleberger both draw from it basic guides to economic policy.[8] So also does Raul Prebisch.[9] And recently a distinguished group of British economists, in a letter to *The Times*, worried over the terms of trade of under-developed areas: 'It is not always realized that a comparatively small fall in commodity prices is equivalent in its effect to a cut of billions of dollars in aid to under-developed countries.'[10]

III. Causes of Changes in the Terms of Trade

Analyses in this century have run in two channels. One is short-run monetary or cycle analysis, classical in inspiration, and once stimulated by a remarkable teacher, Taussig, and once again by a major problem, German reparations payments in the 1920s. The second is longer-run, emphasizing basic productivity and demand trends, and shifts of functions rather than movements along given functions. Some of these longer-run analyses are partial, arguing that some one influence or trend is dominant, at least for a given commodity, period and place. Others are 'complete', or macro-economic, attempting to include in logic, or even empirically, all the supply and demand influences on both the export and import sides, or primary and secondary production sides.

The following table attempts to present in an organized pattern the more conspicuous of these hypotheses. Unless there is explicit exception, the terms of trade are spoken of below with primary products or agricultural products in the numerator, and secondary products or manufactures in the denominator; that is, a 'rise in the terms of trade' means that primary product prices are rising compared to secondary products.

Of the 18 entries below, 4 offer short-run monetary or cyclical explanations, specific to a particular country and time. Of the 14 longer-run interpretations, 10 are 'partial' approaches (as defined above). Among these 10, 3 accept (for their periods or for the 'long run') and explain improving terms of trade for agriculture as compared to manufacturing; 3 more accept and explain heterogeneous experience, and 4 assume and explain worsening terms of trade. Then there are the 4 remaining, whom I have classified as offering a macro-economic or 'complete' analysis: 1 predicts

[7]New York, 1953, p. 13.

[8]*An International Economy,* Harper, New York, 1956, pp. 230 *et seq.,* and *The Terms of Trade, A European Case Study,* Technology Press and Wiley, New York, 1956, pp. 253-7.

[9]*The Economic Development of Latin America,* United Nations, New York, 1950, pp. 8 fol.

[10]October 29, 1957. I have found only one dissenting voice. Frank Graham was a sceptic on this as on other matters, and deprecates the terms of trade between two countries only, as 'irrelevant to almost any conceivable purpose, and probably not susceptible to any form of measurement'. *Theory of International Values,* Princeton, 1948, p. 249.

improving terms of trade for primary products, 1 deterioration, and 1 sees stability in its given time period, and 1 is agnostic.[11]

IV.   World Experience of the Terms of Trade

We will first try to summarize long-run experience up to about 1950; then to present in more detail estimates for the past ten to twenty-odd years.

The Long Run

The frequent generalization that prices of primary products have been falling relative to prices of manufactures has as its substantial basis British terms-of-trade data stretching from 1876-80 to 1938 (and in one series, 1948).[12] The trend downward for primary product prices seems plain despite a wide fluctuation in the 1920s and 1930s.

In addition we have had more recently the major Kindleberger study of the terms of trade of European countries, in which he concludes that in the European context the terms of trade between primary products and manufactures do *not* run against primary products, though they 'favor the developed and run against the underdeveloped countries'.[13]

Any long series is subject to a fringe of uncertainty due to weighting, and qualitative changes, so that only major shifts are to be taken seriously. But in addition the British data have, as a number of economists have pointed out, two systematic sources of bias. (1) Qualitative improvements in products are inadequately accounted for in the data, and these improvements (I should like to assert here, without digressing into evidence) have taken place predominantly in manufacturing. Hence the British and all similar data systematically understate, over a period of time, the relative price position of primary producers. (2) In addition the British (or European or like data) cannot validly be used to measure the price position of primary producers of the world in their own regions and countries. The reason is that transportation costs have been falling over the past century and more; and primary producers have been receiving prices that fell short of British prices by a smaller and smaller amount, while at the same time they have been paying prices for manufactures that were larger than British prices by a smaller and smaller amount. Both distortions work in the same direction: producers of primary goods in the world have been doing much better than the British data

[11]Haberler generalized from these studies in his Cairo lectures: *International Trade and Economic Development,* National Bank of Egypt, Cairo, 1959, p. 19. See also his 'The Terms of Trade and Economic Development', *Round Table,* Int. Econ. Assoc., Rio de Janeiro, August, 1957.

[12]League of Nations: *Industrialization and Foreign Trade,* Geneva,1945, pp. 154-7. The main author is Folke Hilgerdt. The data of this study were reproduced and added to in the United Nations' *Relative Prices of Exports and Imports of Underdeveloped Countries,* Lake Success, New York, 1949, pp. 21-4.

[13]*Op. cit.* pp. 239, 263-4.

Table 1. *Analysis of Changes in Terms of Trade,*
1912–60

	Short-run, Monetary Analysis	Long-run Patterns of Analysis	
		Partial	Complete
1. Keynes, 1912		Terms of trade are rising, due to diminishing returns in primary production	
2. Robertson, 1915		Terms of trade are rising, due to diminishing returns in primary production	
3. Beveridge, 1923			Approx. stability exists in terms of trade: productivity and demand in both industry and agriculture must be taken into account
4. Viner, 1924 (Also the 1920s discussions of German reparations effects)	Presumption terms of trade turn in favor of borrowing or reparations-receiving country		
5, 6, 7. Coates 1915; Carr, 1931; Stovel, 1959	Contradiction to Viner's theory re Canadian 1900–13 experience: not borrowing, but cyclical boom and industrial growth explain terms of trade change		
8. Colin Clark, 1942			Prediction of rising terms of trade; macro-mathematical model
9. Kindleberger I, 1943, 1950			Terms of trade of primary-producing countries are falling due to 'continuously increasing efficiency, and . . . Engel's law'
10. Kindelberger II, 1956		Falling terms of trade of underdeveloped countries (not of primary commodities), due to lack of flexibility in economic adjustments	

Table 1.   *Analysis of Changes in Terms of Trade,*
1912—60 (Cont'd.)

	Short-run, Monetary Analysis	Long-run Patterns of Analysis	
		Partial	Complete
11. Prebisch, 1950		Falling terms of trade, due to wage rises of unionized workers in indus-trialized countries, and monopoly pricing	
12. U.N. experts, 1953			Agnostic judgement: no adequate ground for choos-ing among theories
13. Arthur Lewis, 1955		Poor terms-of-trade experience of under-developed countries due to wages in exports fixed by peasant - earnings' level	
14. Myrdal, 1956		'Under-developed countries have had rather bad luck', plus lack of flexi-bility	
15. Ellsworth, 1956		Trend from 1876 on, partly spurious, and partly explain-able by successive ad hoc causes	
16. Aubrey, 1957		Rising terms of trade expected. Main basis: specific com-modity studies	
17. Morgan, 1959		Heterogeneous ex-perience since 1800. Diverse dominant influ-ences for differ-ent commodities, countries, times	
18. Bernstein, 1960		Falling terms of trade. Chronic sur-plus of primary products, due to secular fall in raw material content of industrial output	

indicate. It is readily possible to find commodities whose prices were at the same time falling in London and rising in Bombay, or falling in New York and rising in Minneapolis.

In addition, it is possible to obtain British data for a much longer period, back to 1801, and reliable domestic primary-manufactured products data for the United States back to 1787. I have found long-run data that I thought acceptably reliable for five other countries besides, three of them now 'under-developed' and two 'developed'.

The over-all impression from these seven series is that of the wide variety of experience of different nations. Primary products had sharply *rising* relative prices in the United Kingdom up to the 1860s or 70s, when the UN series began. Primary producers in the United States have experienced a remarkably favourable trend price-wise since the 1790s—to over three times the relative price position then. The other five countries show extreme fluctuations, and various changes of trend. India, for example, shows amidst its fluctuations a rising relative price trend for primary products up to 1900-10, an irregular fall to the 1930s and a rise since.[14]

The data as a whole underline the prudence of *not* trying to predict, from the experience of one country or region, what is likely to be the experience for others.

Recent Experience with Terms of Trade

Terms of trade of developed and under-developed countries, 1953 and 1937 compared with 1959 or 1960.[15] The following are median values for the terms of trade of 18 'developed' countries, and 29 'under-developed' countries for two periods, 1953 to 1960; and for 15 countries in each classification for 1937 to 1959:

Table 2. Median Value of Terms of Trade

(1953=100)

	1954	1955	1956	1957	1958	1959	1960
Developed countries	100	99	99	96	100	100	101
Under-developed countries	108	106	110	98	90	88	89

(1937=100)

	1948	1950	1951	1952	1953	1954
Developed countries	102	96	98	100	102	102
Under-developed countries	108	130	160	126	125	128

	1955	1956	1957	1958	1959	1960
Developed countries	100	97	97	99	101	102
Under-developed countries	135	131	127	117	123	119

Charts 1*a* and 1*b* reproduce the data of Table 2. The greater stability of the developed countries is apparent throughout. For the under-developed

[14]T. Morgan, 'The Long-Run Terms of Trade Between Agriculture and Manufacturing', *Econ. Develop. and Cult. Change*, Oct. 1959, pp. 1-23.

[15]For Burma, the final year is 1958; for Ecuador, 1957; for Malaya, Sudan and Turkey, 1959.

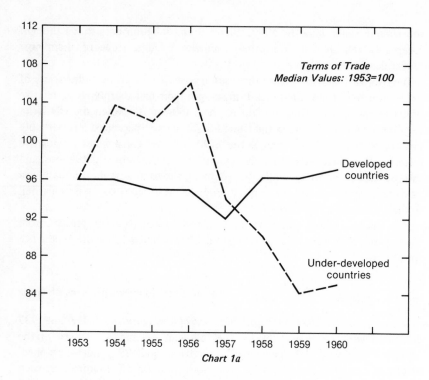

Chart 1a

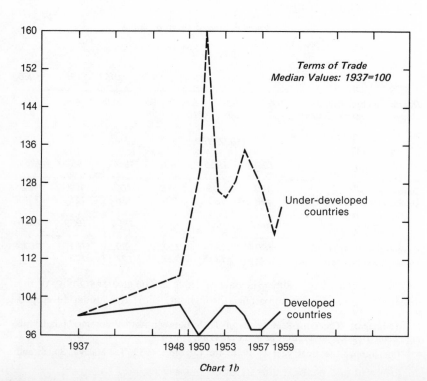

Chart 1b

countries, 1948 data show surprisingly little improvement over 1937 experience. The Korean War brought a major boom to their terms of trade, from which they were receding in the 1950s. But by the end of our period, the terms of trade of four under-developed countries were above 1937 by over 70 per cent, and of two, by over 100 per cent. Among the developed countries, the maximum improvement of the terms of trade was 26 per cent.

We can present a frequency distribution for these same countries, in accord with the change in their terms of trade at the end of each period:

Table 3. Distribution of Changes in Terms of Trade

(1953—60)

| | | Terms of trade | | | | | |
| | | Improved | | | Worsened | | |
	Total number	+20% or better	+10% to 20%	0% to 10%	−10% to 0%	−20% to −10%	−20% or poorer
Developed countries	18	0	4	8	4	1	1
Underdeveloped countries	29	3	1	5	3	7	10

(1937—59)

Developed countries	15	2	0	8	2	2	1
Underdeveloped countries	15	7	3	2	1	0	2

We may generalize that during the more recent period the under-developed countries include more extreme changes, and show more tendency to deterioration. Post-Korean War recession in prices of primary commodities has a relationship to this experience; some relevant data will be given below. For the 1937 to 1959 group, under-developed countries demonstrate major improvement from depression levels for primary products; they again show a tendency towards more extreme changes.

Terms of trade and aid per capita *received.* There is some interest in inquiring into the empirical relationship between aid *per capita* to under-developed countries, which in some has attained relatively high levels, and the terms of trade. Here we are in the classical framework of thinking. The literature left some presumption that the terms of trade would shift in favour of a country receiving capital inflows. The simple presumption does not find support in 1950's data. We have calculated the average terms of trade for a sample of 20 under-developed countries during 1954—1959, compared with their terms of trade in 1953. The 5 countries receiving the highest *per capita* aid show a terms of trade worsening at 2 per cent, the highest 2.5 per cent. The 5 countries receiving the least *per capita* aid show a terms of trade improvement of 2 per cent, the 10 lowest, improvement of 1 per cent.

The results are consistent with the effects of relative supply of *commodities* on domestic prices—but, of course, 'other things' were not equal. . . .

Short-run data on maritime shipping charges show wide variations in flexible response to changes in demand. Secular declines in transportation costs have been drastic—see, for example, the illustrations collected by Ellsworth[16] — and a major influence on commodity terms of trade of distant countries. European terms-of-trade data have negligible value towards indicating the terms of trade of primary producers in their own countries abroad.

The real purchasing power in terms of imports of primary product exports. This series, together with the commodity terms of trade (see Table 2), seems to us the most significant of our data findings. Chart 2 gives Dorrance's 'Income Terms of Trade' for the countries and years in question. The series measures in real terms what could be bought in exchange for primary product exports. The calculation is index of value of exports divided by the price index for imports:

$$\frac{Px_i Q x_i}{Px_o Q x_o} \cdot \frac{1}{Pm_i / Pm_o} ,$$

where P is price, x is exports, m is imports, i is the given year and o the base year. Countries are weighted in their individual groups in accord with their volume of exports.

The position of developed countries *vis-à-vis* under-developed countries looks quite different, by this measure, than it did when we applied the commodity terms-of-trade measure. The increased volume of exports of 'Developed Countries I' dominates the picture from 1937 on and has increased pre-eminently their capacity to buy imports.

'Developed countries II' are Australia, New Zealand and Denmark, whose agricultural exports have exceeded 60 percent of their total exports. The real purchasing power of their exports has increased the least, since 1937, of the three groups. Since 1953, also, these three countries have fared the worst.

V. The Hypotheses Tested
against the Data

It appears to us that no monotonic hypothesis stands up well to the diversity of experience. As soon as we move beyond the tautologous statement that supply and demand influences exist on both the export and the import sides (or primary product and non-primary product sides), we

---

[16]'The Terms of Trade between Primary Producing and Industrial Countries', *Inter-American Economics Affairs*, summer 1956, pp. 51-7. See also Douglass North, 'Ocean Freight Rates and Economic Development, 1750-1913', *Journal of Economic History*, Dec. 1958.

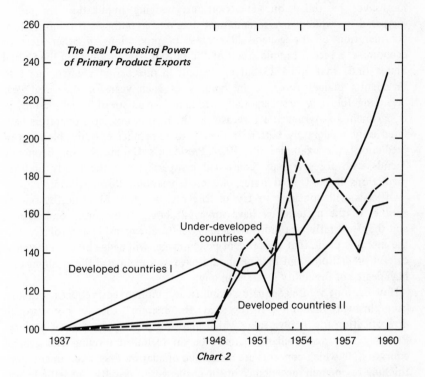

Chart 2

need to look hard to the particular *ad hoc* influences that for a particular commodity, country, and time are relevant. The possibility and various effectiveness of government price stabilization schemes, and commodity trade agreements, are no help to the practicality of narrowly economic analysis. The empirical record is of wide price instability, both short-run and long-run, with a few short-run exceptions where price stabilization programmes have been effective.

VI. Implications for Policy

Suppose that a careful prediction for future terms of trade—for example, like that of Aubrey's—turns out to be accurate. Even so, past experience for all the nations for which we have data indicates we should expect sharp interim fluctuations. And flexibility is needed to cut production and one's losses, if the fluctuation is adverse; or to expand and gain whatever possible, if the fluctuation is favourable.

But it is difficult to know which predictor one should rely on—whether Bernstein (poor terms of trade for primary producers) or Aubrey (sharply rising); or Myrdal or Lewis (poor terms of trade) or Colin Clark (rising); or Kindleberger I or Prebisch (falling); or the 1953 UN experts (agnostic). The policy-maker would find his bets shifting widely, depending on which soothsayer he relied on. The cautious, hedging implication for policy suggested by widely diverse empirical data *and* hypotheses is reinforced by consideration of the general ill success of predictions in other areas of economics: a recent sample study of the fate of new products in the United States finds that some 23 out of 25 fail. In one period studied, the U.S. President's budget forecasts in January of each year for the fiscal year beginning July 1 were substantially wrong in 5 years out of 7, right in only 2. Department of Agriculture forecasts of the incomes of farm operators have fared only moderately better. It is easy to remember extreme blunders of prediction: for example, the 1929 President's Committee on Economic Trends who foresaw only continued prosperity; and the nearly uniform predictions, in the United States, of deep depression following 1945.[17]

Officials will continue to try to forecast the terms of trade, by one or another of the patterns we have surveyed above, or by some combination; and they will influence industrial and agricultural expansion accordingly. But the moral is plain, that the prudent policy-maker will hedge on even the most careful predictions, and that he should have as a main goal the attaining of a high degree of flexibility in his economy.

How can one secure adequate flexibility at minimum cost; equating, that is, gain through flexibility to cost at the margin? Clearly not through diversification for its own sake, which increases poverty for fear of poverty. Probably one main reliance should be on technical training and general education, in which concepts are inculcated of adaptiveness, experimentation, thinking for oneself, acceptance of the challenges of novelty and self-reliance. Such training might well include the history of sciences and of technology, with focus on problem-solving and the origins of innovations in their historical contexts. A pragmatic open-mindedness as to organization, as well as technical possibilities, is desirable. The skills taught should be those adaptable to new functions: increasingly our world is likely to have people at kinds of work that did not exist when they were in training ten or twenty, or more, years back.

Another likely policy is regularly to try out pilot projects in alternative attractive industries—to train people by doing, to obtain actual experience on costs and returns, and to lay the foundation for rapid expansion should the terms of trade and comparative advantage prove favorable in a given line. This follows the venerable counsel that we should aim at 'small mistakes and big successes.'

[17]Hansen summarized several studies of forecasting results in *Business Cycles and National Income*, Norton, New York, 1951, pp. 583-7.

New Perspectives on Trade
and Development

Isaiah Frank

25

The first meeting of the United Nations Conference on Trade and Development (UNCTAD) in 1964 marked a turning point in relations between poor and rich countries. . . .The first UNCTAD dramatized a salient fact about the development process—namely, that the sluggish increase in the poorer countries' capacity to import had become a principal constraint on their economic growth. But the conference went far beyond a diagnosis of the problem and gave expression to some basic policy implications and prescriptions, mainly in the form of measures to be adopted by the advanced countries to increase the foreign-exchange receipts of the less developed countries. . . .

Before assessing the state of current thinking on trade and development, however, I might indicate how the trade of the developing countries has in fact evolved during the first half of the 1960s. A review of the major trends is particularly appropriate because some significant changes have emerged since the decade of the 1950s—the period that served as the main backdrop for the original UNCTAD conference.

Excerpted by special permission from *Foreign Affairs*, April 1967. Copyright by the Council on Foreign Relations, Inc., New York. The author is William L. Clayton professor of international economics, Johns Hopkins University School of Advanced International Studies.

What sparked the concern in the early 1960s about the growth prospects of developing countries was the unequivocally adverse trends in their exports during the latter half of the fifties. In terms of physical volume, exports increased only sluggishly; because of falling prices for many basic commodities, earnings from exports grew at an even slower rate, averaging 3 percent annually. Looking to the future, the United Nations projected a widening gap between the imports needed to support accepted growth targets of 5 percent annually and the capacity of developing countries to pay for such imports from the proceeds of their exports. This gap between required imports and anticipated exports was the point of departure for the entire UNCTAD approach.

In examining the 1960-65 record, however, one finds another type of "gap"– a marked divergence between U.N. projections prepared for the first UNCTAD conference and the actual trends in the foreign trade of developing countries. Exports of developing countries increased at an annual rate of 6 percent during the first half of the sixties, a rate 50 percent higher than the rate projected by the U.N., and twice as great as the corresponding figure for the latter half of the fifties. Pointing out this difference does not imply that the U.N. was "wrong." In no sense did it purport to forecast what would actually happen; it intended merely to project trends based on certain past relationships and assumptions about the future.

As it turned out, demand for certain products was more responsive to increases in income than had been assumed in the U.N. projections. But the main factor that threw the projections off was the unexpectedly high growth rates of the industrial countries comprising the principal export markets of the developing countries. The U.N. assumed that total output in the advanced countries would increase annually by 3.7 percent, the same rate as in the decade 1950-60. Since, in the latter half of that decade, output increased even more slowly, the U.N. projections did not seem unduly pessimistic. In fact, however, the increase in output of the industrial countries in 1960-65 accelerated to 4.7 percent, largely due to the doubling of the growth rate of the United States compared to the preceding five years.

One might well have expected that, in doubling their export growth rate, the low-income countries would also have increased imports substantially. To the surprise of many observers, however, the growth rate of imports did not accelerate but remained at the 4 percent per year figure that obtained in 1955-60. At that rate, the import requirements of sound development plans remained unsatisfied.

Another way of looking at the changing export-import relationship may cast some light on what has been happening. In 1957-59, the developing countries imported an average of $3.2 billion of goods per year in excess of their exports. By 1963-65, however, this net transfer of goods from the outside world had contracted to an annual average of less than $0.6 billion. According to both GATT and the United Nations, if imports as well as exports are measured on an f.o.b. basis, there was actually in 1965 a small net transfer of real resources away from the developing countries, in the sense that their exports of goods exceeded their imports.

How does one explain this anomalous situation? After all, the essential purpose of aid is to permit low-income countries to invest in excess of their own current savings by allowing them to make net drawings on the real resources of the rest of the world. But now we find that, because of a much slower growth of imports than of exports, these net drawings have, for the developing world as a whole, shrunk to zero.

As is true of so many aspects of economic development, it is difficult to evaluate this trend while speaking of "the developing world as a whole." To some extent, the explanation lies in the more rapid expansion of exports of petroleum than of other products from developing countries, and in the channeling by oil countries of a significant part of their proceeds into reserve accumulations. For non-petroleum exporters, however, the most important factor appears to have been the rapidly increasing sums required to service their foreign debts. In Latin America, where the burden is most acute, debt service absorbed 15 percent of export earnings in 1964 as compared to only 6 percent in 1956. For some countries—Chile, Brazil, Turkey—public debt service has grown to 20 percent or more of export receipts. At the same time, payments by developing countries for other "invisible" items in their balance of payments—transport and other services, dividends and other investment income—have increased sharply, correspondingly reducing the sums available to pay for commodity imports.

The disappearance of the import surplus previously enjoyed by the low-income countries may be viewed from another perspective. At the beginning of the sixties aid and other capital flows to developing countries were of sufficient volume to offset net payments for invisible items in the balance of payments, with enough left over to finance a sizeable excess of imports of goods over exports. With the failure of the volume of aid to increase significantly during the first half of the sixties, while financial claims mounted, the low-income countries as a whole have simply had to limit their imports to what they could pay for with the proceeds of their own exports. As put by the World Bank in its most recent annual report, "A shortage of such resources [aid] is reflected most directly by insufficient growth in imports. Barring an unforeseen change in world markets, imports of developing countries cannot be expected to grow sufficiently unless the flow of external funds is increased considerably."

The situation has been further aggravated by the tendency for food production in the low-income countries to lag significantly behind food requirements. The Indian food crises of 1965 and 1966 are dramatic instances, but the problem is widespread. Consequently, food imports have been rising as a proportion of total imports into low-income countries, thereby impairing their capacity to import goods contributing more directly to development.

In sum, despite impressive statistics on the rapid growth of exports from developing countries in the first half of this decade, those countries as a group still face the problem which set the stage for the first UNCTAD conference—namely, a squeeze on their capacity to finance the imports necessary for satisfactory growth.

One line of action to meet this problem is to step up substantially the flow of capital, and particularly the flow of aid on liberal repayment terms. . . . Even if we accept the most optimistic expectations, however, increases in aid are not likely to obviate the need for increasing the earnings of low-income countries from their own exports.

In the foreseeable future, export prospects of low-income countries will depend overwhelmingly on markets for primary products—food, raw materials and fuels. Not that exports of manufactures have been lagging. On the contrary, one of the most impressive achievements of the 1960-64 period was the rapid growth in manufactured exports from developing countries. But they still represent only about 10 percent of total exports.

Given the continuing dominance of primary commodities as a source of export earnings, it is understandable that the main concentration at the first UNCTAD conference was on issues of commodity policy. Since then, much attention has been devoted to this subject; and I believe that real progress has been made, both in understanding what has been happening and in evolving mechanisms for coping with some of the problems.

An important advance is the wider recognition that there is no panacea in this field, and that the beginning of wisdom is to take as hard a look at the differences among commodities and countries as to generalize about the similarities. The dictum that aggregates conceal as much as they reveal is particularly pertinent to international commodity policy. Consider, for example, the growth of the world market for traditional exports in the first half of the sixties. The record varies from an increase in the value of world exports of over 80 percent in the case of maize, tin and zinc to actual declines for other commodities including cocoa, manganese ore and rubber. Among commodities registering increases of between 30 and 50 percent are not only petroleum but also iron ore, wood, rice, lead, meat and livestock, citrus fruit and copper. Even within broad commodity categories there was a significant degree of dispersion. For example, although agricultural raw materials as a group showed the slowest export growth rate, exports of wood were among the fastest growing of all commodity exports.

One might expect, then, that the foreign trade performance of individual countries would be determined largely by the composition of their traditional exports. For a particular country a rapid growth of exports would thus be associated with specialization in commodities for which world exports increase rapidly. One of the most revealing findings of a recent GATT study, however, is that the trade fortunes of a particular country are likely to be dependent less on how its traditional commodities fared worldwide than on changes in its *share* of world trade in these commodities and on its success in developing new lines of production for export. These results—which are broadly substantiated in preliminary studies by the World Bank—underline the importance of a country's own internal and external policies.

A major objective of international commodity policy is the achievement of a higher level of export earnings for developing countries as a whole. Since the first UNCTAD conference, thinking has tended to shift increasingly away from the notion, espoused by the French, that this objective can be universally pursued through commodity agreements or, as the French put it, the "organization of markets." Today it is widely recognized that policy must depend largely upon the market characteristics of the particular commodity in question.

From this viewpoint, UNCTAD, in recent studies, distinguishes three broad categories of commodities by their market characteristics: commodities produced wholly or mainly in developing countries and not subject to serious competition from substitutes (*e.g.* coffee); commodities produced wholly or mainly in developing countries but subject to competition from substitutes, especially synthetics (*e.g.* natural rubber); and commodities produced in substantial quantities by both developed and developing countries (*e.g.* sugar). While some commodities may not fall squarely in any one group, the distinction is nevertheless useful for policy purposes.

Broadly speaking, agreements aimed at raising prices can be effective in increasing producers' incomes mainly with respect to commodities in the first group, for which somewhat higher prices will not significantly reduce demand. For commodities in the second group, higher prices for the natural product would be self-defeating, since the result would be to encourage further substitution. What is required for this group are cost reductions to improve the competitive position of the natural product, and diversification over the longer term into production with more favorable market prospects. Regarding the third group of commodities—those produced in substantial amounts in both developing and developed countries—the main problems arise from import barriers in the advanced countries. Here the principal aim of policy should be to increase the access of low-income countries to the high-income markets.

The scope for commodity price-fixing agreements as a means of raising the export earnings of developing countries is quite limited. Only five major commodities—coffee, tea, cocoa, bananas and tin—clearly meet the two most important conditions: that production take place primarily in developing countries, and that demand for the product be relatively inelastic with respect to price changes. In 1964, exports of these commodities amounted to approximately 12 percent of the total exports of developing countries. If coffee and tin are excluded—since agreements already exist for them—the remaining products account for only about 4 percent of exports. . . .

If there is wider acceptance today of the limited applicability of commodity agreements, there is also franker acknowledgement that their prime purpose is not the traditional one of moderating price fluctuations around a long-term trend. Rather, it is to alter the trend itself in order to increase the export earnings of developing countries, or, as a minimum, to prevent them from falling. This is what is meant in UNCTAD parlance by the objective of "equitable" and "remunerative" prices, and it has been broadly accepted today by all the advanced countries.

To what extent can commodity agreements add to the external resources available to developing countries? According to a recent estimate,[1] if monopoly pricing were pushed to the point of maximum returns for producers, it would add perhaps a billion dollars per year to their revenues. As an increment to export receipts, this theoretically maximum figure would represent only a modest increase of 3 percent, or the equivalent of only half of the average annual increase in export earnings by the developing countries in the period 1960-65. Viewed, however, as a form of aid or net resource transfer from rich to poor countries, the figure is substantial, amounting to 10 percent of the public and private flow of capital to developing countries in 1965.

It is proper to regard international price-fixing agreements as a form of aid, since they are a disguised means of taxing consumers in the developed countries in order to provide resources to the low-income countries— resources which the governments of those countries can, at least potentially, mobilize for purposes of development. However, as Harry Johnson points out, once one begins to think of international taxing mechanisms for financing development, one is struck by the relative inefficiency of commodity agreements.[2] The distribution of neither the burden nor the benefits conforms to optimum tax principles; and such agreements are notoriously difficult to negotiate and administer.

In a rational world, there would be no particular reason for disguising taxation through a price-raising mechanism. Nor would it be necessary to link international taxation exclusively to primary commodities. Any number of other, more general and equally automatic schemes could be devised. For instance, if the advanced countries were to earmark for development assistance a 2 percent tax on imports of all commodities from all sources, it would yield over $2 billion, a sum equal to an increase of one-third in the current volume of bilateral aid to less developed countries. Moreover, because the trade of advanced countries has been increasing rapidly, the yield of the tax would rise by about 9 percent annually. I am not advocating any particular tax, but merely illustrating the theoretical possibilities for simpler and more efficient devices to mobilize resources for development.

In connection with domestic farm-support programs, economists have long urged the superiority of direct subsidies financed through general taxation over indirect transfers through market-support schemes. The widespread

[1]John A. Pincus, "Trade, Aid and Development," New York: McGraw-Hill, 1967. The commodities included in the Pincus estimate are coffee, tea, cocoa and sugar.

[2]Harry G. Johnson, "Economic Policies Toward Less Developed Countries," Washington: Brookings Institution, 1967.

resort to the less efficient technique reflects the farmers' preference for disguising the subsidy and the government's preference for reducing its budgetary cost. Similarly, in the case of foreign aid, practical considerations argue in favor of the commodity agreement where it is feasible. With the volume of bilateral aid remaining virtually stationary at $6 billion for several years in the face of rising prices and an increasing need for assistance, methods such as commodity agreements, whatever their limitations, can provide a much-needed additional transfer of resources to developing countries.

More important over the long run is improved access to the markets of industrialized countries. With the notable exception of petroleum, industrial raw materials move relatively freely in international trade. But primary agricultural products face a wide range of restrictions—tariffs, quotas, excise taxes, as well as preferential trading arrangements benefiting particular low-income countries at the expense of others. Pledges to moderate or eliminate such restrictions were made by the advanced countries both at the UNCTAD conference and, more recently, in the new GATT article on trade and development. Despite high-sounding expressions of principle, little progress can be reported. The basic pattern of restrictions remains—either because of a fiscal interest in maintaining revenues, or more commonly, because of the overriding desire of governments to protect competing domestic producers. Moreover, given the internal political pressures in advanced countries, it is probably unrealistic to expect any major dismantling of agricultural restrictions in the near future.

Although little has been accomplished in easing access to markets for primary products, the first UNCTAD conference did induce a substantial advance in coping with the short-run instability of export earnings. Traditionally, international efforts to moderate export instability concentrated on the commodity-agreement approach. Partly as a result of the complexity and limitations of arrangements tied to individual commodities, a new and more generally applicable technique was adopted in 1963 by the International Monetary Fund. It provides for special drawing rights on the Fund to "compensate" countries for short-falls in their export proceeds below the level of the medium-term trend. At the first UNCTAD conference in 1964, the developing countries pressed for a substantial liberalization of this facility, and in 1966 some of their major recommendations were adopted by the Fund.

As now liberalized, a Fund member may draw up to 50 percent (although ordinarily not more than 25 percent in one year) of its quota to offset export shortfalls as compared to only 25 percent previously. These drawings are additional to a country's normal borrowing rights in the Fund and, as a practical matter, are available on virtually automatic terms. Moreover, compensatory drawings no longer affect the conditions under which members have access to successive "tranches" of ordinary drawings. Like ordinary drawings, however, funds borrowed under the compensatory arrangement are repayable in three to five years.

In assessing the importance of compensatory finance, it would be a mistake to be unduly influenced by the fact that the original fund facility was used only a few times—by Brazil and the United Arab Republic in 1963 and by Sudan in 1965. This infrequency of use reflects partly the improvement in commodity markets after the new facility had been established, and partly the initial reluctance of countries to prejudice the terms of their access to ordinary fund drawings. With the latter consideration no longer applicable under the liberalized rules, and with a softening in a number of commodity markets already in view, there is good reason to expect more active recourse to this facility in the future.

To supplement the I.M.F. scheme, the United Kingdom and Sweden put forward at the UNCTAD conference a proposal for dealing with adverse movements in exports which could not be dealt with adequately by short-term balance-of-payments support. At UNCTAD's invitation, the proposal was examined by the World Bank. Concluding that it was addressed to a major problem confronting the developing world, the Bank staff submitted a specific scheme to the United Nations for carrying it out. The Bank's proposal aims to insure against the disruption of development programs resulting from unpredictable adverse movements in export receipts in cases where those movements are either too sustained or too severe to be dealt with by short-term balance-of-payments assistance.

To be eligible to receive support under the Bank proposal, a country would have to enter into a prior understanding with the administering agency both as to reasonable expectations of export earnings over the period of its development plan and as to the policies to be pursued in carrying out the plan. Provided the country lived up to its policy commitments and had no other readily available source of finance, support from the scheme in the form of long-term loans would be triggered by a deficiency of exports as compared to the agreed reasonable expectations. According to World Bank estimates, between $300 and $400 million per year would be needed to operate the scheme over an experimental period of five years, even after taking account of other possible sources of finance including the I.M.F.

The Bank's proposal would provide a valuable addition to the existing array of international instruments for long-term development finance. Countries ready to meet the disciplines implicit in the scheme would be assured that their development efforts would not be disrupted by export shortfalls due to causes beyond their control. And, as a natural concomitant of the scheme, a new and constructive relationship should emerge between individual developing countries and the international community, a relationship in which "the incentives and prospects for effective internal development performance would be greatly strengthened."[3]

Developing countries are convinced that over the long run they must increasingly become exporters of manufactured products. In their view, no

[3]International Bank for Reconstruction and Development, *Supplementary Financial Measures*, December 1965.

matter what measures are taken to improve the conditions of trade in primary materials, the long-term prospects are not encouraging for most of the basic commodities in which they specialize. Diversification into manufacturing would lead to a more rapid expansion of exports while moderating the sharp short-term swings to which primary commodity trade is peculiarly vulnerable. Even aside from foreign exchange considerations, developing countries regard the growth of manufacturing as essential in the modernization process because of its "linkage" effects in inducing investment in related sectors—that is, in industries supplying the inputs and using the outputs of the manufacturing sector.

Recent trends support the view that manufacturing is the most "dynamic" export sector of the low-income countries. Excluding processed metals, exports of manufactures to the developed countries increased 14 percent annually in 1960-64, outstripping even the growth rate of petroleum exports. But the absolute volume of exports of manufactures is still low and heavily concentrated in a small number of developing countries—Hong Kong, India, Mexico, Taiwan and Pakistan.

Obstructing efforts to broaden and accelerate the expansion of developing countries' exports of manufactures are two main roadblocks: restrictions imposed by the advanced countries, and questionable policies in the developing countries themselves. On the first set of barriers, UNCTAD has had a notable impact. In contrast, the obstacles erected by the developing countries themselves have until recently been regarded in UNCTAD as virtually forbidden territory, the subject being introduced only in connection with the World Bank's proposal for supplementary finance.

In dealing with the first roadblock, one of UNCTAD's accomplishments has been to help dispel a widespread misconception in advanced countries. Until recently, the prevailing view was that, with average rates of duty in the United States and the European Economic Community at only about 12 percent, tariffs did not significantly limit exports from low-income countries. In a report prepared for the first UNCTAD conference, however, the U.N. gave prominence to data assembled from GATT and other sources which showed that figures on average tariff levels substantially understate the degree of protection of manufactured products of the kind originating in less developed countries.[4]

Two reasons explain this underestimation of protection. First, the duties on products which the less developed countries are capable of manufacturing are generally higher than the average of 12 percent. Clothing, for example, is dutiable at 25 percent in the United States, 15 percent in the Common Market, and 25 percent in Japan. Comparable figures for shoes are 17, 20 and 30 percent; for bicycles, 14, 21 and 25 percent; for toys and sporting goods, 25, 18 and 22 percent.

Second, and equally important, is the fact that tariff rates typically increase with the degree of processing. While the Common Market's tariff is zero on

[4]The report was reproduced in 1963 in the United Nations, *World Economic Survey, 1962,* Part II. See especially pp. 66-68 and p. 79.

hides and skins, it is 9 percent on leather and 16 percent on leather manufactures. A similar escalation of duties in relation to the degree of processing is found in the tariff schedules of other industrial countries as they pertain to such products as cocoa, cotton, jute, paper, rubber, wood and others. That this structure of tariffs discourages trade in the more highly fabricated products is obvious. In fact, the deterrent is considerably greater than first appears.

Suppose that unprocessed logs are admitted duty-free; that plywood manufactured from these logs is subject to a duty of 20 percent; and that the logs constitute 50 percent of the value of the finished plywood. In this case, a domestic manufacturer of plywood benefits from a 20 percent duty calculated on the full value of output, not just on the 50 percent of the value which he contributes in the manufacturing process. As a result, the height of the tariff as a percentage of the value added by him is not 20 percent but 40 percent. Thus, tariffs really protect processes rather than products; and the process of manufacturing plywood is protected to the extent of 40 percent.

"Effective" tariffs are generally higher than the "nominal" rates due to the admission of raw materials and semi-finished goods at lower rates than finished goods. Although much of the empirical work in measuring effective tariffs has been carried out in the past few years by university economists independently of UNCTAD, the U.N. conference provided a strong impetus. In a recent study, Professor Bela Balassa of Johns Hopkins has demonstrated that the average effective tariff for consumer goods is 25.9 percent in the United States, 30.9 percent in the European Common Market, 40.4 percent in the United Kingdom and 50.5 percent in Japan. These figures underscore the significance of including in the Kennedy Round, and in subsequent tariff negotiations, reductions in duties on manufactured products important to the present or potential export trade of less developed countries.

Regrettably, UNCTAD's success in highlighting tariff obstacles has not been matched by a comparable impact on what is undoubtedly the most restrictive set of barriers to processed exports confronting the low-income countries. I refer to the Long-Term Cotton Textile Arrangement negotiated in 1962 under GATT auspices. As expressed in the preamble, its purpose is to permit increased access for low-income countries' exports of cotton textiles, while insuring that the growth in this trade takes place in an "orderly manner" so as to avoid market "disruption." However, what started out as an understandable accommodation to certain social and political realities in the advanced countries has in practice become the vehicle through which highly restrictive quotas have been imposed—in Europe as well as in the United States—with little regard to the criteria for determining the existence of market disruption. . . .

In contrast, the continuing interest of developing countries in preferential, rather than simply equal, access for their processed and manufactured goods to the markets of advanced countries has by no means been neglected. At the first conference, the lines seemed tightly drawn, with all developing countries firmly supporting the idea of tariff preferences, and the United States opposing it in principle. In the intervening period, however, one detects a certain convergence of the two positions, with the developing countries displaying a livelier sense of the complexity of the technical and policy issues involved, and the United States, on its side, showing a greater willingness to examine specific proposals on their merits and expressing a more sympathetic attitude toward the objectives of preferences. . . .

The argument for preferences is in some respects an extension into the export sector of the infant-industry argument for protection of the home market. It rests on the need to overcome the initial disadvantages faced by a newcomer in manufacturing, including the high cost of gaining a market foothold. But unlike infant-industry tariffs which can totally insulate inefficient domestic industries from outside competition, preferences extended to all developing countries provide built-in limitations on inefficiency. The exporter in the developing country would have to compete on equal terms with suppliers from other less developed countries, and with domestic producers in the advanced countries to which he seeks to export. He would also continue to compete, although not on equal terms, with exporters of the same product from other advanced countries, who might still be in a position to overcome their tariff disadvantage.[5]

On the other hand, there are also strong arguments against a system of preferences. Once granted, they would tend to create a vested interest in existing levels of protection as among the advanced countries, and would militate against further efforts to liberalize world trade, since lower most-favored-nation tariffs would result in lower margins of preference. Secondly, preferences applying to all developing countries would favor the more advanced among the developing countries, since they would be the ones in a position to take prompt advantage of the new opportunities. If efforts were made to distinguish among developing countries, a preference system would become exceedingly complicated to administer and would tend to fragment the world trading system even further. Lastly, any general preference system adopted by the advanced countries would inevitably be accompanied by quantitative safeguards against "market disruption," and in the end these might leave the developing countries with less effective access than they had before. . . .

Improved access to the markets of advanced countries, whether on a preferential or on a nondiscriminatory basis, is unlikely by itself to be a major stimulus to exports of manufactures from low-income countries. Crucial to

[5]Two other differences should be noted. First, in infant-industry protection, the costs are borne by consumers in the less developed country imposing the tariff; in the case of preferences, the costs would be borne by the developed countries, chiefly those granting the preference. Second, the degree of advantage to particular industries conferred by a system of preferences would depend on the accident of relative tariff levels in the preference-giving countries rather than, as in the infant-industry case, on the potential international competitiveness of the industries receiving the tariff advantage.

the success of such measures are the trade and financial policies of the low-income countries themselves. Because of their sensitivity, however, UNCTAD has thus far scarcely attempted to come to grips with the range of problems in this field.

Policies of import substitution—that is, of manufacturing those products which otherwise have to be imported—frequently operate at cross-purposes with the avowed objective of promoting exports of manufactured products. Reliance on a highly protected domestic market tends to relieve an industry of the disciplines required for achieving international competitiveness. This is not to say that import substitution is undesirable. Newly established industries often do require some initial protection before they can stand on their own feet and compete on equal terms with foreign manufactures. And balance-of-payments considerations often impel developing countries to seek to save foreign exchange by producing at home manufactured goods that were formerly imported.

The issue today is not whether developing countries should pursue policies of protection or of free trade. After all, neither the United States nor Continental Europe industrialized under conditions of free trade. For the developing countries, the issues are rather which industries to protect, by how much, and in what way to effect the transition from import substitution to export promotion. These are questions to which UNCTAD should address itself.

A protective tariff is among the most powerful instruments of economic planning. It is a means whereby a levy is imposed on the community at large in order to permit the establishment or continuation of an industry. Unless a tariff is selective so that it lends support to those sectors where the present or potential comparative advantage is greatest, there will be a misallocation of resources that few poor countries can afford. Yet in many countries the system of protection is often arbitrary and completely independent of the priorities in their development plans. Planning and foreign trade are administered in separate compartments as if they bore no relation to each other.

Research recently undertaken by Hal Lary of the National Bureau of Economic Research provides one promising empirical approach to the identification of manufacturing industries in which developing countries should have a competitive advantage. By using data on "value added" by manufacture in different industries, Lary was able to array various industries in relation to the intensity of their use of the two factors which are typically scarce in less developed countries: labor skills and physical capital. His technique involves separating value added per employee in each industry into its wage and non-wage components, and using the wage part as a measure of skills and the non-wage part as a measure of physical capital. Lary's studies. . . illustrate one possibility of working out a basis for a reasonable policy of protection for low-income countries by concentrating on those industries in which skill and capital requirements are toward the lower end of the scale.

One would hope that UNCTAD, with the help of the newly established U.N. Industrial Development Organization, would turn some of its resources toward developing a basis for a rational foreign trade policy for low-income countries. And as part of such a policy, consideration should be given to techniques for maintaining some pressure of external competition on protected industries, possibly through the gradual lowering of tariffs. In this way, a policy of import substitution can evolve into a growing capacity to export manufactured products.

Foreign trade policies of low-income countries frustrate development in other ways. For example, the importation of luxury goods is typically subject to a high degree of import restriction in order to conserve foreign exchange and encourage saving. Commonly, however, both objectives are defeated by stimulating the production of the same goods at home, using imported raw materials and intermediate products as well as imported capital goods. Luxury consumption continues, and the imports required to sustain domestic production may leave little net saving of foreign exchange. A more effective way of meeting the country's objective would be through a nondiscriminatory internal consumption tax applying equally to domestic production and to imports. Yet very little attention has been given in UNCTAD to the relation between internal tax structure and trade policy.

Internal fiscal and monetary policies are touchy subjects for developing countries. Too often these countries have been at the receiving end of preachments about financial rectitude by governments of advanced countries, including some which themselves have not achieved notable success in maintaining price stability under conditions of strain on real resources. Considering the lesser capacity to save and to tax in low-income countries, and the tremendous pressures on precisely those resources that are essential to a vigorous development effort, one cannot but be impressed with the enormity of the job of managing a development program with a reasonable degree of price stability. Despite the widespread international attention already devoted to this problem, it cannot sensibly be avoided by UNCTAD. For inflationary fiscal and monetary policies operate with special force to frustrate a country's objectives in foreign trade.

Experience has shown that a sustained and rapid rate of inflation under a system of fixed exchange rates results in an almost chronic overvaluation of a country's currency. Whatever correction takes place periodically through devaluation is quickly overtaken by the increase in the domestic price level. The most direct effect of the overvaluation is to encourage imports and discourage exports since, at existing exchange rates, domestic prices will be too high in relation to prices in the world market. As foreign exchange reserves become exhausted, the government has no alternative but to intervene to offset the incentive to import and the disincentive to export. And here is where the difficulties get compounded, because the management of such a "disequilibrium system" tends to get more and more complex and is soon beyond the capacity of most governments.

To encourage exports, special exchange rates may be declared for particular commodities, rebates may be granted on transport charges, special rights may be given to keep or sell on the free market some part of the foreign exchange earned from exports. Yet, while incentives to export are being adopted, other government departments may be leaning in the opposite direction, trying to hold down the volume of exports through taxes or outright prohibitions in order to prevent consumer prices from rising or to insure supplies of materials for domestic processing. On the import side, overvaluation tends to vitiate, in whole or in part, tariff protection intended for domestic industry. To counter the encouragement of imports, tariffs (including surcharges) may be raised to astronomical levels, advance deposits may be required of importers, and, most commonly, a system of quantitative import controls may be instituted.

Controls are, of course, unavoidable in some situations. But as comprehensive controls become the normal way of life because of the persistence of disequilibrium, adverse effects on development are inevitable. The system tends progressively to insulate a country from the competitive pressures of the world market, to introduce wasteful and inequitable distortions, to invite corruption and increasingly to substitute for constructive activity a preoccupation with "beating the system."

According to an UNCTAD report issued in 1966: "The majority of the developing countries, which generally maintain comprehensive control systems, have continued—and in many instances reinforced—their existing import policies, in the form of increased duties, quota or license restrictions. . ."[6] Considering the pervasive effects on foreign trade and development of internal fiscal and monetary policies which give rise to comprehensive controls, it is essential that these policies now be brought within the orbit of UNCTAD's discussions.

As a new organization born in 1964, UNCTAD has not had easy going. It has set as its goal no less than the reshaping of world trade in the interests of developing countries. But, as any practitioner in foreign economic policy will testify, tough as it is to get funds for foreign aid, it is even tougher to bring about changes in trade policy favorable to "low-wage" countries. The domestic interests immediately affected are more concentrated and the political resistance more difficult to overcome.

In focusing world attention on the growth needs of the developing countries, UNCTAD has made a solid contribution toward greater accommodation to those needs by the advanced countries. It can also claim a considerable measure of credit for stimulating such specific advances as the adoption by GATT of a new set of articles on trade and development; the liberalization by the International Monetary Fund of its facilities for compensatory finance; and the pending World Bank proposal for supplementary finance to offset unexpected adverse movements in exports.

[6]UNCTAD, *Review of International Trade and Development 1966,* Part II, p. 23 (Mimeographed report TD/B/82, 20 July 1966.)

UNCTAD is viewed by the developing countries as *their* organization. Unlike GATT, the I.M.F. and the World Bank, which came into being through the initiative of the advanced countries, it was a creature of the less developed countries and was brought to life over the initial indifference or opposition of the advanced countries. Perhaps this explains, at least in part, why its pressures have thus far been directed almost exclusively toward changes in the policies of advanced countries. It remains to be seen whether UNCTAD can evolve into an organization capable of dealing with the totality of the trade problems of the developing world, including those policies of the low-income countries themselves which are so crucial to their development.

Part Five: Education and Growth

The Importance of Education in
National Development

Oliver Popenoe

26

The mid-20th century has been called the era of the educational explosion—the cumulative result of three separate explosions: explosions of population, of knowledge, and of aspirations. During the 1950's, the number of children in primary school throughout the world rose 57%, those in secondary school increased 81%, and those in higher education went up 71%. That is a compound growth rate of between 5% and 7% per annum, yet demand continues to far outrun supply. By 1959 only 35% of the school age group actually went to school, compared with 25% in 1950. So the bulk of the problem still remains to be tackled (8, pp. 96-7).*

Although the industrial revolution took place in Europe from a low base of literacy and popular education, this no longer appears possible. The new nations have a two-fold task of economic and political development which the earlier industrializers did not face in the same acute form. They must simultaneously train their citizens to play a civic role undreamed of by the ordinary European during most of the 19th Century, and must also respond to their insistent political demands for widespread education. But more than

From the *International Development Review,* December 1966. Reprinted by permission. The author is at the London School of Economics.

*Numbers in parentheses identify the references listed at the end of the article.

this, the complex technology communication and record-keeping systems of the modern industrialized world require a much higher level of education to operate them.

During the last five years education has become fashionable among developers—so fashionable that it runs the risk of being oversold. Despite a growing amount of research on the relationship between education and development, we still know very little that can clearly guide the development planner in making the 'right' decisions. This article—written not for the educator but for the development generalist—reviews recent findings and highlights the major problems of education in developing nations. It looks at education first from an economic point of view, next as a producer in innovations and social change, and finally in terms of its role in political development.

Until recently, virtually all Western economists, Adam Smith excepted, shied away from the obvious observation that people invest in themselves and that these investments play a large part in productivity. Men were regarded as the ends of economic activity, not—except in slavery—as capital goods, a form of wealth that can be augmented by investment.

A turning point came in December, 1960, when Theodore W. Schultz, in his presidential address to the American Economic Association, called for a new look at human resources. He noted that the income of the United States had been rising at a much higher rate than the combined amount of the three factors of production: land, man-hours worked, and the stock of reproducible capital. How could this discrepancy be explained? Schultz suggested that it was due partly to economies of scale but primarily to the large improvements in the quality of inputs that had occurred but that had been omitted from the input estimates.

Examining the investment made in human beings in the United States, Schultz found that the stock of education in the labor force rose 8-1/2 times between 1900 and 1956, while the stock of reproducible capital rose only 4-1/2 times. After taking into consideration improvements in health and the share of educational expenditure that might properly be regarded as consumption rather than investment, he concluded that between 36% and 70% of the hitherto unexplained rise in the earnings of labor was explained by returns to the additional education of the workers (19).

Another approach to measuring the contribution of education to productivity and development, called 'the internal rate of return,' involves calculating the rate of interest at which higher incomes obtained later in life would just compensate for the direct expenditure on education and the value of income foregone during the period of schooling. If this interest rate is higher than the interest rate on alternative investments, the investment in education is a superior one from a narrow economic point of view. Several different studies show internal rates of return for primary education of 20% or higher in the U.S. and Mexico; secondary education rates of 10-15% in the U.S., Hyderabad and Mexico; and higher education rates of 11% in the U.S.,

17% in Hyderabad, and 30% in Mexico. (By comparison, in India estimated rates of return on physical capital of 17% to 26% were obtained.) Returns on primary education are higher because costs are lower and little income is foregone (5, p. 69).

Finally, there have been several attempts to correlate educational and economic indices. Mary Jean Bowman and C. Arnold Anderson of the University of Chicago Comparative Education Center examined a number of these studies and concluded that, although there are positive correlations between level or spread of education and economic levels, these connections are loose ones. All countries with literacy rates of 90% or more had per capita incomes of over US $500, while all countries with literacy rates of less than 30% had incomes below $200. But in the 30-70% literacy range there was virtually no correlation with income. Countries with incomes between $100-$200 had literacy rates as high as 70-80% (7).

The most extensive and sophisticated attempt to correlate education and economic growth has been by Frederick H. Harbison and Charles A. Myers of Princeton University. For 75 countries, they collected the best available data on economic development and stock of high level manpower, enrollment ratios for first, second, and third level education, orientation of higher education to science and technology or arts and humanities, and expenditures on education as a percent of national income. In all, 14 different indicators were tabulated and correlated for the 75 countries. Analysis of their data led them to conclude that economic development correlated more strongly with higher education than with primary education or literacy, and from this they developed a composite index of human resource development. This index consists of the percentage of the age group in secondary school, plus the percentage of higher education multiplied by a weight of 5. The correlation between this composite index and gross national product per capita is very high: .888.

On the basis of this composite index, Harbison and Myers ranked the 75 countries and divided them into four levels of human resource development: underdeveloped, partially developed, semi-advanced and advanced. The bulk of their book, *Education, Manpower and Economic Growth* consists of an analysis of the differing types of problems of resource development in the four groups. It is a very useful addition to the cross-country analysis of human resource development.

In making educational investment decisions, the relative costs of alternatives must be considered. Which will give the biggest pay-off: primary, secondary, or higher education? liberal arts or technical education? The cost of educating an engineer or a scientist is three to four times that of educating a man in the humanities. This is one reason why so many developing countries turn out too few dear scientists and too many cheap lawyers.

Similarly, a vast expansion of primary education is relatively cheap and certainly popular, despite the fact that it generally is not the most efficient form of education for a poor country seeking economic development. But even primary education tends to be very expensive in developing countries because the teachers are overpaid relative to the rest of the population.

The UNESCO-sponsored Conference of African States on the Development of Education in Africa, held in Addis Ababa in 1961, recommended a 20-year program of educational expansion. Against a 1960 educational pyramid with 40% of the age group in primary education, 3% in secondary education, and 0.2% in higher education, they called for 1980 levels of 100%, 23% and 2.1%, respectively. However, achieving this goal would require increasing the individual countries' investment in education from 3.9% of national income in 1961, to 8.6% in 1970, falling to 7% in 1980. In addition, it would require foreign aid at the rate of $258 million in 1963, $1,000 million in 1970, and $386 million in 1980 (11, pp. 26-7). And these estimates were optimistic regarding the expansion of national income during this period. By contrast, it should be noted that the United States spends only 4.6% of national income on education and the U.K. spends only 4.2% (14, p. 48).

Why is education so expensive in a poor country? W. Arthur Lewis has graphically brought out the mathematics of the problem. Where education is a scarce resource, it receives a high price. A university graduate in a rich country starts at a salary equal to a miner's wage, but in a poor country he may start at a level five times as high. Giving 8 years of primary schooling to every child would cost .8% of national income in the U.S., 1.7% in Jamaica, 2.8% in Ghana, and 4.0% in Nigeria. The primary teacher is paid 1-1/2 times the per capita income in the U.S., 3 times in Jamaica, 5 times in Ghana, and 7 times the per capita income in Nigeria (16).

We thus see the anomaly that the poorest countries that most need more education are precisely the ones that can least afford to pay for it. In Africa the range of salaries is wider than anywhere else in the world. African primary leavers expect to receive salaries of twice the per capita national income. They have priced themselves out of the market, and the problem of unemployed primary leavers is endemic there. But if by 1980 primary education becomes universal, as planned, it clearly follows that they cannot all receive twice the national average. As their price falls, job skill requirements will be raised and the demand for them will increase. Ultimately an economy can use any number of educated persons. But over the short run, it is better to educate fewer students longer and to restrict the over-production of primary leavers to a level that will not create overwhelming social tensions. Lewis estimates that the limited absorptive capacity of most West African economies makes frustration inevitable if more than 50% of the children enter school.

This might tempt one to say: well then, let's start at the top and work down. But all the universities in Africa started since World War II have been costing three to five times more per student than European ones (15). The most *economic* approach to higher education for an African country appears to be to get as many scholarships as possible for advanced study in Europe, the U.S. and the U.S.S.R., rather than organize one's own university. But this, just as much as restricting primary education, may be politically wholly unfeasible.

Let us now move from an economic to a sociological look at education. Essentially education serves two important social purposes:

1. To convey the accumulated cultural heritage and to socialize the the child into the ways of the society: and
2. To act as a mechanism for role allocation—for moving individuals into different kinds of jobs and different places in the social structure.

In a society which is rapidly changing from a traditional ascriptive one—in which jobs are filled on the basis of ascribed considerations of birth and status—to a modern one in which jobs are filled on the basis of individual achievement, both of these purposes become acutely important.

Many colonial school systems originally were designed to train a few people to be efficient clerks and helpers of the ruling class, but most to do a better job of fishing, farming and hewing wood. The distortions came later, when the voice of the local people was more loudly heard. The people didn't want to be better farmers, they wanted to be like the Europeans; they didn't want a second-rate education, tailored to their then station in life, they wanted the same education as the Europeans.

Today the school, particularly at the secondary level, often exists in isolation from its cultural surroundings and produces a product which is adapted neither to the traditional culture nor to the needs of a modern industrial society. There are many causes for this, rooted both in the subject matter offered and in the pedagogical methods. Most educational systems in the new nations rely heavily on external examinations and the result is a type of education which is effective in teaching students to pass examinations but poor in teaching students to think for themselves and in inculcating the desired new values.

There are good reasons for a national examination system. It insures a common standard of education, usually one which—in its higher reaches—is related to standards in Europe. When not all children can be accommodated in school, it is the most equitable means of selection for further education. But over-emphasis on examinations—and the certificates and diplomas they produce—leads to a slavish adherence to the syllabus and emphasis on rote memorization. Peace Corps science teachers in developing countries have found that many of their students are excellent at memorizing laws and examples of their operation, but quite unable to apply the principles to new examples. And they simply do not want to hear about any new principles that have been discovered since the syllabus was written, since such knowledge is dysfunctional to the goal of passing the examination.

Rigid, examination-oriented educational systems are poor in producing flexible, innovative people who can adapt well to the confusions and opportunities of the business world and who are a necessary ingredient of economic growth. Fortunately, developing countries are now, to a growing extent, breaking away from their former patterns of elitist, white collar education, and looking for a type of education that is more appropriate to their present needs. They are internationalizing their models. For example, in 1965, Malaysia established a new universal system of comprehensive schools for the 7th, 8th and 9th years of school. They drew partly on U.K. ideas—which are not yet fully implemented in the U.K.—and partly on experience in Sweden, Germany and the United States.

Given educational reform, how far can the schools go in creating the type of modern man needed by a developing nation? The schools are just one of the tools of socialization, but for the artisans of social change, they are the most important one.

Harvard psychologist David C. McClelland argues that the chief personality values associated with economic progress are a need for achievement and other-directedness. Although many psychologists believe that motivations are largely established in early childhood and are not very amenable to change in school or adulthood, McClelland thinks that people can be re-educated in this basic way. He suggests three courses of action:

1. Develop a national achievement mystique, through the mass media, the political parties and the schools. Rewrite children's stories to stress achievement, train teachers to promote competitive games and encourage personal commitment to work toward national achievement goals.
2. Promote feminism. No country has yet sustained a long period of rapid economic growth in the modern era that has not also emancipated its women and encouraged them to enter the labor force. Women are the carriers of culture; getting them out of the home and exposed to new ideas will lead to their passing them on to their children.
3. Establish motivation training courses for executives. McClelland and his colleagues at Harvard University have developed experimental courses in India and Mexico to learn how achievement motivation can be stepped up in executives (17).

Some may question the desirability of such a broadscale attack on the problem of changing basic cultural values. Many traditional cultures place a higher value on friendship and getting along with others than they do on competition and achievement. But modern society is, above all, achievement oriented, and only those who can adapt to it will in the long run get their fair share of the fruits of the world.

Another approach is to extend schooling downward, in order to move more of the task of socializing the child from the family to the school. In the United States it has been found that slum children do very poorly in school compared with their suburban, middle-class peers because of the poverty of their early socialization in terms of language ability, ability to generalize, work habits, and a value system which is not consonant with the values of the classroom. At the age of six when they start school they are a couple of years behind, and as time goes on the gap does not narrow—it widens. Recent studies suggest that the earlier years of the child's life are crucial in simply developing his mind to its maximum. Last year a nation-wide attack on this problem was started, called Operation Head Start, and more than half a million pre-school children were enrolled in a two-month summer course. It has proved to be the most popular program in the American 'War on Poverty.'

Israel uses a similar method to assist the children from its Oriental families to catch up educationally with the children from European families. The Communist nations have also gone in heavily for this approach, both in their widespread kindergartens for working mothers, and in the new Russian boarding schools, of which there are currently more than 2,000. A study of Chinese pre-school training programs in Kiangsu Province, utilizing McClelland's theories and methodology, concluded that they were strongly achievement oriented and inculcated self-reliant, competitive behavior to a far greater extent than do Western pre-schools (15).

At a time when developing countries cannot afford universal primary education of the traditional variety, thoughts of such a pre-school program may appear visionary. Nevertheless, some small-scale experimentation with this idea would be worthwhile in any country. It could conceivably lead to a radical reorientation of the concept of primary education in traditional areas.

Social change may be influenced almost as much by who gets educated as by what kind of education he gets. When there is not enough education to go around, some kind of rationing is necessary, and the government is faced with the issue of equity vs. efficiency. The practically potent demand for equity calls for spreading the supply as widely as possible. But efficiency calls for giving educational priority to those groups, areas, or individuals where given inputs will produce the largest response in attendance, educational achievement, and output to meet the growth of the nation.

Let us look at the case for efficiency. Anderson and Bowman have argued in several papers (1, 2, 6, 7) that educational opportunities should be differently provided to those groups who are most interested in education and most prepared to profit from it. They suggest that the concept of balanced growth is almost a contradiction in terms. Economic development, like other social changes, occurs in nodes, in centers displaying high rates of change in interaction with other such centers. This calls for concentrating on the development of growth institutions and centers as models for the whole society, rather than a frontal attack on backwardness throughout the society. It means that in initial stages of development there will be widening educational and income differentials among strata and localities, although eventually these will narrow as the system becomes more highly developed.

The implication for education is that schools should be preferentially located in the centers where the community will make the most effort to have them and that financing of secondary and higher education should rely heavily on loans and fees rather than stipends. Wide variations in standards should be accepted. As appreciation of the value of better schooling becomes more widespread, individuals and communities will make greater efforts to achieve it. An educational system flourishes to the extent that parents become convinced that their children will benefit tangibly from it. At present in many developing nations much of the primary education is almost totally wasted. Dropout rates run higher than 50% in some places and basic literacy barely gained is quickly lost.

One can criticize the Anderson-Bowman approach by noting that it would result in the most education going to those in the social structure who already get the most education because of their favored position. This is a proposition little likely to appeal to the socialistically-oriented new nations. It should be noted, however, that the U.S.S.R. employed local financing of schools in the early years, and fees more recently. During the 1929 school year, only 4.6% of the more than 50,000 schools engaged in the eradication of illiteracy in the U.S.S.R. were financed out of the State budget; 74% were supported by local governments and 21% by trade unions, co-ops, etc. (10). And from 1941-1956 fees were required for higher education. As a result of the combined effect of fees and parental influence, in 1958 an estimated 60-70% of the students in institutions of higher education were children of officials and the intelligentsia (3, pp. 252-3). Similarly, in the West, as schooling is made more widely available, the privileged classes are able to take more advantage of it than the unprivileged ones. Indeed it may be argued that, unless there is a stringent means test, educational stipends actually amount to a subsidizing of the rich by the poor.

Let us now look at the political side of education. A decade ago there was little awareness of the determinants of political development and its relationship to economic development. Developers from the West conveniently assumed that as other countries achieved satisfactory economic growth, stable, democratic systems would somehow evolve as a matter of course.

But a growing amount of instability and a growing number of coups upset this easy assumption. Development is growth plus change and change may be functional or dysfunctional to the political system. Similarly, educational growth may be functional or dysfunctional to the economic or the political systems. And when we talk of national development, we must always think double. National development is economic and political development moving along in tandem.

What do we mean by political development? Can it be viewed in the abstract, shorn of the biases of competing ideologies and power blocs? The Committee on Comparative Politics of the Social Science Research Council in the United States has attempted to do this in a number of recent studies (10, pp. 14-5). It starts with the concept of an emerging world culture, a concept including a scientific and rational outlook, the primacy of secularity in human relations, at least a formal acknowledgment of humane values, the acceptance of rational-legal norms for governmental behavior, and deference to democratic values, at least in the minimum sense of encouraging mass involvement in political activities.

The Committee speaks of a development syndrome with three basic principles:

1. *Differentiations*—such as division of labor, the dominant trend in the historic evolution of human society;
2. *Equality*—the core ethos pervading all aspects of modern life; and
3. *Capacity*—man's enhanced abilities to manage his environment through increasing rationality, applied science, and organizational technology.

Political development, then, is viewed as the acquisition by a political system of a capacity to create new social integration which can regulate and contain the tensions and conflicts produced by increased differentiation, and to create new forms of participation and resource distribution which respond adequately to the demands generated by the ideal of equality.

Using this abstract definition, the advanced Communist countries and the advanced capitalist countries would both score high on political development while the traditional oligarchies and socially fragmented new nations would score low. Education is clearly an important factor in providing the specialized skills increasingly needed by the growing amount of differentiation in a society. Political capacity rests upon mass literacy, which makes a modern communications system possible, and upon the development of rational-secular attitudes. As for equality, education is clearly the major determinant.

While education is clearly an essential pre-requisite for political development, it can also hinder political development if not carefully planned. One of the major aims in the socially fragmented new nations is to build a sense of national unity in place of the existing ethnic and regional divisions. This frequently involves both a new ideology and a new language. The problem is one of balancing the need for homogeneity against other needs for heterogeneity. Tunisia has such a conflict in its desire to establish Arabic language education for the sake of cultural unity. But faced with the practical immediate problem of choosing between cultural unity in Arabic and high educational standards in French, Tunisia chose the latter. At no point has the introduction of a greater degree of instruction in Arabic been permitted at the risk of lowering standards. This dilemma illustrates how education which is economically functional, may be politically dysfunctional, and vice versa.

As I have suggested earlier, the same is true of social mobility—the source of some of the most severe political problems in the new nations. The problem of the unemployed graduates in Egypt and India and the unemployed school leavers in much of Africa is the gap between aspirations and achievement. Their unemployability stems from their unrealistic expectations. The greater the gap in expectations, the greater the risk that these people will be recruited into extremist political organizations.

Rapid educational change frequently creates a critical conflict between the generations. The political leadership of the various national revolutions has frequently been foreign-educated and is replaced by less-educated leaders who speak only the local languages. Conversely, many of the good government jobs are initially filled with people who are poorly educated or very young, or both. As the next generation comes along, there are many more with higher education who see all the good jobs preempted for decades to come by those they consider less worthy. This can be a source of great political tension since it directly concerns so many of the relatively small elite.

The solution is partly one of expanding the number of good jobs available, particularly outside the government sector, and partly one of reducing the emphasis on education as the major criterion of elite status. An expansion of technically relevant education will produce a larger group of what is sometimes called 'the new class'—people who have broken sufficiently from the traditional structure to assume a position in society not determined by birth but by training and ability. This group needs to become large enough to give up the illusion of trying to model its way of life on that of the European colonists or the small educated elite that preceded it. At first it will meet many resistances from both the elite and the traditionalists, but eventually it will become large enough to constitute a true middle class. It will create a new social milieu with the values, aspirations and standards of efficiency on which development depends.

In the early stages of development, teachers may represent the largest group of government employees and the largest group of educated persons in the nation. Because they are widely distributed and highly regarded in rural areas, they often play a large political role. A study of the legislatures of eight African countries showed that former teachers made up from 23% to 46% of the membership (10, p. 368). However, with the introduction of mass education, the teachers' status declines as many younger people are educated to higher levels. The result can be politically dysfunctional, especially since teachers are in such a strategic position to influence their students and their rural communities.

I have tried to indicate in this article ways in which education can be functional or dysfunctional to economic or political development, or both at the same time. In order to maximize the positive contribution a nation must be aware of these effects and must have a manpower plan which relates educational development to economic development. The essence of the problem is balance. The educational system must produce the trained people needed for economic development, but conversely investment in economic expansion must be planned so that large pools of unemployed educated are not allowed to persist.

If education can be said to be the single most important factor in development, it is because it is the most important determinant in creating human and social capacity. A nation—like an individual—that has capacity is more apt to follow a rational realistic course. A nation that lacks capacity is apt to look for short cuts—to be beguiled by the mirage of irrational utopias.

Francis Sutton, Ford Foundation Representative in Nairobi, says: "The seriousness of the pressures to hasty Africanization seems to vary inversely with the level of education attained in a country coming to independence" (10, p. 71). Countries with the least capacity to manage anything are sometimes the first to push out the trained foreigners; to take over their businesses; to amalgamate small businesses into large state enterprises, thereby increasing their requirements for organizational and administrative expertise. The result—as we have seen in many of the countries lowest in education—is chaos.

For these nations, the weakest links in development are the human ones. And for these links, the solder is education.

References

1. Anderson, C. A. and Bowman, M. J. *Education and Economic Development,* Frank Cass and Co., London, 1966.
2. Anderson, C. A. "The Impact of the Educational System on Technological Change and Modernization," In Hoselitz and Moore (Eds.), *Industrialization and Society*, 1963.
3. Azrael, J. A. "Soviet Union," in Coleman (Ed.), *10.*
4. Beraday, G. Z. and Lauwerys, J. A. (Eds.) *The Education Explosion*, Evans Bros. Ltd., London, 1965.
5. Bowman, M. J. "The Requirements of the Labour-Market and the Education Explosion," in Beraday (Ed.) *4.*
6. Bowman, M. J. and Anderson, C. A. "The Role of Education in Development," in Brookings Institution, *Development of the Emerging Countries*, Washington, 1962.
7. Bowman, M. J. and Anderson, C. A. "Concerning the Role of Education in Development," in Geertz, C. (Ed), *Old Societies and New States*, Glencoe Free Press, 1963.
8. Bowles, F. *Access to Higher Education*, UNESCO, Paris, 1963.
9. Burns, H. W. (Ed.) *Education and the Development of Nations*, Center for Development Education, Syracuse University, Syracuse, N. Y., 1963.
10. Coleman, J. S. (Ed.) *Education and Political Development*, P.U.P., Princeton, 1965.
11. Cowan, I. G., O'Connell, J. and Scanlan, D. G. (Eds.) *Education and Nation Building in Africa*, Pall Mall Press, London, 1965 (also Praeger paperback, N.Y.).
12. Curle, A. "Education, Politics and Development," *Comparative Education Review,* Vol. 7, No. 3, February, 1964.
13. Curle, A. *Educational Strategy for Developing Societies,* Tavistock Publications, London, 1964.
14. Harbison, F. H. and Myers, C. A. *Education, Manpower and Economic Growth,* McGraw-Hill Book Co., N.Y., London, 1964.
15. Lewis, J. W. "Party Cadres in Communist China," in Coleman (Ed.), *10.*
16. Lewis, W. A. "Education and Economic Development," in Cowan et al. (Eds.) *11.*
17. McClelland, D. C. "Changing Values for Progress," in Burns (Ed.), *9.*

18. Piper, Don C. and Cole, T. (Eds.) *Post Primary Education and Political and Economic Development,* Duke University Press, Durham, N.C., and Cambridge University Press, London, 1964.

19. Schultz, T. W. "Investment in Human Capital," *American Economic Review*, Vol. 51, No. 1, March, 1961.

20. UNESCO *Economic and Social Aspects of Educational Planning,* UNESCO, Paris, 1964.

Breaking the Credentials Barrier

S. M. Miller

27

[The following was written with reference to the United States, but its main burden appears to be at least equally relevant to many a less developed country.]

Education has in the past helped make our society more democratic by emphasizing qualifications rather than connections. In this way, it has freed us considerably from the rule of nepotism and arbitrariness. Paradoxically, however, this same insistence on education is now becoming a barrier to democracy—particularly to our national effort to remake the social class structure of this country by reducing the number of its poor and underprivileged.

We have built this barrier through our emphasis on credentials. Indeed, we have become a credential society, in which one's educational level is more important than what he can do. People cannot obtain jobs that they could well fill because they lack educational qualifications. Negroes who dropped out of the educational steeplechase before obtaining a high-school diploma cannot get jobs. Employers do not feel that they are discriminating against these dropouts; they merely regard them as "unqualified." And they persist

From an address delivered before the American Orthopsychiatric Association in Washington, D.C., March 1967. Reprinted by permission. The author is a program adviser in the National Affairs Division of the Ford Foundation.

in their beliefs despite a growing body of evidence, analyzed by Ivar Berg at Columbia University, that the higher-educated have a worse record than the poorly educated at every occupational level—more absenteeism, turnover, dissatisfaction, and probably lower productivity. Indeed, few companies even know the connections between the educational level of their employees and their performance. They have not bothered to probe their records to find out if their beliefs accord with the results of their practice.

I focus on the exclusion of the low-educated, but the processes that we are concerned about build Chinese walls of exclusion around an increasing number of occupations. We have a new guild system of credentials, license, certificates—largely built on the base of education—which keeps people out of many occupational channels. There is increasingly, for many occupations, only one route in—that taken when young. Failing to take that route bars one forever from the possibilities of that occupation.

It is assumed that these credentialing procedures assure a better product—that those who receive the credentials can do much better in the occupation than those who do not; that those who successfully go through the steps needed to gain the credentials are better fitted for the occupation than those who are not interested in doing so or fail in the prescribed climb.

I submit that we do not know whether these two assumptions are true. To some extent they are undoubtedly untrue. And a broader assumption—that those who do not go through credentialing activities are unfit for the demands of the occupation—is clearly inaccurate. All of us know of individuals who cannot get jobs that they would be able to perform well because they lack the appropriate credentials—whether it is a high school diploma or a Ph.D.

The Reasons for Credentialism

Schools today are not a humanizing or an educational force as much as a credentialing agency, sorting people out who do not fit into the regular channels of educational development. Schools function to certify that someone is not harmful rather than to develop the potential of all. Many of the poverty and job-training programs serve the same function.

Why is credentialism growing? One reason is that we like to assume that our world is rational and scientific. We invest confidence in the present structuring of occupations as optimal; then the question becomes how best to fit people into these wisely constructed occupations.

Then we presume that we know enough to sort out "potential" and "ability" from their opposites. Consequently, we repose an enormous misplaced confidence in testing and educational achievement, even when we have quivers of doubt about their "real meaning." Objective measures seem to remove irrationality and discrimination in favor of universally applied, objective rules. Where there has been oversupply of labor and talent, then processes of exclusion on some basis will occur. But when shortages occur as now in many professions, maintenance of exclusion as the core process is obviously peculiar. Such peculiarity is undoubtedly based on some fear—a fear of having to make choices and exercise judgment.

This fear is related to the third reason for the spreading tide of credentialism. Increasingly, the results and achievement are difficult to measure in a service-growing society. Norms of production output are difficult to use in the professions or in government service. Ambiguity of purpose further compounds the measurement problems. If 70 per cent of patients seeing a physician have no ascertainable medical reason for being there, how does one measure the achievement and productivity of the physician? Our uncertainty about what is the product and how to measure effectiveness throws us back to the input—that is, what is the training of the occupational incumbent?

A fourth reason for emphasizing exclusion is the "marshal's baton" syndrome. Napoleon asserted that his military prowess was based not only on his kitchens but on his promotion outlook—every soldier carried a marshal's baton in his knapsack, ready to jump into a command position. In many occupations and organizations, the notion, at least for men, is frequently to employ only "top-notchers" who can move to the peak of the pyramid. Yet the possibilities of moving to the top are slim indeed. In many organizations there is enormous turnover; only a very few stay long, and yet the notion is of "long-distance promotability." Furthermore, as Robert K. Merton has pointed out, there is no possible definition of "top-notchers" nor an adequate number of them, so that organizations and professions are doomed to feel that they are being short-changed in their share of "top-notchers." The important thing in this context is that the "marshal's baton" syndrome serves to make it appear wise to exclude many, even when talent and ability are in short supply. And certainly it caters to the yearning for prestige to be able to say that the profession or organization has only top-qualified people.

A fifth reason for credentialism is the importance of social appearance. As organizations and professions not only become more uncertain about criteria or performance, but require more intricate "teamwork," getting along with others, appearing "mature," and more acceptable to the public to be serviced, the desirability of insisting on educational credentials grows. For the credentials certify not educational achievement, but personal serviceability—that one knows how to get by, conform, manage. The educational failures—at whatever level—are social failures, bad risks.

Suggestions for Change

Does my attack on credentialism imply that there should be no standards of training, no qualifications for entrance into occupations? I do not think that these are the implications, but I do think my analysis implies the following:

There should be a general downgrading of the importance of education as the major credential. Experience and performance should gain greater importance. Many people will not be seriously considered for a job because they lack educational credentials; prospective employers will not even pause to investigate whether the low-educated can perform well. The absence of certificates results in automatic exclusion. Individuals should be judged on what they can do rather than where and how long they have gone to school.

If we treated experience and performance seriously, civil service regulations would be changed so that low education was not an automatic bar to many positions. Testing would be downgraded in favor of trying people in jobs and then assessing their performance. Since much of the job training today is not relevant to work, there should be a strong movement toward "Jobs first, training later." The absence of this practice means that many minority group members are now serving lifetime sentences of low-income and unemployment for their educational delinquencies.

"Dropout" is a label assigned at age sixteen; it persists through a lifetime. The consequence is that individuals who may have outgrown the issues which propelled them out of schools or who now have demonstrated and developed considerable skill are still economically disenfranchised because of their youthful educational difficulties. Once a dropout, always a dropout. As in many other aspects of American life, we need a de-labeling procedure which takes the curse off individuals who once ran afoul of conventional styles and were labeled and cast aside—whether the label is "dropout," "delinquent," or "mental patient."

We need deepened awareness of and respect for the abilities of those who have educational difficulties. We should not believe that our educational hurdles infallibly pick those who should be successes and unerringly cast aside those who should be failures. As we increasingly face the manpower problems of scarce talent, the great hope will be in the cultivation of talents among those who are now disadvantaged.

I do not wish to imply that every poor individual deserves and can use a marshal's baton. But many can. The failure is in cultivating these talents. We have much to learn here that we shall not learn if we persist in the new fashion of denouncing poor families for their deficiencies as educational environments. We then excuse the schools for their failure to learn how to adapt to and develop different varieties of students.

The first step of liberation from the shibboleths of invincible ignorance is to recognize the educational and occupational potential of many who have difficulty with educational systems as they are presently conducted.

We need new channels of credentialing and new points at which credentials can be expanded. While I am eager to see reduced emphasis on educational credentials, I am realistic enough to know that this kind of change is slow. Consequently, we must make it easier for individuals to obtain educational credentials.

Today, if one does not get twelve or sixteen or eighteen or twenty years of education in the orthodox way of continuous immersion without a break in the apparatus of formal education, one has much reduced chances of gaining credentials.

We should more effectively develop school programs and procedures so that once out does not mean permanently lost. Education and training will be increasingly a discontinuous process for the highly-educated in American society, as they will need new kinds of education at various points in their careers. The same attitude should prevail towards those who have not successfully weathered the educational system to high school or college graduation or beyond. They should be in practice re-entering and benefitting from education and training at various points in their lives.

To some extent the poverty programs are new credentialing systems in our society. Experience in the Job Corps or in the Neighborhood Youth Corps or in Manpower Development and Training Act programs may not be primarily important in terms of providing skills. Rather, employers may be more willing to hire youth who have gone through one of these self-selection and molding systems. Neighborhood Youth Corps experience may be a new way of getting a credential which employers will accredit and accept.

The Second-Chance University

By multiplying the number of credential channels, we make it easier for individuals to gain them. Those rejected by our educational system at age sixteen might be able to get needed credentials at age eighteen, twenty-two, or thirty. One should have second, third, fourth chances and ways of getting credentials. The more different ways of getting credentials, the fewer the people who would fail to get some brownie points needed for acceptance into the main economy.

What is needed is the idea of a Second-Chance University which permits "dropout" adults to get further and more useful opportunities to get credentials. Experience should be given educational credit; courses should be more relevant to activities—liberal-arts education need not be taught in traditional ways in order to reach traditional ends. While there is need for a formal structure to facilitate re-entry into the educational atmosphere, there is also need to recharge that educational atmosphere so that it is more hospitable and useful to those who have found the established educational practices less than useful or stimulating.

Every credential system should have an escape clause which permits the unusual person to be admitted to the realm of the elect. As professions tighten their qualifications, there is usually a "grandfather clause" which exempts oldtimers from meeting new qualifications. Similarly, at least 5 per cent of each year's entrants into a profession or other highly credentialed occupation should be individuals who have "qualified" in non-usual ways—by taking tests without the traditional educational prerequisites, or by getting credit for enriched experiences, for example. Some collective bargaining contracts have a similar provision: the company is allowed to hire back after a cutback up to 10 per cent of the labor force without paying attention to seniority; the other 90 per cent of the labor force must be rehired according to seniority. The company is permitted some margin of choice and selectivity to meet its production needs.

Without a minimum percentage, it is unlikely that a "creative minority" could in practice obtain unusual entrance into a field. Arbitrariness and favoritism could be avoided by a blue-ribbon panel of decision-makers.

The need here, as in so many other parts of our society, is for making pluralism possible in a complex society. We need a variety of social inventions to provide the structure and the reality of pluralism.

We should not assume that the present structuring of occupations is optimum. Many jobs, for example, call for too many different kinds of skills and too many time-consuming tasks; they should be broken down into finer tasks for many hands. Many jobs, too, should be enlarged so that those holding them can accept greater responsibility.

The emerging position of the nonprofessional is interesting here. The tasks of a professional job—like those of a social worker or nurse or teacher—can often be broken down into smaller units and combined in ways that permit less trained people to perform them. Sometimes the recombination produces services which the professional was not able to provide. These new positions could reduce the great unmeetable demand for professional services. With the tightening up of educational qualifications, it will be increasingly difficult to turn out an adequate number of professionals. As a consequence, the role of professional should increasingly be that of making it possible for less trained people to do effective work.

But this rational role is moving very slowly. There are grave limitations on what nonprofessionals are allowed to do; there is the absence of a career structure that permits many nonprofessionals to move into the middle class and into the elite stratum of the professional activity.

Professionals are increasingly becoming the gatekeepers of the welfare state, deciding on "professional" grounds who receives what kinds of services and who is allowed to perform various services. The pivotal importance of professional and organizational services has led many of the New Left students to focus on the professionals as the "enemy." While the assault is overdone and frequently misguided, there is something to the view that professions are hardening into barriers rather than aids. The guild-like features of professional occupations frequently are more visible than their commitment to broad social concerns, though there does seem to be important growth here. The emphasis on "competence" and "quality" frequently means a lack of attention to the poor or to those who do not easily fit into professional activities.

The slowness with which the nonprofessional is catching on—in being permitted to do broad jobs, in having chances to move up the occupational ladder—is indicative of the failure of professionals to reassess their roles today.

But I do not want to criticize professionals alone. For business deserves criticism here as well. Private enterprise could probably get needed labor (and at high productivity levels) if it restructured jobs so that the less trained could perform at least parts of them. The credentials problem is an issue vital to both the private and public sectors. The national interest of gaining decent employment for the low-educated and the poor could be joined with the private interest of profit.

In summary, we live in a pseudo-meritocracy where individuals are presumed to be selected for talent and placed into appropriate squares. Education becomes the major route to social mobility as the historic alternative routes are shut off. As social mobility becomes more important in our national policies, we narrow down the routes to it.

The general issue which the plight of the poor raises is that of a hardening and narrowing of society into fewer and fewer acceptable routes to economic improvement. We are slowly and rather hazily re-examining the core values and practices of our society. But we must press the search for equity and purpose rather than accept a patina of rationality through reliance on school processes in resolving our value choices.

Part Six: Unemployment

Unemployment and Income Growth in
Less Developed Economies: The
Asian Case

Harry T. Oshima

28

I. Unemployment in Asian Countries:
Present and Future

The measurement of unemployment and the analysis of its causes in developing countries are complex. It is difficult and hazardous to generalize for regions as varied as Latin America, the Middle East, Africa and Asia. In a paper as brief as this, it is possible only to summarize the situation in some of the Asian countries and give a few additional comments on the other developing regions.

Existing figures from the official national accounts show that Asian countries (excluding Japan, and the Communist countries and Indonesia, for which data are not available) were growing at an annual rate of 4 to 5 percent

This paper was written at the Economic Research Centre, University of Singapore, where, during 1967-68, the author was visiting professor of economics. This is its first publication. All rights reserved. The author is now professor of economics at the University of Hawaii.

per year during the period 1950/1952 to 1963/1965.[1] These growth rates of national product were about double the rate of population growth for the period in question. At the same time, unemployment in most of the Asian countries appears to have been increasing during the decade of the 1950's and into the 1960's so that today it is probably at a level high enough to be considered critical.

Unemployment as a magnitude is difficult to measure in developing countries. Incomes are so low in most of these countries that few persons can subsist without working a large part of the year. Present methods of measurement classify a person as unemployed if he is looking and available for work and has done no work (or very little work, say less than 5 hours of work) during the specific week designated by the survey, usually the week prior to the survey week. If some other reference period is selected, the composition of the unemployed group may be different. Also some who are declared to be employed may be working at odd jobs for only a few hours per day during the reference week. These comprise the underemployed labor force.[2] These definitions are applicable for the urban population, but difficulties arise when dealing with the agricultural labor force. During the busy seasons of the year, during planting or harvesting, most adults and older children put in long hours of work, but during slack seasons only few hours of work (on or off the farm) are available even for the male adult of the farm family. Even in urban areas, students and housewives defined to be outside the labor force are likely to work for a few hours per day, especially in family enterprises. These problems relating to the concept of labor force and employment do exist in developed countries but are of relatively minor importance. Such problems are much greater in most underdeveloped countries. There is a wide, gray zone between employment and unemployment (and those in and out of the labor force) and any attempt to measure the size of the unemployed labor force is likely to be somewhat arbitrary.[3]

Nevertheless, it is necessary to get some notion of the magnitude of unemployment, if only to assess its seriousness. Probably the most useful

[1]For a convenient summary of these data, see *National Accounts of Less Developed Countries,* OECD Development Centre, Paris, 1967. These figures exclude Mainland China and Indonesia. Growth rates are compound rates in this paper.

[2]Excluded from the discussion is the disguised unemployed labor force, those who are working but are not contributing to the increase in output. This problem has been the subject of much discussion, partly because disguised unemployment is almost impossible to measure. If such unemployment did exist in any significant degree, some nations would have deliberately shifted such workers out of agriculture and into non-agriculture. But I know of no case where this has been done except in Mainland China during the 1959-1961 Great Leap movement. Agricultural output fell sharply partly as a consequence of this shift and subsequently the policy has been reversed. Another group difficult to measure are persons who are not looking for work but may want to work if appropriate jobs are available. These persons are not included in "the labor force."

[3]For a discussion of problems in the concept and statistics of labor force, employment and unemployment in the collection of these data through censuses and surveys, see Peter You Poh Seng, "Growth and Structure of the Labor Force in the Countries of Asia and the Far East," *Report of the Asian Population Conference and Selected Papers,* New Delhi, India, December 1963.

concept is to measure it in units of full-time equivalent man-months or days to overcome the difficulties inhering in the existing concepts of labor force and employment. But the data for such a concept are not available. The closest approximation is the concept of full-time equivalent employment and unemployment for the reference week, assuming some standard weekly number of hours (such as 40-45 hours) as constituting full-time employment.

We have attempted estimates of full-time equivalent unemployment of several Asian countries, and though these are as yet preliminary, they do show unemployment rates to be 10% or more of the labor force in recent years. And for most of these countries the full-time equivalent unemployment rate appears to have increased from the early 1950's.[4] Even more alarming is the prospect that in the decade of 1970-1980, the unemployment rate is likely to increase still more and perhaps faster than during the 1950's and 1960's.

According to projections of international organizations, the size of the labor force in Asian countries which grew by about 87 million in the period 1950 to 1960, will increase by about 128 million in 1960 to 1970, by about 172 million in 1970 to 1980, and by about 225 million in 1980 to 1990. What is happening is that the population explosion of the immediate postwar years is producing an explosion of the labor force in the decades of the 1960's, 1970's and 1980's.

Surveys in most of these countries indicate that at least one-half of the unemployed population comprise young people below the age of 25. Apparently students coming out of schools are finding it extremely difficult to find jobs and, if the past decade is a guide, the situation is likely to worsen. It is true that many of these youngsters can live with their families for a while but eventually they will have to leave for the cities in search of jobs. Statistics of migration indicate a large movement of young people to the urban areas, especially the large cities. As this occurs, unemployment in the large cities (which already is large) may increase. This younger generation, educated to expect much from national independence, is not likely to remain passive and quietly endure the poverty and insecurity that accompany joblessness. Crimes, racial tensions and political instability may be the outcome.[5]

[4]See *Bulletin of Labour Statistics,* 1967, 4th Quarter, International Labour Office, pp. 21-22, where data from the employment exchanges are reported. From 1957-1959 to 1965-1967, the data shows that unemployment in the cities doubled and tripled for Burma, Ceylon, India, Pakistan, South Korea, Singapore, and Malaya. Despite the many deficiencies in these data, it is hard to dismiss the inference that unemployment is increasing in most of the Asian countries, especially since similar data for Latin America and Africa do not show such increases.

[5]An extensive youth program for those below 20 and single is urgently needed in Asian countries to harness the energy and idealism of young people to the tasks of nation-building. Burma, it is said, has worked out a successful youth movement through a Ministry of Youth.

II. The Relation between the Growth
of Income and Employment

Is it possible that in the coming decades the present unemployed population and the new entrants to the labor force will be absorbed to such an extent that unemployment can be kept at a minimum level, say 5% or less? There is no adequate method of forecasting demand for manpower, so there is no easy answer to this problem. But it may be possible to guess at its magnitude on the basis of past experience. As noted above, the real national income of Asian countries during 1950 to 1965 (excluding Communist countries, Indonesia and Japan) grew at a rate of about 4 to 5%. Aggregate employment (in the full-time equivalent sense) appears to have risen at a lower rate, although it is difficult to obtain data for the necessary calculations. Nevertheless, the estimated labor force for the countries under discussion grew at an annual rate of 1.6 in the period 1950-1965, a time when unemployment as a percent of the labor force seems to have increased. It may, therefore, be justifiable to assume that the growth rate of employment (Rn) was less than the growth rate of the labor force, say 1.5%, at a time when the growth rate of real income (Ry) was 4-5%. Dividing Ry by Rn, one gets a coefficient of about 3, which can be interpreted to mean that in the past decade and a half, for every increase of 1% in the growth rate of employment there was associated a growth rate of real national income of about 3%.[6] According to the best available figures, the labor force (f) of South and Southeast Asian countries grew at a compound rate (Rf) of about 1.0% per annum before 1950, 1.5% per annum in the 1950's, is growing at the rate of 2.1 in the 1960's and will be growing at the rate of 2.2 in the 1970's and 2.5 in the 1980's and 1990's.[7] This will mean that, if the relation between income and employment in the 1950's holds for the 1960's, 1970's and 1980's, the rate of growth of national income will have to be at least 6 or 7% (i.e., Ry/Rn x Rf) in order to absorb the waves of new entrants to the labor force in the next few decades. That is to say, Ry/Rn in the 1950's showed that a 1% increase in employment was associated with 3% increase in income, so that if the Rf of 2.2% is to be employed in the coming decades, an income increase of (3% x 2.2% =) 6.6% is indicated. If the existing level of unemployment is taken into account, the growth rate of income may have to average 8% in the next ten years in order to absorb the already unemployed persons. This rate exceeds the 5% target growth rate of the UN Development Decade for the 1960's and for the next ten years, and is double the rate of growth (4.1%) during 1960-1965. This, in turn, implies that the saving ratio

[6]For a discussion of this coefficient, see my paper "Growth and Unemployment in Singapore," *Malayan Economic Review,* October 1967, p. 38; the coefficient is designated as the income-employment growth coefficient in this paper.

[7]See preliminary estimates of James N. Ypsilantis, "World and Regional Estimates and Projections of Labour Force," International Labour Organization, Geneva, Switzerland, 1966. East Asia is omitted because data for Mainland China on national income are not available and the labor force statistics are too conjectural.

(s/y) must be doubled over the 1960-1965 figure, assuming no change in the marginal capital-output ratio. The latter is likely to rise rather than remain constant if existing rates of migration and urbanization continue into the coming decades.[8] The major determinant in the changes of the overall marginal capital-output in Asian countries is the massive amounts of savings that must go into urban infrastructure—housing, schools, hospitals, roads, public utilities and the like—and though these countries have spent a great deal in the past decade for these, much more may have to be spent if the stream of migrants to urban areas widens as is expected.[9]

Moreover, for the coming decades, Ry/Rn is more likely to rise than remain constant or fall. This is because the coefficient tends to rise with increases in income per worker. Ry/Rn is defined as $\Delta Y/Y \div \Delta N/N$ and this is equal to $N/Y \times \Delta Y/\Delta N$. N/Y may be regarded as the income required to give full-time equivalent employment to one person, and its reciprocal is productivity per worker. $\Delta Y/\Delta N$ is the incremental productivity per worker. Assuming no changes in the income required to give employment to one worker in existing industries, the income-employment growth coefficient may be thought of (a first approximation) as determined by *changes* in income per unit employment in the new industries, relative to that in the existing industries. Productivity per worker in existing industries does not remain unchanged in the real world, so that, strictly speaking, the coefficient is determined by the changes or increment in income per employment in all industries relative to the average level of income per employment in the previous period.

Under present policies, industrialization and modernization are likely to accelerate, raising income compared to employment both in the new industries and in existing industries. With the large investments in education made in the past, young people leaving schools and entering the labor force are better trained for work in new industries. Existing industries built in the recent past will be able to raise their productivity with the realization of increasing scale economies, more experienced entrepreneurship and work force, more extensive external economies, etc. A rise in the income-employment growth coefficient from, say, 3 to 3-1/2 or to 4 in the next couple of decades will mean that the growth rate of national income will have to rise by about one-sixth to one-third to create the same growth in employment, with other things equal.

[8]See *Report of the Expert Working Group on Problems of Internal Migration and Urbanization and Selected Papers*, ECAFE, UN, 1967, pp. 232-233.

[9]Rough estimates from the national accounts for Malaya, Singapore, Philippines, Thailand, S. Korea and Ceylon indicate that something like one-third of gross fixed capital formation appears to comprise urban infrastructure. Since structures rather than equipment predominate in these investments, the impact on the overall capital-output ratio is great.

III. Causes and Consequences
of Unemployment

There is no doubt that the population explosion of the previous decades is the source of the large supply of jobseekers in the present and future decades. But why hasn't the demand for employment kept up with the increase in the supply of workers in developing countries during recent decades, as it appears to have in developed countries where there was also a sizeable "baby boom" in the immediate postwar years? This is a complicated problem and research on it has barely begun; its progress is slow, largely due to the scarcity and inadequacy of statistical information in developing countries, and also to wide variations in the experience of different underdeveloped economies in the postwar decades. In what follows, we speculate about possible sources of unemployment in some of the Asian countries on the demand side. Since the supply of new workers for the next two decades is already born, and their labor force participation rates in future years may not change substantially, it is on the demand side of the problem that solution must be sought.

In the earlier decades, economists working on the problems of developing countries more or less assumed that rapid industrialization would increase not only national income but also create substantial amounts of employment, via linkages and multiplier effects (both internal and foreign). Some like Arthur Lewis depicted the process of development as a movement of surplus labor to the new industries of the cities where, as long as surplus labor existed, wages would not rise so that more new industries could be created until surplus labor decreased substantially, the large and increasing profits generated from the use of modern techniques and cheap labor comprising the source of capital for the new industries. This mechanism failed to produce full employment partly because, as Lewis points out, wages paid in the newer industries rose sharply instead of remaining constant over time. And this is to be expected even without labor unions, for the skills required to operate the modern capital-intensive industries are in short supply.

Others such as Baer and Herve trace the source of unemployment to the tendency of the newer industries to adopt highly capital-intensive techniques (which employ small amounts of labor per unit of capital).[10] No doubt, these are major causes of unemployment. Still, the experience of Japan raises the question: Why didn't the unemployed labor force find jobs at very low wages in the labor-intensive, small-scale industries which are not unionized and where wages can and probably do fall so low that they may be far below subsistence? In principle, and for the short-run, below-subsistence wages are possible because it is to the interest of the unemployed worker to work at wages which just exceed the additional cost of food, clothing, etc. required for the work in question. This additional cost is equal to the difference

[10]See "Employment and Industrialization in Developing Countries," *Quarterly Journal of Economics,* February 1966, pp. 88-107. W. Arthur Lewis, *Development Planning,* N. Y., 1966.

between the total cost of subsistence when the person is at work and when he is not at work. The difference is largely due to the greater food requirements of a person at work as compared to the person at leisure and may be as low as one-fifth to one-fourth of the cost of subsistence. There is a fairly large element of fixed or overhead cost in the production of labor power by the human body, which is mainly due to the minimum basal metabolic needs of the body even at complete rest.[11] In the long run, much of the overhead cost must be paid for and this can be done from the income earned during the busy seasons on the family farm or household enterprises.

The problem of unemployment touches areas beyond wage policy and choice of techniques. Part of the problem has to do with the displacement of labor-intensive traditional industries with which most of the modern, capital-intensive industries compete in the domestic market. A classic, historical example of this is the decline in the hand-loom, hand-weaving activities, particularly of peasants, with the rise of mechanized textile industries in Asia. But the displacement effect is not confined to such industries, whose products are closely similar and therefore highly substitutive, but extends to a greater or lesser extent to nearly all industries which are now being introduced into developing countries. For example the use of kerosene, gas or electric power for cooking from the petroleum and public utilities industries will replace the highly labor-intensive charcoal industry; the use of automobiles from local assembly plants will replace horse-carts, railways, buses and bicycles; the consumption of beer and soft drinks from the modern beverage industries will replace the more labor-intensive traditional and indigenous beverage industries, etc.

This displacement takes place not only between industries at the same stage of production, or horizontally, but also vertically, (i.e. backwardly-linked industries). For, typically, the modern industries established in developing countries are hardly more than semi-assembly plants which import not only their machines, tools, parts, but also the raw materials, semi-processed intermediate materials. The basic tool and material industries such as steel, aluminum, heavy chemicals, rubber, pulp and paper, and the machinery and engineering industries, are extremely costly and/or technologically complex, requiring enormous scale-economies for efficient operation.[12] It is difficult for developing countries (even large ones) with limited industrialization and low incomes to establish such basic industries, so that the equipment and processed materials (intermediate goods) for the modern consumer (or final) industries established in developing countries must be imported, tending to produce balance of payments deficits.

[11]See my paper, "Food Consumption, Nutrition and Economic Development," *Economic Development and Cultural Change*, July 1967, University of Chicago, where the relation between caloric intake and work is discussed. Although physiologists are not yet certain, the additional intake of proteins, calcium and other nutrients required for a full day's work over minimum basal metabolic requirements may be even less than one-fifth.

[12]See *Report of the Asian Conference on Industrialization*, Manila, December 1965, UN, N. Y., 1966, p. 8.

The foregoing discussion on industrial displacement applies to the tertiary industries as well. The use of modern means of communication, e.g., the telephone, and consumer durables (automobiles, washing machines, vacuum cleaners, refrigerators, etc.) in households tends to diminish the use of domestic servants and to rationalize and modernize retailing. The use of typewriters, adding machines and other office equipment in commerce and services tend to substitute machines for workers, thereby reducing the demand for employment. If the equipment is produced domestically, jobs are created in industries which may compensate for the loss of jobs in the service industries, but if they are largely imported (or if most of the parts for their assembly are imported), there is no compensatory creation of employment; instead the developing countries are often left with balance of payment difficulties.[13]

Finally, the attempt to establish modern industries as rapidly as possible entails the creation of a class of industrial workers, managers and professional people, whose consumption patterns are increasingly oriented to modern and westernized patterns and whose incomes are high enough to make effective their demand for newer patterns of living. For the emphasis on science and technology carries with it a modernized set of values looking toward westernized ways of living. Some of the modern consumption goods desired by this class can be produced domestically, but a large miscellany of them must be imported, partly because the internal markets for these varied products are still too small for them to be economically supplied within the developing countries. Accordingly, the rapid shift from traditional to western patterns of food, clothing, housing, recreational and cultural consumption of those engaged in modern industries tends to reduce jobs in the traditional sectors and adds to balance of payments problems.[14] It appears therefore that the policy of emphasizing modern industrialization is largely the cause of unemployment on the demand side, whose counterpart is balance of payments difficulties and requirements of large amounts of savings for highly expensive, long-gestation infrastructure.

Undue emphasis on industrialization-urbanization, in turn implies inadequate attention to the needs of agriculture, which is labor intensive. If sufficient emphasis on developing intensive cultivation in Asia had been given in the early postwar years, there would have been increases in total agricultural production under conditions both of rising employment in the rural areas *and* of rising productivity per worker, i.e., the increase in output exceeding the increment of labor and other inputs. This happened in Japan in

[13]On the other hand, the use of modern consumer durables does create a demand for repairing and servicing of durables, activities which are highly labor intensive.

[14]For a detailed discussion of shifts in the structure of consumption and demand induced by and associated with shifts in industrial structure in the growth of developed countries, see Simon Kuznets, *Modern Economic Growth*, Chapter 3, Yale University Press, 1966; Chapter 4, on income distribution. In the paper on the "International Comparison of Size Distribution of Family Incomes," *Review of Economics and Statistics*, November 1962, Harvard, I tried to show that the lowest income groups in Asian countries are those in agriculture.

the prewar decades and in Taiwan in the postwar period, so that, in 1960, agricultural labor force per 100 hectares of arable land in Japan was three times that of India, Pakistan and the Philippines, and in Taiwan, two times, while agricultural output per worker in U.S. dollars in 1960 was about twice as large in Taiwan and three and a half in Japan compared to the average for India, Pakistan, Philippines and Thailand.[15] And in 1967, the use of the new rice seed developed by the International Rice Research Institute in Los Banos, Philippines, together with the "package" of other inputs, resulted in the doubling of rice yields, and an increase of 25% of labor and inputs.[16] It is said that in the Philippines with the spread of the new rice culture, self-sufficiency in rice is foreseen within the next two or three years, whereas in 1965, the value of rice imports was 7.5% of the value of exports. But even more important, within a few years, a substantial reduction in the level of unemployment can be expected below the 10 to 12% (full-time equivalent) of 1967. In modern industrialization, increased productivity is achieved mainly by using machinery which substitutes for labor (directly and indirectly). In intensive agriculture of the kind discussed above, increased productivity is achieved by the use of more water, fertilizer, insecticide, better seeds, etc., which are complementary to labor. Equipment capital per unit of labor rises in the former but does not in the latter.

The increased labor input is required by the new rice culture (for land preparation, fertilizing, weeding, harvesting, etc.). Just as important is the fact that the increased incomes of peasants due to rising labor productivity will generate larger demands for material inputs and for wage-goods. The agricultural population comprises the lowest income group in developing countries and their consumption needs are generally met from the output of small-scale, indigenous units which are highly labor intensive, using little capital and imported inputs and located in the small towns and rural areas. The greater employment in these indigenous units will in turn increase demand in the towns and, in multiplier fashion, some of these will reach the metropolis where the modern industries (most of which are operating below full-capacity) are located. This process, when continued, may eventually reverse the large outflow of people from the rural areas and small towns to the large cities, thereby reducing the need for the provision of urban infrastructure.[17]

The model implicit in the foregoing argument is not hypothetical but drawn from life, being based largely on the historical experience of Japan

[15]*Changes in Agriculture in 26 Developing Nations*, 1948-1963, Foreign Agricultural Economic Report, No. 7, U.S. Department of Agriculture, Washington, D.C., 1965, p. 64, Table 49.

[16]Randolph Barker and E. U. Quintana, "Farm Management Studies of Costs and Returns in Rice Production," (mimeo.), International Rice Research Institute, 1967.

[17]An official of the Rizal County Agricultural Development Council (Philippines) which spearheaded the use of the new rice culture in Rizal County in 1967 pointed out to the writer that there was observable a tendency for young workers who had migrated to Manila to return to Rizal County in that year.

and, more recently and more pertinently, Taiwan. Agricultural gross output per worker in Taiwan has been rising at a rate of about 9% per year in the 1950's, while output per unit of all inputs has been rising at a rate of 5%.[18] Indigenous small industries (70% of which are located in rural areas) predominate in the industrial structure, although in the 1960's large-scale modern industries are growing rapidly, making Taiwan's industrial and overall growth the most rapid in Asia today. And despite its most rapidly growing labor force, Taiwan's unemployment rate is the lowest in Asia.[19]

In contrast, Puerto Rico achieved rapid growth by emphasizing industrialization. But this success was largely due to U.S. capital, know-how, and, above all, proximity and full access to U.S. markets. And despite the fact that net out-migration equalled the increases in population, unemployment persisted throughout the period, remaining as high as 10% in the 1960's, and this in the face of spectacular increases in tourism which is labor-intensive; without the jobs created by tourism, the rate of unemployment may have been twice as high.[20]

In sum, under Asian conditions, the outcome of a policy overemphasizing industrialization is an imbalance in the economy—an imbalance characterized by food shortages and malnutrition, maldistribution of income and expenditures, balance of payments difficulties, excessive and costly urbanization, and severe unemployment and underemployment of unskilled and semi-skilled labor together with shortages of skilled labor. Increases in productivity in agriculture generate a pattern of effective demand which is different from the pattern originating in productivity increases in modern industry, the former being more oriented to wage-goods consumption patterns in contrast to salary-goods patterns for the latter. Since the wage-goods industries tend to be labor intensive, rural-based, and indigenous raw materials-using as compared with salary-goods industries, more employment is created per unit of income produced.[21]

But it may be objected that an attempt to emphasize agricultural development instead of industries may not produce growth rates of overall

[18]Computed from data in S. C. Hsich and T. H. Lee, *Agricultural Development and Its Contributions to Economic Growth in Taiwan*, JCRR, Economic Digest No. 17, April 1966, Taipei, pp. 110-111, also p. 97.

[19]Unemployment defined to include persons working less than 18 hours per week has been steadily falling from about 6-1/2 of the labor force in 1963 to about 3-1/2 in 1967. Underemployment defined to include persons working less than 42 hours but more than 18 hours has also been declining from 5-1/2 to 3%. See *Quarterly Report on the Labor Force Survey in Taiwan, 1967*, Council for International Economic Cooperation and Development, Taipei.

[20]L. G. Reynolds in the *American Economic Review*, March 1965, pp. 19-39.

[21]I have discussed these and other aspects of an agricultural development strategy in the *Economic Development and Cultural Change*, University of Chicago, April 1962. In that paper I stressed the importance of capital-saving aspect of an agricultural-based growth, i.e., the use of existing tools, equipment, housing, other infrastructure, and building on existing skills and training. With the labor force explosion generated from the previous decades' population explosion *and* the continuing population growth of the present decade, the need to economize on savings is likely to be urgent.

national product high enough to absorb the new entrants to the labor force and existing unemployed population, even though employment per unit of income produced may rise. It is difficult to achieve high overall growth rates with a sluggish and stagnant agriculture even though industrial growth is high, partly because in the developing countries the agricultural sector is two or three times larger than the industrial sector (measured by product originating). And increases in productivity per worker largely confined to the relatively small modernized portions of the industrial sector cannot create an increase in the total volume of effective domestic demand (as distinct from imbalances in the structure of effective demand discussed above) which will enable productive capacity to be fully utilized (in the sense of double shifts in industry, double cropping in agriculture, and full-time work in the service industries).

Not only are there savings in the fuller use of capital and other material-productive equipment in an economy operating at high levels of employment, but also in human labor costs. As mentioned above, the human body requires large quantities of food, clothing and shelter, even when at rest or at leisure or unemployed. The increase in these basic necessities when the body is fully at work (say, 45 hours per week) is mainly in the caloric intake from additional food consumed to provide the energy for the 45 hours of work. But this increase in food intake is considerably less than the increase in output of unemployed people when they are put to work. The reason is that for the basal metabolic functions of the human body (e.g., for the operations of the organs of the body), a large amount of calories are needed anyway, whether one is resting or working. The number of calories required to power the functioning of the body organs and miscellaneous, leisurely activities not related to work, may be as high as 50% or more of a normal working person's calorie needs.[22] This implies that when unemployed workers are put to work, their consumption of basic necessities will not increase by as much as their income, so that a large part of their income may be spent for semi-luxuries (with favorable effects on incentives) and another part saved.[23] High rates of growth can be achieved in this type of development because the economy begins to make fuller use of existing capacities, i.e., as the rate of double-cropping and double-shifts rises and when infrastructural investment

[22]In a paper entitled "Growth and Unemployment in Singapore," *Malayan Economic Review*, October 1967, pp. 47-48, I estimated that the increase in the demand for basic necessities by workers who were previously unemployed may not be more than 20%. On this basis, I estimated that the increase in output of employing unemployed workers may be as large as four times that of the increase in the consumption of basic necessities. In other words, as in machinery and buildings, there is a large element of fixed, overhead cost in human labor.

[23]At the outset, probably the increases in saving will take the form of decreases in dissaving, such as paying back loads and reduction of debts and borrowing. Most of the household income and expenditure surveys in Asia shows much greater dissaving in the lower income groups than in the West. In the case of Ceylon, the dissavings exceed the positive savings of the higher income groups, so that overall, households show negative savings. *Survey of Ceylon's Consumer Finances, 1963*, Central Bank of Ceylon, Colombo, 1964, p. 125.

falls, the capital-output ratio falls and probably the savings rate may rise, especially with favorable interest rate structure. And as full capacity and full employment are approached, the tendency for wages to rise will induce entrepreneurs to substitute equipment for labor, further raising the growth rate. With rising productivity in agriculture, labor will migrate to the cities and industrialization will accelerate.[24]

To what extent the foregoing discussion is relevant for other regions of the developing world it is difficult for the writer with his limited knowledge to judge. There are reports of fairly severe unemployment in Morocco, Nigeria, Caribbean countries, Chile, Honduras, Panama and Venezuela.[25] To the extent that the unemployment may be due to displacement of traditional industries and distortions in the demand structure, both due to rapid industrialization, the analysis in the foregoing pages may be relevant. But the solutions to the problem may be quite different since agricultural structure and conditions in Asia are unique. On the other hand, even in Africa, Latin America, and the Middle East, there may be potentials for agricultural productivity increases with more intensive cultural practices, although output per worker and per hectare is already considerably higher in most of the countries of these regions than in India or Pakistan, Philippines and Thailand. It may be that for these other regions, a combination of agricultural intensification and public works may be necessary to absorb those who are displaced by modern industrialization. It is clear that, even for these other regions, the rate of increase in the labor force in the coming decades is similar to that for Asia, and the continuation of the population explosion and the rise in per capita incomes will call for increased production of food and fibers in the years ahead.[26] The technological (medical) revolution in the production of the labor force which underlies the population explosion in the developing countries must be met by a comparable technological revolution in the production of basic necessities, chief of which is food. The problems of surplus labor force and insufficient food and other basic necessities are closely related.

[24]Such appears to be the pattern of growth of Western countries (and Japan), as Kuznets has shown. See his *Six Lectures on Economic Growth,* Lecture III, N.Y., 1961.

[25]See Fred Dziadek, *Unemployment in the Less Developed Countries,* AID Discussion Paper No. 16, Office of Program Coordination, AID, Washington, 1967, p. A-3.

[26]*Op. cit.,* U.S. Department of Agriculture, Chapter 1. In Latin America the growth rate of the labor force was 2.6 in the 1950's, 2.9 in the 1960's, 3.1 in the 1970's; in Africa it was 1.4 in the 1950's, 2.2 in the 1960's, 2.3 in the 1970's. See Ypsilanti, *op. cit.* Since growth rate of income in the 1950's was around 5% for Latin America and 4.5% in Africa, the income-employment growth coefficient is around 2.5 to 3.0.

Part Seven: Development Policy

Planning and the Market in
Economic Development

Harry G. Johnson

29 Economic development is a field of study in which economists have only recently begun to specialize, and in which consequently there is as yet no settled body of economic doctrine. I must therefore begin with the warning that what I am about to present is not the agreed view of a representative group of economists, but rather my own opinions. Though I have drawn on the literature of development and of economic theory in forming these opinions, I cannot say that the results constitute an authoritative statement of the present position of economics.

The fundamental causes of economic growth are not a subject with which economists have dealt much in the past, and they are not a subject with which economists can claim to be qualified by training and technique to deal now. My subject is not, however, the causes of economic development, but planning and the market in economic development; this involves the theory of markets, and on that subject economists by profession have a great deal to say. Indeed, from the time of Adam Smith, the theory of markets has been the core of economics as a social science.

Reprinted from the *Pakistan Economic Journal*, June 1958. Reprinted by permission of the author and publisher. The author is professor of economics at the London School of Economics and the University of Chicago.

It is true that the full ramifications of the market as an instrument of social and economic organization were not appreciated from the start by the classical economists. The English classical economists understood the functions of commodity markets; but they did not link the theory of distribution to the pricing process. The integration of the theory of factor prices with the theory of commodity markets was left to J. B. Say, and later Walras and Marshall, to work out. But the relation between the market and economic development lay at the centre of the foundations laid by Adam Smith. Smith was concerned with economic development, and at the heart of his work was the market, determining the extent of specialization and division of labour and the limits to increasing productivity.

In recent times, there has been a retreat both in economic theory and in economic policy from the nineteenth-century ideal of the unfettered market as a principle of economic organization. But the economic pros and cons of this retreat have been fully debated, and the economist consequently has a great deal to say about the relative merits of the market as contrasted with other methods of economic organization, and the circumstances appropriate to each.

The subject of planning and the market in economic development is, therefore, one which falls definitely within the field of the economist. Before I go on to discuss it, I must define more precisely what I mean by it. 'Planning and the market' may be interpreted in two different ways. First, it may refer to the contrast between direction of the economy by Government and the policy of *laissez-faire*. This is not my subject, though in a wider philosophical and historical context it offers much to discuss. For example, though *laissez-faire* and direction are often regarded as opposites, if one looks to the history of economic development one finds (as Professor Easterbrook has shown[1]) that economic development is almost invariably a process in which planning and direction on the one hand and freedom of enterprise on the other play their part, and are mixed. There is almost no case in which economic development has been entirely planned or entirely unplanned. The usual pattern is one of some framework of control by Government, within which the entrepreneur provides his services—a mixture of bureaucracy and enterprise, in which bureaucracy takes care of the major risks of development and enterprise faces and overcomes the minor ones. Another relevant point that Easterbrook makes is that an economy which succeeds in finding a formula for growth tends to repeat that pattern after it has become inappropriate. For example, Britain has gone on trying to work the internationally-orientated pattern of her nineteenth-century development; Russia has been very successful in developing heavy industry but has not yet solved the problem of agriculture.

[1]Professor Easterbrook's analysis was presented in the Marshall Lectures at Cambridge University in the spring of 1956. Unfortunately these lectures have not been published, but some of the ideas are available in W. T. Easterbrook, 'Long Period Comparative Study: Some Historical Cases', *Journal of Economic History*, XVII, No. 4, December 1957, pp. 571-95.

The alternative interpretation takes planning, in the sense of a general direction of the economy, as an established principle, and considers the market as an alternative to other and more direct means of detailed control. Given the general framework of economic planning, there is still a choice between two alternative methods of looking after the details. One is by direct detailed planning by a central authority, the other is by leaving the working out of details as far as possible to the operation of the market. (There is a third alternative, in which the Government is itself the entrepreneur and investor, which I shall consider later.)

This alternative interpretation is the one I shall be using: I shall discuss the question of the market mechanism as against detailed planning as an instrument of economic development. I should like to make it clear from the start that I am going to make a strong case for the market, as the preferable instrument of economic development, on two main grounds. The first is that the achievement of the desired results by control methods is likely to be especially difficult and inefficient in an underdeveloped economy; at this point I should like to remind you that a large part of Adam Smith's argument for *laissez-faire* was the inefficiency and corruption he saw in the Governments of his time. The second is that the remedies for the main fault which can be found with the use of the market mechanism, its undesirable social effects, are luxuries which underdeveloped countries cannot afford to indulge in if they are really serious about attaining a high rate of development. In particular, there is likely to be a conflict between rapid growth and an equitable distribution of income; and a poor country anxious to develop would probably be well advised not to worry too much about the distribution of income.

I am going to make a fairly strong case for the market, because the market figures relatively little in the literature of economic development, and the theoretical analysis which economics has developed in relation to markets is often overlooked or disregarded. Before getting down to business on the subject of markets, I should like to explore a little the question why, in the theory and policy of 'economic development', so little scope is usually allowed to the operation of market forces. There have been, I think, three main groups of factors at work.

In the *first place*, there seems to be in human societies a set of social and psychological factors favouring intervention in the market. In this connection it is important to remember that the free market as commonly understood is essentially a characteristic of the nineteenth century—before then, and since, the common feature of economic organization has been intervention in the market. What are these factors? One of them, I believe, is the impatience of idealists and would-be reformers with the working of the market, and their desire to take direct action to improve things, according to their criteria of improvement: this attitude reflects the intellectual arrogance typical of reformers. The attitude is reinforced by the fact that the defects of market organization seem obvious to anyone, or can be made to seem so, whereas the socio-economic functions of the market are obscure and difficult to appreciate. The discovery of these functions was indeed the great achievement of the classical economists, and constitutes the only claim that economics has to the status of a science. The obscurity of the market's functions makes it easy, also, to confuse opposition to unattractive features of the free enterprise system which express themselves through the market, such as inequality of income and wealth, with opposition to the market as a mechanism of organization.

Opposition to and dislike of the market for the reasons I have just discussed are frequently allied with a positive belief in the desirability of Government intervention in the market, and a faith in the disinterestedness and effectiveness of such intervention. Belief in the desirability of Government intervention in the western world is associated with the spread of socialist ideas, and in its modern form can be traced back to Benthamite utilitarianism; elsewhere, it can probably be associated with the nature of the State as the dispenser of justice in primitive economies. Belief in the efficiency and disinterestedness of Governmental intervention is associated with the growth of the modern career civil service, with its standards of incorruptibility, particularly in Britain and countries influenced by the British example. (This explains why the belief is less prevalent in the United States than in other English-speaking countries.) It is, in my opinion, an important question for underdeveloped countries whether their civil services are of the calibre required to administer the kinds of social and economic programmes adopted in the advanced economies.

Opposition to the market as a means of economic organization is also inherent in the characteristics of an established and functioning civil service. One of these characteristics, a corollary of the standards of administrative efficiency and 'public service', is a natural propensity to regulate. A good civil service, or a bad one, is rarely prepared to decide that non-intervention is the best policy; and to the bureaucratic mind the functioning of the price system as a regulator appears mere disorder and chaos. Another characteristic is an antipathy towards entrepreneurship; the entrepreneur is an agent of change, and as such disturbs the orderliness of the economy and makes it more difficult to regulate. This is not, of course, a universally valid generalization: civil services have, at times, played important entrepreneurial roles themselves, though usually under the pressure of political events. One special feature of the generally anti-entrepreneurial attitude of civil servants, noted by P. T. Bauer in his studies of West African trade,[2] is specially relevant to underdeveloped economies. This is the antipathy of the British-trained type of civil servant, literate and 'responsible', to the semi-literate and socially unacceptable type of individual who possesses the knack of making money by trading—the small-scale entrepreneur on whose activities economic development from a low level may well depend.

[2]P. T. Bauer, *West African Trade: A Study of Competition, Oligopoly and Monopoly in a Changing Economy* (Cambridge: Cambridge University Press, 1954), especially Chaps. 11-12, pp. 145-71.

These characteristics of civil services are important in considering the uses and limitations of control methods in economic development. The economist, or any other intelligent man, can easily think up ways in which market processes could be improved on by means of controls, assuming that he administers them himself and has infinite time in which to do so. But would the conclusion in favour of controls be the same if it were accepted that their administration had to be entrusted to a 'responsible' civil servant of the British type, let alone a civil service with a less ingrained tradition of honesty and disinterestedness?

A third factor antithetical to the market has been the character of modern economics itself, as applied to economic planning. Modern economics has been strongly influenced by the theoretical revolutions of the 1930s, which were inimical to competition and the market. On the one hand, both the theory of monopolistic competition and the new welfare economics have been excessively concerned with criticisms of the efficiency of the market mechanism, criticisms formulated from a static viewpoint not obviously relevant to growth problems. On the other hand, the Keynesian revolution fostered aggregative thinking to the neglect of older ideas of substitutability in production and consumption (which in turn have receded into the limbo of mathematical economics); and the habit of aggregative thinking has to some extent been reinforced by the modern emphasis on statistical verification which has necessarily postulated simplicity of economic relationships.

In addition to these theoretical developments, development economics has been strongly influenced by the nature of the major problems with which economics was concerned before it turned to 'development', namely mass unemployment and war finance, which inculcated the habit of thinking about economic structure as given, and of applying other criteria than consumers' choice. Two features of war-time economic planning are frequently over-looked in the attempt to carry over its concepts and techniques to peacetime planning. In the first place, the battery of controls applied in war-time rested very heavily on a strong appeal to patriotism. The application of similar techniques might be possible in an underdeveloped country which could mobilize and concentrate all the instruments of communication and propaganda on the single aim of development; but the capacity of most countries to do this is doubtful, especially as development presents no single dramatic objective comparable to victory. Secondly, in spite of the propaganda and the patriotic appeal, war-time economic policy in most countries ran into serious difficulties with the resurgence of the market in the form of black markets of various kinds, shop shortages, incentive problems, and so on.

I have been discussing various reasons why thinking about economic development has been inimical to, or neglectful of, market considerations. I now want to recapitulate briefly the various economic functions of the market and the price system as a method of economic organization. I shall be brief, as the argument is a familiar one.

In the first place, the market rations supplies of consumer goods among consumers; this rationing is governed by the willingness of consumers to pay, and provided the distribution of income is acceptable it is a socially efficient process. Secondly, the market directs the allocation of production between commodities, according to the criterion of maximum profit, which, on the same assumption, corresponds to social usefulness. Thirdly, the market allocates the different factors of production among their various uses, according to the criterion of maximizing their incomes. Fourthly, it governs the relative quantities of specific types of labour and capital equipment made available. Fifthly, it distributes income between the factors of production and therefore between individuals. Thus it solves all the economic problems of allocation of scarce means between alternative ends.

These are static functions; but the market also serves in various ways to provide incentives to economic growth. Thus the availability of goods through the market stimulates the consumer to seek to increase his income; and access to the market provides an opportunity for inventors of new goods and technical improvements to profit from their exploitation. Moreover, the market serves particularly to provide an incentive to the accumulation of capital of all kinds: first to the accumulation of personal capital in the form of trained skill, since such skill earns a higher reward; and second to the accumulation of material capital, since such capital earns an income.

The argument, then, is that a properly functioning market system would tend to stimulate both economic efficiency and economic growth. And it is important to note that the market does this automatically, while it requires no big administrative apparatus, no central decision-making, and very little policing other than the provision of a legal system for the enforcement of contracts.

All this sounds very impressive; but it is clearly not the whole of the story. What, then, are the objections to the market, how serious are they, and what should be done about them in the context of economic development? I shall discuss these questions in some detail. But first I shall state briefly the central theme of my discussion. It is that in many cases the objections to the market can be overcome by reforming specific markets, so as to bring them closer to the ideal type of market; and that to overcome other objections to the market may be very expensive and may not prove to be worthwhile—in other words, the defects of the market mechanism may on balance be more tolerable than they look at first sight.

Now, what are the objections to the market? They can, I think, be classified into two main types. One type of objection is that the market does not perform its functions properly. The other type of objection is that the results produced by the functioning of the market are undesirable in themselves.

I begin with the first type of objection, that the market does not perform its function properly. Here it is useful to draw a distinction between two quite different sorts of cases—those in which the market operates imperfectly, and those in which a perfectly functioning market would not produce the best results.

Imperfect operation of the market in an underdeveloped country may be attributable to ignorance, in the sense of lack of familiarity with market mechanisms and of awareness of relevant information, or to the prevalence of other modes of behaviour than the rational maximization of returns from effort. In the first case, the appropriate Governmental policy would seem to me to be, not to assume from the market the responsibility for allocative decisions, but to disseminate the knowledge and information required to make the market work efficiently and provide the education required to use it. The second case implies a more fundamental obstacle, not only to the use of the market but also to economic development itself, and suggests that successful economic development requires a basic change in social psychology. To my mind, it raises a serious question of fact. Is it really true that people in underdeveloped countries are strangers to the idea of maximizing gains? The idea that they are is very common in the literature and policy-making of economic development; one of its manifestations is the implicit assumption that both supplies and demands are completely price-inelastic. I am very sceptical about this, partly because of Bauer's work and partly because at least some of the actions of Governments in underdeveloped areas presuppose that even the poorest producers are susceptible to price incentives. I personally do not think one is justified in assuming as a general proposition that ignorance and illiteracy necessarily imply that men are not interested in making money. If it is true, there will be serious difficulties in the way of economic development; but again, the appropriate Governmental policy would seem to be to educate the people in the practice of rational economic behaviour.

Even if the market functions perfectly, it will not produce the best possible results by its own criteria if there is a difference between social and private benefit or cost. This type of case may be particularly relevant to economic development; it includes the case of increasing returns to scale, and can be extended to include the possibility that technical progress or capital accumulation tend to proceed more rapidly in industry than in agriculture. But it raises an immediate question of fact—whether divergences between social and private benefit or cost are numerous and important or not. This is an important question, but one on which we do not know very much for certain. The theory of increasing returns is logically intriguing, but the influence of increasing returns still has to be disentangled from that of technical progress in historical growth. Again, it is a fact that few advanced countries are not industrial; but this by itself does not establish the wisdom of a policy of forced industrialization in an underdeveloped country. Aside from the question of fact, the existence of divergences between social and private returns does not necessarily indicate a need for the Government to replace the market mechanism; instead, the operation of the market can be perfected by the use of appropriate taxes and subsidies to offset any divergences between social and private returns.

I now turn to the second type of objection to the market, the point of which is not that the market does not work in the way it should, but that the results produced are undesirable in themselves. Here, I think, there are two major objections to the market. The first is that the income distribution produced by the market is unjust and socially undesirable. The distribution of income through the market depends on the wealth and talents of different individuals, and on their individual skill in seeing a profitable opportunity of employing their money or labour. If they make a wise or lucky choice, they may obtain a much higher income. The objection is that this method of determining the distribution of income is not just. But if you attempt to intervene in the distribution of income, you immediately encounter the problem that such intervention interferes with the efficiency of the market system. If people are not allowed to enjoy the income they could obtain by their decisions, their decisions in turn will be affected, and the efficiency of the system will be impaired. There is, therefore, a conflict between economic efficiency and social justice. The extent and importance of this conflict is likely to vary according to the state of economic development. The more advanced a country is, the more likely are its citizens to have consciences about the distribution of income, and to accept the high taxation necessary to correct it without disastrously altering their behaviour; and on the other hand, the higher the level of income reached, the less serious will be any slowing down of the rate of growth brought about by redistribution policies. An advanced country can afford to sacrifice some growth for the sake of social justice. But the cost of greater equality may be great to any economy at a low level of economic development that wishes to grow rapidly, particularly as it is evident that historically the great bursts of economic growth have been associated with the prospect and the result of big windfall gains; it would therefore seem unwise for a country anxious to enjoy rapid growth to insist too strongly on policies aimed at ensuring economic equality and a just income distribution. I should add that the problem may not be in fact as serious as I have made it out to be, since in the course of time rapid growth tends in various ways to promote a more equal distribution of wealth.

At this point I should like to digress on a special aspect of the conflict between the market principle and considerations of social justice, which appears in some underdeveloped countries, the conflict created by opposition on moral grounds to the payment and receipt of interest.[3] Now the view that interest is a bad thing is economically nonsensical (unless it is merely a terminological dispute) until the economy has reached a stage at which no more capital can usefully be employed. I am not here referring to the administrative difficulties of removing interest from the economy, but to the economic principle involved. The problem of underdeveloped countries centres around the scarcity of capital. If capital is scarce, there should be both an incentive to the accumulation of it by saving, and a device for rationing supplies of it among alternative uses. These are the functions of

[3]This digression was a response to the seminar discussions that accompanied the Pakistan Refresher Course; in the seminar it became clear that many students were bothered by the conflict between economic principles and the Muslim injunction against the taking of *riba*.

interest. If you 'abolish interest' in the sense of forcing interest to be called by some other name, as was the practice in the Middle Ages, the result will merely be inconvenience; but if you abolish interest in the economic sense, the result will be the loss of the economic services performed by interest. On the one hand, the amount of private saving will be reduced and its allocation to investment distorted by the restriction of investment to activities over which the saver has personal control. On the other hand, insofar as there is a pool of investment funds (created, say, by taxation or monetary expansion, or made available by foreign aid), some method will have to be found for rationing it out among competing claims if it is to be used efficiently. This problem has in fact arisen in Russia, where the engineers and planners who assess investment projects have had to work out concepts which amount to the rate of interest, to fill the gap created by the refusal of Marxian dogma to recognize that capital has a scarcity value and is productive.

The same sort of argument makes it seem undesirable for the Governments of underdeveloped countries to use their monetary policy to favour themselves with low rates of interest. Governments now often enjoy the privilege of paying a rate of interest of 2-1/2 or 3 per cent; this encourages them to think, and to plan, as if capital were easily available. There seems no reason why Governments should enjoy low rates of interest when capital is scarce; on the contrary, it promotes wasteful investment and also, for reasons explained below, tends in the long run to promote inequality of income distribution.

I have been discussing the objection to the results of the market system on the grounds that it produces an undesirable distribution of income. A second objection of the same sort is that the free market will not produce as high a rate of growth as is desirable. I think there is a strong case for this objection, because people's actions in regard to saving and investment depend very much on their guesses about the future. Now people are likely to know their own current requirements better than the Government. But the requirements of the future have to be looked at not from the individual or family point of view or that of the nation as a collection of individuals, but from the point of view of the ongoing society. The needs of society in the future, many economists agree, tend to be underprovided for by the free market.

Even if the conclusion that state action is desirable to raise the rate of growth is accepted, this conclusion nevertheless does not carry with it a number of corollaries which are often attached to it. In particular, it does not necessarily imply that the state ought to undertake development saving and investment itself. Private enterprise may be more efficient than the Government in constructing and operating enterprises, so that the best policy may be to stimulate private enterprise by tax concessions, subsidies, and the provision of cheap credit. Similarly, it may be preferable to stimulate private saving by offering high interest rates, rather than by forcing savings into the hands of the state by taxation or inflation. One argument against a policy of low interest rates and forced saving is that it may in the long run contribute to the inequality of income distribution. The reason is that the poor or small savers are mainly confined to low-yielding fixed-interest investments, directly or indirectly in Government debt, because these are safe and easily available, whereas the larger savers can invest their money in higher-yielding stocks and shares or directly in profitable enterprises. There is, therefore, an opportunity here for Government both to stimulate saving for development and to improve the distribution of income.

There is another reason for being wary of the proposition that the state should undertake development investment itself—the danger that if the Government undertakes investment itself, especially if its administrators are not too clear on their objectives, the result will be the creation of vested industrial interests inimical to further development, and resistant to technical change.

To summarize the foregoing argument from the point of view of development policy, it seems to me that much of development planning could usefully be devoted to the improvement and strengthening of the market system. This does not imply the acceptance of all the results of *laissez-faire*, especially with respect to the rate of growth; but there are reasons for thinking that too much emphasis on a fair or ethical distribution of income can be an obstacle to rapid growth.

The argument I have presented has been concerned mainly with one side of the case for the market. The other side concerns the costs and difficulties of controls, in terms of the manpower costs of the administration they require, and their effects in creating profit opportunities which bring windfall gains to some members of the community and create incentives to evasion which in turn require policing of the controls. I have touched on that side of the argument sufficiently frequently to make it unnecessary to elaborate on it further.

Instead, I shall comment briefly on international markets in relation to economic development, since so far I have been implicitly concerned with internal markets. Economic development planning inevitably has a strong autarkic bias, by reason both of its motivation and of the limitation of the scope of control to the national economy. Nevertheless, international trade can play an important part in stimulating and facilitating the development process. Access to foreign markets for exports can permit an economy with a limited domestic market to exploit economies of scale, and the potentiality of such exports can serve as a powerful attraction for foreign capital and enterprise. Similarly, the capacity to import provided by exports can give a developing economy immediate access to the products of advanced technology, without obliging it to go through the long and perhaps costly process of developing domestic production facilities. Economic nationalism and excessive fear of the risks of international trade, by fostering aversion to exploiting the advantages of the international market, can therefore retard economic development unnecessarily.

One further comment on the international aspects of the market and economic development seems to me worth making. Discussion of the international side of development has been mostly concerned with commodity trade and commercial policy. But in fact one of the most important ways in which the world market system is imperfect is with respect to the international mobility of capital and labour. The problem of international capital movements has received a fair amount of attention, labour mobility and immobility much less. Now, the process of economic development in the past, especially in the nineteenth century, was characterized by vast movements, not only of capital, but also of labour, about the world. The mass movement of labour between countries has now been more or less shut off by the growth of nationalism. I believe it is important to recognize this restriction on international competition, and its implications for programmes of economic development. It means—looking at the world economy as a whole—that the solution to the problem of maximizing world output cannot be approached directly, by bringing labour, capital, technology, and natural resources together at the most efficient location; instead, the other productive factors have to be brought to the labour. To a large extent, 'the economic development of underdeveloped countries' is a second-best policy,[4] in which gifts of capital and technical training by advanced to underdeveloped countries are a compensation for the unwillingness of the former to consider the alternative way of improving the labour to resources ratio, movement of the labour to the resources. The fact that development is a second-best policy in this respect may impose severe limitations on its efficiency and rapidity.

To conclude, I have been concerned with the role of the market in economic development; and I have aimed at stressing the economic functions of the market, in automatically taking decisions about various kinds of allocations of economic resources, and the place in economic development programmes of improvements in market organization and methods. I have been advocating, not a policy of *laissez-faire*, but recognition of the market as an administrative instrument that is relatively cheap to operate and may therefore be efficient in spite of objectionable features of its operations. The general assumption on which I have been arguing is that economic development is a process of co-operation between the state and private enterprise, and that the problem is to devise the best possible mixture.

[4]See J. E. Meade, *The Theory of International Economic Policy, Volume II: Trade and Welfare* (London: Oxford University Press, 1955), and R. G. Lipsey and Kelvin Lancaster, "The General Theory of Second Best', *Review of Economic Studies*, XXIV(1), No. 63, 1956-57, 11-33.

Public Planning and Private
Decision-Making in
Economic and
Social Development

Gerhard Colm
Theodore Geiger

30

Regardless of its name, every modern form of economic system combines some measure of public planning with some latitude for private decision-making. Even in the freest of market economies, the government's own expenditures are planned in accordance with annual requirements and with the anticipated longer-range needs for those services considered appropriate for it to provide, and many large private enterprises plan their investment and market development programs for five or ten years ahead. Even in the most centralized socialist economies, the planning and administering authorities must take into account the probable responses of individuals and of local institutions to central government directives regarding production, consumption, saving, and investment. Hence, the task of

Excerpted from a paper of this title in *Organization, Planning and Programming for Economic Development*, Vol. 8 of *Science, Technology and Development*, United States papers prepared for a United Nations conference on the application of science and technology for the benefit of less developed areas. Reprinted by permission of the authors. The authors are, respectively, Chief Economist and Chief of International Studies at the National Planning Association, Washington, D.C.

harmonizing public and private decision-making confronts every modern economic system, though in different forms and in different degrees.

The less developed countries of Latin America, Asia, and Africa are in the process of working out reconciliations of public and private decision-making which are relevant to the character of their economies, consistent with their social values, and more or less effective in achieving their chosen goals. The variation is very wide, ranging from such countries as Mexico, Brazil, and Argentina, in which private decision-making in the free market plays the major role, to countries like Niger and Chad, in which the modern sector of the economy consists of a few government-owned or foreign-owned enterprises of various kinds. In consequence, it is impossible to discuss public and private decision-making in a way which is equally valid for all less developed countries. While our aim is to present some guidelines and suggestions, the analysis which follows is necessarily cast in the form of a generalized discussion of the subject and is not to be construed as descriptive of any particular country.

Functions of Government Planning and Private Decision-Making in Less Developed Countries

To a greater or lesser degree, the countries of Latin America, Asia and Africa are faced with common difficulties in seeking to accelerate their economic and social advancement. Among the problems relevant to the subject of this paper are: (a) the inadequacy of the existing infrastructure (transportation and communication, energy, and power facilities, etc.) and social capital (education, health, and housing facilities, etc.), (b) the shortage of investment capital, (c) the limited supply of managerial and technical skills, (d) the inadequate incentives and institutions for stimulating productive investment and increasing productivity, and (e) the heavy dependence upon foreign trade and external aid for obtaining the capital funds and the capital goods required for economic and social development. In such circumstances, governments have had to assume responsibility for discharging three types of functions in order to insure that economic and social development would actually occur in their countries.

The first function is that of national development planning. Broadly speaking, this function consists of defining the goals of the national development effort, estimating and mobilizing the necessary domestic and foreign resources of money and skills, and allocating or guiding them to those specific uses which seem likely to make the greatest contributions to achieving the national goals. This function may be carried out by explicit preparation of a long-range national development plan, as has been done in India and Pakistan, and is now beginning in several Latin American countries. Or, it may be done implicitly and unsystematically, as was customary in many less developed countries until recently. Today, most countries have recognized that, to be effective, national development planning must be carried on in a deliberate and systematic way.

The second function of government in economic and social development is to initiate those investments and manage those activities which comprise the public sector of the economy. In every economic system, there are certain essential services which only governments can perform (national defense, maintenance of law and order, etc.). In addition, there are certain types of investments which are so large or so pervasive in their importance to the economy as a whole that it is necessary or desirable for the government to undertake them. These generally include certain kinds of infrastructural and social overhead capital.

However, the public sector may cover a much broader range of economic activities either by deliberate preference, as in socialist countries, or because there are no practical or acceptable alternative ways of conducting them. For example, in some less developed countries, significant accumulations of capital exist in private hands, but these are often not invested in ways which directly and immediately contribute to economic growth. Traditional habits or present uncertainties may cause such private funds to flow into real estate, commodity transactions, money-lending, and other activities promising quick or large returns, which may eventually result in luxury consumption or investment abroad, usually in Western Europe or the United States. In other countries, there is no private capital or private sector of the economy in the modern sense of the term. In default of government initiative, too few private entrepreneurs would come forward to take advantage of such economic opportunities as may exist. Hence, for a variety of different reasons, the governments of many less-developed countries not only invest in essential services and infrastructure but also establish and operate, at least initially, some or all of the new economic activities that are envisaged under the national development plan.

The third function of government in economic and social development is to stimulate, guide, and assist private initiative and activities so that they contribute to achievement of the national development goals. Virtually all the less-developed countries are explicitly or implicitly committed to a significant measure of private economic decision-making as an essential complement to the economic functions of the central government. This results not only from deliberate choosing of the social values served by decentralized, nongovern-mental decision-making in economic life. Paradoxically, it is necessitated by the same scarcities of capital and skills as have impelled governments to assume the national development planning function and the entrepreneurial and managerial functions comprised in the public sector of the economy. In most less developed countries, neither the governments nor the ruling political parties possess the trained supervisory personnel, the technical skills, and the funds necessary to replace all significant privately conducted activities by central planning and government operation of the economy. Determination of the output and consumption of certain types of activities and products—especially those in services and consumer-goods industries—seems to defy the detailed directives of central planners. Moreover, there are always potential sources of capital, talents, and initiative that are unavailable to governments, particularly when they operate by compulsion, but which can be stimulated to manifest themselves voluntarily by appropriate incentives and encouragements. The less developed a country, the less it can afford to neglect the potential resources that could be activated only voluntarily and in decentralized, nongovernmental forms.

In addition, the more numerous and detailed the entrepreneurial and managerial decisions that have to be made by the central government authorities, the slower, more cumbersome, and less flexible the operation of the economy becomes. Most less developed countries have found that the market mechanism is a much less wasteful way of making many kinds of economic decisions and for getting many kinds of economic tasks accomplished. A system of centralized direction of production, investment, and consumption is also susceptible to political pressures and the ponderous inflexibility of bureaucratic control. Some of the socialist countries have recognized this deficiency of a large, centralized public sector, and have tried to solve their problems by decentralizing many economic decisions and activities, and providing market-type incentives and pressures for guiding them. Yugoslavia is the leading example of such a country.

Also, many less developed countries have concluded that there are substantial benefits to be derived from attracting responsible private investment from the more developed countries. Continuing, well-conducted enterprises established by foreign companies and businessmen in less developed countries significantly increase the amount of capital available for productive investment; disseminate much needed managerial and technical skills among the local population; and create opportunities for—and often provide financial and technical assistance to—indigenous enterprises to get started as suppliers of the materials, components, and services required for their own operations.

There is a wide variety of different ways by which the government carries out its third function of stimulating and channelling private economic initiative and activity. Thus, it is able to select the particular combination of policy measures that seems best adapted to achieving national development goals in socially acceptable ways.

The question, then, which each less-developed country must answer for itself is which economic decisions and activities can best be undertaken by the government and which by private institutions and individuals. This choice is sometimes deliberate, but more often it grows out of the historical background and existing socio-political structure of the country.

The Participants in Public Planning
and Private Decision-Making

In order to clarify the interplay between public planning and private decision-making, the actors or participants have to be defined.

In the Public Sector

Though we usually speak of the government, it must be remembered that the term covers a multitude of ministries, departments, and agencies, each engaged in planning its own activities. These include not only the several ministries or departments of the central government, but also those of provincial and local governments, as well as quasi-governmental agencies, such as social security funds, central banks, development banks and corporations, port authorities, railroad administrations, public utilities, highway commissions, government-owned and managed manufacturing enterprises, and so on. The planning of each of these governmental institutions has a greater or lesser effect on consumers, workers, and private enterprises. Each of these units of government is interested in specific policies and often subject to pressures from various groups in the population.

The multitude of activities and effects of the various parts and levels of government can themselves be planned only if there is some central planning agency which coordinates and directs planning for the government as a whole. Such a body is, in effect, responsible for the national development plan, as distinct from the different sectoral, functional, and regional programs, which deal in greater detail with the separable parts of the national economy.

The central planning agency has different locations in various countries. In some, it is located under the jurisdiction of one of the ministries (economics or finance); in others, it is organized as a ministry of its own; and in still others, it is an agency under the jurisdiction of a planning council in the office of the country's Chief Executive. National development planning is not a separate activity isolated from the other functions of government. Like budget-making, it is intimately related to all functions. Therefore, it can be effectively carried out only if, regardless of the location of the planning agency, it has the full backing of the country's Chief Executive, who is responsible for all official policies. This dependence on the highest governmental authority is best symbolized when the national development planning function is performed by an agency in the office of the Chief Executive, or the Prime Minister, and when he is directly involved in the planning process as head of a planning council.

Generally, the sectoral and functional programs contained in the national development plan can best be prepared and implemented in a decentralized manner by the individual ministries, departments, and agencies concerned. However, in some less developed countries with a scarcity of government planning personnel, the central agency may have to take on the additional functions of guiding the programing activities and training the programing personnel of the individual governmental and quasi-governmental agencies of the central administration and of provincial and local authorities.

In the Private Sector

While the participants in the public sector can be readily identified as units of the central and local governments, there is no simple way of defining the many different kinds of non-governmental enterprises and activities that play significant roles in national development efforts. A definition by enumeration will be clearer than a definition by characterization.

In some less-developed countries, non-governmental activities in commerce and industry may take the form of corporate enterprises similar to the business corporations of the United States and Western Europe. In many other less-developed countries, the most important commercial, industrial, and financial activities in the private sector are individual and family proprietorships, like those that predominated in the highly industrialized nations at earlier stages of their development. However, in most parts of Africa, Asia, and Latin America, the numerically largest portion of private economic activity is in agriculture and takes the form of large estates and of small peasant farms, the latter producing either cash crops, or subsistence crops, or a mixture of both.

In recent years, other forms of non-governmental economic activity have been established in less developed countries and have been assuming increasing importance. These include producers and marketing cooperatives, predominantly in agriculture; credit unions and other types of cooperative saving and lending institutions; productive enterprises financed or managed by trade unions, political parties, kinship groups, etc.; and similar institutions. In addition, there are various kinds of local community projects and village organizations. Though many of them may be officially sponsored or government financed, their operations largely depend upon the voluntary initiative and labor of their members, and they may be properly classified as part of the private sector.

Less numerous, but economically more significant, are various forms of joint government/private ventures, involving the participation of local entrepreneurs, and often of foreign companies, which contribute capital and managerial and technical "know-how". When, as is most often the case, the private participants in such joint enterprises are responsible for management, these activities, too, may be considered part of the private sector.

These many and diverse forms of private economic activity play different roles in the national development effort through people's decisions regarding what and when they will produce, consume, save, and invest. In the traditional forms of private economic activity (e.g. peasant farming, latifundia, moneylending, shopkeeping, etc.) these decisions tend to be based upon short-run calculations and on the assumption of static economic conditions, not of dynamic growth. Indeed, by definition, the less-developed and more traditionalist a country, the more private economic activities will be of a subsistence nature in agriculture and characterized by a static outlook in commerce, banking, and industry. If these traditionalist and static enterprises are to contribute more effectively to economic growth, their motivation and decision-making have to be reoriented toward the prospects for future expansion and growth. One essential element in bringing about such a dynamic transformation is to enlist the active participation of the numerous, smaller types of private enterprises in the national planning effort.

Generally, it is only the larger, more modern, and more productive private enterprises, including the subsidiaries of North American and West European companies, that are oriented toward longer-term growth expectations. Some follow the practice, increasingly prevalent in the developed countries, of undertaking their own long-range planning of investment and market development within the framework of the national development plan. Such private planning plays a most important role in ensuring that the private sector will make the fullest possible contribution to achieving the goals of the national development effort.

The Character of Planning in
Less Developed Countries

The publication of a plan is merely one stage in national development planning. The process as a whole consists not only of preparing the plan, but also of debating and adopting it, implementing it, and then comparing actual performance with the plan and revising it periodically on the basis of experience.

A national development plan always should have a long-range perspective covering general goals for at least ten years ahead, and more details of specific objectives for an intermediate period of four or five years. It should be an operational tool, closely related to the annual government budget, particularly for the short-run period of the next year or two. Operational shorter-term and perspective longer-term planning should be in fluid interrelationship, particularly through the "feed-back" effect made possible by effective progress reporting and evaluation, and periodic revisions.

In an economy in which private decision-making plays the major role, the national development plan establishes goals for social and economic development; determines the programs in the public sector; presents forecasts of agricultural, industrial, and commercial investments in the private sector; and estimates the international transactions needed to realize the objectives. These estimates of investments in the private sector and of international transactions are of a different character and significance from the detailed investment programs prepared for the public sector.

In the public sector, the government can determine the specific programs needed and can then direct the execution of these programs. However, even in the public sector, there is an important qualification. These programs are financed either by voluntary private savings and taxation, or by forced savings of various kinds, such as inflation, restriction of consumption, compulsory labor, etc. While the programs are determined in part on the basis of estimates of the productive facilities, manpower, and skills needed to achieve the national development objectives, the expected growth in turn is the most important factor determining the financial resources which will become available.

In the private sector there is the additional task of estimating the likelihood that private domestic and foreign decision-makers will in fact engage in the activities postulated by the plan. In addition, it is important to know the amounts and kinds of consumption which would be compatible with the national development goals and with the public programs subject to government direction. For this purpose, the plan has to contain consistent relationships among investments in public undertakings (infrastructure); in social capital (education, health, housing); in directly productive enterprises (public and private); and among government and private savings, consumption, and the other major components of the national domestic and external accounts. For the private sector, the estimates have not only to be consistent with the public sector and with the plan as a whole; they must also be realistic—that is, they must represent realistic forecasts of consumer actions, personal and private institutional savings, etc.

The government can influence consumption by price, tax, wage, and other policies and by a number of other devices discussed in the next section. For the determination of these policies, the plan has to serve as a guide. Thus, the estimates of the sectors in the economy which are not under direct government control commonly consist of forecasts of actions of private decision-makers as they are likely to behave under the influence of government policies specifically designed to affect their behavior. The realism of the forecast depends in part on the degree of influence the government can and intends to exert over the behavior of the private sector.

The uncertainty is inevitably greater with regard to the estimates of international transactions embodied in the plan. A country that depends largely on exports of a few primary products traded on world markets can usually exert little influence on the prices and quantities of these exports. Hence, this item in the plan will always be purely a forecast, and it must be treated as independently given data. In contrast, other variables in the plan are subject to a greater or lesser degree of direct or indirect control (e.g. imports), and can be so adjusted as to be compatible with the independent factors. Because forecasts of the more or less independent factors may turn out to be erroneous and because these factors themselves cannot be significantly influenced by government policies, it is always prudent to provide contingency measures for adjustment in the other, controllable sectors in case adverse developments occur; for example, if export earnings are less than expected.

In forecasting investments in the private sector, an important distinction needs to be made between what may be called "strategic" investments and "collateral" investments. The former relate to increases in capacity in key industries which are essential for the fulfillment of other parts of the plan. These private investments are often projected on the basis of actual negotiations between the planning agency and the private enterprises concerned. As to the collateral investments, they may be estimated on the basis of surveys of the intentions of private enterprises, taking into account the fact that new investment opportunities arise with expanding markets. Thus, the collateral investment decisions will generally be made automatically as the economy expands in the course of economic development. Inclusion of a projection of collateral investment in the plan is necessary in order to estimate the total demand for funds and the total increase in productive capacity which are likely to be forthcoming. These estimates are, however, less firm than those for the strategic investments and are subject to a considerable margin of error.

It has not been possible in the short space available to indicate more than a few of the many ways in which goal setting, program determination, forecasting, and choice of implementation policies interact with one another in the complex process of planning for economic and social development. The essential role which the forecasting, or projection, of the main components of the national accounts and balance of payments plays in the planning process is not always sufficiently recognized. Conversely, it is sometimes denied that any process which relies so heavily upon forecasting can legitimately be called planning. Those who hold this view maintain that national development planning is only possible if the government has, and is willing to use, the power of directly determining all significant decisions in the economy concerning production, consumption, saving, and investment.

Such a narrow definition of planning is neither accurate nor useful. It is not accurate because all national economic plans, even those of the most centralized and authoritarian socialist countries, contain an important element of forecasting the probable future behavior of individuals and organizations. The level and composition of consumer demand as specified in the plans of centralized socialist economies are essentially estimates of the likely behavior of consumers under certain conditions fixed by the government, rather than directives that will inevitably be obeyed, or which could be exactly enforced. The production goals fixed by central socialist planners, particularly in agriculture, contain a large measure of uncertainty—and to that extent are forecasts—because they are based upon assumptions about the effects on productivity not only of the weather and other natural phenomena but, more importantly, of the attitudes and motivations of farmers and other producers. The external transactions posited in the plans of socialist economies also contain a large element of forecasting. Their inability to control the behavior of world markets and of other governments is one reason why these countries strive to minimize their dependence upon imports—especially from noncommunist economies—despite the higher costs often involved in such autarkic policies.

Indeed, planners of all ideological persuasions have to recognize the fact that governments have only a limited capacity to influence or offset the effects of certain developments, such as a drop in the world prices of primary products, natural catastrophes, the initiative and conscientiousness of the individual citizen, and the variability of producer and consumer responses. Also, a country cannot enjoy the advantages of vigorous innovation and enterprise without giving the managers of private and public enterprises a high degree of freedom from bureaucratic regulations and political interference.

However, no country pursuing a determined policy of social and economic development could expect that all required adjustments in the plan would be made only in the public sector. A successful economic and social development plan depends on the ability to work out a constructive relationship between government planning and private decision-making, particularly with respect to strategic investments.

Techniques for Harmonizing Public Planning and Private Decision-Making

For each country, the major elements in its national development plan can be ranged from those which are most independent of control, such as foreign trade and the weather, to those which are susceptible of control by the government, such as public expenditure programs. In between, are the many factors in which private decision-making predominates but is subject to more or less influence by government policies. Thus, every plan implies some combination of direct implementation through government action, and indirect implementation through the guidance provided by government policies and by the planning process itself for the actions of private decision-makers.

While public and private economic activities should be conducive to realization of the goals of the national development effort, they do not always have this character. In the public sector, governments may not make the necessary decisions or may not carry them out effectively, for a variety of political and social reasons. Similarly, the results of private decision-making may not always contribute to economic and social advancement, and in some cases may be counter to it, again for a variety of reasons. Insofar as the causes are accessible to remedial action—and this is not always possible at any given stage of a country's political and social evolution—there is a variety of techniques for harmonizing public planning and private decision-making with one another and with the goals of the national development effort.

The Announcement Effect of the Plan

A national economic development plan will generally specify the amounts of investments in the different branches of industry in the private sector which are consistent with the other elements of the plan and are required for the increase in production posited as a goal for a future year. The problem is to maximize the probability that private decision-makers will actually undertake the investments proposed in the plan.

A major factor working toward this result is what has been called the "announcement effect" of the plan. If the managers of private enterprises are convinced that the government is determined to execute the programs and actions required of it in the public sector and, hence, that there is a good chance that the development goals could be achieved, then the plan for the private sector represents not only what is required of private enterprises but also reveals the opportunities for expansion likely to occur in various industries. In effect, it becomes a matter of self-interest on the part of entrepreneurs to increase productive capacity in line with the opportunities highlighted in the plan. This result depends, of course, on the conviction that the plan is feasible and that the government and other private decision-makers will play their respective roles. Success breeds success, and the "announcement effect" can be a continuing one rather than a one-time event.

It is particularly important for the success of the "announcement effect" that the investments be made which provide the transportation and energy facilities and other elements of infrastructure required for expansion of the private sector. Public educational and training programs, and housing for additions to the work force, are often required for labor mobility and industrial expansion. Confidence in the plan can also be strengthened if representatives of private enterprises are consulted in the planning process so that they have a sense of participation and have an opportunity to explain the kinds, locations, and timing of the infrastructure and social capital investments they believe are needed for the success of their own efforts. Such private participation in national development planning is discussed below.

Government Policies in Support of Private Investments

Important as it can be, the announcement effect of the plan is not sufficient by itself to induce the required investments by the private sector. Assuming that the reasons for the lag are not primarily deficiencies in infrastructure or social capital, they are usually caused by a lack of capital available to the private sector; by absence of the required technology, skills, or manpower; or by attitudes and motivations which are not conducive to increased investment or increased productivity. There is a variety of government policies which can help to fill these gaps, and provide incentives and pressures for more productively oriented behavior by private individuals and organizations.

Fiscal and monetary policies of various kinds are important means by which governments can support the private sector. The government's budgetary policy has a major influence on the activities of the private sector through the size and timing of a surplus or deficit. Special tax benefits can be provided for stimulating productive investments, and differential rates may be used to discourage traditional kinds of investments which make little or no direct contribution to the national development goals. In providing such tax incentives, however, care must be taken to prevent possible misuse of them as tax "loopholes." Sometimes, the entire tax system needs to be reformed in order to ensure that all groups in the population contribute equitably to the national development effort.

Through its ability to influence long- and short-term interest rates, the government can ease the shortage of investment or operating capital available to the private sector from the commercial banks and other private lending institutions. More important in many less-developed countries than interest rate policy are the ways in which the government exercises direct control over credit availability, investment licensing, construction permits, rationing of capital obtained as foreign aid, etc.

Governmental policies relating to prices and wages can help to maintain the profitability of efficient enterprises within a framework of reasonable price stability. In addition, price policies for public enterprises can be designed which will improve the performance and prospects of private enterprises. Import and foreign-exchange policies can help the private sector to obtain the quantities and kinds of capital goods, materials and components, and operating supplies which can only be purchased abroad; and they can also provide protection against foreign competition for "infant" industries.

Agricultural policy is particularly important in less developed countries, for the agricultural sector often provides the major source of domestic savings for investments in infrastructure, social capital, and new industries; of the foreign-exchange earnings needed to import capital goods; of labor for new factories and service trades; of food to feed the growing population of the towns; and perhaps also of some of the raw materials required for manufacturing. The capacity of the agricultural sector to fulfill these functions exercises a major influence on the development of industry and other new activities. Hence, it is generally necessary to undertake extensive and continuing programs of technical assistance and vocational training in the countryside; to provide adequate credit facilities for agricultural improvement; to encourage the development of producers' and marketing cooperatives and other new forms of cooperation among small farmers; to build farm-to-market roads, irrigation systems, and other installations; and to institute other measures required to increase agricultural productivity. In some countries, basic reform of the whole agrarian system is required before agriculture can begin to play its proper role in the national development effort.

Often, however, more direct measures of specific assistance to the private sector are needed. Development banks—sometimes operating through industrial development corporations—serve as important instruments for extending loans, and in some cases equity capital, to enterprises wishing to expand, or to new ventures which lack the financial resources required for investment in accordance with the plan. Government subsidies have also been used, either in the form of low-interest loans or of outright grants to cover the initial deficits of new enterprises, public and private. Whether institutionalized in development banks and corporations or administered by regular government agencies (e.g. ministries of finance or industry), such government loans and grants form an important link between the public planning process, on the one hand, and the decisions of private enterprises, on the other. Their effectiveness is increased when development banks and corporations provide not only funds but also managerial advice, particularly to new enterprises.

A major contribution to the development of the private sector is made by government policies and measures for mobilizing external resources of funds, commodities, and technical assistance, and making them available by various devices to private enterprises. These external resources may take the form of aid from international organizations and the governments of other countries, or they may be obtained through private foreign investment and the nonprofit activities of educational, research, and philanthropic institutions, trade unions, cooperative societies, and other voluntary private groups in the developed countries.

There is also a regulatory or restrictive group of government policies, in addition to the measures of positive stimulation and assistance just outlined. It may sometimes happen that enterprises will invest faster than envisaged in the plan in order to gain an advantage over competitors or for other reasons. This may be beneficial except where, as in countries with a basic shortage of capital, it may divert resources from higher priority purposes. In such cases, funds for financing "excess" expansion may have to be restricted.

Alternatively, it more often happens that, despite the government's incentives and subsidies, traditionally oriented enterprises—indigenous and foreign—may not invest in the expansion or modernization of their facilities, which may play a strategic role in achieving the objectives of the plan. In this case, new entrepreneurs may be encouraged by the government, or it may itself have to make and initially operate the investments which the private sector is unwilling or unable to undertake.

Other types of limitations on the freedom of action of the private sector imposed by governments include the regulation of the monopolistic and restrictive practices of private—and sometimes public—enterprises, the protection of labor and consumers, the maintenance of public health and safety, and the elimination of other activities and conditions considered socially undesirable.

Governments have to consider not only the impact of restrictive or compulsory measures on the specific enterprises that have provoked them but also the broader effects on attitudes and motivations in the private sector as a whole, as well as the implications for achievement of the national development plan. Since inconsistencies between the objectives of the plan and private decisions are bound to arise from time to time, it is essential that machinery be provided for resolving those conflicts that are of strategic importance in a manner which is just to the individual enterprises involved and is in the best interest of the national development effort as a whole.

In this brief space, it has been possible only to list the main kinds of policy instruments at the disposal of governments for stimulating the private sector to grow and to contribute as effectively as possible to the national development effort and for harmonizing private activities with those of public authorities. In many ways, this is the crucial portion of the strategy of economic and social development. Selecting the proper combination of policy measures and direct subsidy programs is an exceedingly difficult task in most less developed countries not only because of the scarcity of the required financial resources and administrative skills but, more fundamentally, because of social and political obstacles. As already explained, national economic projections or forecasts are most useful tools for helping governments to determine the particular combination of public policies and programs needed to assist the private sector to perform its functions more effectively. But, whether these policies and programs will actually be carried out depends upon the willingness and ability of the government to overcome the political and social resistances to change, the weaknesses in its own administrative capabilities, the resentment of influential special interest groups, and sometimes even the apathy of the people themselves. However, all of these difficulties can be significantly eased to the extent to which the private sector and the people generally become voluntary participants and partners in the national development effort.

Private Planning and Participation in Public Planning

The harmonization of public planning and private decision-making is not a one-sided process involving only policy choices and actions by the government. It also requires appropriate measures by private decision-makers.

In order to contribute most effectively to the national development effort, private enterprises need to engage in their own long-range planning, particularly of their investments in plant and equipment. It is desirable for large enterprises of all types to calculate the productive capacity, manpower, import, and financial resources they are likely to require during the planning period. These private plans should then be made available on a confidential basis to the government planning agency and revised periodically. This applies particularly to what we have called strategic investments in the private sector. Mention has already been made of the desirability of meetings between government planners and the managers of such strategic private enterprises. These negotiations are important not only to ensure consistency in the requirements of the public and private sectors but also to foster constructive attitudes on both sides and mutual understanding.

If the private sector is to make the greatest possible contribution to the national development effort, the many different kinds of private decision-makers, large and small, have to be permitted and encouraged to participate actively in the public planning process so that they can acquire a sense of voluntary commitment to achieving the objectives of the national development plan. One method used in a number of countries is for the planning agency to establish advisory committees composed of representatives of industries, the farmers, the trade unions, and other significant private groups. In addition to such direct participation of the private sector in the planning process, each country will, of course, officially review and legally adopt its national development plan in accordance with its constitutional and political procedures.

Ultimately, the success of a national development plan depends upon the basic attitude toward it. To the extent that both public planners and private decision-makers recognize that the planning process is a tool, not an end in itself, the task of harmonizing public planning and private decision-making will be less difficult in practice and more fruitful in results. Successful fulfillment of this task will make a most important contribution to social and economic progress within a framework of democratically developing institutions.

Multiple Gaps

John Pincus

31 How much aid do developing countries need? There have been a number of estimates of the savings gap—the difference between investment levels needed to sustain a specified rate of economic growth and the estimated funds available from a combination of domestic saving and probable capital inflows from abroad. There have also been estimates of the trade gap—the difference between estimated import level required to maintain the specified growth rate and probable foreign exchange revenues available from a combination of exports and capital inflows. More recent analysis is based on a so-called two gap approach, in which the larger of the two gaps is applied on a country-by-country basis to emerge with a combined world total. Those of the estimates that are roughly comparable emerge with a total requirement for anywhere from $10 billion to $20 billion annually by 1970, and $16 billion to 34 billion by 1975. The variation is accounted for by differences in target growth rates in the world economy (ranging in the estimates from 4.1 to 5.5 per cent per year for LDC's), in behavior of exports and imports, in assumption about savings propensities in developing countries and about the relation between investment and changes in output.

Excerpted from a paper entitled "How Much Aid for Underdeveloped Countries" from *Columbia Journal of World Business* (Sept.-Oct. 1967). Reprinted by permission of the author and publisher. The author is an economist with the Rand Corporation, Washington, D.C.

A good deal of effort and analytical refinement have been injected into the analysis of LDC requirements for foreign capital, and, in the process, economists have been able to apply an increasingly sophisticated technique to measurement of the gap. I suggest, however, that further refinements of the aggregate gap analysis are virtually valueless as guides to policy, although they may be of considerable professional interest. Nor are the existing estimates, despite the great differences among them in input of effort and intellectual novelty, of much more value than the casual observation by Mr. George Woods that underdeveloped countries could today effectively use an additional $3 to $4 billion annually of capital from abroad . . . .

Gap estimation exercises are essentially a political arithmetic, a technique for quantifying discontent. They put the seal of rationality on donors' charitable inclinations, or on the aspirations of nations that receive aid. A nation with an average annual income of $150 per head has an economic plan aimed at raising real income by say 3 per cent per head per year—a goal that, according to the planners, requires $50 million annually in gap-filling aid. Is there anyone so naive as to imagine that the contentment of its people or the stability of its government or social system will be assured by the gap-filling aid endowment? In the brief silence that follows, let me point out the obvious: the pause ensues because the gap that we are dealing with is the one that separates the aspirations of governments and people in underdeveloped countries from their present realities. This gap is not only vast, but multidimensional. It cannot be encompassed by any computations of the margin that separates savings from investment targets or exports from import requirements. This is not to say that it lacks any measurable dimensions; as we shall see, there are some. But first, let me enumerate the dimensions. All of them are all too obviously interrelated.

1. The aid requirement is usually discussed in terms of an economic gap. The size of this gap can roughly be measured by the difference between average income in developing countries and that in industrial nations. The economic gap also includes an element of domestic income distribution. Oil-rich countries for example have high per capita income, but very inequal distribution, and an aspect of the economic gap thereby remains unfilled.

2. Another gap is social. The developing countries aspire to build modern urbanized societies, moving, in the well worn phrase, from status to contract in social relations.

3. A third gap is political, reflecting a desire for mass participation in a stable political system, either in the form of parliamentary democracy, or of various forms of state socialism.

4. A fourth gap is psychological, built from a consciousness of representing nations that are not "modern," where people are less able to utilize the mixed blessings of contemporary technology; of belonging to colonial societies with their heritage of inferior status, often with overtones of racial inferiority; of belonging to social groups that maintain, despite themselves, feelings of inferiority born from the awareness of educational and cultural deprivation.

5. A fifth gap, incorporating elements of all the others, is the gap in the quality of life. In industrial countries, life is usually long and reasonably healthy; people spend from ten to twenty years as students, developing their intellectual and technical skills; the majority of them are relatively insulated from real poverty; leisure time and means to enjoy it are normal constituents of life; the majority, whatever their doubts and insecurities, do not feel that other contemporary societies are clearly superior to modern industrial ones; and finally, with obvious serious exceptions, most people feel that they hold in their own hands at least some share in determining their material destiny. By and large, only a tiny fraction of people in poor countries can boast these advantages; and that minority serves to make its countrymen more aware of the gap in the quality of their own lives.

6. The first five gaps are overlapping differences that many people in poor countries are either directly aware of, or, in the case of certain social or psychological elements, express through hostility to the policies of rich nations. The sixth gap, if we can call it one, is often not something that people in poor countries seek to close, despite its adverse effects on the quality of life and on economic standards. This is the gap in population growth rates. Governments of developing countries would generally prefer to bring population growth down to the levels prevailing in industrial countries, but individuals do not necessarily share this opinion. In many countries, family limitation is far from a universal quest; and it would require an obsessive attachment to social goals for people to wish to shorten their own life expectancies as a substitute for family planning.

Now that we know that multiple gaposis is a condition of the world community, what does it have to do with how much aid developing countries need? The answer is that it depends on what gaps you want to fill. In terms of costs, the cheapest to fill is probably the population gap. It has been estimated that investments in birth control . . . are of the order of one hundred times as profitable as investments in production. But this gap may be hardest of all to fill presently, in view of the existence of the first four gaps.

The Economic Gap

How much would it cost to fill the economic gap? It depends on the time horizon. Filling it halfway at once by raising per capita incomes to say $1000 a year, the bill would come to about $1.4 thousand billion, a sum roughly equal to the combined annual gross national product of the industrial countries, and more than two hundred times as much as the current aid flow. . . .

We could . . . achieve an average level of world income at about $630 per capita (1963), if the rich countries transferred about $600 billion annually to poor countries. . . .

Prospects for World
Population Control

J. Mayonne Stycos

32

A decade ago the population debate centered around resources and population growth, with the optimists insisting that resources and technology would keep well ahead of population. Such optimists are many fewer in number today, and the debate is now centered around the question of *how* or how soon widespread birth control practices will be effected in the underdeveloped areas. The optimists regard the ideological, technological, and organizational explosions in family planning as at least matching the population explosion, and soon to overtake it. They believe that just as contemporary mortality levels can be achieved by modern medical science with a minimum of social and economic change, so can modern fertility levels be achieved without such changes. Opponents of this view feel either that birth control *will* not really take hold until broad socio-economic changes occur in underdeveloped areas, or that it *should* not be encouraged until such changes occur. A brief historical review should clarify this.

A paper presented at the Indiana University Conference on World Population Problems, May 1967, and reprinted in *World Population: The View Ahead*. Reprinted by permission of the Bureau of Business Research. The author is Director, International Population Program, Cornell University.

Under the conditions of high mortality characteristic of most of man's history, sheer replacement of the population (plus a margin of safety for catastrophes) requires high fertility. Accordingly, we would not expect a successful society to show a high incidence of birth control practices prior to the achievement of modern mortality levels. On the other hand, the reduction of mortality would appear to be a necessary but not sufficient cause for widespread fertility reduction. In Europe the gradual reductions in mortality which occurred in the last two centuries were a consequence of such broad social changes as the agricultural, industrial, and scientific revolutions and the improvement of socio-economic conditions. These general forces directly affected not only mortality but fertility, probably by altering the perceptions of costs and benefits of children. Although the transition from high to low levels of fertility lagged considerably behind mortality declines and often took as long as 150 years, it is noteworthy that they were generally achieved without modern birth control technology, without systematic publicity on family planning, and in the face of opposition from church and state.

In the underdeveloped areas today, declines in mortality are not normally the product of broad social changes, but are much more efficiently being effected by the application of medical technology. That high fertility has in fact persisted for decades in countries with rapidly declining mortality (e.g., many Latin American countries) lends some empirical evidence to the argument that basic socio-economic changes are necessary pre-conditions for fertility decline. The unique case of Japan, with its successful demographic transition and socio-economic modernization would also support this hypothesis.

More optimistic experts, however, view the contemporary situation as ripe for rapid declines in fertility prior to modernization. They can point to: (1) recent breakthroughs in contraceptive technology; (2) the legitimation of birth control by churches and states; (3) improved methods of disseminating information; and (4) the desire for small families on the part of even poorly educated populations around the world.

Technology

There is no doubt that modern female methods require far less motivation than was ever the case with classical technology. Contrasting the IUD with the diaphragm, for example, the former requires only one decision every year or two, is not associated with the sexual act, and, since it is inserted by physicians, shares both the glamour and the medical neutrality of an inoculation. In these respects it has all the advantages of sterilization, without the disadvantages of irreversibility and possible post-operative complications. Just as Puerto Rican women responded enthusiastically to sterilization prior to the development of IUD's, so many women in other regions can be expected to respond to IUD's. It is not likely, however, that current modern methods alone will be adequate to bring fertility down rapidly in the underdeveloped areas. Quite aside from the question of the number of women for whom such methods are not advisable (because of side effects, medical contra-indications, expulsions, etc.) there is the question of whether there is not a "hard core" of women who cannot be influenced, or who cannot be influenced early enough. The hypothesis should be entertained that it would be cheaper and more effective to reach their husbands, and to reach them with male contraceptive methods: new and better ones when they are developed, but the classical male methods in the meantime. It is entirely possible that after the first enthusiastic group of higher parity, older, and better educated women have been reached, that the second round efforts might profitably be directed at males, who are more likely to see the salutary economic consequences of early spacing than are their wives. Clearly there is an important area here for research, involving both technological and sociological considerations.

Communication

In earlier days, information on birth control was spread almost entirely by word of mouth, often surreptitiously. This was the case not only because of illiteracy, but because birth control was not a permissible subject for the printed page. There is some evidence, however, that on the few occasions when literature on birth control was widely read, it was not without effect. Thus, when British sales of Knowlton's *Fruits of Philosophy* jumped from about 1,000 per year to over 100,000 per year in the years immediately following the Bradlaugh-Besant trial in 1877, we cannot help but wonder whether the long-term decline in British fertility which began in 1876 was not accelerated by the huge increase in public information.[1] And one cannot help but wonder whether, in non-puritanical and highly literate post-war Japan, the more precipitous decline in birth rates was not in part due to the greater dissemination of printed information via newspapers and women's magazines.

In more than half of the Latin American countries today literacy exceeds 50 per cent of the adult population and the potential for the printed page is greater than in England of the 1870's. It is generally believed that the subject of birth control is unmentionable in Latin American publications. In what he believed to be a crusading article in 1964, the ex-President of Colombia and editor of *Vision* magazine complained that the subject of population and birth control was "the great tabu" of our time. If the subject was ever tabued in the press it was a tabu fast disappearing, for during the year in which Lleras made his statement, the Cornell International Population Program collected from Latin American newspapers no less than 6,000 articles dealing with population, over three-fourths of which mentioned birth control. Of those articles which mentioned birth control, less than a fifth were unfavorable to it. There is no doubt that those who read today are learning far more about fertility control than readers of newspapers in any previous point in history.

[1]Parker G. Marden, "The Bradlaugh-Besant Trial: A Case Study in Declining Fertility", unpublished M.A. Thesis, Brown University, 1964.

Further, and in the light of the current legitimation of family planning, mass media never before available for such purposes are at the disposal of family planning programmers. A good example is provided by the media treatment of a three-day visit of a Mexican priest to Costa Rica in January, 1967. Father Orozco, who named overpopulation as the number one world problem, and who maintained that the right to limit births is absolute and unconditional, received no less than three and one-half hours of national TV time and recorded three fifteen-minute radio programs. (In addition, he received 609 inches of newspaper publicity.)[2] Of greater long range significance are the 13-episode soap-opera series on problems of excessive family size sponsored by the Population Reference Bureau and currently being broadcast by at least 20 Central American radio stations. "When the imminent arrival of a seventh child into an already crowded household becomes known, the topic of abortion is raised and counsel is sought from a social worker who advises that the mother seek further advice from a doctor and a priest. The dialogues bring to light sound medical thinking on the topic of abortion and responsible parenthood, as well as liberal Catholic counsel. For the latter dialogue, actual advice given for use in the program by a Catholic priest is incorporated in the script."[3]

In Eastern countries everything from puppet shows to popular songs are utilized as educational media. In a family planning program in East Pakistan, "Publicity and information were disseminated by a singing team . . . recruited from local artists who performed in towns, villages and bazaars . . . the troup composed songs in the local medium, some in a question and answer format (emphasizing) the economic and family health aspects of family planning."[4] Such an approach has received the highest blessings. Last month *The New York Times* reported that Pakistan's president Ayub Khan urged that Pakistan produce "songs in simple language on subjects like 'grow more food', 'family planning and national integration'."

Legitimation

While the Eastern religions have never been a major stumbling block to family planning, the Christian churches have traditionally bitterly opposed it. The consequences for fertility, however, have not been particularly striking. All the Catholic countries of Europe have low levels of fertility, and in the United States and Latin America both the ideal family size and contraceptive practice of Catholics are surprisingly close to that of non-Catholics.

Nevertheless, that many Protestant churches have declared themselves in favor of family planning, and that many Catholic churchmen have become

[2]*Planifamilia* (Costa Rica), February 1967.

[3]Alvaro Garcia-Pena, "National and International Informational Programs on Population Problems", PASB Conference on Population Dynamics, February 1967, mimeographed.

[4]Harvey M. Choldin in *Studies in Family Planning*, No. 13, August 1966, pp. 8-9.

more permissive about it makes the situation in Christian underdeveloped nations much more propitious for family planning than was ever the case in the past. Probably the major impact of the more liberal views characteristic of this decade will be in drawing public attention to the problem, allowing free discussion, and softening governments' attitudes toward national policies.

At the same time, the indecisiveness of the leaders of the Catholic Church leaves the door open for the more conservative bishops to take a hard line which can put obstacles in the way of government programs. While such actions will at least slow the pace of government programs, they may also crystallize public opinion and mobilize pro-family planning groups in a way not possible without opposition. In the past the battle was so one-sided that it was suicidal to elicit church opposition. At the present time, some countries, particularly in Latin America, *need* to make birth control a public issue in order to make the matter salient through the mass media, and to arouse courageous public spirited citizens to take political and social action. An interesting test case is being provided in Colombia, where the announcement of a government program of family planning caused a concerted attack by the Catholic Church, which had been previously quite permissive. Two entire issues of the influential Catholic weekly, *El Catolicismo,* were devoted to presenting a conservative Catholic position, and in March of this year, Cardinal Concha had a pastoral letter read in all of the nation's Catholic Churches, condemning all forms of contraception and strongly reaffirming the traditional Catholic position. While at first sight these actions were damaging to the cause of birth control, they in fact will probably accelerate the program. As a result of the opposition, leaders of the family planning movement became "news," were interviewed at length, and their side of the story given far more coverage in the press than would ever have been possible without the creation of an issue. However, in other countries, where the birth control movement is only beginning, such opposition could crush it rather than strengthen it.

In the long run it may be that the Catholic Church will legitimate the use of modern birth control techniques. In the short run it seems more likely that what can realistically be expected is a legitimation of the *goals* of contraception (i.e., "responsible parenthood") and a relaxation of the insistence on the illegitimacy of mechanical and chemical means of curbing reproduction. The Papal encyclical of March 1967, which recognizes both the population problem and the legitimacy of governmental activity to solve it, is consistent with this expectation.

The greatest shifts in the legitimacy of family planning, however, are being made more by states than by churches. Up until the last decade, the only nations in the world with any experience in attempting to influence fertility were those European nations which tried, and continue to try, to *increase* it. Comparable in importance to the revolution in contraceptive technology is the growing trend for nations to formulate explicit policies for the reduction of fertility. Perhaps the most remarkable document of the century was published on Human Rights Day, December 10, 1966. The heads of twelve national states, subsequently joined by at least four others, declared their belief that "the population problem must be recognized as a principal element in long range national planning," . . . that "the opportunity to decide the number and spacing of children is a basic human right," and that "family planning . . . frees man to attain his individual dignity and reach his full potential."

Signed by the leaders of nations as diverse as Ghana, the Netherlands, United Arab Republic, Morocco, and Colombia, the statement was a clear indication that the world-wide legitimation of birth control is not far off. In the same century, what sent Margaret Sanger to jail is extolled as a basic human right by the leaders of the world.

While words do not necessarily mean action, they can certainly hasten it. An increasing number of nations are adopting national programs specifically designed to curtail human fertility. Whether or not they can succeed depends in part on the demand for the services they supply. What do we know about this demand?

Popular Demand for Family Planning

Over the past decade an unusually large number of studies of attitudes toward family size and contraception have been conducted around the world. Uniformly they have disclosed that women would prefer a moderate number of children, and know little about birth control but would like to learn. Such studies have utilized public opinion polling techniques, and typically employ such questions as "Do you want any more children?" and "If you could live your life over, how many children would you like to have?" It is usually found that women regard as ideal about a quarter fewer children than they in fact have by the end of their child-bearing period. The responses to such questions have led to great optimism on the part of family planners concerning the probable outcome of contraceptive programs. Critics of these studies feel that such questions often fail to tap the true attitudes of people, who may be much more indifferent to the question of family size than their responses to simple queries indicate.

My own studies have produced convincing evidence that uneducated women in underdeveloped areas do not in fact give much thought to these matters and that the intensity of their desire for a small to moderate number of children is not great. But I do not regard as tenable the hypothesis that they are merely trying to "please the interviewer" by saying they want few children. One measure of this is provided by data on stated intentions to use birth control. If respondents *really* want to please the interviewer they should overstate their interest in or intention to use birth control, since this is usually the direct aim of much action research in this field. Of course, a failure to realize one's intentions can be due to many factors other than the intention itself, but there should be some correspondence between the verbal statement and subsequent behavior. Thus, while it should come as no surprise to find that not everyone who says he wants birth control in fact uses it when it is made available, there is nevertheless a strong correlation between the expressed attitude and actual behavior. Thus, in a study in Korea, while only 14 per cent of those who said they did not want contraception actually accepted it subsequently, 48 per cent of those who did express an interest in fact accepted it.[5] In Jamaica, under less favorable conditions, while only 6 per cent of those who said they had not thought of using birth control in fact reported use six weeks later, 25 per cent of those who had thought favorably subsequently reported its use. (In the urban area the two figures were 6 per cent and 35 per cent.) The women who were not using birth control in the latter period were asked about their intention to use it in the future, and were again followed up two years later. Less than 10 per cent of those who had no intention to use birth control were using it, but 30 per cent of those who did intend were found to be using birth control two years later. Finally, of those women who reported that they had attended the family planning clinic, a check of clinic records showed that 97 per cent had in fact done so.[6] In short, people's stated intentions and statements of behavior are predictive of their behavior, though the predictability falls short of 100 per cent.

In the absence of public discussion of the question, and in the light of general ignorance about the "controllability" of human fertility, it is not surprising that women's attitudes are not intense, not crystallized, and not unswerving. But at the same time there is little doubt that there is a latent preference for a moderate family size rather than for a large one.

There are at least three things which can be done with such a latent preference: (1) we may leave it as it is and make the technology so easy that little more motivation is required. For example, if there were a temporary sterilizing pill which could be taken annually, accompanied by an effective system of distribution, I believe that most of the women in the world would take it after having three or four children; (2) we may wait for the latent preference to become activated "naturally" as a product of social and economic changes which will alter aspiration levels; (3) by means of direct education it may be reinforced, crystallized and intensified to the extent that the individual will act.

The "great debate" today is between the latter two alternatives. In the scientific world, the hypothesis that the demographic transition can be achieved by means of direct educational techniques is typified by Bogue: "Most (traditional demographic theories) are based on correlations between fertility and other variables that are incapable of being manipulated rapidly .... Family planning research ... begins with the assumption that by the discovery of new principles we may be able to devise programs that can

---

[5]B. Berelson, "KAP Studies on Fertility," in *Family Planning and Population Programs,* Eds., B. Berelson, *et al.* (Chicago: Chicago University Press, 1966).

[6]J. Mayone Stycos and Kurt W. Back, *The Control of Human Fertility in Jamaica* (Ithaca: Cornell University Press, 1964), pp. 233-235. All differences reported are statistically significant at the 0.05 level. For more detailed considerations of methodological problems of the KAP survey, see K. W. Back and J. M. Stycos, *The Survey Under Unusual Conditions—Fertility Research in Jamaica,* Human Organization Monographs, No. 1, 1960.

accomplish the desired results more quickly than would be possible if we waited for the solution along the lines of increased literacy—rising urbanization, improved levels of living, increased contact with technological-cultural change.[7] We should note that Bogue is not only propounding a theory of social change, but an *ideology*. It is not surprising that it collides with at least one other combined theory of social change and action ideology—Marxism.

Ideological Conflict

Throughout most modernizing countries, and especially in Latin America, we can distinguish at least three major ideological types—the conservative, the social reformist, and the revolutionary. The conservative puts the status quo first and revolution last with social change a reluctant second place. The reformer puts social change first and the status quo last, with revolution occupying a second place. The revolutionary puts revolution first and social change last. He prefers the status quo to social change because the latter might stem the revolution, while the former, the more intolerable it becomes, can only precipitate it.[8]

Increasingly economists are of the opinion that population control can accelerate economic development by such means as decreasing the dependency ratio, reducing the cost of social services, decreasing unemployment and raising per capita product. In addition to spreading the benefits of economic development less thin, there should be positive generation of economic development as a result of increased savings for investments in capital producing enterprises. Finally, by alleviating food shortages and other pressures attributable to population increase (e.g., rural over-crowding and urban migration) social tensions might be eased. It should be noted that the gains from population control can occur without any basic changes in the economic and social structure, e.g., without any radical change in the distribution of wealth, ownership of the means of production, etc. Strictly rationally, population control should be of the highest priority to conservatives, of importance but secondary importance to social reformists, and anathema to revolutionaries.

As usual, the revolutionaries have reacted most consistently, and have resisted population control as another palliative of the social reformist ilk which will ease the pressures leading to revolution, diverting attention from the true source of society's ills—the capitalist economic system. More recently, some Communist spokesmen have softened the traditional Marxian hostility to Malthusian theory to the extent of admitting that population growth can impede economic progress and that birth control can alleviate population growth. They feel that birth control, however, will be and *should*

[7]Donald J. Bogue, "Family Planning Research: An Outline of the Field", in *Family Planning and Population Programs, op. cit.*, p. 724.

[8]See Albert O. Hirschman, *Journeys Toward Progress* (New York: The Twentieth Century Fund, 1963), pp. 276-297.

be a natural response to the necessary revolutionary changes in society. That Communist nations have some of the most efficient birth control programs in the world while condemning population control is proof that they are not opposed to birth control per se, but only to the *ideology* of population control and to its proposed sequence in the development of societies.

The conservatives, who should be most enthusiastic about birth control, are split because of conflicting ideologies and credos. In Latin America they tend to be the more traditional and orthodox Catholics who may have moral objections to family planning, and they are also from the business world which sees more consumers and a cheap labor supply as the very fuel of industry. An example of how these conflicting ideologies lead the conservatives to a negative position on population control is provided in the recent report of the Inter-American Council for Commerce and Production. It maintains that "population growth should be considered a sign of progress . . . a legitimate and welcome price for improvement in sanitary and living conditions." A dim view of birth control is taken, and the report notes somberly that "Relations between young people are acquiring great freedom under protection of modern means and for purposes, needless to say, that are not those mentioned when economic development is being discussed." It concludes that "the solution is not birth control but increased food production and economic development."[9] Finally, many conservatives are strongly nationalistic, and they view with pride a populous nation, regarding population control as a new method of the colonial powers to emasculate the nations they hope to continue to dominate. A good example of the blend of economic conservatism and nationalist "populationism" is provided by the following statement by the editor of El Salvador's *Diario de Hoy*, Napoleon Viera Altamirano. He warns his readers about ". . . the true conspirators against our America, who come with a plan of massive destruction! The plan to destroy the capital of Latin America, to frighten away private investment, to socialize us before we have capitalized, and to block our growth, cutting the wombs of Latin mothers, castrating Latin males, before we have grown sufficiently or taken possession of the vast empty lands of the continent."[10]

In point of fact birth control is making greatest headway among the liberals or social reformers who are gradually becoming convinced that it can speed the economic development they desire without jeopardizing any of the social reforms they espouse. Of equal or even greater importance, they see birth control as a social measure, as a means of reducing abortion and illegitimacy, and as a way of increasing human freedom and control over man's nature. Since they tend to be nominal Catholics or leftist activist Catholics, moral-religious considerations are not of paramount importance. Their main preoccupation about family planning is with respect to its suspiciously

[9]Committee for Economic Development, *How Low Income Countries Can Advance Their Own Growth*, September 1966, pp. 45-46.

[10]*Diario de Hoy* (El Salvador), June 21, 1963, Cited in J. M. Stycos, "Opinions of Latin-American Intellectuals on Population Problems and Birth Control", *Annals of the American Academy of Political and Social Science*, Vol. 360, July, 1965.

enthusiastic promotion by the United States. The more they are convinced, by President Johnson and others, that $5 invested in birth control is worth $100 invested in economic development, the more concerned they are that the bargain loving U.S. will choose the $5 investment. In addition, unaware that the conservatives are confused on the issue, they are afraid that both American and local conservatives will substitute Lippes loops for agrarian reform. These concerns have led to the performance of a verbal ritual, performed whenever population control is advocated, which seems to relieve anxieties somewhat. A recent report of the United Nations *ad hoc* Committee of Experts on Programmes in Fertility provides us with a good example. Advisory services in family planning, they warned, should not be regarded as a substitute for energetic efforts to expand production, reduce unemployment and underemployment, and provide adequate facilities for education, public health, and other essential social services.[11]

In sum, there is not only academic debate over whether or not direct education and services can bring down birth rates; there are definite ideological differences concerning its desirability, sequence, and overall place in the strategy of development. Given the present trajectory of technological and communications advances in birth control programs, I believe that such ideological obstacles will loom larger in the future, even affecting the vitality of family planning programs among the countries where these are initiated.

In this context it is important to understand that the task of family planning programs of the future will become more difficult. This is due to the fact that in the underdeveloped areas there is still a great deal of slack in mortality. In many of them the declines in fertility foreseen by family planners may be offset by declines in mortality. As infant mortality approaches insignificance, the three to four children desired by most couples in the modernizing countries will be too many to keep world population growth at a low level. At the present time, since fertility performance is in excess of people's wishes, the task of planned parenthood is relatively simple—that of activating people's own goals and teaching them how their own goals can be realized. But assuming the goals do not change, the task of the future will be not only teaching people to have less, but to *want* less—a matter not only more difficult operationally, but subject to even greater ideological controversy than is characteristic today.

The sample surveys of the past decade have taught us a great deal about people's actual fertility, their knowledge of contraception and their attitudes toward it, but they have taught us much less about human motivation, and nothing about political or other ideologies. Further, they have taught us little about the moral context of birth control. As religious objections to birth control decline in importance, planned parenthood groups become more and more utilitarian and technocratic, adopting a "let's get the cookies on the shelf" approach. The hard headed approach to the distribution of

[11]United Nations Economic and Social Council, Population Commission, December 1966. E/CN9/203.

contraceptive devices will undoubtedly be as effective in this area as it has been in the commercial world generally; but if birth control is a way to increase the freedom and dignity of man, one wonders whether it should not be viewed in a broader context of sexual, conjugal, and familial love. If this be the case, then research should go well beyond the technological, and even beyond the motivational and ideological, to include broad moral considerations. One obvious example would be to evaluate the effects on family and other interpersonal relations of birth control education that is purely technical as opposed to that which places it in a context of human morality.

The weakest part of such a research design would be precisely the moral context. So long has Christianity stressed the negative morality of fertility control, that it is unprepared, in my opinion, to offer us a comprehensive positive morality. Even the most liberal religions can go little beyond the abstractions of responsible parenthood. I present this challenge then to the great religions. Rather than follow the world on this issue, lead it. If birth control is more than plastic and pills, then show us how it is. And if the lives of the peoples of the world can be enriched by such knowledge, then teach them.

Population Policy: Will Current Programs Succeed?

Kingsley Davis

33

Throughout history the growth of population has been identified with prosperity and strength. If today an increasing number of nations are seeking to curb rapid population growth by reducing their birth rates, they must be driven to do so by an urgent crisis. My purpose here is not to discuss the crisis itself but rather to assess the present and prospective measures used to meet it. Most observers are surprised by the swiftness with which concern over the population problem has turned from intellectual analysis and debate to policy and action. Such action is a welcome relief from the long opposition, or timidity, which seemed to block forever any governmental attempt to restrain population growth, but relief that "at last something is being done" is no guarantee that what is being done is adequate. On the face of it, one could hardly expect such a fundamental reorientation to be quickly and successfully implemented. I therefore propose to review the nature and (as I see them) limitations of the present policies and to suggest lines of possible improvement.

This article is abridged from a paper presented at the annual meeting of the National Research Council, 14 March 1967. It appeared in *Science*, Vol. 158, 730-739, 10 November 1967. Copyright 1967 by the American Association for the Advancement of Science. The author is professor of sociology and Director of International Population and Urban Research, University of California, Berkeley.

The Nature of Current Policies

With more than 30 nations now trying or planning to reduce population growth and with numerous private and international organizations helping, the degree of unanimity as to the kind of measures needed is impressive. The consensus can be summed up in the phrase "family planning." President Johnson declared in 1965 that the United States will "assist family planning programs in nations that request such help." The Prime Minister of India said a year later, "We must press forward with family planning. This is a programme of the highest importance." The Republic of Singapore created in 1966 the Singapore Family Planning and Population Board "to initiate and undertake population control programmes" (*1*).*

As is well known, "family planning" is a euphemism for contraception. The family-planning approach to population limitation, therefore, concentrates on providing new and efficient contraceptives on a national basis through mass programs under public health auspices. The nature of these programs is shown by the following enthusiastic report from the Population Council (*2*):

> No single year has seen so many forward steps in population control as 1965. Effective national programs have at last emerged, international organizations have decided to become engaged, a new contraceptive has proved its value in mass application, . . . and surveys have confirmed a popular desire for family limitation. . . .
>
> An accounting of notable events must begin with Korea and Taiwan . . . . Taiwan's program is not yet two years old, and already it has inserted one IUD [intrauterine device] for every 4-6 target women (those who are not pregnant, lactating, already sterile, already using contraceptives effectively, or desirous of more children). Korea has done almost as well . . . has put 2,200 full-time workers into the field, . . . has reached operational levels for a network of IUD quotas, supply lines, local manufacture of contraceptives, training of hundreds of M.D.'s and nurses, and mass propaganda. . . .

Here one can see the implication that "population control" is being achieved through the dissemination of new contraceptives, and the fact that the "target women" exclude those who want more children. One can also note the technological emphasis and the medical orientation.

What is wrong with such programs? The answer is, "Nothing at all, if they work." Whether or not they work depends on what they are expected to do as well as on how they try to do it. Let us discuss the goal first, then the means.

Goals

Curiously, it is hard to find in the population-policy movement any explicit discussion of long-range goals. By implication the policies seem to promise a great deal. This is shown by the use of expressions like *population control*

*Numbers in parentheses identify the references listed at the end of chapter.

and *population planning* (as in the passages quoted above). It is also shown by the characteristic style of reasoning. Expositions of current policy usually start off by lamenting the speed and the consequences of runaway population growth. This growth, it is then stated, must be curbed—by pursuing a vigorous family-planning program. That family planning can solve the problem of population growth seems to be taken as self-evident.

For instance, the much-heralded statement by 12 heads of state, issued by Secretary-General U Thant on 10 December 1966 (a statement initiated by John D. Rockefeller III, Chairman of the Board of the Population Council), devotes half its space to discussing the harmfulness of population growth and the other half to recommending family planning (*3*). A more succinct example of the typical reasoning is given in the Provisional Scheme for a Nationwide Family Planning Programme in Ceylon (*4*):

> The population of Ceylon is fast increasing. . . . [The] figures reveal that a serious situation will be created within a few years. In order to cope with it a Family Planning programme on a nationwide scale should be launched by the Government.

The promised goal—to limit population growth so as to solve population problems—is a large order. One would expect it to be carefully analyzed, but it is left imprecise and taken for granted, as is the way in which family planning will achieve it.

When the terms *population control* and *population planning* are used, as they frequently are, as synonyms for current family-planning programs, they are misleading. Technically, they would mean deliberate influence over all attributes of a population, including its age-sex structure, geographical distribution, racial composition, genetic quality, and total size. No government attempts such full control. By tacit understanding, current population policies are concerned with only the *growth* and *size* of populations. These attributes, however, result from the death rate and migration as well as from the birth rate; their control would require deliberate influence over the factors giving rise to all three determinants. Actually, current policies labeled population control do not deal with mortality and migration, but deal only with the birth input. This is why another term, *fertility control*, is frequently used to describe current policies. But, as I show below, family planning (and hence current policy) does not undertake to influence most of the determinants of human reproduction. Thus the programs should not be referred to as population control or planning, because they do not attempt to influence the factors responsible for the attributes of human populations, taken generally; nor should they be called fertility control, because they do not try to affect most of the determinants of reproductive performance.

The ambiguity does not stop here, however. When one speaks of controlling population size, any inquiring person naturally asks, What is "control"? Who is to control whom? Precisely what population size, or what rate of population growth, is to be achieved? Do the policies aim to produce a growth rate that is nil, one that is very slight, or one that is like that of the industrial nations? Unless such questions are dealt with and clarified, it is impossible to evaluate current population policies.

The actual programs seem to be aiming simply to achieve a reduction in the birth rate. Success is therefore interpreted as the accomplishment of such a reduction, on the assumption that the reduction will lessen population growth. In those rare cases where a specific demographic aim is stated, the goal is said to be a short-run decline within a given period. The Pakistan plan adopted in 1966 (*5*, p. 889) aims to reduce the birth rate from 50 to 40 per thousand by 1970; the Indian plan (*6*) aims to reduce the rate from 40 to 25 "as soon as possible"; and the Korean aim (*7*) is to cut population growth from 2.9 to 1.2 percent by 1980. A significant feature of such stated aims is the rapid population growth they would permit. Under conditions of modern mortality, a crude birth rate of 25 to 30 per thousand will represent such a multiplication of people as to make use of the term *population control* ironic. A rate of increase of 1.2 percent per year would allow South Korea's already dense population to double in less than 60 years.

One can of course defend the programs by saying that the present goals and measures are merely interim ones. A start must be made somewhere. But we do not find this answer in the population-policy literature. Such a defense, if convincing, would require a presentation of the *next* steps, and these are not considered. One suspects that the entire question of goals is instinctively left vague because thorough limitation of population growth would run counter to national and group aspirations. A consideration of hypothetical goals throws further light on the matter.

Industrialized Nations as the Model

Since current policies are confined to family planning, their maximum demographic effect would be to give the underdeveloped countries the same level of reproductive performance that the industrial nations now have. The latter, long oriented toward family planning, provide a good yardstick for determining what the availability of contraceptives can do to population growth. Indeed, they provide more than a yardstick; they are actually the model which inspired the present population policies.

What does this goal mean in practice? Among the advanced nations there is considerable diversity in the level of fertility (*8*). At one extreme are countries such as New Zealand, with an average gross reproduction rate (GRR) of 1.91 during the period 1960-64; at the other extreme are countries such as Hungary, with a rate of 0.91 during the same period. To a considerable extent, however, such divergencies are matters of timing. The birth rates of most industrial nations have shown, since about 1940, a wave-like movement, with no secular trend. The average level of reproduction during this long period has been high enough to give these countries, with their low mortality, an extremely rapid population growth. If this level is maintained, their population will double in just over 50 years—a rate higher than that of world population growth at any time prior to 1950, at which time the growth in numbers of human beings was already considered fantastic. The advanced nations are suffering acutely from the effects of rapid population growth in combination with the production of ever more goods per person (*9*). A rising share of their supposedly high per capita income, which itself draws increasingly upon the resources of the underdeveloped countries (who fall farther behind in relative economic position), is spent simply to meet the costs, and alleviate the nuisances, of the unrelenting production of more and more goods by more people. Such facts indicate that the industrial nations provide neither a suitable demographic model for the nonindustrial peoples to follow nor the leadership to plan and organize effective population-control policies for them.

Zero Population Growth as a Goal

Most discussions of the population crisis lead logically to zero population growth as the ultimate goal, because *any* growth rate, if continued, will eventually use up the earth. Yet hardly ever do arguments for population policy consider such a goal, and current policies do not dream of it. Why not? The answer is evidently that zero population growth is unacceptable to most nations and to most religious and ethnic communities. To argue for this goal would be to alienate possible support for action programs.

Goal Peculiarities Inherent in Family Planning

Turning to the actual measures taken, we see that the very use of family planning as the means for implementing population policy poses serious but unacknowledged limits on the intended reduction in fertility. The family-planning movement, clearly devoted to the improvement and dissemination of contraceptive devices, states again and again that its purpose is that of enabling couples to have the number of children they want. "The opportunity to decide the number and spacing of children is a basic human right," say the 12 heads of state in the United Nations declaration. The 1965 Turkish Law Concerning Population Planning declares (*10*):

> *Article 1.* Population Planning means that individuals can have as many children as they wish, whenever they want to. This can be ensured through preventive measures taken against pregnancy. . . .

Logically, it does not make sense to use *family* planning to provide *national* population control or planning. The "planning" in family planning is that of each separate couple. The only control they exercise is control over the size of *their* family. Obviously, couples do not plan the size of the nation's population, any more than they plan the growth of the national income or the form of the highway network. There is no reason to expect that the millions of decisions about family size made by couples in their own interest will automatically control population for the benefit of society. On the contrary, there are good reasons to think they will not do so. At most, family planning can reduce reproduction to the extent that unwanted births exceed wanted births. In industrial countries the balance is often negative—that is, people have fewer children as a rule than they would like to have. In underdeveloped countries the reverse is normally true, but the elimination of unwanted births would still leave an extremely high rate of multiplication.

Actually, the family-planning movement does not pursue even the limited goals it professes. It does not fully empower couples to have only the number of offspring they want because it either condemns or disregards certain tabooed but nevertheless effective means to this goal. One of its tenets is that "there shall be freedom of choice of method so that individuals can choose in accordance with the dictates of their consciences" (*11*), but in practice this amounts to limiting the individual's choice, because the "conscience" dictating the method is usually not his but that of religious and governmental officials. Moreover, not every individual may choose: even the so-called recommended methods are ordinarily not offered to single women, or not all offered to women professing a given religious faith.

Thus, despite its emphasis on technology, current policy does not utilize all available means of contraception, much less all birth-control measures. The Indian government wasted valuable years in the early stages of its population-control program by experimenting exclusively with the "rhythm" method, long after this technique had been demonstrated to be one of the least effective. A greater limitation on means is the exclusive emphasis on contraception itself. Induced abortion, for example, is one of the surest means of controlling reproduction, and one that has been proved capable of reducing birth rates rapidly. It seems peculiarly suited to the threshold stage of a population-control program—the stage when new conditions of life first make large families disadvantageous. It was the principal factor in the halving of the Japanese birth rate, a major factor in the declines in birth rate of East-European satellite countries after legalization of abortions in the early 1950's, and an important factor in the reduction of fertility in industrializing nations from 1870 to the 1930's (*12*). Today, according to *Studies in Family Planning* (*13*), "abortion is probably the foremost method of birth control throughout Latin America." Yet this method is rejected in nearly all national and international population-control programs. American foreign aid is used to help *stop* abortion (*14*). The United Nations excludes abortion from family planning, and in fact justifies the latter by presenting it as a means of combating abortion (*15*). Studies of abortion are being made in Latin America under the presumed auspices of population-control groups, not with the intention of legalizing it and thus making it safe, cheap, available, and hence more effective for population control, but with the avowed purpose of reducing it (*16*).

Although few would prefer abortion to efficient contraception (other things being equal), the fact is that both permit a woman to control the size of her family. The main drawbacks to abortion arise from its illegality. When performed, as a legal procedure, by a skilled physician, it is safer than childbirth. It does not compete with contraception but serves as a backstop when the latter fails or when contraceptive devices or information are not available. As contraception becomes customary, the incidence of abortion recedes even without its being banned. If, therefore, abortions enable women to have only the number of children they want, and if family planners do not advocate—in fact decry—legalization of abortion, they are to that extent denying the central tenet of their own movement. The irony of anti-abortionism in family-planning circles is seen particularly in hair-splitting arguments over whether or not some contraceptive agent (for example, the IUD) is in reality an abortifacient. A Mexican leader in family planning writes (*17*):

> One of the chief objectives of our program in Mexico is to prevent abortions. If we could be sure that the mode of action [of the IUD] was not interference with nidation, we could easily use the method in Mexico.

The questions of sterilization and unnatural forms of sexual intercourse usually meet with similar silent treatment or disapproval, although nobody doubts the effectiveness of these measures in avoiding conception. Sterilization has proved popular in Puerto Rico and has had some vogue in India (where the new health minister hopes to make it compulsory for those with a certain number of children), but in both these areas it has been for the most part ignored or condemned by the family-planning movement.

On the side of goals, then, we see that a family-planning orientation limits the aims of current population policy. Despite reference to "population control" and "fertility control," which presumably mean determination of demographic results by and for the nation as a whole, the movement gives control only to couples, and does this only if they use "respectable" contraceptives.

The Neglect of Motivation

By sanctifying the doctrine that each woman should have the number of children she wants, and by assuming that if she has only that number this will automatically curb population growth to the necessary degree, the leaders of current policies escape the necessity of asking why women desire so many children and how this desire can be influenced (*18*, p. 14: *19*). Instead, they claim that satisfactory motivation is shown by the popular desire (shown by opinion surveys in all countries) to have the means of family limitation, and that therefore the problem is one of inventing and distributing the best possible contraceptive devices. Overlooked is the fact that a desire for availability of contraceptives is compatible with *high* fertility.

Given the best of means, there remain the questions of how many children couples want and of whether this is the requisite number from the standpoint of population size. That it is not is indicated by continued rapid population growth in industrial countries, and by the very surveys showing that people want contraception—for these show, too, that people also want numerous children.

The family planners do not ignore motivation. They are forever talking about "attitudes" and "needs." But they pose the issue in terms of the "acceptance" of birth control devices. At the most naive level, they assume that lack of acceptance is a function of the contraceptive device itself. This reduces the motive problem to a technological question. The task of population control then becomes simply the invention of a device that *will* be acceptable (20). The plastic IUD is acclaimed because, once in place, it does not depend on repeated *acceptance* by the woman, and thus it "solves" the problem of motivation (21).

But suppose a woman does not want to use *any* contraceptive until after she has had four children. This is the type of question that is seldom raised in the family-planning literature. In that literature, wanting a specific number of children is taken as complete motivation, for it implies a wish to control the size of one's family. The problem woman, from the standpoint of family planners, is the one who wants "as many as come," or "as many as God sends." Her attitude is construed as due to ignorance and "cultural values," and the policy deemed necessary to change it is "education." No compulsion can be used, because the movement is committed to free choice, but movie strips, posters, comic books, public lectures, interviews, and discussions are in order. These supply information and supposedly change values by discounting superstitions and showing that unrestrained procreation is harmful to both mother and children. The effort is considered successful when the woman decides she wants only a certain number of children and uses an effective contraceptive.

In viewing negative attitudes toward birth control as due to ignorance, apathy, and outworn tradition, and "mass-communication" as the solution to the motivation problem (22), family planners tend to ignore the power and complexity of social life. If it were admitted that the creation and care of new human beings is socially motivated, like other forms of behavior, by being a part of the system of rewards and punishments that is built into human relationships, and thus is bound up with the individual's economic and personal interests, it would be apparent that the social structure and economy must be changed before a deliberate reduction in the birth rate can be achieved. As it is, reliance on family planning allows people to feel that "something is being done about the population problem" without the need for painful social changes.

Designation of population control as a medical or public health task leads to a similar evasion. This categorization assures popular support because it puts population policy in the hands of respected medical personnel, but, by the same token, it gives responsibility for leadership to people who think in terms of clinics and patients, of pills and IUD's, and who bring to the handling of economic and social phenomena a self-confident naivete. The study of social organization is a technical field; an action program based on intuition is no more apt to succeed in the control of human beings than it is in the area of bacterial or viral control. Moreover, to alter a social system, by deliberate policy, so as to regulate births in accord with the demands of the collective welfare would require political power, and this is not likely to inhere in public health officials, nurses, midwives, and social workers. To entrust population policy to them is "to take action," but not dangerous "effective action."

Similarly, the Janus-faced position on birth-control technology represents an escape from the necessity, and onus, of grappling with the social and economic determinants of reproductive behavior. On the one side, the rejection or avoidance of religiously tabooed but otherwise effective means of birth prevention enables the family-planning movement to avoid official condemnation. On the other side, an intense preoccupation with contraceptive technology (apart from the tabooed means) also helps the family planners to avoid censure. By implying that the only need is the invention and distribution of effective contraceptive devices, they allay fears, on the part of religious and governmental officials, that fundamental changes in social organization are contemplated. Changes basic enough to affect motivation for having children would be changes in the structure of the family, in the position of women, and in the sexual mores. Far from proposing such radicalism, spokesmen for family planning frequently state their purpose as "protection" of the family—that is, closer observance of family norms. In addition, by concentrating on *new* and *scientific* contraceptives, the movement escapes taboos attached to old ones (the Pope will hardly authorize the condom, but may sanction the pill) and allows family planning to be regarded as a branch of medicine: overpopulation becomes a disease, to be treated by a pill or a coil.

We thus see that the inadequacy of current population policies with respect to motivation is inherent in their overwhelmingly family-planning character. Since family planning is by definition private planning, it eschews any societal control over motivation. It merely furnishes the means, and, among possible means, only the most respectable. Its leaders, in avoiding social complexities and seeking official favor, are obviously activated not solely by expediency but also by their own sentiments as members of society and by their background as persons attracted to the family-planning movement. Unacquainted for the most part with technical economics, sociology, and demography, they tend honestly and instinctively to believe that something they vaguely call population control can be achieved by making better contraceptives available.

The Evidence of Ineffectiveness

If this characterization is accurate, we can conclude that current programs will not enable a government to control population size. In countries where couples have numerous offspring that they do not want, such programs may possibly accelerate a birth-rate decline that would occur anyway, but the conditions that cause births to be wanted or unwanted are beyond the control of family planning, hence beyond the control of any nation which relies on family planning alone as its population policy.

This conclusion is confirmed by demographic facts. As I have noted above, the widespread use of family planning in industrial countries has not given their governments control over the birth rate. In backward countries today, taken as a whole, birth rates are rising, not falling; in those with population policies, there is no indication that the government is controlling the rate of reproduction. The main "successes" cited in the well-publicized policy literature are cases where a large number of contraceptives have been distributed or where the program has been accompanied by some decline in the birth rate. Popular enthusiasm for family planning is found mainly in the cities, or in advanced countries such as Japan and Taiwan, where the people would adopt contraception in any case, program or no program. It is difficult to prove that present population policies have even speeded up a lowering of the birth rate (the least that could have been expected), much less that they have provided national "fertility control."

Let us next briefly review the facts concerning the level and trend of population in underdeveloped nations generally, in order to understand the magnitude of the task of genuine control.

Rising Birth Rates in Underdeveloped Countries

In ten Latin-American countries, between 1940 and 1959 (*23*), the average birth rates (age-standardized), as estimated by our research office at the University of California, rose as follows: 1940-44, 43.4 annual births per 1000 population; 1945-49, 44.6; 1950-54, 46.4; 1955-59, 47.7.

In another study made in our office, in which estimating methods derived from the theory of quasi-stable populations were used, the recent trend was found to be upward in 27 underdeveloped countries, downward in six, and unchanged in one (*24*). Some of the rises have been substantial, and most have occurred where the birth rate was already extremely high. For instance, the gross reproduction rate rose in Jamaica from 1.8 per thousand in 1947 to 2.7 in 1960; among the natives of Fiji, from 2.0 in 1951 to 2.4 in 1964; and in Albania, from 3.0 in the period 1950-54 to 3.4 in 1960.

The general rise in fertility in backward regions is evidently not due to failure of population-control efforts, because most of the countries either have no such effort or have programs too new to show much effect. Instead, the rise is due, ironically, to the very circumstance that brought on the population crisis in the first place—to improved health and lowered mortality. Better health increases the probability that a woman will conceive and retain the fetus to term; lowered mortality raises the proportion of babies who survive to the age of reproduction and reduces the probability of widowhood during that age (25). The significance of the general rise in fertility, in the context of this discussion, is that it is giving would-be population planners a harder task than many of them realize. Some of the upward pressure on birth rates is independent of what couples do about family planning, for it arises from the fact that, with lowered mortality, there are simply more couples.

Underdeveloped Countries
with Population Policies

In discussions of population policy there is often confusion as to which cases are relevant. Japan, for instance, has been widely praised for the effectiveness of its measures, but it is a very advanced industrial nation and, besides, its government policy had little or nothing to do with the decline in the birth rate, except unintentionally. It therefore offers no test of population policy under peasant-agrarian conditions. Another case of questionable relevance is that of Taiwan, because Taiwan is sufficiently developed to be placed in the urban-industrial class of nations. However, since Taiwan is offered as the main showpiece by the sponsors of current policies in underdeveloped areas, and since the data are excellent, it merits examination.

Taiwan is acclaimed as a showpiece because it has responded favorably to a highly organized program for distributing up-to-date contraceptives and has also had a rapidly dropping birth rate. Some observers have carelessly attributed the decline in the birth rate—from 50.0 in 1951 to 32.7 in 1965—to the family-planning campaign (26), but the campaign began only in 1963 and could have affected only the end of the trend. Rather, the decline represents a response to modernization similar to that made by all countries that have become industrialized (27). By 1950 over half of Taiwan's population was urban, and by 1964 nearly two-thirds were urban, with 29 percent of the population living in cities of 100,000 or more. The pace of economic development has been extremely rapid. Between 1951 and 1963, per capita income increased by 4.05 percent per year. Yet the island is closely packed, having 870 persons per square mile (a population density higher than that of Belgium). The combination of fast economic growth and rapid population increase in limited space has put parents of large families at a relative disadvantage and has created a brisk demand for abortions and contraceptives. Thus the favorable response to the current campaign to encourage use of the IUD is not a good example of what birth-control technology can do for a genuinely backward country. In fact, when the program was started, one reason for expecting receptivity was that the island was already on its way to modernization and family planning (28).

At most, the recent family-planning campaign—which reached significant proportions only in 1964, when some 46,000 IUD's were inserted (in 1965 the number was 99,253, and in 1966, 111,242) (29; 30, p. 45)—could have caused the increase observable after 1963 in the rate of decline. Between 1951 and 1963 the average drop in the birth rate per 1000 women (see Table 1) was 1.73 percent per year; in the period 1964-66 it was 4.35 percent. But one hesitates to assign all of the acceleration in decline since 1963 to the family-planning campaign. The rapid economic development has been precisely of a type likely to accelerate a drop in reproduction. The rise in manufacturing has been much greater than the rise in either agriculture or construction. The agricultural labor force has thus been squeezed, and migration to the cities has skyrocketed (31). Since housing has not kept pace, urban families have had to restrict reproduction in order to take advantage of career opportunities and avoid domestic inconvenience. Such conditions have historically tended to accelerate a decline in birth rate. The most rapid decline came late in the United States (1921-33) and in Japan (1947-55). A plot of the Japanese and Taiwanese birth rates (Fig. 1) shows marked similarity of the two curves, despite a difference in level. All told, one should not attribute all of the post-1963 acceleration in the decline of Taiwan's birth rate to the family-planning campaign.

Table 1.   Decline in Taiwan's Fertility Rate, 1951 through 1966

Year	Registered births per 1000 women aged 15-49	Change in rate (percent)*
1951	211	
1952	198	−5.6
1953	194	−2.2
1954	193	−0.5
1955	197	+2.1
1956	196	−0.4
1957	182	−7.1
1958	185	+1.3
1959	184	0.1
1960	180	−2.5
1961	177	−1.5
1962	174	−1.5
1963	170	−2.6
1964	162	−4.9
1965	152	−6.0
1966	149	−2.1

*The percentages were calculated on unrounded figures. Source of data through 1965, Taiwan Demographic Fact Book (1964, 1965); for 1966, Monthly Bulletin of Population Statistics of Taiwan (1966, 1967).

The main evidence that *some* of this acceleration is due to the campaign comes from the fact that Taichung, the city in which the family-planning effort was first concentrated, showed subsequently a much faster drop in fertility than other cities (30, p. 69; 32). But the campaign has not reached throughout the island. By the end of 1966, only 260,745 women had been fitted with an IUD under auspices of the campaign, whereas the women of

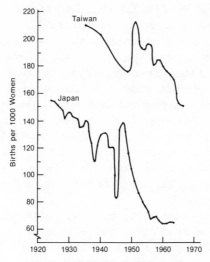

Figure 1. Births per 1000 Women Aged 15 through 49 in Japan and Taiwan.

reproductive age on the island numbered 2.86 million. Most of the reduction in fertility has therefore been a matter of individual initiative. To some extent the campaign may be simply substituting sponsored (and cheaper) services for those that would otherwise come through private and commercial channels. An island-wide survey in 1964 showed that over 150,000 women were already using the traditional Ota ring (a metallic intrauterine device popular in Japan); almost as many had been sterilized; about 40,000 were using foam tablets; some 50,000 admitted to having had at least one abortion; and many were using other methods of birth control (*30*, pp. 18, 31).

The important question, however, is not whether the present campaign is somewhat hastening the downward trend in the birth rate but whether, even if it is, it will provide population control for the nation. Actually, the campaign is not designed to provide such control and shows no sign of doing so. It takes for granted existing reproductive goals. Its aim is "to integrate, through education and information, the idea of family limitation *within the existing attitudes, values, and goals* of the people" [*30*, p. 8 (italics mine)] Its target is *married* women who do not want any more children; it ignores girls not yet married, and women married and wanting more children.

With such an approach, what is the maximum impact possible? It is the difference between the number of children women have been having and the number they want to have. A study in 1957 found a median figure of 3.75 for the number of children wanted by women aged 15 to 29 in Taipei, Taiwan's largest city; the corresponding figure for women from a satellite town was 3.93; for women from a fishing village, 4.90; and for women from a farming village, 5.03. Over 60 percent of the women in Taipei and over 90 percent of those in the farming village wanted 4 or more children (*33*). In a sample of wives aged 25 to 29 in Taichung, a city of over 300,000, Freedman and his co-workers found the average number of children wanted was 4; only 9 percent wanted less than 3, 20 percent wanted 5 or more (*34*). If, therefore, Taiwanese women used contraceptives that were 100-percent effective and had the number of children they desire, they would have about 4.5 each. The goal of the family-planning effort would be achieved. In the past the Taiwanese woman who married and lived through the reproductive period had, on the average, approximately 6.5 children; thus a figure of 4.5 would represent a substantial decline in fertility. Since mortality would continue to decline, the population growth rate would decline somewhat less than individual reproduction would. With 4.5 births per woman and a life expectancy of 70 years, the rate of natural increase would be close to 3 percent per year (*35*).

In the future, Taiwanese views concerning reproduction will doubtless change, in response to social change and economic modernization. But how far will they change? A good indication is the number of children desired by couples in an already modernized country long oriented toward family planning. In the United States in 1966, an average of 3.4 children was considered ideal by white women aged 21 or over (*36*). This average number of births would give Taiwan, with only a slight decrease in mortality, a long-run rate of natural increase of 1.7 percent per year and a doubling of population in 41 years.

Detailed data confirm the interpretation that Taiwanese women are in the process of shifting from a "peasant-agrarian" to an "industrial" level of reproduction. They are, in typical fashion, cutting off higher-order births at age 30 and beyond (*37*). Among young wives, fertility has risen, not fallen. In sum, the widely acclaimed family-planning program in Taiwan may, at most, have somewhat speeded the later phase of fertility decline which would have occurred anyway because of modernization.

Moving down the scale of modernization, to countries most in need of population control, one finds the family-planning approach even more inadequate. In South Korea, second only to Taiwan in the frequency with which it is cited as a model of current policy, a recent birth-rate decline of unknown extent is assumed by leaders to be due overwhelmingly to the government's family-planning program. However, it is just as plausible to say that the net effect of government involvement in population control has been, so far, to delay rather than hasten a decline in reproduction made inevitable by social and economic changes. Although the government is advocating vasectomies and providing IUD's and pills, it refuses to legalize abortions, despite the rapid rise in the rate of illegal abortions and despite the fact that, in a recent survey, 72 percent of the people who stated an opinion favored legalization. Also, the program is presented in the context of maternal and child health; it thus emphasizes motherhood and the family rather than alternative roles for women. Much is made of the fact that opinion surveys show an overwhelming majority of Koreans (89 percent in

1965) favoring contraception (*38*, p. 27), but this means only that Koreans are like other people in wishing to have means to get what they want. Unfortunately, they want sizable families: "The records indicate that the program appeals mainly to women in the 30-39 year age bracket who have four or more children, including at least two sons . . ." (*38*, p. 25).

In areas less developed than Korea the degree of acceptance of contraception tends to be disappointing, especially among the rural majority. Faced with this discouragement, the leaders of current policy, instead of reexamining their assumptions, tend to redouble their effort to find a contraceptive that will appeal to the most illiterate peasant, forgetting that he wants a good-sized family. In the rural Punjab, for example, "a disturbing feature . . . is that the females start to seek advice and adopt family planning techniques at the fag end of their reproductive period" (*39*). Among 5196 women coming to rural Punjabi family-planning centers, 38 percent were over 35 years old, 67 percent over 30. These women had married early, nearly a third of them before the age of 15 (*40*); some 14 percent had eight or more *living* children when they reached the clinic, 51 percent six or more.

A survey in Tunisia showed that 68 percent of the married couples were willing to use birth-control measures, but the average number of children they considered ideal was 4.3 (*41*). The corresponding averages for a village in eastern Java, a village near New Delhi, and a village in Mysore were 4.3, 4.0, and 4.2, respectively (*42, 43*). In the cities of these regions women are more ready to accept birth control and they want fewer children than village women do, but the number they consider desirable is still wholly unsatisfactory from the standpoint of population control. In an urban family-planning center in Tunisia, more than 600 of 900 women accepting contraceptives had four living children already (*44*). In Bangalore, a city of nearly a million at the time (1952), the number of offspring desired by married women was 3.7 on the average; by married men, 4.1 (*43*). In the metropolitan area of San Salvador (350,000 inhabitants) a 1964 survey (*45*) showed the number desired by women of reproductive age to be 3.9, and in seven other capital cities of Latin America the number ranged from 2.7 to 4.2. If women in the cities of underdeveloped countries used birth-control measures with 100-percent efficiency, they still would have enough babies to expand city populations senselessly, quite apart from the added contribution of rural-urban migration. In many of the cities the difference between actual and ideal number of children is not great; for instance, in the seven Latin-American capitals mentioned above, the ideal was 3.4 whereas the actual births per women in the age range 35 to 39 was 3.7 (*46*). Bombay City has had birth-control clinics for many years, yet its birth rate (standardized for age, sex, and marital distribution) is still 34 per 1000 inhabitants and is tending to rise rather than fall. Although this rate is about 13 percent lower than that for India generally, it has been about that much lower since at least 1951 (*47*).

Is Family Planning the "First Step"
in Population Control?

To acknowledge that family planning does not achieve population control is not to impugn its value for other purposes. Freeing women from the need to have more children than they want is of great benefit to them and their children and to society at large. My argument is therefore directed not against family-planning programs as such but against the assumption that they are an effective means of controlling population growth.

But what difference does it make? Why not go along for awhile with family planning as an initial approach to the problem of population control? The answer is that any policy on which millions of dollars are being spent should be designed to achieve the goal it purports to achieve. If it is only a first step, it should be so labeled, and its connection with the next step (and the nature of that next step) should be carefully examined. In the present case, since no "next step" seems ever to be mentioned, the question arises, Is reliance on family planning in fact a basis for dangerous postponement of effective steps? To continue to offer a remedy as a cure long after it has been shown merely to ameliorate the disease is either quackery or wishful thinking, and it thrives most where the need is greatest. Today the desire to solve the population problem is so intense that we are all ready to embrace any "action program" that promises relief. But postponement of effective measures allows the situation to worsen.

Unfortunately, the issue is confused by a matter of semantics. "Family *planning*" and "fertility *control*" suggest that reproduction is being regulated according to some rational plan. And so it is, but only from the standpoint of the individual couple, not from that of the community. What is rational in the light of a couple's situation may be totally irrational from the standpoint of society's welfare.

The need for societal regulation of individual behavior is readily recognized in other spheres—those of explosives, dangerous drugs, public property, natural resources. But in the sphere of reproduction, complete individual initiative is generally favored even by those liberal intellectuals who, in other spheres, most favor economic and social planning. Social reformers who would not hesitate to force all owners of rental property to rent to anyone who can pay, or to force all workers in an industry to join a union, balk at any suggestion that couples be permitted to have only a certain number of offspring. Invariably they interpret societal control of reproduction as meaning direct police supervision of individual behavior. Put the word *compulsory* in front of any term describing a means of limiting births—*compulsory sterilization, compulsory abortion, compulsory contraception*—and you guarantee violent opposition. Fortunately, such direct controls need not be invoked, but conservatives and radicals alike overlook this in their blind opposition to the idea of collective determination of a society's birth rate.

That the exclusive emphasis on family planning in current population policies is not a "first step" but an escape from the real issues is suggested by two facts. (i) No country has taken the "next step." The industrialized countries have had family planning for half a century without acquiring control over either the birth rate or population increase. (ii) Support and encouragement of research on population policy other than family planning is negligible. It is precisely this blocking of alternative thinking and experimentation that makes the emphasis on family planning a major obstacle to population control. The need is not to abandon family-planning programs but to put equal or greater resources into other approaches.

New Directions in Population Policy

In thinking about other approaches, one can start with known facts. In the past, all surviving societies had institutional incentives for marriage, procreation, and child care which were powerful enough to keep the birth rate equal to or in excess of a high death rate. Despite the drop in death rates during the last century and a half, the incentives tended to remain intact because the social structure (especially in regard to the family) changed little. At most, particularly in industrial societies, children became less productive and more expensive (*48*). In present-day agrarian societies, where the drop in death rate has been more recent, precipitate, and independent of social change (*49*), motivation for having children has changed little. Here, even more than in industrialized nations, the family has kept on producing abundant offspring, even though only a fraction of these children are now needed.

If excessive population growth is to be prevented, the obvious requirement is somehow to impose restraints on the family. However, because family roles are reinforced by society's system of rewards, punishments, sentiments, and norms, any proposal to demote the family is viewed as a threat by conservatives and liberals alike, and certainly by people with enough social responsibility to work for population control. One is charged with trying to "abolish" the family, but what is required is selective restructuring of the family in relation to the rest of society.

The lines of such restructuring are suggested by two existing limitations on fertility. (i) Nearly all societies succeed in drastically discouraging reproduction among unmarried women. (ii) Advanced societies unintentionally reduce reproduction among married women when conditions worsen in such a way as to penalize childbearing more severely than it was penalized before. In both cases the causes are motivational and economic rather than technological.

It follows that population-control policy can de-emphasize the family in two ways: (i) by keeping present controls over illegitimate childbirth yet making the most of factors that lead people to postpone or avoid marriage, and (ii) by instituting conditions that motivate those who do marry to keep their families small.

Postponement of Marriage

Since the female reproductive span is short and generally more fecund in its first than in its second half, postponement of marriage to ages beyond 20 tends biologically to reduce births. Sociologically, it gives women time to get a better education, acquire interests unrelated to the family, and develop a cautious attitude toward pregnancy (*50*). Individuals who have not married by the time they are in their late twenties often do not marry at all. For these reasons, for the world as a whole, the average age at marriage for women is negatively associated with the birth rate: a rising age at marriage is a frequent cause of declining fertility during the middle phase of the demographic transition; and, in the late phase, the "baby boom" is usually associated with a return to younger marriages.

Any suggestion that age at marriage be raised as a part of population policy is usually met with the argument that "even if a law were passed, it would not be obeyed." Interestingly, this objection implies that the only way to control the age at marriage is by direct legislation, but other factors govern the actual age. Roman Catholic countries generally follow canon law in stipulating 12 years as the minimum *legal* age at which girls may marry, but the actual average age at marriage in these countries (at least in Europe) is characteristically more like 25 to 28 years. The actual age is determined, not by law, but by social and economic conditions. In agrarian societies, postponement of marriage (when postponement occurs) is apparently caused by difficulties in meeting the economic prerequisites for matrimony, as stipulated by custom and opinion. In industrial societies it is caused by housing shortages, unemployment, the requirement for overseas military service, high costs of education, and inadequacy of consumer services. Since almost no research has been devoted to the subject, it is difficult to assess the relative weight of the factors that govern the age at marriage.

Encourage Limitation of Births within Marriage

As a means of encouraging the limitation of reproduction within marriage, as well as postponement of marriage, a greater rewarding of nonfamilial than of familial roles would probably help. A simple way of accomplishing this would be to allow economic advantages to accrue to the single as opposed to the married individual, and to the small as opposed to the large family. For instance, the government could pay people to permit themselves to be sterilized (*51*); all costs of abortion could be paid by the government; a substantial fee could be charged for a marriage license; a "child-tax" (*52*) could be levied; and there could be a requirement that illegitimate pregnancies be aborted. Less sensationally, governments could simply reverse some existing policies that encourage childbearing. They could, for example, cease taxing single persons more than married ones; stop giving parents special tax exemptions; abandon income-tax policy that discriminates against couples when the wife works; reduce paid maternity leaves; reduce family allowances (*53*); stop awarding public housing on the basis of family size; stop granting fellowships and other educational aids (including special allowances for wives and children) to married students; cease outlawing abortions and sterilizations; and relax rules that allow use of harmless contraceptives only with medical permission. Some of these policy reversals would be beneficial in other than demographic respects and some would be harmful unless special precautions were taken. The aim would be to reduce the number, not the quality, of the next generation.

A closely related method of de-emphasizing the family would be modification of the complementarity of the roles of men and women. Men are now able to participate in the wider world yet enjoy the satisfaction of having several children because the housework and childcare fall mainly on their wives. Women are impelled to seek this role by their idealized view of marriage and motherhood and by either the scarcity of alternative roles or the difficulty of combining them with family roles. To change this situation women could be required to work outside the home, or compelled by circumstances to do so. If, at the same time, women were paid as well as men and given equal educational and occupational opportunities, and if social life were organized around the place of work rather than around the home or neighborhood, many women would develop interests that would compete with family interests. Approximately this policy is now followed in several Communist countries, and even the less developed of these currently have extremely low birth rates (*54*).

That inclusion of women in the labor force has a negative effect on reproduction is indicated by regional comparisons (*18*, p. 1195; *55*). But in most countries the wife's employment is subordinate, economically and emotionally, to her family role, and is readily sacrificed for the latter. No society has restructured both the occupational system and the domestic establishment to the point of permanently modifying the old division of labor by sex.

In any deliberate effort to control the birth rate along these lines, a government has two powerful instruments—its command over economic planning and its authority (real or potential) over education. The first determines (as far as policy can) the economic conditions and circumstances affecting the lives of all citizens; the second provides the knowledge and attitudes necessary to implement the plans. The economic system largely determines who shall work, what can be bought, what rearing children will cost, how much individuals can spend. The schools define family roles and develop vocational and recreational interests; they could, if it were desired, redefine the sex roles, develop interests that transcend the home, and transmit realistic (as opposed to moralistic) knowledge concerning marriage, sexual behavior, and population problems. When the problem is viewed in this light, it is clear that the ministries of economics and education, not the ministry of health, should be the source of population policy.

The Dilemma of Population Policy

It should now be apparent why, despite strong anxiety over runaway population growth, the actual programs purporting to control it are limited to family planning and are therefore ineffective. (i) The goal of zero, or even slight, population growth is one that nations and groups find difficult to accept. (ii) The measures that would be required to implement such a goal, though not so revolutionary as a Brave New World or a Communist Utopia, nevertheless tend to offend most people reared in existing societies. As a consequence, the goal of so-called population control is implicit and vague; the method is only family planning. This method, far from de-emphasizing the family, is familistic. One of its stated goals is that of helping sterile couples to *have* children. It stresses parental aspirations and responsibilities. It goes along with most aspects of conventional morality, such as condemnation of abortion, disapproval of premarital intercourse, respect for religious teachings and cultural taboos, and obeisance to medical and clerical authority. It deflects hostility by refusing to recommend any change other than the one it stands for: availability of contraceptives.

The things that make family planning acceptable are the very things that make it ineffective for population control. By stressing the right of parents to have the number of children they want, it evades the basic question of population policy, which is how to give societies the number of children they need. By offering only the means for *couples* to control fertility, it neglects the means for societies to do so.

Because of the predominantly pro-family character of existing societies, individual interest ordinarily leads to the production of enough offspring to constitute rapid population growth under conditions of low mortality. Childless or single-child homes are considered indicative of personal failure, whereas having three to five living children gives a family a sense of continuity and substantiality (56).

Given the existing desire to have moderate-sized rather than small families, the only countries in which fertility has been reduced to match reduction in mortality are advanced ones temporarily experiencing worsened economic conditions. In Sweden, for instance, the net reproduction rate (NRR) has been below replacement for 34 years (1930-63), if the period is taken as a whole, but this is because of the economic depression. The average replacement rate was below unity (NRR = 0.81) for the period 1930-42, but from 1942 through 1963 it was above unity (NRR = 1.08). Hardships that seem particularly conducive to deliberate lowering of the birth rate are (in managed economies) scarcity of housing and other consumer goods despite full employment, and required high participation of women in the labor force, or (in freer economies) a great deal of unemployment and economic insecurity. When conditions are good, any nation tends to have a growing population.

It follows that, in countries where contraception is used, a realistic proposal for a government policy of lowering the birth rate reads like a catalogue of horrors; squeeze consumers through taxation and inflation; make housing very scarce by limiting construction; force wives and mothers to work outside the home to offset the inadequacy of male wages, yet provide few child-care facilities; encourage migration to the city by paying low wages in the country and providing few rural jobs; increase congestion in cities by starving the transit system; increase personal insecurity by encouraging conditions that produce unemployment and by haphazard political arrests. No government will institute such hardships simply for the purpose of controlling population growth. Clearly, therefore, the task of contemporary population policy is to develop attractive substitutes for family interests, so as to avoid having to turn to hardship as a corrective. The specific measures required for developing such substitutes are not easy to determine in the absence of research on the question.

In short, the world's population problem cannot be solved by pretense and wishful thinking. The unthinking identification of family planning with population control is an ostrich-like approach in that it permits people to hide from themselves the enormity and unconventionality of the task. There is no reason to abandon family-planning programs; contraception is a valuable technological instrument. But such programs must be supplemented with equal or greater investments in research and experimentation to determine the required socioeconomic measures. 57

References and Notes

1. *Studies in Family Planning*, No. 16 (1967).
2. *Ibid., No. 9* (1966), p. 1.
3. The statement is given in *Studies in Family Planning* (*1*, p. 1), and in *Population Bull.* 23, 6 (1967).
4. The statement is quoted in *Studies in Family Planning* (*1*, p. 2).
5. *Hearings on S. 1676, U.S. Senate, Subcommittee on Foreign Aid Expenditures, 89th Congress, Second Session, April 7, 8, 11* (1966), pt. 4.
6. B. L. Raina, in *Family Planning and Population Programs*, B. Berelson, R. K. Anderson, O. Harkavy, G. Maier, W. P. Mauldin, S. G. Segal, Eds. (Univ. of Chicago Press, Chicago, 1966).
7. D. Kirk, *Ann. Amer. Acad. Polit. Soc. Sci.* **369**, 53 (1967).
8. As used by English-speaking demographers, the word *fertility* designates actual reproductive performance, not a theoretical capacity.
9. K. Davis, *Rotarian* **94**, 10 (1959); *Health Educ. Monographs* **9**, 2 (1960); L. Day and A. Day, *Too Many Americans* (Houghton Mifflin, Boston, 1964); R. A. Piddington, *Limits of Mankind* (Wright, Bristol, England, 1956).
10. *Official Gazette* (15 Apr. 1965); quoted in *Studies in Family Planning* (*1*, p. 7).
11. J. W. Gardner, Secretary of Health, Education, and Welfare, "Memorandum to Heads of Operating Agencies" (Jan. 1966), reproduced in *Hearings on S. 1676* (*5*), p. 783.
12. C. Tietze, *Demography* **1**, 119 (1964); *J. Chronic Diseases* **18**, 1161 (1964); M. Muramatsu, *Milbank Mem. Fund Quart.* **38**, 153 (1960); K. Davis, *Population Index* **29**, 345 (1963); R. Armijo and

T. Monreal, *J. Sex Res.* **1964**, 143 (1964); Proceedings World Population Conference, Belgrade, 1965; Proceedings International Planned Parenthood Federation.

13. *Studies in Family Planning, No. 4* (1964), p. 3.

14. D. Bell (then administrator for Agency for International Development), in *Hearings on S. 1676 (5)*, p. 862.

15. *Asian Population Conference* (United Nations, New York, 1964), p. 30.

16. R. Armijo and T. Monreal, in *Components of Population Change in Latin America* (Milbank Fund, New York, 1965), p. 272; E. Rice-Wray, *Amer. J. Public Health* **54**, 313 (1964).

17. E. Rice-Wray, in "Intra-Uterine Contraceptive Devices," *Excerpta Med. Intern. Congr. Ser. No. 54* (1962), p. 135.

18. J. Blake, in *Public Health and Population Change*, M. C. Sheps and J. C. Ridley, Eds. (Univ. of Pittsburgh Press, Pittsburgh, 1965).

19. J. Blake and K. Davis, *Amer. Behavioral Scientist,* **5**, 24 (1963).

20. See "Panel discussion on comparative acceptability of different methods of contraception," in *Research in Family Planning*, C. V. Kiser, Ed. (Princeton Univ. Press, Princeton, 1962), pp. 373-86.

21. "From the point of view of the woman concerned, the whole problem of continuing motivation disappears, . . ." [D. Kirk, in *Population Dynamics*, M. Muramatsu and P. A. Harper, Eds. (Johns Hopkins Press, Baltimore, 1965)].

22. "For influencing family size norms, certainly the examples and statements of public figures are of great significance . . . also . . . use of mass-communication methods which help to legitimize the small-family style, to provoke conversation, and to establish a vocabulary for discussion of family planning" [M. W. Freymann, in *Population Dynamics*, M. Muramatsu and P. A. Harper, Eds. (Johns Hopkins Press, Baltimore, 1965)].

23. O. A. Collver, *Birth Rates in Latin America* (International Population and Urban Research, Berkeley, Calif., 1965), pp. 27-28; the ten countries were Colombia, Costa Rica, El Salvador, Ecuador, Guatemala, Honduras, Mexico, Panamá, Peru, and Venezuela.

24. J. R. Rele, *Fertility Analysis through Extension of Stable Population Concepts* (International Population and Urban Research, Berkeley, Calif., 1967).

25. J. C. Ridley, M. C. Sheps, J. W. Lingner, J. A. Menken, *Milbank Mem. Fund Quart.* **45**, 77 (1967); E. Arriaga, unpublished paper.

26. "South Korea and Taiwan appear successfully to have checked population growth by the use of intrauterine contraceptive devices" [U. Borell, *Hearings on S. 1676 (5)*, p. 556].

27. K. Davis, *Population Index* **29**, 345 (1963).

28. R. Freedman, *ibid.* **31**, 421 (1965).

29. Before 1964 the Family Planning Association had given advice to fewer than 60,000 wives in 10 years and a Pre-Pregnancy Health Program had reached some 10,000, and, in the current campaign, 3650 IUD's were inserted in 1965, in a total population of 2-1/2 million women of reproductive age. See *Studies in Family Planning, No. 19* (1967), p. 4, and R. Freedman *et al., Population Studies* **16**, 231 (1963).

30. R. W. Gillespie, *Family Planning on Taiwan* (Population Council, Taichung, 1965).

31. During the period 1950-60 the ratio of growth of the city to growth of the noncity population was 5:3; during the period 1960-64 the ratio was 5:2; these ratios are based on data of Shaohsing Chen, *J. Sociol. Taiwan* **1**, 74 (1963) and data in the United Nations *Demographic Yearbooks.*

32. R. Freedman, *Population Index* **31**, 434 (1965). Taichung's rate of decline in 1963-64 was roughly double the average in four other cities, whereas just prior to the campaign its rate of decline had been much less than theirs.

33. S. H. Chen, *J. Soc. Sci. Taipei* **13**, 72 (1963).

34. R. Freedman *et al., Population Studies* **16**, 227 (1963); *ibid.,* p. 232.

35. In 1964 the life expectancy at birth was already 66 years in Taiwan, as compared to 70 for the United States.

36. J. Blake, *Eugenics Quart.* **14**, 68 (1967).

37. Women accepting IUD's in the family-planning program are typically 30 to 34 years old and have already had four children [*Studies in Family Planning No. 19* (1967), p. 5.]

38. Y. K. Cha, in *Family Planning and Population Programs,* B. Berelson *et al.,* Eds. (Univ. of Chicago Press, Chicago, 1966).

39. H. S. Ayalvi and S. S. Johl, *J. Family Welfare* **12**, 60 1965.

40. Sixty percent of the women had borne their first child before age 19. Early marriage is strongly supported by public opinion. Of couples polled in the Punjab, 48 percent said that girls *should* marry before age 16, and 94 percent said they should marry before age 20 (H. S. Ayalvi and S. S. Johl, *ibid.,* p. 57). A study of 2380 couples in 60 villages of Uttar Pradesh found that the women had consummated their marriage at an average age of 14.6 years [J. R. Rele, *Population Studies* **15**, 268 (1962)].

41. J. Morsa, in *Family Planning and Population Programs,* B. Berelson *et al.,* Eds. (Univ. of Chicago Press, Chicago, 1966).

42. H. Gille and R. J. Pardoko, *ibid.,* p. 515; S. N. Agarwala, *Med. Dig. Bombay* **4**, 653 (1961).

43. *Mysore Population Study* (United Nations, New York, 1961), p. 140.

44. A. Daly, in *Family Planning and Population Programs,* B. Berelson *et al.,* Eds. (Univ. of Chicago Press, Chicago, 1966).

45. C. J. Goméz, paper presented at the World Population Conference, Belgrade, 1965.

46. C. Miro, in *Family Planning and Population Programs,* B. Berelson *et al.,* Eds. (Univ. of Chicago Press, Chicago, 1966).

47. *Demographic Training and Research Centre (India) Newsletter* **20**, 4 (Aug. 1966).

48. K. Davis, *Population Index* **29**, 345 (1963). For economic and sociological theory of motivation for having children, see J. Blake [Univ. of California (Berkeley)], in preparation.

49. K. Davis, *Amer. Economic Rev.* **46**, 305 (1956); *Sci. Amer.* **209**, 68 (1963).

50. J. Blake, *World Population Conference* [*Belgrade, 1965*] (United Nations, New York, 1967), vol. 2, pp. 132-36.

51. S. Enke, *Rev. Economics Statistics* **42**, 175 (1960); ————, *Econ. Develop. Cult. Change* **8**, 339 (1960); ————, *ibid.* **10**, 427 (1962); A. O. Krueger and L. A. Sjaastad, *ibid.,* p. 423.

52. T. J. Samuel, *J. Family Welfare India* **13**, 12 (1966).

53. Sixty-two countries, including 27 in Europe, give cash payments to people for having children [U.S. Social Security Administration, *Social Security Programs Throughout the World, 1967* (Government Printing Office, Washington, D.C., 1967), pp. xxvii-xxviii].

54. Average gross reproduction rates in the early 1960's were as follows: Hungary, 0.91; Bulgaria, 1.09; Romania, 1.15; Yugoslavia, 1.32.

55. O. A. Collver and E. Langlois, *Econ. Develop. Cult. Change* **10**, 367 (1962); J. Weeks [Univ. of California (Berkeley)], unpublished paper.

56. Roman Catholic textbooks condemn the "small" family (one with fewer than four children) as being abnormal [J. Blake, *Population Studies* **20**, 27 (1966)].

57. Judith Blake's critical readings and discussions have greatly helped in the preparation of this article.

Financial Development and Economic
Growth in Underdeveloped Countries

Hugh T. Patrick

34

An observed characteristic of the process of economic
development over time, in a market-oriented economy using the price
mechanism to allocate resources, is an increase in the number and variety of
financial institutions and a substantial rise in the proportion not only of
money but also of the total of all financial assets relative to GNP and to
tangible wealth.[1] However, the causal nature of this relationship between
financial development and economic growth has not been fully explored
either theoretically or empirically.

Excerpted from an article of the above title in *Economic Development and Cultural Change*, January 1966, by permission of The University of Chicago Press. The author is attached to the Development Center, Yale University.

[1]See, for example, the work of Raymond Goldsmith, particularly his *Financial Intermediaries in the American Economy since 1900* (Princeton: Princeton University Press, 1958); and "Financial Structure and Economic Growth in Advanced Countries," in Moses Abramovitz, ed., *Capital Formation and Economic Growth* (Princeton: Princeton University Press, 1955). For an empirical treatment for Japan see David J. Ott, "The Financial Development of Japan, 1878-1958," *Journal of Political Economy*, LXIX, No. 2 (April 1961).

Demand-Following and Supply-Leading
Phenomena

Typical statements indicate that the financial system somehow accommodates—or, to the extent that it malfunctions, it restricts—growth of real per capita output. For example,

> It seems to be the case that where enterprise leads finance follows. The same impulses within an economy which set enterprise on foot make owners of wealth venturesome, and when a strong impulse to invest is fettered by lack of finance,[2] devices are invented to release it . . . and habits and institutions are developed.

Such an approach places emphasis on the demand side for financial services; as the economy grows it generates additional and new demands for these services, which bring about a supply response in the growth of the financial system. In this view, the lack of financial institutions in underdeveloped countries is simply an indication of the lack of demand for their services.

We may term as "demand-following" the phenomenon in which the creation of modern financial institutions, their financial assets and liabilities, and related financial services is in response to the demand for these services by investors and savers in the real economy. In this case, the evolutionary development of the financial system is a continuing consequence of the pervasive, sweeping process of economic development. The emerging financial system is shaped both by changes in objective opportunities—the economic environment, the institutional framework—and by changes in subjective responses—individual motivations, attitudes, tastes, preferences.

The nature of the demand for financial services depends upon the growth of real output and upon the commercialization and monetization of agriculture and other traditional subsistence sectors. The more rapid the growth rate of real national income, the greater will be the demand by enterprises for external funds (the saving of others) and therefore financial intermediation, since under most circumstances firms will be less able to finance expansion from internally generated depreciation allowances and retained profits. (The proportion of external funds in the total source of enterprise funds will rise.) For the same reason, with a given aggregate growth rate, the greater the variance in the growth rates among different sectors or industries, the greater will be the need for financial intermediation to transfer saving to fast-growing industries from slow-growing industries and from individuals. The financial system can thus support and sustain the leading sectors in the process of growth.

The demand-following supply response of the growing financial system is presumed to come about more or less automatically. It is assumed that the supply of entrepreneurship in the financial sector is highly elastic relative to the growing opportunities for profit from provision of financial services, so

[2]Joan Robinson, "The Generalization of the General Theory," in *The Rate of Interest and Other Essays* (London: Macmillan, 1952), pp. 86-87.

that the number and diversity of types of financial institutions expands sufficiently; and a favorable legal, institutional, and economic environment exists. The government's attitudes, economic goals, and economic policies, as well as the size and rate of increase of the government debt, are of course important influences in any economy on the nature of the economic environment. As a consequence of real economic growth, financial markets develop, widen, and become more perfect, thus increasing the opportunities for acquiring liquidity and for reducing risk, which in turn feeds back as a stimulant to real growth.[3]

The demand-following approach implies that finance is essentially passive and permissive in the growth process. Late eighteenth and early nineteenth century England may be cited as a historical example. In fact, the increased supply of financial services in response to demand may not be at all automatic, flexible, or inexpensive in underdeveloped countries. Examples include the restrictive banking legislation in early nineteenth century France, religious barriers against loans and interest charges, and Gerschenkron's analysis of the abortive upswing of Italian industrial development in the 1880's "mainly, it is believed, because the modern investment bank had not yet been established in Italy."[4] In underdeveloped countries today, similar obstacles, together with imperfections in the operation of the market mechanism, may dictate an inadequate demand-following response by the financial system. The lack of financial services, thus, in one way or another restricts or inhibits effective growth patterns and processes.

Less emphasis has been given in academic discussions (if not in policy actions) to what may be termed the "supply-leading" phenomenon: the creation of financial institutions and the supply of their financial assets, liabilities, and related financial services in advance of demand for them, especially the demand of entrepreneurs in the modern, growth-inducing sectors. "Supply-leading" has two functions: to transfer resources from traditional (non-growth) sectors to modern sectors,[5] and to promote and stimulate an entrepreneurial response in these modern sectors. Financial intermediation which transfers resources from traditional sectors, whether by collecting wealth and saving from those sectors in exchange for its deposits and other financial liabilities, or by credit creation and forced saving, is akin to the Schumpeterian concept of innovation financing.

[3]Cf. W. Arthur Lewis, *The Theory of Economic Growth* (London: George Allen & Unwin, 1955), pp. 267-86.

[4]Alexander Gerschenkron, *Economic Backwardness in History Perspective—A Book of Essays* (Cambridge: Harvard University Press, 1962), p. 363. See also Ch. 4.

[5]The difference between traditional and modern sectors is that the former are dominated by elements (attitudes, forms of economic organization, production technology) inherited from the pre-modern economy, whereas modern sectors are dominated by internationally modern technology, rationality (maximization behavior and attitudes) and modern institutions and other forms of economic organization. See, for example, K. Ohkawa and H. Rosovsky, "A Century of Japanese Economic Growth," in W. W. Lockwood, ed., *The State and Economic Enterprise in Modern Japan* (Princeton: Princeton University Press, forthcoming).

New access to such supply-leading funds may in itself have substantial, favorable expectational and psychological effects on entrepreneurs. It opens new horizons as to possible alternatives, enabling the entrepreneur to "think big." This may be the most significant effect of all, particularly in countries where entrepreneurship is a major constraint on development. Moreover, as has been emphasized by Rondo Cameron,[6] the top management of financial institutions may also serve as entrepreneurs in industrial enterprises. They assist in the establishment of firms in new industries or in the merger of firms (the advantages of economies of scale may be more than offset by the establishment of restrictive cartels or monopolies, however), not only by underwriting a substantial portion of the capital, but more importantly by assuming the entrepreneurial initiative.

By its very nature, a supply-leading financial system initially may not be able to operate profitably by lending to the nascent modern sectors.[7] There are, however, several ways in which new financial institutions can be made viable. First, they may be government institutions, using government capital and perhaps receiving direct government subsidies. This is exemplified not only by Russian experience in the latter half of the nineteenth century, but by many underdeveloped countries today. Second, private financial institutions may receive direct or indirect government subsidies, usually the latter. Indirect subsidies can be provided in numerous ways. Commercial banks may have the right to issue banknotes under favorable collateral conditions; this technique was more important in the eighteenth and nineteenth centuries (national banking in Japan in the 1870's; wildcat banking in the United States) than it is likely to be in present underdeveloped countries, where this right is reserved for the central bank or treasury. Nonetheless, modern equivalents exist. They include allowing private financial institutions to create deposit money with low (theoretically, even negative) reserve requirements and central bank rediscount of commercial bank loans at interest rates effectively below those on the loans. Third, new, modern financial institutions may initially lend a large proportion of their funds to traditional (agricultural and commercial) sectors profitably, gradually shifting their loan portfolio to modern industries as these begin to emerge. This more closely resembles the demand-following phenomenon; whether such a financial institution is supply-leading depends mainly on its attitude in searching out and encouraging new ventures of a modern nature.

It cannot be said that supply-leading finance is a necessary condition or precondition for inaugurating self-sustained economic development. Rather, it presents an opportunity to induce real growth by financial means. It thus is likely to play a more significant role at the beginning of the growth process than later. Gerschenkron implies that the more backward the economy relative to others in the same time period (and the greater the forced-draft

[6]Rondo Cameron, "The Bank as Entrepreneur," *Explorations in Entrepreneurial History*, Series 2, I, No. 1 (Fall 1963), 50-55.

[7]Except in the extreme case where inherent profit opportunities are very high, and supply-leading stimulates a major entrepreneurial effort.

nature of the economic development effort), the greater the emphasis which is placed on what I here term supply-leading finance.[8] At the same time, it should be recognized that the supply-leading approach to development of a country's financial system also has its dangers, and they should not be underestimated. The use of resources, especially entrepreneurial talents and managerial skills, and the costs of explicit or implicit subsidies in supply-leading development must produce sufficient benefits in the form of stimulating real economic development for this approach to be justified.

In actual practice, there is likely to be an interaction of supply-leading and demand-following phenomena. Nevertheless, the following sequence may be postulated. Before sustained modern industrial growth gets underway, supply-leading may be able to induce real innovation-type investment. As the process of real growth occurs, the supply-leading impetus gradually becomes less important, and the demand-following financial response becomes dominant. This sequential process is also likely to occur within and among specific industries or sectors. One industry may initially be encouraged financially on a supply-leading basis and as it develops have its financing shift to demand-following, while another industry remains in the supply-leading phase. This would be related to the timing of the sequential development of industries, particularly in cases where the timing is determined more by governmental policy than by private demand forces.

Japan between the 1870's and the beginning of World War I presents an excellent example of the sequence of supply-leading and demand-following finance.[9] A modern banking system was created in the 1870's, subsidized by the right to issue banknotes and by government deposits. These banks, in the absence of large-scale industrial demand for funds, initially concentrated their funds on financing agriculture, domestic commerce, and the newly important foreign trade. However, they also became the locus for much of the early promotional and entrepreneurial talent which initiated the industrial spurt beginning in the mid-1880's, especially in railroads and in cotton textiles (at first import-competing, and later export-oriented). The banks also became an early important source of industrial funds, albeit *via* an indirect route. The modern financial system thus was not only created in advance of Japan's modern industrialization, but, by providing both funds and entrepreneurial talent on a supply-leading basis, contributed significantly to the initial spurt. By the mid-1890's, the emphasis apparently moved from supply-leading to demand-following in the financing of the textile and other consumer goods industries. On the other hand, the financing of most heavy manufacturing industries continued on a supply-leading basis perhaps until World War I, with a considerable portion of external funds provided through the long-term loans of special banks established at government initiative and utilizing government funds.

[8]*Op. cit.*

[9]For greater detail on the Japanese case, see Hugh T. Patrick, "Japan," in Rondo Cameron, ed., *Banking in the Early Stages of Industrialization* (Oxford University Press: forthcoming).

Finance and the Real Capital Stock

The nature of the connection between financial growth and economic development may be examined from a somewhat different approach. One can conceive of a variety of relationships between the financial system and growth-producing real factors. However, probably the most important is the relationship of the stock of financial assets and liabilities to the real capital stock—its optimal composition and rate of growth and its efficient allocation and utilization. I assume the relationship between the capital stock and real output is strong, direct, and monotonic.[10] The growth objective of the financial system is to achieve the structure and rate of growth of various financial assets and liabilities which are consonant with and even induce the optimal characteristics of the real capital stock.

There are three major ways in which the financial system can influence the capital stock for growth purposes. First, financial institutions can encourage a more efficient allocation of a given total amount of tangible wealth (capital in a broad sense), by bringing about changes in its ownership and in its composition, through intermediation among various types of asset-holders. Second, financial institutions can encourage a more efficient allocation of new investment—additions to capital stock—from relatively less to relatively more productive uses, by intermediation between savers and entrepreneurial investors. Third, they can induce an increase in the rate of accumulation of capital, by providing increased incentives to save, invest, and work.

These effects can be analyzed by an approach blending the Gurley-Shaw model[11] with a portfolio analysis of the behavior of saving-type and investing-type asset holders. The composition of individual wealth portfolios consists of non-reproducible tangible assets (land and precious metals), reproducible tangible assets (producer durables, consumer durables, and inventories), and financial assets (currency, deposits, bonds, stock, loans, insurance, etc.), minus financial liabilities. Individual units hold varying proportions of real and financial assets (and financial liabilities), based on their own preferences and on an asset's specific characteristics of safety, liquidity, and yield (of money income and/or real services). Most theoretical work on portfolio analysis has focused on the composition of financial assets, with little emphasis on the choice between financial and real assets.[12] This latter choice, of course, is of prime importance for growth.

[10]I do not here consider in other than broad outline what constitute the optimal characteristics of the capital stock for growth.

[11]See John G. Gurley and E. S. Shaw, "Financial Aspects of Economic Development," *American Economic Review* XLV, No. 4 (September 1955), "Financial Intermediaries and the Saving-Investment Process," *Journal of Finance*, XI, No. 2 (May 1956); and *Money in a Theory of Finance* (Washington: Brookings Institution, 1960). For explicit adaptations and developments of this model to the process of growth, see Rondo Cameron, "Theoretical Bases of a Comparative Study of the Role of Financial Institutions" in the Conference of Economic History, Aix-en-Provence, France, 1962; and Robert L. Bennett, "Financial Innovation and Structural Change in the Early Stages of Industrialization: Mexico, 1945-59," *Journal of Finance*, XVIII, No. 4 (December 1963).

[12]See, however, James Tobin, "A Dynamic Aggregative Model," *Journal of Political Economy*, LXIII, No. 2 (April 1955); James Tobin and William Brainard, "Financial

Allocation of a Given Amount
of Tangible Wealth

In this section, the focus rests on changes in a given aggregate amount of tangible wealth under the assumption of no net additions to this stock. Unfortunately, definitive capital stock or wealth estimates are not yet available for any underdeveloped country over time, or even for any single point in time.[13] Nonetheless, flow characteristics of saving provide some indication of stock characteristics of wealth. For example, the findings for a sample of underdeveloped Asian countries that between one-half and two-thirds of gross saving is done by households, and that between one-half and three-fourths (and perhaps more, due to under-reporting of increases in tangible assets) of household net saving is in the form of increases in tangible assets,[14] probably well reflects the structure of ownership and composition of wealth for these countries. It is notable that most of the assets held by savers are under their own direct control. In general, the composition of individual real wealth holdings in underdeveloped countries typically consists mainly of land and land improvements, simple agricultural and handicraft tools, livestock, inventories (notably foodstuffs), and durable consumer goods (especially housing, but in some countries precious metals[15] and jewelry, as well). The share of producer durables is relatively low,[16] while that of traditional consumer durables may be relatively high.

In part, this composition of wealth results from a lack of productive investment opportunities or ignorance of their existence. As the economy undergoes change and brings out productive investment opportunities, pressures develop to improve the wealth composition. Moreover, while an individual's initial portfolio composition may be inefficient in terms of the possibilities for selecting among a full range of financial assets as desirable

Intermediaries and the Effectiveness of Monetary Controls," *American Economic Review*, LIII, No. 2 (May 1963); and P. R. Brahmanand, "Some Issues of Monetary Theory and Policy in a Real Liquidity-Conscious Economy," *Commerce* [India] (1960 annual special issue).

[13]Estimates have been made for India; cf. "Estimates of Tangible Wealth in India," Reserve Bank of India *Bulletin* (January 1963), pp. 8-19. Gold, silver, and jewelry are not included (they are approximately 10 percent of total tangible wealth), and the inventory estimates are crude. For a criticism of these estimates see Uma Datta, "The Capital Structure of the Economy," *Economic Weekly*, XVI, Nos. 5-7 annual issue (February 1964), 301-10.

[14]UN ECAFE, "Measures for Mobilizing Domestic Saving for Productive Investment," *Economic Bulletin for Asia and the Far East*, XIII, No. 3 (December 1962), 3-8. The classification of saving sources is into government, government enterprise, private corporate, and household sectors, so households include unincorporated enterprises and farming. For our purposes, this does not pose a major problem.

[15]Precious metals may be processed into jewelry as a consumer good, as well as being held in bulk form as a store of value. Cf. Hugh T. Patrick, "The Mobilization of Private Gold Holdings," *Indian Economic Journal*, XI, No. 2 (October-December 1963). Private foreign exchange and other foreign asset holdings should be included in real wealth, since they represent a direct claim on foreign goods; probably netted against this should be foreign claims upon the country.

[16]See Raymond W. Goldsmith, *The National Wealth of the United States in the Postwar Period* (Princeton: Princeton University Press, 1962), pp. 96-97, for cross-country comparisons.

alternatives, the composition may not be inefficient relative to the alternative financial asset choices which actually exist. Thus, creating additional types of financial assets and making them available to potential holders provides the opportunity for more efficient portfolio selection.

A considerable portion of tangible wealth in underdeveloped countries is held in forms unproductive of sustained growth. Some can fairly readily be transformed into productive capital goods. This is especially true of precious metals, excess holdings of inventories, and the replacement in an aggregative context of the depreciating portion of the capital stock. The amounts involved could be significant. It is not unreasonable to think of ratios of tangible wealth to GNP, even excluding land, of 2 or 3. A re-allocation of as much as 10 percent of this wealth to more productive forms would be equivalent to 20 or 30 percent of GNP and would raise the level of output by about 10 percent.[17] It should be recognized that changes in the composition of a given stock of wealth to more productive forms are a once-and-for-all adjustment, even though they may take some time, so that the level of output is raised, but continued growth does not result.

In many underdeveloped countries, wealth is held in the form of inventories of foodstuffs, other primary products, and, in some cases, even finished manufactured goods, in amounts considerably in excess of normal consumption or production requirements. An important reason[18] for this behavior is that, in the absence of suitable financial asset alternatives, inventories are the only assets which are relatively liquid, divisible, and offer some protection against general consumer goods price inflation. On the other hand, storage and spoilage costs are high, and, for individual commodities, risks (as measured by variance) of price fluctuation are high.

I conjecture that in the early stages of development individuals shift their asset portfolios, relatively, from holding inventories in excess of their normal production or consumption requirements to holding newly-created financial assets which have more attractive terms. In real terms, these inventories are freed to be transformed into productive fixed capital goods, either *via* the foreign trade route, or as consumer goods for workers who produce the capital goods.[19] This hypothesis is virtually impossible to verify by direct empirical evidence, since satisfactory data on inventories in underdeveloped countries do not exist. Consequently, it is possible that there is some

[17]Based, obviously, on highly simplistic assumptions that the marginal capital-output ratio for such reallocated capital is on the order of 2 to 3, and that this wealth prior to reallocation made no contribution to output; a more general assumption would be that the difference between the capital-output ratios of this capital before and after reallocation would be 2 to 3.

[18]Probably the most important reason is the inadequacy, and especially the uncertainty, of supply lines. Thus, improvements in distribution systems probably are the most important single factor in making feasible a reduction in holdings of inventories.

[19]There is also the danger that after financial intermediation the inventories will simply continue to be held, but by a different group (speculators), who finance their holdings by borrowing (short-term) from the financial intermediaries.

overestimation of gross domestic investment in such developing economies, since statistical coverage is likely to be more complete for fixed investment than for inventories, especially where there may be widespread small declines in inventory holdings by a large number of individual units. Part of the recorded fixed investment is thus derived from and offset by unrecorded declines in inventories.

Individual holdings of precious metals and foreign exchange and other foreign assets also can be transformed directly into socially productive fixed assets by the foreign trade route, with imports of capital goods being paid for by a reduction in the net domestic holdings of precious metals or foreign exchange. An important mechanism in the past, whereby countries have freed domestic holdings of precious metals, has lain in the shift from a currency system based in effect upon a commodity (such as specie) as money (where its value in exchange as a monetary unit is equal to its value in alternative uses) to a system based on token currency (where the value in exchange is derived from a guarantee by government or private financial institution, and the value of the token in alternative uses is negligible relative to its monetary value). A further refinement is the development of deposit money.[20] Such token money has the advantages of very low resource costs of production and of greater potential for control over its elasticity of supply. At the same time, it frees the commodity (specie) for alternative uses; using commodities as a domestic means of payment has a high opportunity cost.

An example of such a transformation in the composition of wealth is Japan at the beginning of its modernization effort. Between Japan's opening to foreign trade in 1853 and and 1881, almost all of the domestic supply of gold and silver, which had gradually accumulated through limited domestic production during 250 years of isolation for use as circulating coin, was shipped abroad to pay for a substantial import surplus. Good estimates of Japan's stock of gold and silver as of 1853 do not exist, and the data on the net outflow of specie in the turbulent years of foreign trade prior to the Restoration in 1868, and even during the early years of the new government, are inadequate. Between 1872 and 1881, the new outflow of specie amounted to 71 million yen, 24 percent of total imports during the period. For the entire period, the outflow was on the order of 220 million yen. This was equivalent to perhaps half of her national income in an average year during this period.[21]

It could be argued that a similar shift in the composition of wealth is not open to contemporary underdeveloped countries, since in virtually all countries specie has been eliminated as circulating medium and token money has been substituted. While this is true, in some countries (notably India, but probably also Burma and Pakistan) immense amounts of gold and silver are held by individuals, in part as attractive assets, rather than solely for

---

[20]This process was particularly important in the nineteenth century. Cf. Robert Triffin, *The Evolution of the International Monetary System: Historical Reappraisal and Future Perspectives,* Princeton University Essays in International Finance (1964).

[21]Cf. Patrick, "Japan," *op. cit.*

consumption purposes. In other countries, especially in Latin America and the Middle East oil countries, rich individuals evidently hold a considerable portion of their wealth in the form of liquid foreign assets, at yields below what could be (socially) achieved by stimulating domestic economic development. One of the problems (from a growth perspective) in such a transformation of inventories, precious metals, foreign exchange, or other liquid assets into other forms is that, possibly, they will be used for consumption purposes, with a net decrease in the wealth stock, rather than for creating new productive capital goods. Such living off a country's wealth stock is difficult to document, except in blatant cases. For example, even the use of exports of such assets to finance the import of consumption rather than capital goods does not necessarily mean that consumption increases at the expense of wealth stocks, since the imported consumption goods may replace domestic consumption goods production, thereby freeing domestic resources for production of capital goods or exports.

With reference again to the Japanese case, 1853-81, initially, a high proportion of Japan's imports were manufactured consumer goods, especially cotton textiles, which substituted for domestic handicrafts. It is not clear where and how the domestic handicraft resources found productive alternative uses. The share of investment goods did rise steadily, from 5 percent of imports in 1868-72 to 10 percent of a much larger volume of imports in the next five-year period.[22] More important, perhaps, Japan's stock of specie provided the new growth-oriented government with a breathing period, during which the country's balance of payments pressures were less severe than they might have been and the government's position could be consolidated.

A more pervasive mechanism whereby the composition of a given stock of wealth is altered to produce a higher level of output is through the investment replacing the annual amount of depreciation. While in aggregative terms the wealth stock does not change, in micro terms the replacement investment is often in new sectors, for new uses, and with a higher embodied technology, so it is more productive than the depreciated portion of the wealth stock had been. Measurement of the extent of this allocative effect is extremely dependent upon the definition used for capital consumption allowances. However, the importance of capital consumption and its replacement is well recognized and does not require further comment here.

By what means does the development of financial assets assist in this process of transformation of a given total amount of tangible assets into more productive form? The main point is that individuals who hold tangible assets capable of being transformed are not necessarily those who are willing to hold productive fixed assets. The ownership of productive fixed assets in underdeveloped countries usually entails entrepreneurial and managerial functions as well, especially since equities markets are not well developed.

---

[22]See M. Shinohara, "Economic Development and Foreign Trade in Pre-War Japan," in C. D. Cowan, ed., *The Economic Development of China and Japan* (London: George Allen & Unwin, 1964), p. 234.

Not all wealth-holders are willing to engage in these functions. The opportunity to hold financial assets of superior characteristics to inventories and specie as a store of wealth enables holders of such tangible assets to give them up for financial assets,[23] and for others to arrange the transformation of these freed, tangible assets into a more productive form. What is crucial is, on the one hand, substituting financial assets for real assets in the portfolios of certain individuals and, on the other, permitting entrepreneurs to incur financial liabilities in order to enable them to hold a larger amount of productive assets than they could have otherwise.

In this context, the important point is the substitution between real assets and financial claims. Substitutions among various kinds of financial assets in portfolios of individuals are relatively less important. Their main function is to enhance the efficiency of financial markets by developing various alternative financial assets and liabilities with differing characteristics to meet the variegated preferences of individuals.

In summary, while data are not sufficient to provide an adequate test, I suggest that in the early phases of development such an improvement in the composition of wealth can be quite important. It is one aspect of taking up the slack, as Ranis had aptly phrased it; output is increased by moving toward existing production frontiers through the improved allocation of resources, including tangible assets. This more efficient composition of real wealth is obtained through the creation of financial assets and liabilities which provide the incentive for savers to hold (at least part of) their wealth in financial form and investors to hold more productive real assets than they could have in the absence of a financial system.

More Efficient Allocation of Investment

The foregoing discussion on increasing the level of output by improving the composition of a given amount of wealth through the substitution of financial assets for relatively unproductive tangible assets is essentially an extension of the Gurley-Shaw analysis of the role of financial intermediation in improving the efficiency of investment. In this section, emphasis is placed on the flow of gross additions to the capital stock through the process of saving and investment out of current production. The Gurley-Shaw theory rests on two important assumptions: individual savers (surplus spending units) are not all the most efficient investors (deficit spending units), in terms of the optimum allocation of investment, and savers are not willing to make the full amount of their saving (in excess of their own efficient investment) directly available to the most efficient investors.

The reason that the distribution of saving differs from the most efficient distribution of investment is that saving depends primarily upon income, while efficient investment depends upon entrepreneurial talents, knowledge,

[23]The point should be emphasized that, in order for such a substitution to take place, the financial assets must have sufficiently desirable characteristics of safety, liquidity, and yield.

and willingness to take risk. Several corollaries follow. Savers in under-developed countries, especially in rural areas, tend to invest in real assets, often of relatively low social productivity.[24] Contrarily, efficient investors are not able to invest as much as they would like; in portfolio terms they are unable to increase sufficiently their holding of productive tangible assets and their issuance of financial liabilities. In other words, savers are not entrepreneurs, and entrepreneurs cannot save enough to self-finance their desired investment expenditures. Consequently, marginal rates of return are not equated for different uses or among different users. This deficiency could be remedied without recourse to financial intermediation if savers were willing to purchase the primary securities from (i.e., make loans to or purchase the bonds or stock of) efficient entrepreneurs. However, the characteristics of primary securities do not coincide fully with the preferences of savers, especially in terms of liquidity, safety, divisibility, diversification of assets, and the special services specific financial assets provide (e.g., money as the medium of exchange, insurance, etc).

Under these circumstances, financial intermediaries have an important function in providing a market mechanism for the transference of claims on real resources from savers to the most efficient investors. The more perfect are financial markets, the more nearly optimum allocation of investment is achieved. In this way, the financial system accommodates economic growth; on the other hand, to the extent that the financial system is underdeveloped and/or inefficient, it restricts growth below what optimally could be achieved. The mechanism whereby financial institutions effect this transfer is to issue their liabilities (sell indirect securities) to savers, in exchange ultimately for their real saving (assets) or monetary claims upon such assets, and to provide the assets so accumulated to investors by purchasing their primary securities. The financial system can create a wide variety of financial claims (indirect securities) to serve as assets for savers, with claims differentiated by liquidity, yield, maturity, divisibility, risk of default or change in value, and other services. In this way, the financial system obtains claims to resources which it provides, under optimal market conditions, to the most efficient user. Hence, the most efficient allocation of investment results.

In addition to this major function, financial institutions can achieve economies of scale in the costs of transferring saving to investors through the pooling of default risks of individual deficit spending units, in carrying out investigations of the characteristics of deficit spending units in order to determine the most appropriate terms of issuance, and in engaging in transactions among saving and spending units of diverse location, size, or other characteristics. These economies offset the net risk the financial

---

[24]For example, rural saving in India is predominantly in kind. There is a tendency to hold increased saving in the form of foodstuffs in excess of normal consumption demand, in order that it may be used later to pay for the purchase of durable capital goods or to allow extra consumption (such as for festivals) later. Cf. Wilfred Malenbaum, *Prospect for Indian Development* (London: George Allen & Unwin, 1962), p. 142. See also UN ECAFE, *op. cit.*

institution usually assumes by purchasing direct securities of higher risk than the indirect securities it creates and sells. The margin between the interest rate at which it buys primary securities and at which it sells indirect securities is the compensation a financial institution receives for its services.

Hence, an important function of the financial system is the transmutation of relatively safe, liquid, short-term financial claims into riskier, less liquid, longer-term real assets. We must distinguish between the degree of risk for individuals and for society as a whole in examining specific projects, and also between two types of risk—insolvency and illiquidity. For both types the degree or risk is less for society than for individuals. Risks of insolvency (unprofitability) of specific investment projects are pooled for society, but not for (all but the wealthiest) individuals, unless by financial intermediaries. Risks of illiquidity in the economy can be eliminated or substantially reduced by appropriate action of the monetary authorities as the lender of last resort. Accordingly, financial intermediation allows society to assume the appropriate degree of risk, which would be too high if it were assumed directly by saving individuals. At the same time, financial intermediation provides the mechanism for the reallocation and spreading of risk among individuals.

As an underdeveloped country grows, the composition of its tangible wealth is altered to a more growth-productive mix, both by the once-and-for-all shifts and by the differential composition of the gross additions to wealth. With the growth of financial intermediation, during the neo-classical growth phase (in which the major problem is to increase the supply of productive capital and other factors of production), funds are channeled mainly to finance productive industrial and infrastructural investment. Accordingly, the proportion of producer durables and business structures in total wealth rises, while land and consumer durable assets decline. Later, in what may be termed the Keynesian growth phase (in which the major problem is to assure adequate demand for output), a higher proportion of funds may be channeled into financing the purchase of (new-style) consumer durables,[25] and their proportion rises in total real assets. This is particularly likely to be the case where the government maintains aggregate demand by techniques which directly encourage consumption (such as reductions in personal income taxes) rather than investment. However, a country's economy will have to be relatively advanced before this phase is likely to be reached; in the interim, investment in consumer durables will compete directly with productive investment for growth.

Provision of Incentives to Growth

It is asserted that the development of a financial system and the associated provision of financial claims and services has positive incentive effects for

[25]Cf. Harry T. Oshima, "Consumer Asset Formation and the Future of Capitalism," *Economic Journal,* LXXI, No. 281 (March 1961), 20-35. For example, Oshima estimates that consumer asset formation in the late 1950's was 12 percent of GNP in the United States and 3 percent in Japan.

growth, though these effects have not been analyzed in great detail. The standard approach has been to point out that financial intermediation narrows the differential between the interest rate savers receive and that which investors have to pay.

Gurley and Shaw suggest that by offering a wide array of financial assets, financial institutions stimulate saving,[26] but without further elaboration. A higher, and rising, saving rate relative to GNP correlates well, for a sample of Asian countries, with an increase in the proportion of saving held in the form of financial assets relative to tangible assets.[27] Presumably, the major rationale of the stimulus to saving is that with new assets having higher yield, lower risk, and/or other desirable characteristics, the return on saving is higher than it was heretofore. With the terms of the trade-off (the exchange ratio) between saving and present consumption relatively more favorable to the former, individuals substitute increased saving for consumption out of current income.[28]

Offsetting somewhat this favorable substitution effect on saving are the effects of increased real income (or wealth) derived from having a wider selection of assets in which to hold wealth. Having the additional alternative of holding financial assets makes an individual better off, and he likely will utilize some of this increased income in the form of consumption. This is especially important where the individual is a target saver.[29] Target saving is a shorter-run characteristic of some rural savers in underdeveloped countries. The (subsistence) farmer wants to be certain of adequate saving to provide for consumption until his next crop is harvested, plus a margin to cover the possibility of adverse crop conditions.[30] However, in the longer run, the horizon of conceivable alternatives expands, targets are raised, and the beneficial substitution effects on saving will probably substantially outweigh offsetting income effects.

The specific characteristics of certain financial assets may result in increased total saving. For example, term life insurance may not be sold,[31] so that the buyer has to purchase an annuity as well as pure life insurance when he wants to obtain life insurance coverage. In this case, the lack of a perfect

[26]*Money in a Theory of Finance*, p. 55.

[27]UN ECAFE, *op. cit.*, p. 8. The causal relationship is not explained, however; both the saving rate and proportion held in financial form may be a consequence of the level and the rate of economic growth.

[28]It should be noted that this is different from the wealth (or liquid asset) effect on consumption, in the analysis of which it is usually assumed that there are no changes in the exchange ratio between saving and present consumption.

[29]By improving the return on saving, the target saver is encouraged to save relatively less and to consume more. At the limit, the target saver would not increase his saving, but would consume his full increase in welfare resulting from opportunities of financial intermediation.

[30]Having the possibility of holding even currency, rather than a specific foodgrain, improves a farmer's position under conditions of general price stability, since he can reduce storage and spoilage costs (for which there are economies of scale) and protect himself against relative price movements in the specific commodity he holds.

[31]This apparently is the case in many underdeveloped countries.

market—the tying of financial services to saving, rather than separating them—encourages additional saving, even though less of the services may be bought, since the price is higher.

Financial intermediation also provides a variety of incentives to investors. The reduction in the effective interest rate reduces the cost of investment; the strength of the demand response depends on the elasticity of the marginal efficiency of capital schedule. It should be pointed out that financial intermediation does not mean that "the" interest rate necessarily declines over time, since in a growing economy investment demand may become increasingly strong.[32] However, increased effective financial intermediation will produce a narrowing of the dispersion of interest rates among different types and levels of creditworthiness of users, among geographical regions, and over periods of seasonal fluctuation. This is a consequence of the improvement in financial markets. The development of a wide array of financial assets (and primary securities) provides a more finely delineated spectrum of asset alternatives, with greater possibilities for substitution among assets (since there can be a series of shifts among close substitutes). This allows an increased supply of funds to users who had been starved for funds under imperfect market conditions and who would be willing to pay relatively high interest rates.[33]

For many entrepreneurs, the increased availability of funds as a result of financial intermediation may be considerably more significant than simply the reduction in costs.[34] This is probably particularly true in underdeveloped countries, where most markets are much less perfect than in developed countries. The availability of funds from financial institutions enables the efficient entrepreneur to assume a greater debt position than he could otherwise and concurrently to engage in a larger amount of productive investment. Moreover, as noted earlier, newly developed access to funds on reasonable terms from financial institutions can induce or encourage entrepreneurs to expand their horizon of conceivable opportunities. Not simply access to funds, but the entire financial milieu, and the rationalism it implies, triggers creative entrepreneurial responses.

This is true not only in industry, but also in other, more traditional sectors. A simple but highly important example for underdeveloped countries is the monetization of subsistence sectors, notably in rural areas. Monetization encourages the shift from subsistence to commercial production, with attendant increases in output due to specialization, increased work efforts

[32]That is, the amount of shift of the investment schedule to the right per unit of time becomes increasingly large, for a variety of reasons.

[33]This assumes that funds do become decreasingly rather than increasingly compartmentalized, as a consequence of intermediation. The latter is a real possibility, however; risk-averting bankers in underdeveloped countries may efficiently collect saving through deposits and use the funds to invest in prime commercial bills or foreign liquid assets.

[34]While availability can be thought of in cost terms, (an infinite interest rate at the limit), this results in misplaced emphasis on the actual behavior of lenders, who certainly use credit-rationing criteria, as distinct from interest-rate criteria, in the allocation of funds.

(and increased saving and investment), emphasis on high-income crops,[35] and enhanced responsiveness to changes in relative prices of different crops. The opportunities of commercial production, at least in the early phases of development, improve the terms of the trade-off between income from work and leisure and result in increased labor inputs.[36]

Financial institutions provide services that reduce the risks or increase the profitability of productive real investment projects. Insurance is an obvious example. In underdeveloped countries, another important example is the service related to the financing of trade, as one aspect of the provision of readier access by producers to markets, both domestic and foreign.

Development of the financial system in these ways not only accommodates but even induces growth, by generating incentives to savers to increase their rate of saving, to entrepreneurs to invest more, and to producers to work harder.

[35]See, for example, Walter P. Falcon, "Farmer Response to Price in a Subsistence Economy: The Case of West Pakistan", *American Economic Review*. LIV, No. 3 (May 1964).

[36]This is not true, of course, where the supply schedule of labor is backward-bending. For peasant agriculture, this does not seem frequently to be the case. Good examples are the response of Japanese farmers to the possibilities of export of silk and of Nigerian farmers to the export of cocoa.

Inflation and Growth

Graeme S. Dorrance

35

In a developing economy, the government has a grave responsibility to make certain that its financial policies are directed primarily toward overcoming the basic problems that such an economy is likely to face. These structural problems—so-called because they appear rather as elements in the structure of the economy than as incidents in its history—are often very serious. In most less developed countries, the vast majority of the people are not as yet educated to take their place in a modern technological society. In fact, the most serious problem in many of them is the problem of illiteracy. An inability to take advantage of simple opportunities to fight disease and to overcome poor nutrition is often almost as serious a social problem. Government institutions are frequently inadequate to meet the problems of a rapidly changing society. As populations grow and gather in cities, the basic sanitary facilities become inadequate, and more expensive housing is required than may be the minimum necessary in country districts. In many of the countries where progress has been slow in the past, businesses are not used to taking the risks which must be faced in

From *Finance and Development*, a publication of the International Monetary Fund and the International Bank for Reconstruction and Development. Reprinted by permission of the author and publisher. The author is Advisor, Research Department, International Monetary Fund.

his money to such institutions. He may feel that the future is so uncertain that he might as well spend his money now and let the future take care of itself—in which event, savings will fall. Or, if he saves, he can protect his future by buying gold or foreign currencies. As the Fund said in its *Annual Report* for 1962: "A particularly unfortunate feature of the international scene in the last decade has been the large flow of private capital from those less developed countries which have tolerated inflation to countries, frequently wealthy, which have maintained monetary stability."

These same reasons which lead people to wish to buy foreign currency when they expect prices to rise will lead foreigners to be less anxious to invest in the inflating country, because they are running the risk of their investment losing value through deterioration of the exchange rate. The net result of this two-way process is a loss of capital in the inflating country. A developing country wants the rest of the world to invest in it; but an inflating country tends to be a net investor in the rest of the world.

A private individual may also build up his savings by buying real estate. Insofar as he merely buys land from someone else there is no serious problem. It is the use made by the former landowner of the receipts from the sale of his land that raises problems. However, in cities the purchase of real estate usually means the purchase of a house or an apartment. An individual can see a house or an apartment not only as a place to live in but also as a possession which is likely to rise in price as long as inflation continues. He may well buy a house or an apartment as much to provide protection for his future as to provide shelter for his family. In doing so he will try to buy the biggest house or apartment that he thinks he can possibly afford. That is, he is likely to buy a house or an apartment larger than that which would fit his needs if there were other forms of saving which he trusted. Thus, with an inflation, resources will go into the building of houses and apartments on a greater scale than would otherwise happen. Resources which could have been used to increase the community's capacity to meet its wants will be wasted on the building of houses and apartments larger and more luxurious than people really want. The real satisfaction of the community will be less than it would have been if price increases had not been expected. It might be thought that instead of building a larger house than he desired, a small individual might put his savings in a house or apartment which he could rent. However, in modern societies, when inflation occurs, governments quite rightly try to protect the small individual from the worst effects of the inflation. It is common for the government to impose rent controls in an attempt to protect individuals from profiteers. Unfortunately, one of the effects of these controls is that they treat the small individual who buys a house to rent in fact as a "profiteer," and as a result such houses or apartments become no better than bonds or insurance policies as protection against the future.

the development of new products and new methods of distribution. There is also the need to develop basic community requirements, such as roads, bridges, power, and other public utilities.

Faced with these and other serious problems, the government of a developing country should consider the basic question of its financial policy so that victory over the fundamental structural difficulties may be made more likely.

About inflation itself various questions may be asked:

Does inflation help ease the problems of a developing country?

Is inflation an inevitable result of rapid development?

Or: Are the effects of inflation so harmful that the government of a developing country should fight it with enthusiasm?

The Background

In a country which is trying to develop rapidly, there are always fewer resources (of goods or skilled workers) than are wanted. If development is to be rapid, there is a tendency for the community as a whole (including the government as well as individuals and businesses) to try to spend more than is currently produced by home industries or available as imports. If a community tries to do this, inflation becomes likely. This happens most frequently when governments have committed themselves to spend more than they receive from taxes, or can borrow from the genuine savings of the population. The competition resulting from the attempt to buy more goods and services than are available raises the prices of goods, and the competition for the services of skilled workers raises wages. Then the government itself, however reluctantly and belatedly, also has to pay higher prices and wages and so has to spend even more beyond its means. As long as people in general—which includes the government—try to spend more money than the production costs of the goods and services available at a particular time, so long will prices tend to rise and an inflation will be present.

Not all price rises are signs of dangerous inflation. Food prices may rise because of a bad harvest, for instance, but if a good harvest follows, the situation corrects itself. The inflation that causes concern is a continuing rapid inflation; in this, there are increases in prices which increase incomes but do not correspondingly increase supplies. In that case, prices tend to continue rising. Common sense suggests and experience shows that the problems created by such an inflation may be so great that they make it impossible for a government to speed development. In fact, if a country embarks on a rapid development program without taking steps to restrain inflation, the end result of the program may be progress less rapid than it would have been if the program had not been attempted. If a severe inflation continues, and prices rise rapidly year after year, not only will development slow down, but the social fabric will be severely strained. In recent years there have been many such occurrences, and even at the present time there are a number of countries where these tensions are apparent. Thus, at the moment, prices are more than doubling every year in Brazil and Indonesia, and rising at a rate which would result in their doubling in less than two years in the Congo, and every three years in Argentina, Chile, Colombia, Korea, and Uruguay, to name only a few such countries. It is not unlikely that similar price rises will appear in other developing countries which are trying to catch up with the more fortunate parts of the world, unless their governments stand firmly resolved to fight inflation with enthusiasm.

Danger Signals

There are two danger signals that inflation has gone too far. One is the appearance of a wage-price spiral. When the cost of living is rising rapidly, wage earners and pensioners justifiably refuse to be satisfied with their lot unless they receive frequent large increases in their incomes. Yet large wage increases raise costs, and hence lead inevitably to further upward price changes. The second danger signal is a distrust of money. Once people lose faith in their money because they see that money savings held in bank deposits, insurance policies, social security funds, government securities, or similar forms, melt away in terms of what they can buy, they cease to hold such things and the entire financial structure of the country is strained. Further, they cease to have faith in the real meaning of money promises; workers fight not for wages high enough to meet the present increase in the cost of living but for wages high enough to meet the expected *future* increases in the cost of living. Strikes become widespread and prolonged, and struggles between employers and workers embitter the political scene.

Diversion of Investment

In these circumstances, people see that it is foolish to hold money in bank accounts, savings deposits, life insurance, government securities, or similar forms. Rather than trying to work for a better future for themselves and their families by saving in these forms, they will use in other ways what savings they may already have. It must be remembered, however, that for the vast majority of people in every country there are relatively few ways in which they can hold savings. They can hold such things as savings deposits and insurance policies, gold and foreign currencies, or real estate. Unless they own their own businesses, it is difficult for them to buy other assets which are likely to rise in price. One of the important roles of banks and savings banks (including government development banks) and insurance companies is to gather the relatively small savings of individuals and enable them to be used in the relatively large blocks that are required for productive investment, while providing protection to the small individual which he can use at a time of family crisis or can build up in the hope of providing a better future for himself and his family. However, if prices are going to rise, he will not entrust

Hoarding of Stocks

In the business world there is a parallel to the accumulation of real estate by individuals. The businessman will expect that prices and wages are going to rise in the future. However, he cannot be certain whether they will rise more in the immediate future than they have in the recent past, or whether they will rise somewhat less rapidly; and there is always the ever present chance that the government will have the courage to stop inflation. It must be remembered that governments universally view inflation in the same way that people view sin: they are opposed to it and never do more than accept it as an "inevitable evil." Further, the businessman will be most uncertain about the rate of increase in the prices at which he can sell his products compared with the rate of increase in the prices he must pay for his supplies, and also about the rate of increase in the wages he must pay, or the bonuses he must grant, to his workers to keep them in his employment or to satisfy government decrees intended to protect workers from the worst effects of inflation. While he may be certain that prices will rise, he may be most uncertain as to what his immediate prospects are: As a result, he will be hesitant regarding the future, but will wish to hold some things which he expects to rise in price. He can do this by accumulating stocks of goods, either by buying raw materials which he is likely to need at some time in the future, or by being unenthusiastic about selling all the goods which he produces, in the expectation that he can get a better price for them than their present price. Thus resources which might be used to provide goods to satisfy the desires of the people will be used to build up hoards by businesses, and the general welfare of the community will be worsened.

Government Expedients

In addition to controlling rents, the government may seek to limit the inflation by fixing the prices of socially important goods and services. These expedients deal with symptoms, not with the root trouble. Unless the government subsidizes the production of these controlled goods and services, businessmen will be frightened away from their production, and will strive to produce those goods and services which are not controlled—usually the least important. At the same time, the very fact that the prices of some goods are controlled when the prices of others are rising makes the controlled goods more attractive; people will try to buy more of them. Unless they are subsidized, lines will form in front of shops when small deliveries arrive, black markets will develop, and social dissatisfaction will be common when people are unable to obtain goods that they think should be theirs by right. Some of these problems are most evident in countries where transport and public utility services have deteriorated because fares and rates have been held down while costs have risen. In these circumstances, the economic structure becomes distorted in such a way as to necessitate painful adjustments when inflation is eventually brought to an end. If the government subsidizes the production of essential goods, the problems are avoided. However, equally severe ones take their place. The payment of subsidies will eat up the government's revenues and leave less available to finance development, or lead to further inflationary financing.

The International Consequences

Serious inflation does not limit its ravages to those on the home economy. It also leads to a worsening of a country's international position. It has already been pointed out that constantly rising prices lead to a flight of money abroad and discourage an inflow of capital. This is bad enough, but inflation also encourages people to import goods from abroad and discourages them from exporting. Because domestic prices are rising, imports available from countries with stable prices will become more attractive. Hence people will buy them, rather than goods produced at home. At the same time, a country's exports will suffer when prices are rising, partly because home demand is diverted to them and partly because they become too expensive to be sold in foreign markets.

The only way to avoid these trading disadvantages is to let the exchange rate worsen as rapidly as, or more rapidly than, prices rise. However, a worsening exchange rate tends to encourage the export of capital, so that the government of an inflating country finds itself in a dilemma. If it allows the exchange rate to fall, capital will flee the country; if it does not, the country will sell fewer exports and buy more imports. What often happens in practice is that the exchange rate is supported for a time, and then allowed to deteriorate sharply to a lower level, where it is pegged again. This tends to combine the two disadvantages. As long as the exchange rate is better than is appropriate for prices, the balance of payments will be under pressure. The fact that it has once been altered will induce wary owners of capital to expect it to be changed again.

As long as the exchange rate is pegged at the wrong level, it is necessary to cut down imports as far as possible. Restrictions of various kinds are accordingly placed upon them. This exclusion results in yet another misdirection of effort within the country. In order to replace the goods which formerly were imported, facilities have to be created or diverted. Clearly this must be costly to the inflating country, since if it had been economic to produce the goods at home this would already have been done. The goods which are substituted for the former imports accordingly rise in price.

When all the worst factors combine, an inflation may move very rapidly. Developments combine to depress the exchange rate; and as it declines fresh pressures develop at home, since imports now cost more, and this adds to the forces raising domestic prices.

It Can Be Stopped

Though an inflation tends to be cumulative, and may eventually move with great rapidity, it can be stopped, although the task of stopping it is always difficult and even in the earlier stages is liable to cause a temporary fresh dislocation. Suppose, however, that by one means or another the excess of purchasing power over current prices is eliminated—whether by equating government expenditures with revenues, or by borrowing abroad enough to purchase imports sufficient to fill the gap between demand and supply. What might be called the mechanical result will then have been achieved: there will be no pressures left to raise prices. But the psychological result will not have been achieved until people are convinced that the mechanical one has been, and here there is a gap. For some time to come people will expect prices to continue to rise, and they will continue to act as though prices were going to do so, which in itself may prove an obstacle to price stability. To instill a conviction that the end of price increases has really come is one of the government's most difficult and most important tasks. What adds to the difficulty is that some prices—of food, of transportation, and of public services (such as electricity)—will have to be raised from the artificially low level at which they have been held. But a firm declaration of intent, backed up by effective steps to prevent prices from rising—by avoidance of wage increases and probably by changing the exchange rate sufficiently to close the gap in the balance of payments—will sooner or later achieve the desired results. The inflation is brought to a standstill—or at any rate near enough to a standstill to be no longer a threat to development. There is still an aftermath. All the effort that has been misdirected throughout the inflation has now to be redirected. This second step is difficult. For the immediate result of instilling a conviction that prices will stop rising is to discourage all those types of investment which have expanded as a result of the inflation. However quickly people realize that in the new conditions there will be a growing demand for production appropriate to stable incomes, it takes time to organize the production of such goods; meanwhile, there will be a shortage both of the goods and of jobs. Moreover, those who have been holding stocks of goods as a safe form of investment realize that the prospect of continuing profits from increases in their prices has now been brought to an end, and as the storing of these goods is a costly matter they try to dispose of them, at the expense of current production of the same goods. In the same way those who have been producing exportable goods, and selling them at home, find that the demand for them is much lessened. They withdrew from the export market because they found it difficult in comparison with the home market, and markets which are fairly difficult to retain are naturally exceedingly difficult to re-enter. These are some of the dislocations which hamper and embarrass a government that is trying to stabilize its economy.

The only alternative is to let the inflation continue, and this is worse. Only in a stable economy can effort be effectively directed to the kinds of long-run investments which are needed for economic growth. It is therefore a matter of the most vital importance for governments to persevere in the measures that will end inflation and maintain stability. The measures themselves depend to some extent on the country concerned. But the avoidance of a government deficit, the encouragement of savings, and the control of bank credit will most certainly all be necessary. None of these is easy to administer, but economic growth is a difficult objective which becomes a mere mirage without stability from which to grow. Once the initial difficulties of stabilizing are overcome, true growth can begin, and investors will not be long in taking advantage of the new opportunities which stability affords, provided they are convinced that the government is resolved to push forward resolutely with programs designed to foster development in an atmosphere of financial stability.

Inflation and Growth—
Empirical Evidence

K.C. Sen

36

It is generally believed that inflation is a necessary cost of economic growth. Yet, there is no conclusive empirical evidence supporting this view. "Rapid economic growth has at different times been associated with rising, constant, and falling price levels, just as periods of slow growth, or indeed, of no growth, have been marked by every manner of price behavior."[1] "It is thus a question of Progress versus Stability," says Kaldor, but he also observes that "indeed the development of trade cycle theories . . . has proved to be inimical to the idea that cycle and dynamic growth are inherently connected analytically."[2] "There is no clear international evidence that countries with stable prices grow fast and those with inflation grow more slowly. Some theorists would hold the reverse view, but there are few data

An excerpt from "Economic Growth and the Price Level—An Analysis of Some Asian Data, 1950-63," Research Paper 13 of AID, University of Wisconsin research project on economic interdependence in Southeast Asia. Reprinted by permission of the author. The author is associate professor of economics at the University of Illinois.

[1]Otto Eckstein, "Staff Report on Employment, Growth, and Price Levels," Joint Economic Committee, U.S. Congress (Washington, 1959), p. 11.

[2]Nicholas Kaldor, *Essays on Economic Stability and Growth* (London: 1960), p. 118.

that clearly support these opposite notions."[3] The heterogeneity of experience may be gauged from the following studies.[4]

A. The Less Developed Countries (LDC's)

1. From a study made by U Tun Wai of 3 less developed countries in Latin America, the Middle East, and Asia and the Far East (1938-54),[5] the general conclusion emerged "that for the LDC's the findings proved to be inconclusive in general; but for most of the small number of individual countries for which the available statistics cover periods in which the rates of price increases differ significantly, the evidence suggests that the rate of growth was higher when the rate of inflation was lower."[6]

2. The United Nation's data for Latin America (1946-55) show that whereas prices rose only about 3 percent per annum in Venezuela, they rose over 20 percent per annum in Peru and Brazil, though the rates of growth of real income per head were roughly the same in the two cases. On the other hand, the rate of inflation was particularly high in those countries—Argentina, Chile, and Paraguay—in which growth was very slow, and moderate rates of inflation of 3 to 5 percent per annum generally seemed to go with moderate rates of growth.

3. After analyzing the statistical data for relatively long periods for the Latin American countries (1945-59), Benjamin Higgins concludes: "the Latin American data provide examples of every conceivable combination: monetary stability with high rates of growth; monetary stability with stagnation; inflation with rapid growth; and inflation with stagnation."[7]

B. The Developed Countries (DC's)

1. Rattan Bhatia concluded from his study of five DC's that no systematic relationship between price changes and rate of growth existed; that "the relationship, if any, has differed from country to country. The rates of growth were inversely related to the rate of change in prices in Germany and Japan, whereas in Sweden and Canada the two tended to move together. However, in most cases, the correlation coefficients were low, so that no

---

[3]Lawrence R. Klein and Ronald G. Bodkin, et al., "Empirical Aspects of the Trade-Offs among Three Goals: High Level Employment, Price Stability, and Economic Growth," *Inflation, Growth and Employment*, in the Commission on Money and Credit (New York: Prentice-Hall, 1964), p. 403.

[4]Note that several authors draw from much the same data sources.

[5]U Tun Wai, "A Relation Between Inflation and Economic Development: A Statistical Inductive Study," *International Monetary Fund Staff Papers*, Vol. VII (1959-60), pp. 302-17.

[6]*Ibid.*, p. 302.

[7]Benjamin H. Higgins, "Financing Accelerated Growth," in *Government Finance and Economic Development* (Paris: OECD, 1965), p. 21.

conclusion about the relation regarding the rate of price change can be drawn from the statistical data examined here."[8] The results pertain to a long period (1860-1930), but the short period results are little different: The rate of growth was inversely related to the rate of price change in Germany and Japan. In Sweden and Canada, higher rates of price change were accompanied by higher rates of growth. In the U.K., contrary to what was found for the long periods, there was a *positive* relationship between the rate of price change and the rate of growth. At the 5 percent level of significance, the *r* was significant only for Germany; for each of the other four countries it was too small to justify any firm conclusion.

2. Long-term data for the U.S. and the U.K. further substantiate the lack of a systematic relationship between growth rate and rate of change in prices.

In the U.S., during the three decades (1884-93, 1904-13 and 1944-53) in which the average annual growth rates were almost identical, the price level moved erratically. In the first decade it declined by 2 percent per annum; in the second it increased by 2 percent per annum; and in the third it rose by 9 percent per annum.

In the U.K., a fall in output during the decade 1915-24 of nearly 1 percent coincided with an increase in prices by 106 percent, whereas during 1925-34, prices fell by 17 percent at a time when output increased by 21 percent.

3. In hearings before the Joint Committee on Employment, Growth, and Price Levels, the late Professor Sumner Slichter presented evidence regarding "the increase in the consumer price levels and the increase in real product per capita in 15 countries." His thesis was that a sustained "slow rise in price level (creeping inflation) is an inescapable cost of the maximum rate of growth."[9] Yet he characterized as "a widely disseminated bit of nonsense" the statement that "creeping inflation inevitably ... becomes a gallop."[10] He was of the view that whether or not creeping inflation becomes a gallop rests in the last analysis with the monetary authorities.

---

[8]Rattan Bhatia, "Inflation, Deflation, and Economic Development," *IMF Staff Papers*, Vol. VIII (1960-61), pp. 101-104. Bhatia fitted a linear equation relating rate of growth (Y) to the rate of price change (X) for each country separately and came out with the following results:

Country	No. of Observations	Regression Equation	Correlation Coefficient (r)
U.K.	5	$Y = 2.32 - 0.20 X$	−0.47
Germany	3	$Y = 3.75 - 0.64 X$	−0.75
Sweden	4	$Y = 2.89 + 0.42 X$	0.96
Canada	3	$Y = 4.19 + 0.45 X$	0.85
Japan	5	$Y = 4.67 - 0.12 X$	−0.95

No standard errors are given.

[9]Hearings, *Joint Committee on Employment, Growth, and Price-Levels*, 86th Congress, 1st Session, Part 1, p. 11.

[10]*Ibid.*, p. 12.

C. All Countries

The strongest categorical statement available regarding a systematic relationship between the growth rate and inflation is the one made by Dorrance of the International Monetary Fund. "An examination of the available data, stratified to recognize the effects of wealth on comparative rates of progress," he holds, "indicates that recent experience supports the view that, while a declining price level inhibits growth, and while relatively slowly rising prices, particularly in the wealthier countries, may have a stimulating effect, beyond a certain rate, rising prices discourage economic development, and rapid inflation seriously inhibits growth.[11]

Dorrance offers what he calls the "family of profiles of inflation,"[12] one each for every country, varying with its level of wealth. He also emphasizes the role of "price flexibility," as provided by a mild rise in prices in a growing economy, for bringing about desired structural change.[13] There is, according to Dorrance, "an inverse relation between the relative price flexibility and the acceptability of inflation in any economy," and this, he suggests, depends upon the "traditionality of (the) price structure." Thus, if the traditional price structure is flexible, upward and downward, as in the less developed countries which have not very strong trade unions, . . . the acceptable rate of inflation tends to be very low compared to the more advanced economies which have strong labor unions, complex productive patterns, and hence negligible price flexibility. Consequently, "it follows that price stability will approximate the optimum 'level of inflation' in very poor countries, with rising 'optimum' levels as progress is achieved." His conclusion is that the "countries with average income levels maintaining relatively stable monetary conditions may be expected to achieve the highest level of economic progress. The problems facing both poorer and more wealthy countries will make it less likely that they will be able to achieve the rates of progress attained by the 'average' countries. However, the progress actually achieved by any country will be strongly influenced by its financial policies. Both monetary stagnation and undue inflation will lead to lower levels of achievement: relatively stable prices will be consistent with the highest levels of progress."[14]

In summary, neither on the basis of the time series data, nor on the basis of the cross-section data can we say that economic growth and price level changes are uniquely related. Furthermore, whatever generalizations are actually made must rest on certain very strong assumptions relating to institutional factors. In fact, both price increases and real output increases can go hand in hand and can change together as a result of common causes.

[11]Graeme S. Dorrance, "Inflation and Growth, the Statistical Evidence," *Document of International Monetary Fund* (May 26, 1965), p. 1. Also, see his "The Effect of Inflation on Economic Development," in *Inflation and Growth in Latin America*, Werner Baer and Isaac Kerstenetzky, eds. (Homewood: Richard D. Irwin, 1964), pp. 37-88.

[12]*Ibid.*, p. 6.

[13]*Ibid.*, p. 3.

[14]*Ibid.*, p. 11.

Applications of Development Administration

George F. Gant

37

Development Administration Closes Gaps in
Development Performance

Most countries these days have more or less ambitious plans for social and economic development. Many of these countries, however, are frustrated by a lag between plan and accomplishment. Of the several causes of this lag, inadequacies of administration are among the most prominent. This note will explore ways of using the concept of "development administration" to locate and remedy these inadequacies of administration and to strengthen the application of management skills to the planning and execution of development programs.

The primary functions of public administration in colonies and dependencies before those areas became independent were to maintain law and order, collect taxes, settle disputes, and manage the essential services of

Reprinted by permission of the publishers from John D. Montgomery and Arthur Smithies, eds., *Public Policy,* Volume XV. Cambridge, Mass.: Harvard University Press. Copyright 1966 by the President and Fellows of Harvard College. The author is Director of the Ford Foundation Regional Programs in South and Southeast Asia.

government. These are also the chief functions of public administration in countries which have not gone very far toward the modernization of their agriculture and toward industrialization. The cadres of personnel assembled and trained to perform the duties involved in these functions were, and still are to a large extent, commonly organized into such services as general administration, police, and revenue. The duties themselves, by their very nature, consist very largely of securing compliance with rules and regulations and obedience to authority. Civil servants performing such duties must quite properly observe a certain aloofness in relations with the public. Their sanctions are those of threat and punishment. Most of the career services providing the personnel for this kind of administration rotate their officers quite frequently, largely in order to avoid personal and subjective involvement with the interests of the community of residence.

Among the first tasks confronting a newly independent country, and any other which proposes to modernize its government, is not only to nationalize its civil service but also to improve the integrity and efficiency of its bureaucracy. Most of the attention given to improving the quality of public administration has been directed toward methods and techniques of management—personnel administration, financial management, office management, procurement, and the internal organization and processes of decision-making and delegation in the several public agencies. Specialists in these various aspects of administration can be and are being trained to apply management principles and skills to increase the efficiency and effectiveness of government and agency performance. These are technical skills. Those who possess them can work with approximately equal facility in any government agency.

As countries progress, or desire to progress, from traditional agricultural societies to modern industrial societies, their governments and their administrative structures become larger and more complex. This change is more than a change in degree; it is a change in kind. Public administration in a complex society requires more than additional law and order. It requires more and different kinds of agencies whose functions and relationships are quite different from those of police and regulation. It requires the decentralization of heretofore tightly controlled authorities; and it requires a vastly larger number of skilled managers. This dimension of public administration, as a matter of convenience, can be called "development administration."

"Development administration" is that aspect of public administration in which the focus of attention is on organizing and administering public agencies in such a way as to stimulate and facilitate defined programs of social and economic progress. It involves the adaptation and application of management skills directly to the development process. Development administration thus encompasses the organization of new agencies such as planning organizations and development corporations; the reorientation of established agencies such as departments of agriculture; the delegation of administrative powers to development agencies; and the creation of a cadre of administrators who can provide leadership in stimulating and supporting programs of social and economic improvement. It has the purpose of making change attractive and possible to farmers, industrialists, businessmen, and to the population generally.

Development is, of course, dependent upon public order, and it is affected by the degree of efficiency, economy, and integrity with which the public business is conducted. This aspect of public administration can be characterized as "internal" administration—that is, the process of doing business within an agency with optimum efficiency. The effectiveness of this internal administration is or should be of concern to all public agencies. It is the major concern of purely operating or producing or servicing agencies such as domestic water systems and sanitation departments, tax agencies, and census bureaus. "External" administration, on the other hand, which characterizes development administration, is the process of actively encouraging, stimulating, and assisting institutions and groups outside the government agency to undertake development programs and of creating or encouraging the creation of supporting management services. This kind of administration is indirect rather than direct. Its methods are those of appeal to self-interest, of reward, of promise rather than those of command and reprisal. Development administration requires close identification with, rather than aloofness from, the community or communities of interest. Effective development administration depends not only upon authority and efficiency but more largely upon mutual interest and confidence and ability to provide motivation and management support to the relevant segment of the population embarked upon a program of development. Civil servants engaged in development administration should not be rotated from location to location too frequently. Their tenure should be long enough to instill the confidence and establish the constructive relationship required to get a program going and to keep it going.

Much attention has been devoted to reforms and improvements in internal administration. Analyses of administrative systems, and the resulting modifications, have tended to focus on tax and police administration, fiscal management, and personnel systems. In many countries programs of training and research of a variety of kinds have been introduced and are being strengthened to improve the quality of public administration in its traditional form. These include new courses in public administration in universities; institutes of management and executive development for private as well as public personnel; institutes of public administration; staff colleges for senior and middle-level civil servants and sometimes private executives; and academies for the pre-service and in-service training of civil servants—chiefly for the foreign, revenue, police, and general administrative services.

But failures in the execution of development programs persist. A review of the adequacy of planning and execution of development programs from the point of view of development administration uncovers significant gaps in the application of requisite management skills. Three such gaps and suggestions for closing them are described in this note: the lack of adequate management analysis in the planning process; the insufficiency of management competence in "nation-building" departments; and the short supply of managers needed for local enterprise.

Management Analysis is Needed in the
Planning Process

A not uncommon pattern of country planning machinery, with many variations of course, includes a central planning body; a planning unit in each "nation-building" department such as agriculture, industries, education, and health; and counterparts of these planning agencies in states or provinces and major metropolitan areas. The central and state planning bodies are typically staffed by economists and experts in agriculture, industry, transport, social service, and other sectors of development. The departmental planning units are staffed by experts of the same specialization as the department and often include an economist or at least someone with the skills of economic analysis. Most plans are expressed in fiscal terms, and they are usually tested in terms of financial feasibility. Much less frequently are plans expressed in operational terms or adequately tested from the point of view of administrative feasibility.

It is an anomaly that planning agencies of this kind, although themselves primarily concerned with "development administration," rarely include experts in management and operational analysis. Yet allocations of funds for development programs and projects are realistic only if such programs and projects are operationally feasible; only if the personnel and resources are available and assigned to agencies with such abilities and delegated powers as to be able to function effectively. In fact the competence of planning agencies should include not only economic but also management analysis. Management analysis should be applied to each proposed development project, and to the development plan as a whole, to ascertain whether (1) the skilled personnel and material requirements are or can be made available; (2) the agency or agencies within which these resources are assembled for use, whether public or private, are specifically responsible for results and have all the requisite delegated authority to operate efficiently; and (3) the managerial personnel have the knowledge, ability, and integrity to utilize their authority and resources to accomplish the assigned goals.

Such analysis should be positive rather than negative in character. That is, management skills in planning units should be used to find solutions to operating defects in development proposals and not merely to point out failures in the tests of administrative feasibility. This function should therefore include examination of government-wide administration policies and processes and the making of recommendations for adjustments to meet the requirements of the development program. The patterns of delegation within a country's bureaucracy, for example, and the nature of fiscal authorities given under a country's annual budget are directly relevant to the operating capacity of a development agency.

Management Skills Are Needed in Nation-Building Departments

A second deficiency in development administration in many countries is the comparative weakness of nation-building departments in the field of management. The brunt of development is borne by the nation-building departments, chiefly agriculture, industries, education, and health. Upon them falls the burden not only of determining what should be done to achieve progress but also of planning how it should be done and, in varying ways and degrees, of doing it. The discharge of these functions requires an effective blend of technical and administrative skills. By and large, the strengths of these departments are technical; their weaknesses in accomplishment are often in execution, in management.

Agricultural development provides an illustration. To increase food production, a management link is required between technical knowledge and production, on the one hand, and the informed farmer, on the other. Let us assume that the agricultural department and its associated research agencies have extended their technical knowledge of seeds, fertilizers, water use, and insecticides to the point that production will clearly increase if the knowledge is applied. We will assume also that the seeds, fertilizers, water, and insecticides are being or can be produced and that increases in production from their use would be so great as to provide attractive incentives to the farmers (both of these assumptions would be tested by management analysis). Nevertheless, these inputs will have to be made available to the farmers at the right time and at the right place every year if they are to be useful. Availability will need to be combined with sensible arrangements for credit and for storage, not to mention access to tools and equipment.

Some of the many tasks of administration involved in solving the above problems might be undertaken by private enterprise, some by new agencies, both public and private, and some by the government departments themselves. An understanding of development administration involves the foresight to anticipate the many requirements of supply and distribution, to assign the several management responsibilities involved, and to create the best environment possible for the discharge of these responsibilities. The competence of the agricultural department should therefore include not only technical but also administrative knowledge and skill—administrative skill not only for internal efficiency in the management of technical affairs but administrative skill in the application of technical knowledge through many agencies not immediately under its control and by thousands and even millions of farmers to whom the applications must be both attractive and possible.

In many countries the senior administrative officers of the nation-building departments and programs are drawn from the same civil services which provide staff for the performance of general administrative, regulatory, and police functions. There are cases where district commissioners are at the same time responsible for both police and tax collecting functions and the conduct of development programs. As has been pointed out, the methods of discharging these disparate functions and the bases for effective relationships with the public are quite different. It is the exceptional civil servant who can perform both sets of duties simultaneously. Also the training for development administration and the policies of rotation and tenure for development administrators by no means coincide with the training and rotation arrangements for tax collectors and administrators responsible for internal agency efficiency.

In some systems of public administration the senior administrative posts in agriculture, industries, education, and health agencies come under the technical or professional services in these several fields. But a highly skilled specialist in some profession is not *ipso facto* a good administrator. It does not follow that because he possesses technical knowledge he also has administrative knowledge or the talent to communicate and work effectively with others or the ability to give vigorous leadership to a program.

Actually, development administrators can be drawn either from a traditional general administrative service, in which case supplementary training should be given in the unique development requirements of the relevant field, such as agriculture, or from the appropriate technical service, in which case supplementary training should be given in the principles of administration. In other words outstanding persons from both the traditional administrative services or the technical services who have demonstrated their potential capacity for development administration could be selected for special training and subsequent assignment to key posts in the nation-building departments. In the training, special attention should be given to the art of external administration—that is, to the process of encouraging and supporting progressive change in social and economic behavior.

The selection of development administrators should be based upon demonstrated capacity to instill confidence and give leadership in programs involving innovation and decisive action. Such persons will be found in both the administrative and technical services. Once selected, tested and trained, these administrators might be placed in a "development administration cadre" or some similarly named service for assignment and rotation at such places and for such periods of time as the nature of the development program requires.

Development Administration in Staff Colleges and Academies

Most countries are establishing and strengthening their basic institutions for research and training in general administration. Administrative staff colleges, for example, have been established in many countries to provide in-service training and to conduct the research involved in such training for civil servants and general administrative officers. The programs of these colleges, by the addition of development administration, could help train the management analysts of central and state planning agencies and those selected for the administrative posts in nation-building departments.

Instruction in development administration might emphasize:

> The nature and importance of responsibility and accountability within development agencies, the necessity for making delegations and granting authority commensurate with defined responsibility and accountability.
> The nature and process of synthesizing the technical, economic, and administrative aspects of a development program or project.
> The nature and process of innovation and motivation in assisting private and public agencies within their cultural and political settings.
> The process of applying foresight to the management requirements of a development enterprise.
> The unique powers and relationships of public corporations and other agencies established to conduct some parts of a development program.

These subjects are common to the concern of all nation-building departments and to the agencies involved in planning nation-building programs. At the level of generalization involved, the understandings and skills which are required are common to the several departments and indeed would gain for purposes of teaching and research by comparative rather than individual and isolated treatment. The inclusion of such work in development administration in institutions would serve also the in-service needs of general administrators. It would have the advantage of bringing those involved in general administration and those involved in the administration of development to a closer appreciation of one another.

Staff colleges are often limited to senior personnel. Some countries have training agencies for local and middle-level administrators in addition—sometimes called academies. These academies should also add the subjects of development administration to their curricula and extend their service to the personnel of specialized agencies in agriculture, industries, health, and education as well as to administrative officers in the civil service. The need and opportunity for training and research are uniquely great at the academy level because it is the point at which the bureaucracies of the several departments come together at the local level and where they mesh, or should mesh, with instruments of local self-government and development in their varying stages of emergence. It is here that the process of development may be seen at the point of application and therefore where programs of training and research in development administration can be most instructive.

More Managers Are Needed for
Local Enterprise

A third weakness in administration for development is the short supply of managers for those local agencies which provide the essential services for development programs at the final point of application. These are the managers of cooperatives, of utilities, of feed and seed stores, of public works programs, of small industries and malaria eradication and family planning enterprises. The ultimate success of most of the development programs of most countries, whether their execution is through public or private channels, depends upon the integrity and down-to-earth skills of the managers of local enterprises. However, this category of personnel is generally overlooked in plans for training. Most of the many training centers being created for such programs as community development, rural cooperatives, and family planning emphasize the ideological and technical aspects of their agencies' missions and neglect the management and operational phases; they customarily try to cover too much material in too short a time. While many countries are now establishing and strengthening facilities for training executives for public and private enterprise, these facilities are usually too sophisticated in their approach and too few in number to train the personnel of local enterprise in the basic skills of managing the supply and distribution of materials, of accounting, of supervising staff, and of dealing harmoniously with the relevant clientele.

Most countries could accelerate their development programs by facing up to this manpower problem and providing the recruiting and training mechanisms to solve it. The technical institute is a widely found and rapidly growing type of educational institution to train the very large numbers of technical personnel required in an expanding economy—technical personnel for industry and agriculture. These institutes typically offer a two- or three-year program beyond matriculation or the high school diploma. One method of meeting the need for managers in a country is to add to the programs of these technical institutes a solid course in management. Both the technical and the management training would be strengthened by association in the same institute because of the close relationship between the acquisition of skills for application.

Universities and Development Administration

Although universities have a major contribution to make to development administration, many administrative staff colleges, academies, centers, and institutes have been established outside the universities. This suggests that the universities have not in many cases been willing or able to make their contributions. In many countries the universities have only recently begun to orient their programs systematically to development needs. Even when they do so, it will take some time for them to acquire the competence which is required to be of direct and immediate assistance in all fields, of which development administration is one. Recognition of the universities' potential contribution to development is also being given only slowly by some governments which are not accustomed to rely upon academic institutions to meet their needs for training, research, and consultative services. In other countries university teaching and research in "public administration" has been so narrowly defined in terms of the efficient internal management of public agencies that it has not met the needs of "development administration."

However, the universities are the best point at which the interdisciplinary resources of political science, law, management, economics, sociology, and psychology can be brought to bear on problems of research and training in administration for development. They are also the point at which the professional fields of agriculture, engineering, commerce, education, and health can be enriched by the joint study of the process and technique of executing development programs and projects. Many universities offer general courses in public administration. For the most part, however, these courses are offered to undergraduate and graduate students, whereas most training in administration is and should be at the in-service level. Also, these courses tend to deal with internal administrative staff services and specialized techniques of administrative management and are inclined to neglect the concepts and methodology of development administration.

A university which wishes to inaugurate or strengthen a program of research and training in administration which includes development administration might consider the following points:

a. A large part of the training would be of an in-service character, based upon research which heavily emphasizes the means of activating and conducting programs of development.
b. This kind of program needs to be interdisciplinary because it requires the contribution of political science, law, economics, sociology, and psychology as well as management.
c. This kind of program needs to be interprofessional because it involves the activation of programs in such substantive fields of development as agriculture, education, industries, and health.

The training of teachers of management for technical institutes is another university function, distinct from but closely related to the broader program of development administration outlined above. A university which is bent on furthering its country's development would not wish to neglect facilities for training teaching personnel for management as well as for other subjects in technical institutes or equivalent training programs.

Although this note has more or less relevance to most countries and most universities, it has additional relevance to those universities which are or may become involved in technical-assistance projects overseas. When planning and negotiating projects of assistance in planning, education, and administration,

for example, the following needs and opportunities might be considered—
needs and opportunities which perhaps have been overlooked too often in the
past:

a. Assistance to planning agencies, at whatever level, should include
    aid in management as well as in economic analysis.
b. Assistance to administrative staff colleges and academies should
    include development administration, should serve nation-building
    departments, as well as the administrative services, and should be
    related to universities.
c. Assistance to universities should include assistance with in-service
    programs in development administration and with the training of
    teachers of management.
d. Assistance to technical institutes should include assistance with
    management as well as technical subjects.

Summary

In summary, looked at from the point of view of development administration:

1. Country planning processes should include management as well as
    economic analysis.
2. Nation-building departments should develop competence in man-
    agement to match and apply technical competence.
3. A country's educational system should provide for the training of
    large numbers of managers of local enterprise, possibly in technical
    institutes.
4. Training and research institutions in the field of administration
    should enrich their programs by adding the dimension of develop-
    ment administration.
5. Universities should establish programs of development administra-
    tion to meet the needs of planning bodies and nation-building
    departments and to strengthen the programs of autonomous
    training agencies.
6. Universities should also train the teachers of management for
    technical institutes.
7. Universities engaged in technical assistance should incorporate
    development administration in projects involving planning agencies,
    nation-building departments, universities, management training
    agencies, and technical institutes.

The Impulse to Modernize

David C. McClelland

38 Why do some nations "take off" into rapid economic and social growth, while others stand still or decline? The question has always fascinated historians. Why did the Greek city-states, and particularly Athens, begin expanding in the sixth century B.C., until a couple of centuries later they had spread their culture unforgettably across the origins of Western civilization? Why did the landlubberly Romans, defeated again and again in their naval battles with the Carthaginians in the fourth century B.C., persist in finding the money to build new fleets until they finally won? The Romans were in an expansionist phase that not even costly defeats could stop. Or, to move to more modern times, why did one part of North America, first settled by the English, develop rapidly economically, and another part, settled initially by the Spaniards, who thought they had a richer piece of real estate, develop slowly until recently? Why did Japan take off economically in the nineteenth century, but not China? The comparisons can be multiplied endlessly, but the questions are always the same: What impulse produces economic growth and modernization? What is it like, and where has it come from?

Chapter 2 of *Modernization,* edited by Myron Weiner, © 1966 by Basic Books, Inc., Publishers, New York. The author is professor of psychology and chairman of the Department of Social Relations at Harvard University.

Psychologists have made an unexpected contribution to this ancient mystery—unexpected in the sense that they were not working directly on this problem when they made the discovery that ultimately shed some light on the process of economic growth. They were working in the laboratory to isolate what might be called, for the sake of convenience, a certain type of "mental virus," that is to say, a certain way of thinking that was relatively rare but which, when it occurred in an individual, tended to make him behave in a peculiarly energetic way. Following the course of this discovery for a moment will help us understand in more detail what the impulse to modernization is and where it comes from.

The mental virus received the odd name of *n* Ach (short for "need for Achievement") because it was identified in a sample of a person's thoughts by whether the thoughts had to do with "doing something well" or "doing something better" than it had been done before: more efficiently, more quickly, with less labor, with a better result, and so on. For instance, individuals may be asked to tell a story to get samples of their spontaneous thoughts: Individual A tells a story about "a young man who is studying for an exam but finds it hard to concentrate because he keeps thinking about his girl." Individual B tells a story about "a young man who is determined to get a high grade on the examination because he wants to go on to professional school. He is studying hard late at night, is worried that he won't do well enough, and so forth." Individual B clearly has more *n* Ach thoughts than Individual A and gets a higher score. He is more infected by this particular mental virus. The methods of detecting the virus—the presence of such thoughts—are quite accurate and objective. They can even be applied by machine to samples of thoughts from individuals or from the mass media or other forms of popular literature.

It was when samples of popular literature were coded for the presence of *n* Ach over long periods of time that the relation of this mental virus to economic growth began to be apparent. For example, it was found that the *n* Ach content of early Greek literature (seventh to sixth century B.C.) was much higher than for later Greek literature (from the fifth century B.C. on) and that the *n* Ach content of English popular literature in the sixteenth century was much higher than in similar Spanish literature at the same time. Could it be that *n* Ach was the mental virus that made the early Greeks economically so much more successful than the later Greeks and the English in North America so much more economically successful than the Spanish? More striking results followed: the *n* Ach content in England of folk ballads, sea captains' letters, and popular plays was coded every quarter-century roughly from 1400 to 1800, from the Tudor kings to the Industrial Revolution. At the same time, a rough index of *rate* of economic growth was computed from coal imported at London. Twice, a rise in *n* Ach in popular thought was followed about fifty years later by a rapid rise in the rate of economic growth—once around 1525 and again around 1725-1750—and twice declines in *n* Ach were followed by periods of relative economic stagnation.

It began to look as if *n* Ach might be a part of the impulse to economic growth—an identifiable, measurable part. Nowhere did this become more apparent than in a couple of more ambitious studies, described in my book *The Achieving Society,*[1] in which a nation's "infection level" with the *n* Ach virus was estimated by coding the imaginative stories the country used to teach its third- and fourth-grade children to read. These estimates of *n* Ach infection levels turned out to be significantly correlated with subsequent rates of economic growth, taking either a 1929 or a 1950 base line. That is, a country that was high in *n* Ach level in its children's texts around 1925 was more likely to develop rapidly from 1929 to 1950 than one that was low in *n* Ach in 1925. The same result was obtained when 1950 *n* Ach levels were related to rates of economic development in the late nineteen-fifties for a sample of some forty countries. Nations higher in *n* Ach developed faster.

But suppose for the moment that the psychologists have found a way to measure a part of the impulse to do better, to grow economically; just exactly how does the process operate? There has been much theorizing on the subject, but the simplest way to understand and summarize it is to take an actual community and see the impulse at work in concrete ways. Several years ago, it was decided that if the *n* Ach virus was important for economic growth, one ought to try to infect a community with it to see if it would produce the effects so often described retrospectively after a take-off has begun. One could run a controlled experiment, so to speak, in which one community is infected and a comparable one is not, to see if in fact it is a crucial factor in the take-off process. The experimental community chosen was Kakinada, a town of about 100,000 population in Andhra Pradesh, India, on the Bay of Bengal. Previous research had established that businessmen are the best "hosts" for this virus: they are most likely to harbor some *n* Ach already and most likely to benefit concretely from being infected with more of it. So the businessmen of Kakinada were invited to participate in this experiment, which involved a 350-mile trip to Hyderabad, the capital city, to attend a ten-day self-development course at the Small Industries Extension Training Institute designed to increase their *n* Ach and otherwise give them insight into themselves and their work. In all, fifty-two in four groups trained at intervals during 1964.

It would be impossible to describe in any detail the nature of the course. It will have to suffice to say that it was voluntary, residential, intensive, and made use of every scrap of information we had collected about the nature and functioning of *n* Ach in seventeen years of research: that is, the participants learned how to think easily in terms of *n* Ach, to act in lifelike games like a person with high *n* Ach, to reconcile *n* Ach with their self-image and conflicting cultural values, to form a self-perpetuating interest group (The Kakinada Entrepreneurs Association) that would keep the idea alive, and so on.

[1]David C. McClelland, *The Achieving Society* (Princeton, N. J.: O. Van Nostrand Company, 1961).

What is more germane here is the outcome of the course: on the whole, it was fairly successful in implanting the n Ach virus in these businessmen. Based on studies here and elsewhere in India, we have estimated that in any given two-year period about one-third of such a group of businessmen will show signs of *unusual* or *innovative* business activity—for example, start a new product line, do something that results in a big salary raise, or take a course in accounting. After our courses, two-thirds of the businessmen of Kakinada showed such signs of unusual entrepreneurial activity. In other words, the courses had *doubled* the normal or spontaneous rate of innovative activity for India. We obtained the same result following some courses in Bombay.

But the statistics hide the interesting part. What did individual businessmen do? Let us consider some cases.

1. Many of the men paid more attention to business after the course. Some of them had inherited family businesses, like cycle shops, that gave a fair return if entrusted to assistants while the owner relaxed and enjoyed life. A change in n Ach stimulated their attendance at work. They came early, stayed late, paid attention to customers, and found their businesses improving. The view of a businessman as someone driven to work hard by a desire for profits simply had not occurred to many of these businessmen. They had enough money to be comfortable. Why exert themselves? After the course they did, not to make money as such, but because they were determined to do a better job, to make a better showing for themselves, for Kakinada, and for India. Note that a "love of work or industriousness" was not inculcated nor an interest in profit as such. They did not "love" work or money any more afterward than before; they worked longer hours because that seemed the appropriate way for them to do a better job and get more satisfaction out of life.

2. Other men started innovating. Endless discussions can take place as to what constitutes a "real" innovation; but in simple business terms, it means doing something new or different for a particular time and situation. What is an innovation for Kakinada is not an innovation for Bombay. Most of the innovations were extensions of work the man was already doing. A photographer decided to go into lens grinding because spectacles could not be ground locally; a dealer in grains investigated various types of dal mills to find the one that could be used most profitably for the local market; a cycle-shop owner decided to manufacture cycle stands locally; efforts were being made to discover how the Japanese formed the indigenous palmyra fiber into brushes so that the latter could be made locally instead of simply exporting the raw material. One of the leaders of the group egged the others on by pointing out he had been put out of the castor-oil business because someone in Bombay had developed a technique for producing a purer product. These men were intensively active in searching for new ways of doing old things, or at least doing locally what could now be done only at great expense and delay by sending away to the big urban centers. The innovation that people with

high *n* Ach engage in is not real artistic creativity; it is more simply motivated by the desire to find a *better* way of getting a job done.

3. Several men began investing money differently. Most conspicuous was the manager of a local bank who says that before the course he lent money solely in terms of the security provided. Usually this meant putting up land as collateral, which meant in turn that money could be lent only to the wealthy landowners who (*a*) did not need loans and (*b*) were generally not entrepreneurially active anyway and would need to borrow only for some extraordinary expense like a wedding. As a result, his bank did not lend much money and was rather a static affair. After the course, he decided he should lend not only in terms of the security provided but also in terms of the quality of the man requesting the loan and the quality of the project for which he wanted the money. Accepting these two new "revolutionary" loan criteria led him to accept some greater risks than he would have taken by the old standard of absolute security; but so far they had paid off handsomely, not only in greater activity in the commercial loan department but in more deposits, for example. His bank had become a force for promoting change in the town; he had been offered a better job in Calcutta, but had decided to stay to continue helping the community to develop. He had found a great new pride in what he was doing for Kakinada. Note how a small shift in attitude toward doing a better job had a tremendous economic impact locally, when it occurred in a man in a position to make important decisions.

Another type of banker, a traditional moneylender, came to me and asked, "Why should I invest in industry for this town, when I know I can lend out money at 2 per cent a month with absolute security? I might lose my money in industry. Also I have to wait a long time before I get any return at all." Why, indeed, should he invest in business? I should like to hear anyone give an *economic* answer to his question that would persuade him to give up earning 24 per cent a year, payable immediately at 2 per cent a month, with absolute security, in favor of a long-term investment in industry that *might* start paying off in three to five years at perhaps 10 to 15 per cent a year *at best*. Yet this is the basic problem in Kakinada. There are many wealthy families in the community, so there is no lack of capital to finance new ventures. Yet there are simply no financial reasons why the money should be used for development purposes. The prevailing attitude is that money is to be stored and turned into gold for the most part. My answer to this particular moneylender was already implicit in his question. I told him he was going to invest in developing businesses "because he couldn't help it; now that he had been infected with *n* Ach he would simply never respect himself again if he sat around and did nothing, which bored him anyway." In other words, he got an irrational answer, and he is beginning to behave irrationally (in strictly economic terms) by investing in such enterprises as a small papermaking concern that was initiated at one of the courses when he provided the money for an inventor (who had discovered a new papermaking process) and a manager to go into business together.

4. A few started entirely new enterprises. The owner of a small radio shop decided to set up a paint and varnish factory, which appears to be a large and growing concern. He raised the money, hired a chemist who knew the business, acquired a plant, and began operation and sales all within a few months. He exemplified all the characteristics found in the laboratory to be associated with high *n* Ach. He took a calculated risk only after he had carefully researched the situation as to the profits that might be expected in selling various products. He took active personal responsibility for seeing the project through and was doing something new and different that others were not doing. In all this, he was gaining achievement satisfaction—carrying out, by himself, a slightly risky venture that not everyone could handle and assessing concretely his progress in terms of sales and profits. Furthermore, he also started a branch radio shop in which he installed a woman as manager—quite a startling innovation in his town. This illustrates nicely how the restless desire for constant improvement may break up strong social traditions in the search for new ways of doing things better. Here, in part, is why businessmen have tended to be unpopular from Plato's time to the present: they often break with tradition when infected with *n* Ach.

In short, a minor economic revolution appears to be in the making in Kakinada which, if the *n* Ach virus remains firmly implanted, may in time produce a take-off into rapid economic development. Note particularly that what came from the outside was not material aid or technical instruction—all of which the businessmen of Kakinada have or can obtain from the government—but an idea, the motive, the spark, the impulse, that seems to be necessary to set such a process in motion. But note also how far-reaching its effects can be, because these businessmen control most of the institutions that matter in the town: the banks, the cinemas, the shops, the foundries, the mills. Their actions and decisions will vitally affect employment income, levels of demand, the prices farmers get for some of their crops—all aspects of the community's economic life.

But *n* Ach is by no means all there is to modernization. It is only one key ingredient. To balance the picture a little, it is worth describing one other input, not so well researched as yet, but almost certainly as important. *n* Ach by itself is an individual virtue; it does not automatically lead one into socially useful activities or projects. In the absence of conscience, it could lead to success in crime, for example. Yet in the Kakinada study it was apparent from the outset that the men wanted to do something not just for themselves but for Kakinada, for India, and possibly even for the whole world of stagnant communities like theirs. It was only as their "conversion" took on this larger social significance that it really gripped them. Furthermore, they wanted to join together actively: to plan an industrial estate, for example, for the town. Anyone familiar with India knows how limited is this type of cooperative action across caste lines; yet these men were strongly moved by the desire to do something in unison for the common good.

This theme of concern for the common good was also found more often in the children's textbooks (referred to earlier) used by those countries that subsequently developed more rapidly. That is, their stories more frequently described people being influenced by the wishes and needs of others. In the stories for children from more slowly developing countries, on the other hand, there were more references to traditions or habitual ways of doing things. A person in the story did something because it had always been done that way, not because of the needs of some other character. It was almost as if some countries realized that in order to get people thinking about modernization, they had to replace their normal traditionalism with a concern for the welfare of others who might even be strangers to them. Furthermore, it is probably in this way that one may most easily explain the correlations that have been found between investments in health and education and subsequent rates of economic growth. Why should investments in health speed economic growth? Rationally, one might expect they would slow it down by decreasing infant mortality and therefore increasing the population faster than the active portion of the populace could produce food. Yet careful study of the history of some thirty to forty developed countries shows that in nearly every case a minimum public health standard was achieved before the country could break through to a rapid rate of economic growth. One explanation may be that public health care directly reflects man's concern for his fellow man, and this, in turn, is that other key psychological ingredient essential for modernization. Similarly, investments in education, even at the secondary-school level (to say nothing of primary school), do not accelerate rates of economic growth immediately, but they do in the long pull—that is, some twenty years later, when the secondary-school graduates are at the height of their powers. Again, it cannot be immediate economic gain or even n Ach that leads people to start stressing education for their young. It must be this other ingredient, which might be called the "concern for the common welfare of all." Eventually, such a concern pays off economically.

In short, the impulse to modernization in ideal psychological terms seems to consist in part of a personal virtue—n Ach—and in part of a social virtue—interest in the welfare of the generalized other fellow. But where does such an impulse come from? To judge mostly from our knowledge of n Ach, which is more detailed, it is not a racial or environmental characteristic, since clearly a given culture can be infected with the virus at one moment in history and not at another. It does not derive from military conquest. In fact, the reverse seems more often to have been the case: the conquered seem more often to have developed n Ach, perhaps because power was denied them. It does not result from the spread of education, technology, or economic growth; at least, not in a simple way. Here is one example of behavior, which every development economist can illustrate a hundred times over. The government of India decided to help the fishermen of Kakinada by providing them with nylon fishing nets, which were a clear technological improvement. For instance, they required less mending and did not break or tangle easily. The idea was that the fishermen would catch more fish, make more money, and buy more consumer goods, leading the businessmen of Kakinada to expand their business, and so on. The fishermen caught more fish, to be sure; but two unexpected things happened. Some stopped fishing as soon as they had caught as much as they were used to catching (they worked less); and others made more money, which they spent on bootleg liquor (the state is dry). This is probably not the end of the story, but over and over again technological innovation has been shown *not* to produce attitude change. Better fishing nets did not increase the *n* Ach of the fishermen: their desire to do better, to save, to invest. All through the Industrial Revolution on the northern shore of the Mediterranean, the inhabitants on the southern shore simply failed to get really interested in all the technological innovations taking place up north, even though they had plenty of exposure to them. At that time, the Arabs were not much interested in the machine culture the Europeans were developing. On the other hand, improved motives clearly lead to rapid adoption of technological changes, just as our radio-shop owner, after the *n* Ach course, decided to import technicians who could make paint and varnish.

But where do the motive changes come from, if not from obvious happenings "out there" in the environment? If opportunities do not create the impulse to take advantage of them, what does? Sometimes *n* Ach levels are clearly the result of local history. For example, lower-class Negro Americans are generally low in *n* Ach, a fact that seems clearly to be the result of the near-slave status of such groups, particularly in the South, for we know that dependent peoples are usually rewarded for being obedient and responsible rather than self-reliant and achievement-oriented. On the other hand, what is to account for the fact that in Nigeria the Ibo and Yoruba are both highly infected with the *n* Ach virus, while the Hausa are hardly infected at all? Only careful local historical analysis could give the reasons, which are often based on different migratory patterns.

However, one generalization can be made. Zealous, reformist religious groups—or at least the children of the first generation—are nearly always highly infected with *n* Ach. The best-documented case is that of the early days of the Protestant Reformation in the West, which produced an *n* Ach-infected business behavior like that of the Kakinada businessmen just described. But there had been other religious minorities, like the Parsis or the Jains in India, the Jews in many countries, the Zen-oriented Samurai in Japan, or the overseas Indians in East Africa or Asia, that have shown extraordinarily high business success and presumably high *n* Ach. What is characteristic of all these communities is an intense, religiously based feeling that they are *superior* to other people living around them and that in one sense or another they hold the key to salvation, perhaps not only for themselves but for all mankind. Thus the two psychological elements essential to economic success are there: the desire to prove oneself better than others and the need to promote the common good—at least of their minority group, which is often somewhat persecuted. The Communists have managed to create these psychological convictions strongly in their adherents in the present century, and it is therefore not surprising to find that the n Ach infection level rose in Russian and mainland Chinese literature after their Communist revolutions. It is a curious paradox that the Communists have managed to produce rapid economic growth in a country like Russia, not, as they believe, because of socialism, but because of their fanatical belief in its superiority. That is, here, as elsewhere, a conviction in one's superiority has spread the n Ach virus, which is more directly responsible for accelerating the rate of economic growth than the socialist type of economic organization.

Must we, then, encourage people to embrace rigid, doctrinaire, minority convictions so that they may feel superior and develop n Ach? Fortunately, science has provided us with an alternative that is less dangerous to the peace of the world and probably more effective. By direct training, we can apparently infect the people who need it with both n Ach and a sense of public responsibility, just as we did in Kakinada. Science has provided at least some of the information needed by a people who wish, by taking thought, to increase the strength of their own impulse to modernize.

A Hard Look at Development Planning

Albert Waterston

39

In an attempt to determine where, when, how, and why development planning has been successful, a small group within the World Bank has since 1958 been examining data for countries throughout the world—over 100 countries, developed and less developed, in Africa, Asia, Europe, and the Americas, including socialized as well as mixed-economy countries. Out of this great assemblage of raw material, a comprehensive comparative study was published in December 1965.[1] Those who are interested in development planning are now able to consider not only how it *might* be done but how in fact it *has* been done.

While countries about to start planning their development can learn much from the planning experience of other countries, few make use of this experience: this is the first lesson of the study. The reason, in part, is that the experience of other countries is not known; but mostly, it is because countries will not be guided by the experience of other countries, since they consider their own political, economic, and social conditions to be unique.

Yet the study reveals that most countries not only encounter the same planning problems; they make the same mistakes. They frequently confuse

From *Finance and Development,* June 1966. Reprinted by permission. The author is an officer of the International Bank for Reconstruction and Development.

[1]Albert Waterston, *Development Planning: Lessons of Experience* (Baltimore, 1955).

the mere formulation of a plan with planning, fail to take adequate account of what can be done, and hence plan for less than is realistic in others. They have their planners take on extraneous tasks which divert them from planning, set up unsuitable planning machinery, set it up in the wrong places, and so forth.

Plans Versus Planning

Planning has undoubtedly promoted development in many countries. But postwar history reveals that there have been many more failures than successes in carrying out development plans. Indeed among developing nations with some kind of market economy and a sizable private sector, only one or two countries seem to have been consistently successful in carrying out plans.

Except for short periods, most countries have failed to realize even modest income and output targets. What is even more disturbing, the situation seems to be worsening instead of improving. In Asia, where countries' experience with planning has been greater than that in any other region, the rates of growth in the early 1960's fell short not only of targets but even of the growth rates of the 1950's. The situation is not very different in the other continents.

While most countries with development plans have not succeeded in carrying them out, some countries without national development plans or national planning agencies have been developing rapidly. For example, Mexico between 1940 and 1955, when it had no planning agency or plan (and even until now, since in fact it has no plan to which the Government adheres), maintained an annual average rate of growth of 5-6 per cent. Israel, which had no plan before 1961 and still does not have one which the Government follows, has been able to maintain an even higher growth rate. Puerto Rico has become a showcase of development without benefit of a development plan. And among the more developed countries, Germany, without plans, has increased income and output at least as rapidly as France with plans.

It could be contended—and I do contend—that if these countries had had development plans they might have done even better. But the fact is that a country can develop with or without a plan.

A development *plan*, however, is not the same as development *planning*. Planning as a process involves the application of a rational system of choices among feasible courses of investment and other development possibilities based on a consideration of economic and social costs and benefits. These may or may not be put into writing in a "plan." Those who equate a development plan with development planning—and they are many—confuse what should be a product of the planning process with the process itself. A plan can play an important part in the planning process when it makes explicit the basis and rationale for planning policies and measures. But if a plan is prepared before the process has begun in earnest or is unable itself to generate the process, it is likely to have little significance for development.

Importance of the Political Factor

Why are so few development plans carried out? Lack of government support is the prime reason. This lack of support manifests itself in many ways, among them the failure to maintain the discipline implied in plans and the failure to adopt appropriate policies for carrying them out.

Sustained governmental commitment is a *sine qua non* for development; this is cardinal. Pakistan's experience, for example, gives dramatic evidence of the overriding importance of government support. Although the planners of Pakistan's First Five-Year Plan produced a development plan with targets well within the limits set by economic and financial resources, the Plan did not get very far because it did not have help from the Government. Given support from a strong and stable leadership, the Second Five-Year Plan overfulfilled its main targets.

Experience in other countries has been similar. In the nineteenth century, Japan, with fewer resources than Burma, China, India, or Indonesia, nevertheless became the most industrialized country in Asia. In large part, this was because of sustained effort supported by a determined Government. In the twentieth century, the histories of such diverse countries as the Republic of China, Israel, Mexico, Mainland China, the U.S.S.R., and Yugoslavia give ample evidence of the importance to a country's development of firm and continuing support from a stable government.

Economic Incentives

Until the political leaders of a nation become committed to development, the people themselves are unlikely to show much interest. If a country's leaders make development one of their central concerns, experience shows that the people's interest can be obtained. But except on occasion—for example, during or immediately after a war or other catastrophe or upheaval—interest is not likely to be obtained through appeals to their patriotism, devotion to abstract ideals or altruism, or panegyrics about individual or group accomplishments. Direct government controls over economic activity, or threats of imprisonment or other punishment, are also generally ineffective.

The evidence teaches that the best long-run method of getting people to act in such a way as to achieve plan objectives is to make it profitable for them. Where governments have replaced administrative controls by economic incentives, the result has usually been accelerated economic activity. In Pakistan, for example, government officials as well as outside observers agree that administrative restraints hampered industrial growth during the First Plan period. They also agree in attributing the high rate of industrial progress during the Second Plan period largely to the reduction of government controls over imports and foreign exchange and the introduction of a system of tax incentives and bonuses which encouraged businessmen to expand capacity and output. In Pakistan's agriculture, also, the use of incentive prices played an important part in increasing production.

Since the early 1950's, when Yugoslavia replaced centralized controls based on the Soviet model with decentralized management of the economy, that country has evolved a system of economic incentives based on tax, credit, and price policies by which workers and enterprises are rewarded in accordance with their efficiency. These incentives have done so much to raise production that other Eastern European countries, notably Czechoslovakia, but also Poland and Hungary and even the U.S.S.R., are moving toward the Yugoslav system.

In contrast, many governments in countries with mixed economies rely on direct controls and administrative intervention in the private sector in preference to incentives, and often depress their economies as a result. The problem now is how to get the mixed-economy countries to readopt the system of economic incentives that the socialized countries seem to be taking over from them.

Separation of Plan Formulation from Implementation

Economic development is so difficult that, if political leaders are not very deeply committed to it, the plans which they approve are not carried out because no provision is made for carrying them out. Prime Minister Jawaharlal Nehru of India, who as Chairman of the Indian Planning Commission showed an uncommon grasp of planning problems, once pointedly remarked, "We in the Planning Commission and others concerned have grown more experienced and more expert in planning. But the real question is not planning, but implementing the Plan . . . . I fear we are not quite so expert at implementation as at planning. . . ." This statement is notable not only because it recognizes—correctly I think—that the problems of plan implementation are more difficult than those of plan formulation, but also because it distinguishes—wrongly I believe—"planning" from "implementation."

The word "planning" is often used, as it was by Prime Minister Nehru, to refer to the formulation of plans, but not to their implementation. The conceptual separation of "planning" from "implementation" is more than a question of semantics: it is symbolic of an attitude which is unfortunately prevalent among planners. Experience shows that nothing hampers the success of development plans more than the separation of plan formulation from provision for implementation. Planning cannot leave off where plan formulation ends and action to execute a plan begins. Every target must be accompanied by policies and measures which have been devised specifically to fulfill it; otherwise it becomes only a forecast or projection.

The link between the targets of a plan and the policy and other measures required to attain them is one which many planners and political authorities find difficult to grasp. There is frequently a lack of understanding in developing countries that investment is not enough to ensure ¡rowth, that appropriate policy, administrative, and organizational measures are almost always more important for development than is higher investment.

Most plans are prepared in central planning agencies whose officials have little authority over economic policy that is formulated elsewhere. Consequently, one often finds countries where tax, price, monetary, and credit policies impede rather than help to realize plan objectives. For instance, in Pakistan's First Plan, agricultural price policy discouraged farmers from planting crops whose output the Plan sought to increase.

Discounting Overambitious Plan Targets

A planner may not be able to do much about a government's administrative inefficiency and its lack of political commitment or will to develop. But if in preparing his plans he ignores these critical factors, which together constitute the main limitations on the ability of most less developed countries to realize their economic possibilities, he ends up by separating his activities and the plans he formulates from the real world that has its being outside of national planning agencies.

This is precisely what happens in many less developed countries. National development plans are based on a country's economic potentialities or its needs as determined by population growth, and are little related to the country's administrative capacity, or to the government's will, to carry them out. In these countries, plans are not so much blueprints as hortatory instruments. It can hardly be surprising, therefore, that most planning aims are never achieved. Because the aims are related to what is possible or desirable, with little regard to what is likely, they are usually set so unrealistically high that they never have a chance. For instance, in Bolivia's Ten-Year Development Plan for 1962-71, the target of average annual increases of 9.2 per cent in gross national product in the first five years may have been economically possible, but it was far beyond the country's administrative and political capacities. The Government wisely abandoned it as overambitious.

If planners are to set realistic targets in their plans, they must somehow find means to *measure* administrative inadequacy and the lack of political will to develop, so that they can "discount" the unduly optimistic targets set when plans are formulated solely on the basis of economic potentiality. This sounds difficult, but it is not impossible. For example, it is possible to quantify the cost of administrative inefficiency, in terms of money and time, on the basis of past discrepancies between original estimates and actual performance in projects and programs. By deflating the estimates by a factor based on past errors, such adjustments can go a long way toward closing the gap between promise and performance.

Similarly, it is possible to quantify a country's political will to develop if planners set up for each major area of policy (e.g., taxation, credit, investment, money, and incomes) feasible alternatives, including the effects of each on development, from which political authorities can make a choice before a plan is drafted. In the process of selecting the alternatives which best suit them, the political authorities will be supplying specific information about the extent to which they are prepared to adopt policies and other measures for furthering development which, collectively, can be said to constitute a veritable measure of their "will to develop."

If the three basic elements that enter into the planning process—economic potential, administrative capacity, and political will to develop—are all taken into account in formulating plans, planning aims are bound to be more in line with a country's real capacity to achieve its economic potentialities.

The Projects Problem

The current artificial separation between the formulation and implementation of plans accounts for the failure of planners, concentrating as they do on aggregative planning, to recognize soon enough that the weakness in most developing countries is not the lack of an elegantly integrated comprehensive plan based on economic potentialities but the lack of well-planned individual projects that can really be carried out. For example, after 18 months of work on Bolivia's Ten-Year Plan, the planners found themselves in the embarrassing position of conceding that "the principal deficiency that will be noted in the formulation of the present Plan is the small number of specific investment projects . . ."[2] needed to execute it. Similar statements can be found in the plans of many other countries.

Because it usually takes several years to identify and prepare a sufficiently large number of good projects needed to implement a plan, it is too late for planners to become concerned about them after a plan has been prepared or even when it is being formulated. Unless preinvestment and investment studies of projects for implementing a comprehensive plan are sufficiently advanced, it does little good to prepare such a plan. Yet all too often this is exactly what happens. Few projects are carefully worked out before the work of implementing them begins. As a result, many projects and programs are not carried out at reasonable cost and in reasonable periods of time. Attempts to reduce the time spent in preparing projects frequently result in the choice of low-yield projects; substantially increased costs and delayed construction because of technical or other problems that were not foreseen; poor phasing of raw material, transport, staffing, or other requirements; failure to provide

[2]Junta Nacional de Planeamiento, *Plan Nacional de Desarrollo Económico y Social, 1962-1971: Resumen* (La Paz, Bolivia, 1961), p. 24. (Author's translation)

adequate financing; shoddy construction; and inability to make full use of completed projects.

Only a few of the less developed countries are fully aware of the need for selecting soundly conceived projects with potentially high yields, defining their scope with clarity, estimating their national currency and foreign exchange requirements with a sufficient degree of accuracy, and laying down realistic schedules for their execution; even fewer have the administrative capacity and the political will to cope with these needs and, especially, to carry out the projects in accordance with carefully developed programs of action.

Changing the Planning Mix

One reasonable conclusion to be drawn from experience is that it may be desirable to reverse the usual proportions of the planning mix. Planners have almost invariably concentrated on aggregative planning rather than on the proper preparation and execution of projects, but experience shows that countries with well-prepared projects coordinated by sound budgetary procedures and controls can dispense with comprehensive plans, at least for a time, and still maintain high rates of growth. It seems clear, therefore, that improvements in project preparation and budgetary controls, where needed, are at least as urgent as the preparation of aggregative plans.

These findings obviously have an important bearing on the sequence in which planning problems ought to be attacked. If the planning process is to be realistic, planners must not start, as they often do, with a series of theoretical abstractions of planning as it *ought* to be, and they must not try to force these ideas in an inhospitable environment where governments are unstable, not genuinely committed to development, or otherwise unready for aggregative planning. Instead, while not forgetting the long-run objectives that theory demonstrates to be desirable, they must—at least at first—attune their plans to "things as they are."

Improving Planning Organization

Since effective projects should be prepared in the agencies that will actually carry them through, the organization of programing units in these agencies should get much higher priority than it now has in many developing countries, perhaps even higher than central planning agencies. Improved budget offices also may be more important in these countries than improved central planning agencies.

Changing Technical Assistance

The type of technical assistance needed for preparing technically and economically sound projects, and executing and operating them, differs from the type of technical assistance that has been supplied for aggregative or comprehensive planning. Aggregative planning is a business for economists who need only a modest knowledge of agricultural and industrial techniques; but project preparation requires engineers, agronomists, and other technicians, including some who are capable. of translating financial costs and benefits into economic costs and benefits.

Because the preparation, execution, and operation of projects involve many people in a government, it is becoming imperative that foreign technical assistance be largely made up of "demonstrators" rather than "doers." Doers can be used for a few special purposes, but only demonstrators working on the job with groups of government employees actually engaged in project preparation and execution can hope to train in a reasonable period the large numbers of workers who must become involved in project preparation, execution, and operation.

What I have written is not an attack on comprehensive planning. Ideally, planning should be undertaken "from the top down" as well as "from the bottom up." But experience reveals that in most countries planners begin with the first and rarely get around to the second. Since planning from the bottom up is essential to development, while planning from the top down is not, it seems sensible for a country to begin with the preparation of sound projects and sector programs and, with these as a foundation, to advance toward comprehensive planning as rapidly as circumstances permit.

Planning: The Savings Gap and the Foreign Exchange Gap

Douglas S. Paauw
Forrest E. Cookson

40

Development planning at the *aggregate* level is frequently based on a simple national income accounting framework. One common framework comprises the following aggregate variables: total resources available (Y), national income (X), consumption (C), investment (I), domestic savings (S), imports (M), exports (E), and an import surplus or foreign capital (D). These variables form a system of national income accounting as defined by four accounting equations:

$$Y = C + I + E \quad \text{(aggregate demand for resources)} \tag{1.1a}$$
$$Y = X + M \quad \text{(aggregate supply of resources)} \tag{1.1b}$$
$$M = E + D \quad \text{(foreign exchange condition)} \tag{1.1c}$$
$$X = C + S \quad \text{(disposition of income)} \tag{1.1d}$$

Such a system is pictured in Figure 1, the arrows designating the direction of monetary flows.

From *Planning Capital Inflows for Southeast Asia*, published by the Center for Development Planning, Planning Methods Series No. 3, National Planning Association. Reprinted by permission. The authors are both attached to the National Planning Association.

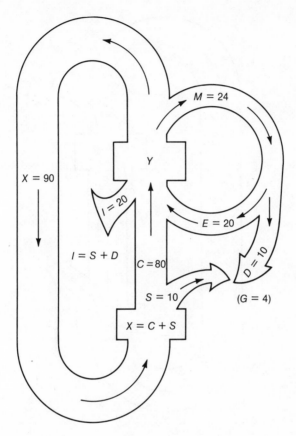

Figure 1

From the equations in (1.1) it is readily deduced that:

$$I = S + D \qquad (1.2a)$$
$$D = I - S \qquad (1.2b)$$

i.e., total investment (I) is financed by domestic savings (S) or foreign capital (D). In the form of (1.2b), the right-hand term $(I - S)$ defines a savings gap; i.e., the excess of investment over domestic savings.

Moreover, we know from equation (1.1c) that:

$$D = M - E \qquad (1.2c)$$

the right-hand term now defining D as a foreign exchange gap, i.e., the excess of imports over exports.

These accounting relations logically imply equality of the magnitude of the two gaps—the savings gap and the foreign exchange gap. Thus, ideally this relationship must be satisfied if consistent economic planning is to be undertaken within this framework. Consistency would seem to imply no divergence between the two gaps.

The divergence in the values of the two gaps arises from the procedures employed for solving practical planning problems. The tendency of planners

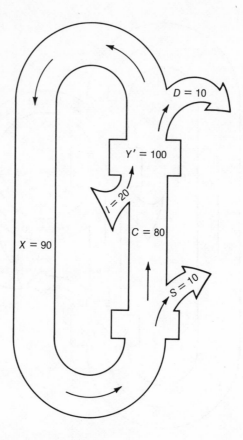

Figure 2

to assume, implicitly or otherwise, that these gaps diverge emphasizes the need for exploring the problem as an issue of both methodology and practical planning. The application of practical methods to estimate the gaps for planning purposes, in fact, amounts to an approximation of "ideal" procedures. Yet it is precisely in the application of these methods of approximation that the apparent inconsistency between the ideal and actual procedure arises. We will elaborate on this problem by examining the essence of the practical methods employed in order to evaluate these procedures from the viewpoints of methodology and policy.

National Income Accounting Framework

We begin by accepting the national income accounting framework summarized in (1.1). By further aggregation, we establish a still simpler national income accounting system, as shown in Figure 2. The simple framework in this diagram may be summarized in the following system of accounting equations:

$$Y' = C + I \tag{1.3a}$$
$$Y' = X + D \tag{1.3b}$$
$$X = C + S \tag{1.3c}$$

As compared with the more detailed system in equation (1.1) and Figure 1, this system singles out one major aspect, the *overall adequacy of resources* to cover investment and consumption demand. From equations (1.3) we can deduce:

$$I = D + S \tag{1.4a}$$

or

$$D = I - S \tag{1.4b}$$

As in equation (1.2b), the right-hand term of equation (1.4b) may be viewed as the savings gap, as filled by external resources (D).

The problem of the foreign capital inflows required to maintain a specified per capita income target at this level of aggregation was analyzed in an earlier paper. By employing the per capita marginal savings ratio (*PMSR*) model developed in that paper, the gap between required investment and domestic savings (the "savings gap") is calculated.

This allows us to determine overall resource availability according to the equations in (1.3), yielding values for all the basic parameters in this system.

We now shift our attention back to the more "complete" national income accounting system presented in the equations in (1.1) and Figure 1, transferring the parameter values, as determined above, to this system. The parameters X, I, C, S, and D have been determined, while Y, M, and E are still undetermined. They must be determined subject to the constraints already derived, i.e., the values of X, I, C, S, and D. This poses the aspect of the problem of disaggregation on which discussion in this study is focused.

The Disaggregation Problem

In approaching this disaggregative aspect of the problem, we note that although there are three remaining undetermined variables (M, E, Y), the necessity of consistency in accounting allows only one degree of freedom. When the value of any of three remaining variables is obtained, the other two are automatically determined. This condition presents us with three choices:

1. Postulation of an import demand condition (emphasizing, for instance, the complementarity of imported goods on both current and capital account in the production process). This will give us the value of M, and the values of E and Y will then be determined residually.
2. Postulation of exogenously determined export values, which will give us E and yield the values of M and Y residually.
3. Postulation of Y, thus determining M and E.[1]

---

[1]We mention this possibility for purposes of mathematical completeness. In practical planning situations, it is unlikely to be as useful as postulating (1) or (2).

Hence, as long as one condition is postulated either as a behavioristic assumption or exogenously, we confront no problem. The problem arises when, for planning purposes, it appears desirable to emphasize more than one of the three conditions listed above. For example, if we emphasize both (1) and (2) above, we are likely to find not only that the values of M and E are different but also that this difference, the *foreign exchange gap* $(G = M - E)$, has another value from that of the savings gap (D), determined at the higher level of aggregation. Clearly, we have precipitated this problem by overdeterminancy when we postulated two of the conditions above although only one was required for a consistent solution.

As an illustration of this procedure, we determine the numerical values at the aggregate level (as indicated in Figure 2) to be $Y' = 100$, $C = 80$, $I = 20$, $S = 10$, and $D = 10$. With the exception of Y', these values are transferred into Figure 1 and, thus, partially determine the system pictured in that diagram.

Suppose now, at the second stage of planning, we make the following independent assumptions:

1. The value of exports is independently projected to be 20;
2. The value of imports, based on estimation of imports required on both current and capital account, is 24.

When these latter numbers are transferred into the system in Figure 1, we find that the value of G is determined as 4, which differs from the value of D $(= 10)$. Hence, a divergence $(= 6)$ occurs between the values of G, the foreign exchange gap, and D, the savings gap. Correspondingly, we find a similar difference between the values of total demand $(I + C + E = 120)$ and total supply $(X + M = 114)$.[2]

The time paths of the diverging gaps may be calculated, and, as an example, we show one possibility of diverging time paths of the two gaps in Figure 3.

To pose the planning problem on which we focus, we add to Figure 3 the projected time path of the expected inflow of foreign capital (A). We emphasize that the addition of this new parameter is exogenous, based on an independent estimate of "likely" capital inflow. It is not explicitly recognized within the first model discussed below (the Fei-Paauw model), which estimates *required* foreign capital inflows, a concept quite different from *likely* or anticipated foreign capital inflows.

In the example shown in Figure 3, we perceive the planning problem as one of reconciling the two gaps—D (the savings gap) and G (the foreign exchange gap)—at some level consistent with the anticipated availability of foreign capital and domestic planning of parameters, including the target growth rate. Positing the estimated inflow of foreign capital at the level A in Figure 3, the savings (overall resource availability) condition required to achieve the target

[2]Methodologically, we see that the consistent national income accounting framework causes the discrepancy between the values of the foreign exchange gap and the savings gap to produce an equivalent discrepancy between the total demand for resources $(I + C + E)$ and the total supply of resources $(X + M)$.

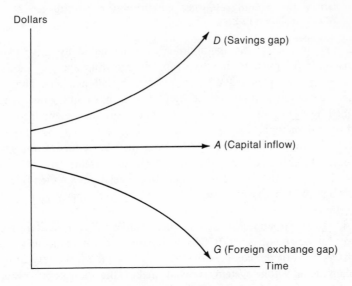

Figure 3.   Hypothetical Time Paths of
Savings Gap, Foreign Exchange Gap,
and Anticipated Capital Inflow

growth rate will not be satisfied although the foreign exchange condition (technical complementarity between foreign and domestic resources) will be more than satisfied. This situation is similar to the case described in the numerical example above, inasmuch as the savings gap is larger than the foreign exchange gap.

The possible cases that may emerge in this analytical framework may be reduced to four, depending on whether D is above G or vice versa and on the position of A relative to D and G.[3] These cases may be listed as:

1. A level of foreign capital inflow adequate to satisfy both the overall resources condition (i.e., to fill gap D) and the technical complementarity condition (i.e., to fill gap G);
2. A level of foreign capital inflow inadequate to meet either the overall resource condition (i.e., to fill gap D) or the technical complementarity condition (i.e., to fill gap G);
3. A level of foreign capital inflow adequate to satisfy the overall resources condition (i.e., to fill gap D), but inadequate to satisfy the technical complementarity condition (i.e., to fill gap G);
4. A level of foreign capital inflow adequate to satisfy the technical complementarity condition (i.e., to fill gap G), but inadequate to

[3]The relative positions of D, G, and A may assume the following possible orders:

	(1)		(2)		(3)	(4)
	(a)	(b)	(a)	(b)		
	A	A	G	D	G	D
	G	D	D	G	A	A
	D	G	A	A	D	G

satisfy the overall resources condition (i.e., to fill gap D)–the situation shown in Figure 3.

We now return to the methodological issue raised by this "two gap" approach. It is apparent that two gaps emerge from applying methods of approximation in planning used in practice by all planners. The national income accounting system defined by (1.1) and shown in Figure 1 is actually obtained by aggregating a more detailed micro system, e.g., by incorporating input-output relationships. Hence, the acceptance of (1.1) as a *preliminary* framework for planning amounts to what may be termed a *disaggregative* approach. In this approach, the overall resource framework of (1.1) and Figure 1 is estimated first. The detailed micro relations are then filled in at a later stage, within the constraints imposed by preliminary planning at the aggregate level.

A disaggregative approach of this kind is not an ideal procedure from the theoretical viewpoint, since it fails to incorporate, simultaneously and with consistency, all of the complexities of the problem. Yet the very complexity of planning a whole system is what makes the disaggregative approach essential as a practical planning device. We note, however, that the disaggregative approach offers a number of practical advantages. It allows the planner to rely on the skills of specialists in parts of the total problem. It also emphasizes to the planner the problem of consistency itself. We will see later that policy decisions are sharply posed to bring consistency to the results of the disaggregative approach. It is our contention that conscious policy decisions which make planning objectives feasible are essential to good planning. Consistency forced by a model, without making the required policy decisions explicit, is likely to do more harm than good to the realization of plan objectives.

In this approach, however, errors and gaps in the system are inevitable. The elimination of these discrepancies calls for adjustment and compromise among the relationships in the system. We must accept the necessity of relying on judgment to make adjustments needed to obtain consistency. Such judgment will be based on extra-model considerations, and in this aspect of planning it must be regarded as more of an art than a precise science.

Reconciliation of Discrepancies

The problem of divergence between the magnitude of the savings gap and the foreign exchange gap, therefore, is an example of *ex ante* inconsistency arising from the application of the disaggregative approach. The divergence emerges from this approach itself; but in resolving the problem and moving toward consistency, planning is kept realistic. Reconciliation of the discrepancies brings the results of specialized research together and forces the planner to resolve the problem in terms of the practical policy constraints under which he operates. Reconciliation requires that some or all of the behavioral or exogenous postulations must be violated. The obvious over-determinancy of the system implies that at least some of these assumptions must be changed.

It is important to note that this analysis cannot be dynamic in the full sense of that word. It must be carried out for specific target years in the future; i.e., it is *projective* in nature. Although the two components of the analysis used in this paper (the savings model and the foreign exchange model) are dynamic, there is no consistent transition growth path leading to the target.

We view these problems as inevitable to establishing consistency between an overall planning framework and its component parts—a problem implicit in moving beyond an aggregate framework to specific aspects of the planning problem by disaggregation. In fact, we believe the point can be made even more strongly. In the process of recognizing these inconsistencies and resolving them, important policy issues are placed before the planner in sharp focus, and the points in the process at which judgment must be introduced are clarified. Judgment is required to recommend which behavioral and exogenous relationships can be affected by policy actions and how much specific initial forces can be altered to achieve a compromise solution where the gaps diverge. There is every advantage to facing these problems consciously as policy issues on which judgment must be brought to bear rather than as problems of forcing the gaps into *a priori* coincidence by formal, possibly unrealistic, assumptions.

The policy implications of this approach, therefore, relate to the problem of making the necessary compromises among the underlying forces in specific situations in order to reconcile the gaps at one planned level. . . .

The Impact of Underdevelopment on Economic Planning

Andrew M. Watson
Joel B. Dirlan

41

In this section we shall focus attention on certain key shortages, or constraints, which tend to defeat the planner's efforts and to inhibit growth. The existence of these shortages in less developed regions has been noted by other writers, but only in passing. In most cases, they have been regarded—wrongly—as peripheral aberrations, temporary and capable of being surmounted if planners are aware of them, and if a "sense of crisis" is present. In reality, they are the essence of underdevelopment.[1]

Reprinted by permission of the publishers from Andrew M. Watson and Joel B. Dirlan, *The Quarterly Journal of Economics.* Cambridge, Mass.: Harvard University Press, copyright 1965 by the President and Fellows of Harvard College. The authors are at the University of Toronto and the University of Rhode Island, respectively.

[1] See E. Hagen, *Planning Economic Development,* Irwin, 1963, p. 362. Hagen quite carefully pulls together what he calls the "difficulties" revealed by his case studies, but does not appear to regard them as much more than incidental obstacles, mostly capable of being overcome by good "planning organization" (principles for which he briefly lists in *ibid.,* pp. 333-35). In his view they do not seem to call for shrinking the area of the economy to be planned or lowering targets. On the contrary, he proposes that in spite of their conspicuous success in developing their economies, the Mexicans and Japanese should change to hortatory, comprehensive development programs. *Ibid.,* p. 360. (cont.)

A. Lack of Information

Under this heading may be included a multitude of evils, one or other of which will dog the planner all along the way—in preparing the plan, in implementing it, and in revising it through its lifetime. Most crucial, at the outset, will be the lack of statistics. Even the most advanced countries may lack many of the statistical series which planners require, but the shortage is much more serious in an underdeveloped nation: some countries attempt comprehensive plans without even tolerably reliable estimates of population or national income, and no information on their past rates of growth. Other fundamental series, concerning cost of living, agricultural prices, indebtedness, land tenure, and so on, will almost certainly be lacking.[2] On occasion, data in the possession of other agencies will not be furnished to the planners.

In searching for other kinds of information the planner will find that library facilities are inadequate and works he wishes to consult cannot be obtained. This is one of several reasons why there is so little effective pooling of the experience of underdeveloped countries with similar problems. Even reports made by visiting experts a few years earlier may have vanished. Files and other records may have been lost. When projects get under way, the planner may be in the dark about their progress, there being no regular machinery for collecting and feeding back information.[3]

B. Lack of Suitable Projects Ready
for Implementation

Perhaps a special case of the lack of information, this constraint deserves special mention on account of its importance. Because enough projects have

---

Walinsky, in his full-dress review of the experience of the Nathan consultants in Burma (*Economic Development in Burma*), quotes with approval the significant warning of the report which preceded the participation of the consultants in the planning process: "Success of the development program hinges more on this (adequate manpower) than any other single factor." Yet after hundreds of pages of confirmation of this very point, showing the impossibility of implementing a plan in the face of incompetence, dogmatism and corruption, he manages to remain optimistic about what can be done: "To a far greater extent than in the more advanced democratic societies, governments in underdeveloped countries must take major responsibility for initiating and carrying through accelerated economic development." *Ibid.*, p. 586.

[2] A notorious example is the Nigerian population figure. After the first "complete" census, there was no agreement on whether the population was 41.4 or 53.2 million. See W.G. Stolper, "Economic Development in Nigeria," *Journal of Economic History*, XXIII (Dec. 1963), 396. The Third Indian Plan was severely distorted by the planners' ignorance, until very late in the planning process, of the rapid increase in population that had taken place during the period of the Second Plan. The latest Turkish plan, according to one observer, is a workmanlike job, complete with intersectoral input-output tables. But it has one defect: the underlying statistics are either unreliable or absent. See J.K. Eastham, "The Turkish Development Plan: The First Five Years," *Economic Journal*, LXXIV (Mar. 1964), 132-36.

[3] According to Lewis, projections of specific industry growth used in the Indian Third Five-Year Plan were not based on actual accomplishments under the Second Five-Year Plan. Malenbaum states that in India material for studying outputs and operational behavior is "elusive at best."

not been prepared in sufficient detail, much of the time and the staff of the planning division will be occupied in working up more projects. Nevertheless, the plan, when it emerges, may be less specific than desired, and it may include some projects of questionable value merely because these *had* been prepared in detail.

In certain areas, the plan may have to be kept deliberately vague, since the desirable course of action will not be known until the results of a feasibility study or a resource survey are available; estimating the required investment or setting goals for output is not possible in such areas, and another element of uncertainty creeps into the whole plan. Again, if additional funds for development become available, and for budgetary reasons have to be appropriated quickly, it will sometimes be discovered that no suitable projects are ready. The funds may go begging, or will be applied to hastily conceived schemes on which they and other scarce resources are wasted.

C. Lack of Qualified Personnel

The lack of skilled human resources is generally more serious than any other resource lack, and is at the root of all the other main shortages characteristic of underdevelopment. To glimpse its importance, we need only imagine the effect of transferring populations from developed to underdeveloped nations.

High administrative officials attend to petty details. This practice occurs partly because of a shortage of trained and trustworthy assistants, and partly because of an inability to delegate power. The consequence is a minor vicious circle: underlings are not trained to accept responsibility, and their superiors neglect the most important work.[4] The few able people at the lower levels of the civil service are often less effective than they could be, owing to incompetent superiors or colleagues, or because of unwieldy procedures (sometimes left over from colonial days).

The results are everywhere apparent. Schedules for such relatively simple tasks as committee reports cannot be followed. Projects do not produce according to plan. The potential output of a mine, for instance, cannot be realized, because the acceleration of production presents a series of interrelated problems that defy solution. (These may range from the unwarranted interference of directors in matters of office routine to the selection of new sites for exploitation.) Similarly, a potential increase in agricultural output from irrigation remains potential, because, even if the necessary construction is completed, it is a difficult and time-consuming

[4]Cf. Olsen and Rasmussen, in Hagen, *op. cit.*, p. 237. The Burmese Economic and Social Board, whose membership included ministers concerned with economic activities, did not meet frequently, did not delegate responsibility, and was so concerned with the operating function that it could not plan development, or even review and appraise performance. A board of enquiry to improve implementation was composed of key civil servants who already had full-time jobs.

process to work out and get accepted the most desirable live-stock and cropping patterns.[5]

Large-scale projects, unless carried out by foreign personnel, can seldom be incorporated with assurance in a plan. This fact is sometimes temporarily obscured by the letting of major construction projects to foreign concerns, and by the underplaying of projects which make heavy demands on local administrative talent. All too often, the really difficult, *but strategic*, programs which promise to establish bases for continuing growth —community development, the organization of agricultural cooperatives, the creation of agricultural extension and research stations in effective concert, the training of technicians and administrators, and the like—are sacrificed to projects such as highways and dams that can be built under contract with foreign firms.[6]

Attempts to move ahead intensify shortages in personnel. Agencies expand and proliferate, there are frequent changes in jobs, and people shift so often that they fail to acquire a knowledge of their jobs. Able civil servants move up to head ministries, and with a change in the party in power move out of government, never to return (since they cannot re-enter as juniors). Changes in foreign personnel, who are frequently in key positions, aggravate the problem.[7] Foreigners who first conceive the ideas for programs are seldom around when they finally take shape; and those who start projects off have been posted thousands of miles away by the time they are in full-scale operation (if the project is not abandoned before this point has been reached). Since the chances are that one will not be around to be taxed with their failure, there is a temptation to plump for schemes on very short-run grounds.

The "solutions" which have been devised for overcoming shortages of personnel have not been conspicuous for their success; each tactic, if it

[5]In northeast Brazil the construction of numerous large dams over a period of years has been unattended by the development of agriculture. See the summary in Hirschman. In Iraq, according to one well-informed writer, the building of irrigation works became an end in itself, with little attention being paid to subsequent agricultural development. See M. Ionides, *Divide and Lose* (London: Geoffrey Bles, 1960), Chap. 15.

[6]The problem of establishing an effective community development project is perhaps typical. In most countries where the program has been attempted, it has been impossible to train a sufficient number of dedicated and capable persons, to keep them in the villages, and to overcome the hostility of the older and more specialized branches of the civil service to what is regarded as encroachment. See, e.g., H. Tinker, "The Village in the Framework of Development," in R. Brabanti and J. Spengler, *Administration and Economic Development in India* (Durham: Duke University Press, 1963), pp. 94-133.

[7]Even staunch supporters of the U.S. foreign-aid program have been disturbed by the rapid turnover of personnel. See *Personnel Administration and Operations of Agency for International Development. Report of Senator Gale W. McGee*, Senate Doc. No. 57, 88th Congress, 2d Session (1963), *passim*. According to Hubert Humphrey, the job cannot be done with two-year personnel who leave the program six months after they have learned their job. "Two-thirds of the loan officers experienced in Latin-American affairs who were with the Development Loan Fund at the time it was absorbed into AID in November, 1961, have now left the Agency and those who left were among the ablest. . . ." *A Report on the Alliance for Progress,* 1963, Senate Doc. No. 13, 88th Congress, 1st Session (1963), p. 11.

does not fail utterly, at least has serious drawbacks. In the case of projects which require prolonged experience of local conditions, contracting projects or parts of projects to foreign firms adds greatly to the cost without ensuring that the work will be well done. When the foreigners withdraw on the expiration of their contract, the residue of local training will be minimal and, after the initial thrust by the foreigners, local follow-through may not be forthcoming. The importation of foreign experts to work alongside local personnel may overcome some of these disadvantages, but much will depend on the quality of these "experts" and the duration of their stay.[8] Those whose expertise is confined to a knowledge of how things are done in an advanced country, those who do not easily adapt themselves to the conditions of the underdeveloped country, and those who stay only a short time will contribute little. Those who stay only long enough to make recommendations, and do not remain to see to the establishment of an organization to implement these recommendations, will not have much effect, even where there existed a prior determination to carry out reform. On the other hand, if experts *are* able to get results, there are other dangers: lacking a sense of economic timing, they may try to do too much, and draw too much money and manpower into their own sphere. Other areas, perhaps even more important, but lacking an expert, may be neglected.

Nor, in our opinion, is the training of local personnel abroad (known in the trade as the "Holiday on Ice") often a satisfactory solution.[9] Inevitably, a trip abroad is regarded as a prize in itself: it is a chance to leave a dirty, hot, culturally backward area for New York, London, or Paris, with the additional lure of a faintly possible permanent residence abroad. Selection is frequently made on the basis of the political connections of the candidates, not their ability. The people chosen, if competent, are desperately needed on the job. It seems unlikely that the marginal social benefit of a Ph.D. for a geologist with a M.A. who knows the local conditions, exceeds the cost of waiting another two years to locate water-bearing strata for 100 villages. But U.S. AID officials do not make their selections on such bases. Very often, the training received is of little value in the context of the underdeveloped nation and may actually disorient the trainee. Or if the training has some application, it may not be used: on his return the trainee is given another job, either through bureaucratic inefficiency or jealousy.[10]

[8]To give only one example, the French government has found that newly independent nations in what was formerly French Africa are unwilling to accept technicians who had African experience during the colonial period. It has therefore been necessary to send experts with no previous African experience, and the result, according to one writer, has been the repetition of many old mistakes. See E. Bonnefous, *Les milliards qui s'envolent* (Paris: Fayard 1963), p. 188. See also Dudley Seers' "Why Visiting Economists Fail," *Journal of Political Economy,* LXX (Aug. 1962), 325-38, which aptly pinpoints the difficulties facing foreign advisers and experts.

[9]Cf. R. Brabanti, "Reflections on Bureaucratic Reform in India," in Brabanti and Spengler, *op. cit.,* pp. 50 and 59.

[10]The writers are acquainted with an individual who was regarded as the most highly trained tannery manager in the world. He had studied for several years in the United

In most cases, it seems best to train on the job, with whatever local teachers can be recruited and foreigners where they are really needed. Such training can sometimes be effectively supplemented by short study trips to countries which are just one notch up the scale in development and have made conspicuous progress with the very problems with which the trainee will be dealing. Short-term, practically oriented courses in regional training centers can also yield good results, but until now this kind of training (which for many kinds of work could be organized at a fraction of the cost of scholarships to the United States) has been little used.[11]

Regardless of what "solutions" are used, however, only limited progress can be expected in overcoming this crucial shortage.[12] While a country is underdeveloped, the shortage of competent personnel will remain a persistent, hard-core problem to which all attempts to accelerate growth will be vulnerable. This obstacle will not disappear until the larger problem, of which it is a part, has been solved.

Conclusion: The Orientation of Planning

Economic, administrative, and statistical underdevelopment constitutes a syndrome, and as development proceeds these symptoms will clear up. While a country remains in an underdeveloped condition, however, the difficulties which confront the planner—the ideological climate, organizational weaknesses, the lack of information and projects, and the shortage of competent personnel—are not merely symptoms of the underlying condition: *they are also crucial obstacles to changing that condition.* Indeed, we venture to suggest that in the great majority of underdeveloped nations today the operative constraints on development are not, as is widely held, the shortage of capital or foreign exchange or natural resources, but rather these other obstacles. It is they which slow down the rate of growth and limit the capacity to absorb increments in foreign aid. And it is they which should be the focus of the planner's attention.

We are led to conclude that in most underdeveloped nations the orientation of planning—and of all attempts to develop economically—should be changed so that a far greater part of the total development effort

---

States, Germany, France, England and Jugoslavia, while waiting for a tannery to be approved, financed and built. When it was finally completed and ready to go into production, he was fired by the directors in a trivial dispute. In another case the director of an agricultural research station and his chief assistant, both highly competent men with M.A.'s, were sent to the United States for a three-year Ph.D. program. The work of the station, which had previously been the only station carrying out important research, came to a standstill.

[11] A good example of a successful venture of this kind is the British Forestry Training Centre in Cyprus to which civil servants from a number of Eastern Mediterranean countries are sent for short-term courses. Since the conditions in Cyprus, unlike those found in most parts of the United States, are similar to those in the trainee's homeland, the chances that the training will be transferable are greater.

[12] It cannot be overcome simply by more education *per se.* Middle Eastern countries are today afflicted by unemployment of high school and university graduates who have concentrated on arts courses.

is directed to removing, or at least weakening, these constraints. In particular, we feel that projects of the following kinds merit far more attention: the development of essential statistical series and the making of reasonable projections; the survey of essential resources such as minerals, ground water and soils; the study, evaluation and, where suitable, detailed programming of the widest possible range of projects (including those for legal, fiscal and administrative reform); and, *above all*, the development of a more enlightened and capable labor force at all levels, for both the government and the private sectors. Tall orders these, which cannot be filled overnight. But everything suggests that in most underdeveloped nations these are the areas where the long-term yields from investment will be greatest. Without a strenuous effort in this direction, it will be on precisely these obstacles that efforts to speed up growth will founder.[13]

What cannot be easily removed, however, must be lived with and should be taken into full account. As long as these *are* the operative constraints on growth, it is a costly error to pretend that they do not exist. Effective planning will tailor the program of development to achieve the most that is possible within the limitations beyond the planner's control. Broadly speaking, this means scaling down the program for the public sector so that the energies of capable civil servants are not spread too thinly over a large number of projects, but rather concentrated on essential projects which *collectively* are both strategic and within the realm of the possible.

Ordinarily, there will be a few significant outlets for funds which no one doubts will be beneficial, given the population and geography, no matter what is to be the ultimate industrial pattern: the linking of portions of infrastructure, such as highways and ports; basic water supply; loans to new business ventures that promise to pay off; loans to farmers who qualify under terms of sound agricultural credit; education, geared to the needs of the economy; and so forth. These can be safely pursued, and can, if it is desired, be articulated into a "plan."[14] If more can be achieved, other projects may be added. But care should be exercised to ensure that the country's capabilities are not so overburdened that ultimately less is achieved than was possible.

Politicians, untutored in the harsh realities of economic life, and dissatisfied with such modest goals, may, if they belong to one end of the

[13]Donald Wilhelm Jr. concludes that "the experience in Burma suggests the need for nothing less than a wholesale revision of the priorities of technical assistance .... There emerges a strong case for placing administrative training and improvement near the top of, instead of, as in Burma, toward the bottom of any list of urgent technical measures." "The Place of Public Administration in Overseas Technical Assistance Programs," in C.J. Friedrich and J.K. Galbraith (eds.), *Public Policy* (Cambridge: Harvard University Press, 1955), Chap. VI, p. 208.

[14]This is the type of planning, we take it, that is envisaged by A.G. Papandraeou in *A Strategy for Greek Economic Development* (Athens: Center for Economic Research, 1962), Chap. 2. It may be the type of planning that is carried on in Israel; it has been argued, however, that planning in Israel amounts to little more than subsidization of consumption and agriculture by capital imports. S. Riemer, "Israel: Ten Years of Economic Dependence," *Oxford Economic Papers*, Vol. 12 (June 1960), p. 141, and A.J. Meyer, "The Economic Problems of Israel," *Economic Development and Cultural Change*, X (April 1962), 331-33.

political spectrum, be consoled to learn that more *can* be achieved if the government creates conditions which will encourage maximum activity in the private sector—that is, if the greatest possible amount of talent and capital, which for one reason or another lie beyond the government's direct control, is mobilized. To obtain such increments, however, the government may have to be content to lose much control over the economy. It may even have to reconcile itself to a considerable measure of foreign domination of economic life, to seeing some of the most important decisions being made by the "neocolonial" or "imperialist" sector. But it may be this or nothing. Unfortunately, this sad fact is obscured by the propaganda of both aid-givers and aid-receivers, which makes excessive claims for what has been achieved. Failures, which might be more instructive, are never mentioned.

The generally prevailing overoptimism indicates that much more pooling of experience is needed, particularly of unsuccessful experience. Economists in both donor and recipient countries would profit greatly from detailed and critical appraisals of what has and what has not been achieved by planning in underdeveloped nations by aid-giving programs, and by other attempts to force growth. At present, few such studies are available, and the hazards are not well understood. For the politicians of the underdeveloped nation, we should like to organize an educational Cook's tour which would take in such noteworthy archaeological sites as completed factories which have never produced, housing projects which are uninhabited, unfinished water-spreading dams whose initial purpose and design have been forgotten, tracts of virgin soil cleared and now reverting to waste, superhighways used mainly by donkeys and mules, and the countless villages untouched by developmental efforts and in full decay. Wishful it is, no doubt, to imagine that such an itinerary could ever be arranged. But if a concerted attempt is not made to disabuse the decision-makers of their more fanciful notions, we shall be condemned to watching history needlessly repeat itself.

The Breakthrough Plan

Lauchlin Currie

42

... [I have argued] that a large proportion and, in some of our countries, even a majority of the workers are, economically speaking, virtually unemployed. These are the people engaged in a primitive type of agriculture, as well as the workers in small towns who are dependent on this form of agriculture. To this total may be added many more workers in towns and cities which have no industrial base. Owing to the frequent holidays, the minority who have regular employment probably work no more than some 220 days a year. It is obvious that people out of work, or working little, cannot enjoy a high standard of consumption.

[I have] also argued that remunerative employment in agriculture could not be created for this labor force—that the future of agriculture, as in developed countries, lies in mechanization and technification, requiring much less land and much fewer people. Further, it was pointed out that the translation of felt demand into effective demand and hence remunerative employment—an effective working out of Say's Law—is prevented by numerous powerful elements which impede mobility of labor, as well as by mistaken government policies.

[I have] argued that the failure to break the circle engendered by intense and hopeless poverty could bring the whole development process to a stop—that the forces of regression can be as self-generating as constructive forces. Finally, it was implied that the various approaches or programs that have or are currently being tried offer little hope of success . . . Therefore a breakthrough plan is necessary to attain quickly a higher level from which the constructive self-generating forces can gain the ascendancy.

Even if a country has arrived at a point where continuing development appears assured, a policy of acceleration may still be justified to relieve misery and suffering. Thus in the United States a program to abolish the remaining poverty has been adopted. If this is a desirable and humane objective in such a relatively rich country as the United States, there would appear to be hardly a country in the world where an acceleration in the production of goods and services and more equality in consumption are not desirable. Thus the approach suggested here does not depend exclusively on the breakthrough argument.

The nature of the problem suggests the elements of a plan. It is simply to bring together idle men and idle equipment to produce goods and services to satisfy felt needs, to channel resources to this end, and to subordinate other objectives to the early attainment of a decent minimum standard of living for the masses. Stated thus, there can surely be little disagreement. It is in the elaboration of a program to accomplish these objectives that difficulties arise.

Elements of a Plan

The program described here is in essence a very simple one. Instead of trying to secure an increase in productivity of all workers in their present occupations, it proposes that the least productive (the virtually unemployed) be given an opportunity to secure more remunerative work. It suggests that we provide incentives or a pull to overcome the sluggishness in the mobility of labor and that we remove existing deterrents to such mobility. Instead of setting the objective as a certain rate of growth in the GNP, it proposes to tackle directly the problems of wider employment and inequality by setting the objective as the creation of a certain number of new nonagricultural jobs in a given time. It also suggests taking action to ensure that the bulk of these jobs will be in the provision of urban housing, public services, and wage goods, so that the additional people will be in part employed in making additional goods they themselves need. Insofar as the objective is attained, the overpopulation in rural districts is reduced and the effective demand for foodstuffs is increased. The plan proposes that the initial major emphasis be placed on raising the consumption of the poorest sectors of the community rather than on increasing investment. It seeks to achieve a greater measure of equality in consumption by a process of upgrading on the one hand and a better enforcement of progressive individual taxation on the other.

This, then, is the objective based on the diagnosis of widespread under-employment, particularly in rural areas and small towns. In general terms, the objective would be the same for our whole group of developing countries; in specific terms (such as the number of jobs and the length of the work year), it would vary according to the degree of underutilization of existing equipment, the availability of foreign exchange resources, the magnitude of the problem, and the will to do. When the breakthrough plan was first proposed in summary fashion in Colombia in 1961, the public impression, perhaps because of faulty presentation, was that the essential point consisted of the migration of labor to the cities. Actually, of course, the keystone is the provision of new and better-paid jobs. Migration would be a consequence rather than the initiating factor. It is just as important to provide work for the urban unemployed as for the rural.

Presented in this way, the plan appears perhaps deceptively simple. Actually it would require economic programming of a high level of technical competence. Just as its inspiration owes a good deal to wartime experience, so in its mechanics it relies more heavily on direct controls and rationing than most economists in developed countries would probably care to invoke in the absence of war.

For example, to restrain the importation and/or production of luxury goods (expensive homes, cars, and so on) little reliance could be placed initially on the taxing arm. Stopping tax avoidance and closing up loopholes are the fruit of persistent years of effort. A short-term program would depend mainly on the exercise of the authority to grant or withhold building licenses, to control imports, and to ration available exchange.

The exchange licensing authority would be confronted with many applications claiming that they would save x exchange in the form of future importations, create x jobs, utilize national raw materials, and so forth. Such applications would have to be subjected to a very close study. The following questions should be the main criteria for this type of war in which the enemy is dire poverty: (1) How much use of existing equipment can the applicant show? (2) How much more use of the existing equipment will the new imports permit? (For example, will they enable the applicant to pass from one shift to two?) (3) Will the imports increase the capacity to produce wage goods or goods of mass consumption immediately?

Applications receiving high priority would be spare parts in general; goods that permit passing from one to two or three shifts daily; new cotton textile machinery in cases where operations are already on a three-shift basis; equipment for water, sewer, and electric plants in cities expected to show large population increases; hand tools; equipment for the construction industry; and so on. If capital is scarce, preference should be given to investments yielding immediate returns. When the emphasis in exchange rationing is shifted from more roundabout capital investments to those permitting intensive use of existing capital, the increase in returns can be enormous.

If criteria such as these were adopted, I believe that the ratio of production to the stock of capital could be sharply raised, the productivity of new investment could be greatly increased, and the ratio of employment to capital could be radically altered in a short period.[1] It seems to me that the limitation on production imposed by shortage of foreign exchange suggested by a study of historical relationships would not apply, at least for a time. Exchange licensing, then, would become one of the chief arms of policy.

Another main policy instrument would be housing, a topic which brings us to the actual mechanics of getting the program under way. Although the plan's overall objective is the creation of nonagricultural jobs for agriculturalists (which could well be an objective for developed countries also), we are in a moving situation, with population and the working force increasing at a rapid rate. Thus before we can effect a net shift of population from rural to urban surroundings, we must first provide, say, a yearly 3 percent increase in jobs for the natural increase in the working force. If the gainfully employed are distributed roughly 50-50 between urban and rural activities, and it is desired to reduce the rural force from 50 to 40 percent of the total in three years, there would have to be an increase in urban jobs of around 15 percent of the total working force, or 30 percent of the original urban working force. Though not an impossible goal, this is certainly one requiring a tremendous effort, and an effort which few countries would probably be prepared to embark upon. Yet if the goal is set too low, we may do little more than provide for the natural increase in the working force. An objective that would show great results would be, say, a 4½ percent decrease per annum in rural employment continued for three years—the breakthrough period—and lowered to 3 percent thereafter. Even this program would, under our assumptions above, mean an increase of 31 percent in urban jobs and a decline in the rural population only to a little below 40 percent of the total. In countries with a lower rural excess, the numerical objectives would be reduced.[2]

If this should be chosen as an overall objective, then the immediate aim would be the provision of adequate urban housing for the expected addition. And here we come to a very important difference between the breakthrough program and the New Deal problem of providing employment. In the New Deal's case, the listed unemployed

[1]Some writers seem to think that the ratio of capital to employment—the amount of capital it takes to create one new job—is fixed and is so high as to make it impossible to have many new jobs without a tremendous increase in saving and borrowing. They are unconsciously postulating the continuance of present inefficient practices and patterns.

[2]As this study was being completed, references were appearing in the press to the Spanish Plan of Development, designed to reduce the proportion of rural population from 40% to 33% in four years.

were already in the cities, with housing of a sort. Hence the pump priming had to be sought in public works of various kinds. But in the breakthrough program, housing and public services provide the obvious object of pump priming. This phrase is perhaps not very appropriate, since housing and public services would remain the main items in the investment segment as long as the program continued . . . .

The Contriving of Reform

Albert O. Hirschman

43

. . . The problem-solving process was described [above] in terms of concurrent or sequential advances in understanding and motivation. For an important group of problem-solving situations these two elements are overshadowed by, and indissolubly linked with, a third condition for advance: the ability to enact and carry through certain measures, remedies, or *reforms*, in spite of the resistance which they evoke. We now turn to such situations; they are of special interest in Latin America today and occupy a prominent place in each one of our country studies.

The Reformer's Initial Handicap

Faced with the claims of the Cuban revolution on the one hand, and with the demands and promises of the Alliance for Progress on the other, Latin Americans appear to have been placed squarely before the familiar, if stark, alternative: change through violent revolution or through peaceful reform?

Excerpted from chapter 5 of *Journeys toward Progress*, Twentieth Century Fund, New York, 1963. Reprinted by permission. The author is professor of economics, Harvard University.

On the basis of the country studies it will be argued in the following pages that this traditional dichotomy does very poorly at catching the reality of social and economic change. But first it should perhaps be explained that, contrary to what might be expected, a strong initial advantage for the advocates of revolution results from formulating the choice facing the developing countries of Latin America in this bipolar fashion.

Social reform and social revolution are usually distinguished by the manner in which a given change is brought about as well as by the extent of that change. But they have in common the nature of the change, since both propose a shift in power and wealth from one group to another. Hence they are varieties of what we shall call *antagonistic* solutions to problems in contrast to *non-antagonistic* solutions which consist of measures that are expected to leave each group better or at least as well off as before.

A proposed change can be thought of as non-antagonistic by its advocates, but may turn out to be antagonistic and to be perceived as such. In fact, any "progress," however non-antagonistic it was meant to be, will almost always hurt the absolute or relative position of *some* social group, at least initially. Anthropologists have shown that all aspects of the status quo, even those that seem wholly undesirable, have their defenders and profiteers who are going to fight the proffered improvements. Unrealistic expectation of universal cooperation with measures which in the mind of their sponsors had no antagonistic component has spelled the failure of many a technical assistance project. Such disappointments have been well documented even in the ostensibly most non-antagonistic field of public health.[1] Thus we tend consistently to *underestimate* the difficulties of change in the case of (subjectively) non-antagonistic measures and we are constantly surprised and chagrined by the resistances which they encounter.

The opposite bias—overestimate of the difficulties of change—frequently affects measures which are openly and avowedly antagonistic. We know and expect that land expropriation, nationalization of industries or progressive income taxation will be strongly opposed by well-entrenched groups.[2] Hence, when it comes to such measures, the revolutionary who is out to ridicule the peaceful reformer has an easy task indeed. He will show that a basic transformation of existing power relationships is a prerequisite to adopting and enforcing any measure that threatens the interests and privileges of the ruling class. He will deride the argument that the establishment of democratic

[1]Oscar Lewis, "Medicine and Politics in a Mexican Village," in Benjamin D. Paul, ed., *Health, Culture, and Community,* Russel Sage Foundation, New York, 1955.

[2]It is usual, but no longer justified, to limit discussion of such measures to those that are antagonistic to the interests of the older and wealthier ruling groups. More and more frequently, some Latin American countries such as Argentina and Brazil have found it imperative to tackle pressing problems of efficiency and financial solvency by curtailing the privileges of stragetically located groups among the middle or working classes. What experience we have with this variety of antagonistic measures shows that they are no less difficult to push through than those directed against the older ruling groups.

institutions and of universal suffrage will allow basic reforms to be adopted legally since, so he will argue, democratic trappings will be discarded as soon as the real powerholders find them no longer convenient. . . .

The idea of revolution as a prerequisite to any progress draws immense strength from the very limited human ability to visualize change and from the fact that it makes only minimal demands on that ability. All we are asked to imagine by the revolutionary is the tumbling down of the old regime in a total upheaval which will give birth to the new order. Revolution thus conceived is essentially a quite brief, though cataclysmic interlude between two static societies: one, unjust and rotten, which is incapable of being improved, and the other, rational and harmonious, which has no further need to be improved upon. Sorel, the apostle of the violent general strike as an energizing myth, clearly had this concept of revolution in mind when he wrote:

> . . . the general strike must be considered as an undivided whole; consequently, no detail about ways and means is of the slightest help for the understanding of socialism. It must even be added that there is always danger of losing something of this understanding, if one attempts to split this whole into parts . . . the transition from capitalism to socialism must be conceived as a catastrophe whose process defies description.[3]

Sorel thus understood perfectly the dual function of the ideal of revolution to gratify the desire for change and to dispense with the need to visualize the process of change in its intricate and perhaps unpleasant details by telescoping it into an "undivided whole."

The neat trick involved in this operation, while intellectually not very respectable, goes far toward explaining the drawing power of the idea of revolution. But the reformers are also to blame. They have made themselves particularly vulnerable to the charge of being unrealistic by failing to explore how social change short of cataclysmic revolution actually happens. Thus they have permitted the revolutionists to set up a caricature of "change via reform" where the latter follows smoothly (and unbelievably) upon the 51 per cent election victory of the Reform Party or, more modernly though even more naively, upon the recommendations of international experts or the offer of finance. Actually there are a good many intermediate stations between this kind of effortless and painless reform at one extreme and total revolution at the other and our studies permit us to map out a few of these stations.

Events of recent years have created a somewhat similar continuum between total peace and total war (cold, phony, brushfire, limited war), and political scientists have identified various types of political regimes (tutelary democracy, modernizing oligarchies) filling the void between Western-type parliamentary democracy and totalitarian autocracy. In contrast to these efforts, our observations do not lead to the firm establishment of a typology. Rather, ... elements of both reform and revolution are present in the sequences of policy-making. . . . We hope to provide basic materials for what may eventually go into a "reformmonger's manual"; perhaps it is time that such a text be written and offer some competition to the many handbooks on the techniques of revolutions, coups d'état, and guerrilla warfare.

This section stands in need of an important postscript. Our argument, as developed so far, does not mean to imply that any reform whatever can always be introduced without revolution, i.e., without the prior, violent, wholesale overthrow of the current power holders. Certainly many situations have existed and still exist in Latin America as elsewhere in which power is so concentrated, opposition to change so fierce, and the social and political structure so rigid that any non-revolutionary change is, short of a miracle, impossible, *besides* being inconceivable. The point we have been trying to make is that there are many other, less rigid situations in which change by methods short of revolution is or has become possible, but where, because of the force of habit or some similar cultural lag, change is still visualized primarily as something that requires a prior revolution. . . .

The discovery that non-antagonistic remedies are available after antagonistic measures have held sway should in principle be greeted as just as stunning an intellectual discovery as the opposite feat. It requires at least as much imagination and sophistication to perceive that two groups whose interests were universally assumed to be wholly divergent actually have some important interests in common as to notice an opposition of interests between groups that were hitherto thought to be, and thought of themselves as, partners traveling along the same road toward common objectives.

To illustrate, we recall the sweeping victory of Free Trade with its doctrine that foreign trade is mutually beneficial over mercantilism's dogma that one trading partner's gain is the other's loss. The similar discovery that Russia and the United States actually share one overriding interest, namely survival, while it has not created international harmony, has nevertheless had a profound effect, not only on the debates about nuclear strategy and disarmament, but on the behavior of the two super-powers as well.

[In Latin America, however,] we are dealing with societies where the existing social order had not been seriously disturbed or questioned at the point of departure of our stories. The remedies then proposed were those advocated by the well-entrenched upper classes who had no doubts about the identity of their interests with those of society at large. Only later was this assumed harmony questioned, and the discovery that an antagonistic treatment might be required came as a blinding insight after so long a period of firm belief in, and practise of, the non-antagonistic therapy. This must be understood if the depth of antagonistic feeling in Latin America today is to be correctly gauged. . . .

Much has been made in the preceding pages of the opportunity to gain new allies which becomes available to today's reformmongers in Latin America. But even with those allies, the margins with which the battles for reforms are won are narrow indeed. It is therefore easily understood why reformmongers dare not cut themselves off from any actual or potential group support of substantial size even though they may disagree with the final objectives of that group. Clearly it would be foolish for them to gain allies on the Center and Right at the cost of losing the Left.

This need to spread his net as wide as possible will make the reformmonger appear to be quite naive once again, this time about the dangers of Communist infiltration. Often this is so because the most effective reformmongers are to be found amongst erstwhile revolutionaries who notice, much to their own surprise, that some of the social changes they have been seeking can be achieved without that "prior" revolution in whose necessity they had long believed. To turn such private insights into the collective experience of a group that has long remained in a position of pure protest against the established order is perhaps even more important than the achievement of any single reform in itself, if Latin American societies are ever to become "integrated." From this point of view also, the effective reformmonger must delay as long as possible, and perhaps avoid altogether, any break with his radical followers. Frequently this will not require any special effort or dissimulation on his part since he is himself still doubtful—quite rightly so until the returns are in—that it is possible to dispense with revolution.

At his best, our reformer-revolutionary will therefore retain the trust of his old followers even as he enlists aid and support from new quarters. He will now have to play to several quite different galleries; he will contrive change by negotiating for new allies while not ceasing to agitate for it. These two tasks are of course so different that they are best performed if they can be dealt out to *several* principal actors who feel quite independent of each other, in the manner of the struggle for Italian unification which was able to draw on the highly diverse talents of Cavour, a master contriver, and of Mazzini and Garibaldi, who filled the roles of conspirators and agitators. But sometimes there is only one chief actor who, to be successful, must combine both roles, appear in the guise of Necker and Stolypin one day and in that of Danton or Lenin the next—a highly risky assignment, though perhaps also rather an entertaining one!

In fine, the roads to reform are narrow and perilous, they appear quite unsafe to the outside observer however sympathetic he may be, *but they exist*. Having become acquainted with their twists and turns throughout this book, we emerge with a heightened consciousness of the difficulties facing Latin American policy-makers; but also and foremost, with a new appreciation of the many unsuspected and unorthodox opportunities for maneuver and advance.

The Requirements for Development

Maurice Zinkin

44

The qualities required for economic development are not the highest of which man is capable; for both the individual and the nation there are more important ends in life than becoming rich. It is still pleasanter and more proper to die for one's country than to save for it; and loving our neighbour, not making money, is the way to salvation.

Economic progress is, in short, only doubtfully also moral progress. Riches subject man to nearly as many temptations as poverty. Economic development is only good in so far as it is achieved without an increase in envy, uncharitableness and exploitation. The sweating of labour in the first half of the nineteenth century in England permitted some very necessary accumulation, the enclosures of the second half of the eighteenth century saved England from starvation in the Napoleonic Wars; but they were not good for the souls of the sweaters and enclosers.

Economic development, therefore, would appear at first sight something over which no one could get excited; and so it was, on the whole, in ancient India or mediaeval Europe. But today it has become mixed up with a whole series of moral considerations to which it is somewhat doubtfully relevant.

From Maurice Zinkin, *Development for Free Asia* (London: Chatto & Windus Ltd., 1956). The author was in business in India for many years.

Those who love their country now believe that to be great she must be powerful; and to be powerful she must first be rich. Those who love their neighbour now regard the salvation of his body as more important than the salvation of his soul; there is much rejoicing over a 5 per cent increase in the national income, little over new endowment for temples. Those who love God often feel that He is better worshipped by high taxes than by prayer.

Economic progress is, therefore, sought today, in Asia as elsewhere, for reasons which are not economic. That provides a drive profounder than any known before, for the sacrifices men will make for religion are far greater than those they will make for riches. But it also has its dangers. Because the qualities and the policies required for development are so often religiously uninspiring, the resources needed for economic progress are perpetually being diverted to satisfy some non-economic principle, often with only the dimmest idea of the economic sacrifice involved. High cost industries are built up, because they are thought to contribute to national power. Amenities for labour more expensive than productivity justifies are enforced, so that labourers shall have a better life. High incomes are taxed almost out of existence to increase equality. Location of industry is interfered with so that every part of the country shall have its 'fair' share of development. Such large farmers as know about agriculture have their holdings cut down so that more of the landless can enjoy the pleasures of ownership. And so on. The criteria applied in judging economic problems mostly have nothing to do with economics; and the result is naturally that, though there may be more equality, or greater regional fairness, or possibly, fewer revolutions, there is also less development.

That does not necessarily mean that these non-economic criteria are wrong. Economic and non-economic standards of value are not better or worse than each other, they are different. Which should be applied in any particular case is for a man's conscience rather than his reason to decide. It is an irrelevance to tell those who believe cows to be sacred that they would be better off if useless cattle were killed. All that can properly be said is that sometimes those who apply non-economic criteria are not altogether aware of their economic cost. Those who shout for equality now might do so less loudly if they knew it would make their children poorer. Those who build high cost factories to make their country more powerful today might be less enthusiastic if they realized how much weaker the waste of resources will make their country in the long run. Any major decision, national or personal, should in the end be guided by men's beliefs, and not their interests; but before the decision is made the facts should be understood.

The requirements which have to be fulfilled for Asia to get rich are clear. Getting rich must be a major objective, for which people are prepared to sacrifice old habits as well as present consumption. They must save instead of hoarding, or spending on festivals or ceremonies. They must invest productively instead of buying jewellery and brocades. They must admire innovations, and inventions, and successful entrepreneurs rather than writers of commentaries and men who conform to perfection to the methods of their ancestors. Business must become as respectable as administration. The State must take the initiative in change, it must develop public utilities, put through social reform, make available extension services and widen the scope of co-operation; but, because it has so much it ought to do, it must refrain from doing what can be done by others. It must restrain itself from unnecessary nationalisations and meddling controls. There must be politicians who can lead their people to change, and bureaucrats who can make actual the politicians' dreams. There must be equality for women and the traditionally oppressed, so that society may draw upon the initiative of all, but economic equality must not be excessive, so that some will have the leisure and the money to study or take risks. Education must be reformed to bring forward an adequate supply of the technically trained and economically adaptable. Above all, in deciding between alternative possibilities of action, the most profitable should be chosen, not that which will be most advantageous to a special interest, or will benefit the most backward, or the best behaved, or the largest number. If wealth is the aim, wealth must be the criterion, not power, or autarchy or even fairness.

The needs of development cannot be absolute. There must be occasions when defence or justice will override them with propriety. But for that there is a price. The poor will remain poorer for longer.